GERMAN–POLISH
RELATIONS, 1918–1933

Harald von Riekhoff

GERMAN–POLISH RELATIONS, 1918–1933

The JOHNS HOPKINS PRESS, Baltimore and London

The Johns Hopkins Press, Baltimore, Maryland 21218
The Johns Hopkins Press Ltd., London

Library of Congress Catalog Card Number 73–141999

International Standard Book Number 0–8018–1310–7

To my parents

Contents

Preface

IN COMPARISON to the richly documented works on German–Soviet relations in the inter-war period which have been published after World War II, the related subject of German–Polish relations during the same period has received scanty treatment. What has appeared on the subject has generally dwelled on the more dramatic events which preceded the outbreak of the 1939 catastrophe rather than focussed on German–Polish relations during the Weimar period. The vast amount of primary source material from public and private archival collections—most of which is still unpublished—which has recently become available for scholarly investigation invites a detailed and objective examination of the diplomatic, economic, and military relations which evolved between Weimar Germany and the restored Polish Republic during the 1918–33 period.

In this study, German–Polish relations between the 1918 armistice and Hitler's accession to power are projected onto a wider screen that features the inter-war diplomacy of the European powers. There is probably a greater need to treat this particular subject in a broader context than would be the case for most other dyadic relationships. Most of the key issues between Berlin and Warsaw arose specifically from an international settlement—the Versailles treaty—which provided an international division between its supporters and opponents. To protect herself from Germany's revisionist aims, Poland became part of the web of alliances which France wove to restrain Germany and other revisionist powers. Just as Poland was driven to internationalize her security needs, Germany tried to make an international issue of her territorial claims against Poland and to win international sympathy and support for her revisionist aspirations. In this way even routine and minute matters in German–Polish relations tended to be elevated to the status of general issues of European diplomacy.

Needless to say, I have tried throughout this work to provide a truly objective assessment of events and personalities. This is the duty of the diplomatic historian, and in this particular case it is all the more necessary because the controversial subject matter has tended to produce highly biased versions and polemics at the expense of scholarship. I have used the German name and spelling for places lying inside the territorial boundaries of the Weimar Republic and Polish names for places inside Polish territorial limits.

This work has grown out of a Yale University doctoral dissertation which was directed by Professor Hajo Holborn. I am indebted to George Kennan for having first aroused my interest in the subject. No words can describe my gratitude, admiration, and affection for the late Hajo Holborn who offered unfailing guidance, inspiration, and cheerful encouragement. None of his students could evade the impact of his wisdom and personal charm and his influence on the life of all persons who had the great privilege to work under his direction will be permanent.

I would also like to acknowledge my appreciation for the many useful comments and suggestions that emerged from interviews with Immanuel Birnbaum (Foreign Affairs editor of *Die Süddeutsche Zeitung* and formerly Warsaw correspondent of the *Vossische Zeitung*), Gotthold Starke (formerly editor of the Bydgoszcz *Deutsche Rundschau*), and Professor Hans Roos of Bochum University.

I am greatly indebted to the directors and staff of a number of archives and libraries for giving me access to their collections and providing exemplary assistance. The following were of particular value to this study: the National Archives in Washington, D.C.; the Archiwum Akt Nowych in Warsaw (Dr. Bronisława Skrzeszewska); the archives of the Auswärtiges Amt and of the Bundes Presse-und Informationsamt in Bonn (Dr. Seeberg-Elverfeldt); the Bundesarchiv in Coblenz (Dr. Hans Booms); the Public Record Office in London. Dr. Ulrich Sahm of the German Foreign Ministry kindly let me use the unpublished papers of his father, Heinrich Sahm, the president of the Danzig senate. The Arbeitsgemeinschaft für Osteuropaforschung in Tübingen generously allowed me the use of its excellent collection of newspaper clippings. Other valuable collections were found in the Library of Congress in

Washington, the British Museum in London, and the university libraries of Yale, Columbia, Bonn, Göttingen, and Toronto.

Dr. Tadeusz Rakowski (former Polish Consul General) and John Hay, my personal research assistant at Carleton University, greatly facilitated the task of writing and revising the manuscript. M. Wróblewski's help proved invaluable in going through the massive files of the Polish Foreign Ministry. Professor Piotr Wandycz of Yale University made detailed comments on an earlier draft which guided my revisions. The editorial suggestions of John Gallman and Nancy Middleton Gallienne of The Johns Hopkins Press did much to trim and clarify the text.

Finally, I wish to acknowledge the generous financial assistance which I received from the Woodrow Wilson National Fellowship Foundation, the Canada Council, and Carleton University.

Abbreviations

AA   Auswärtiges Amt (German Foreign Ministry)
AMSW   Archiwum Ministerstwa Spraw Wewnętrznych (Records of the Ministry of Interior)
AMSZ   Archiwum Ministerstwa Spraw Zagranicznych (Records of the Ministry of Foreign Affairs)
BBWR   Bezpartyjny Blok Współpracy z Rządem (Nonpartisan Bloc for Co-operation with the Government)
DDP   Deutsche Demokratische Partei (German Democratic Party)
DNVP   Deutschnationale Volkspartei (German National People's Party)
DVP   Deutsche Volkspartei (German People's Party)
FO   Foreign Office (British Foreign Office)
IMCC   Inter-Allied Military Control Commission
KPD   Kommunistische Partei Deutschlands (German Communist Party)
NPR   Narodowa Partia Robotnicza (National Labor Party)
NSDAP   Nationalsozialistische Deutsche Arbeiterpartei (Nazi Party)
POW   Polska Organizacja Wojskowa (Polish Military Organization)
PPRM   Protokoły Posiedzeń Rady Ministrów Rzeczypospolitej Polskiej (Protocols of the Council of Ministers of the Polish Republic)
PPS   Polska Partia Socjalistyczna (Polish Socialist Party)
SA   Sturmabteilung (Storm Troopers)
SD   State Department (U.S. State Department)
SPD   Sozialdemokratische Partei Deutschlands (German Social Democratic Party)
SS   Schutzstaffel (Protection Squad)

GERMAN–POLISH RELATIONS, 1918–1933

I

The Peace Settlement and Its Impact

THE PEACE SETTLEMENT OF PARIS exercised a more predominant influence on almost every facet of German–Polish relations during the inter-war period than any other single factor or combination of factors. Historical resentments, contrasts in temperament and personality, economic disputes, and cultural differences had their share in shaping the course of relations between the two neighbors. But in the web of their routine interactions factors of the latter category could mitigate each other or could be modified gradually. The Versailles treaty offered no such prospects.

In view of its significance to their subsequent relations, it strikes us as an historical irony that neither side played a very active role in shaping the treaty as the principal Allied and Associate Powers determined the restructuring of the political forces on the European continent. In this process of power redistribution, Germany became the object of the punitive decree of a victorious military coalition, while Poland was the object of support and solicitous concern by France and the other coalition partners. Poland had too recently reappeared on the international scene and was internally too weak to allow her to play a major role in the negotiations. By the curious proceedings which marked the conference, Germany was altogether excluded from the actual negotiations and her role was restricted to making counterproposals to a completed treaty proposal. While the outcome of the settlement affected the two powers in almost diametrically opposite ways, they both shared an object relationship to the treaty, and both Germans and Poles were accustomed to speak of the Versailles *Diktat*.

1

Despite certain Polish reservations about the outcome of the peace settlement, no objective historical observer can fail to be impressed by the enormous gains which Poland derived from the treaty at the very outset of her career as a restored power. Several factors contributed to this success. In the first place, Poland enjoyed the sponsorship of France. In a rare marriage of sentiment and *Realpolitik,* France backed Poland's claims as part of her own search for an East European ally that could fulfill the dual role of isolating Bolshevist Russia and encircling Germany.

Furthermore, the great historical dilemma which had plagued Poland ever since her partition, whereby a war among the three partitioning powers would not lead to her restoration but merely to a redistribution of Polish territory in favor of the victorious power, had finally been resolved. By a most unusual constellation of historical forces, the three partitioning powers, Austria, Germany, and Russia, simultaneously emerged as vanquished nations after a catastrophic war.

Finally, Poland's restoration under such propitious auspices was assisted by the remarkable skill and energy of her diplomatic representatives in the different European capitals during World War I.[1] During the first years of the war, Polish political feelers operated on almost every front, in the capitals of the Entente no less than in Vienna and Berlin. Such diversity of approach has often been interpreted as a reflection of the fundamental division in Polish politics and the capriciousness of the Polish character. It would be more accurate to view this as the natural behavior of an occupied country seeking to exploit an enormously complex and entirely unpredictable international situation to its fullest advantage.

By the end of 1916, the thrust of Polish diplomacy seemed to have become crystallized in two principal, and seemingly contradictory, directions which duplicated the division of Europe into two hostile coalitions.

In terms of the military investment and administrative personnel, the stronger effort was no doubt made by those groups seeking a solution in conjunction with the Central Powers in order to defeat Russia. This particular effort involved the activities of the Polish Legion under the direction of Piłsudski. While these forces pursued independent political goals and operated largely autonomously in the military sphere, they

---

[1] For a discussion of Polish diplomacy during World War I, see Roman Dmowski, *Polityka polska i odbudowanie państwa* (2nd ed,; Warsaw, 1926); Werner Conze, *Polnische Nation und Deutsche Politik im Ersten Weltkrieg* (Cologne, 1958); Tytus Komarnicki, *Rebirth of the Polish Republic* (London, 1957).

were subordinated to the Austrian General Staff, from which they received much of their material and equipment.

The impressive performance of Piłsudski's forces in the Volhynian summer campaign of 1916 so whetted the appetite of the German General Staff to tap this rich source of unexploited military manpower that it pressed for the creation of a Polish army in return for some political concessions to the Poles. The scheme met with strong opposition from such quarters as Count Burian, the Austrian Foreign Minister, who wanted to undertake nothing that might impair his dream of an Austrian solution to the Polish problem. Germany's Chancellor, von Bethmann-Hollweg, feared that even the semblance of a restoration of an independent Polish state might encourage irredentist demands among the Polish population in Prussia. Also, Bethmann-Hollweg did not want to foreclose the option of a separate peace with Russia by an adventurist initiative on the Polish question. However, as on most other disputed issues during the war, military rationale prevailed over civilian objections. The outcome was the Two-Emperor Proclamation of November 5, 1916, in which both Germany and Austria–Hungary proclaimed the existence of a Polish state that was to have a monarchical constitution. Initially, the proclamation had little more than symbolic value, but it subsequently acquired more concrete political significance when the Central Powers agreed to the establishment of a Polish Regency Council in September 1917. Under the direction of the Regency Council, Polish authorities gradually assumed responsibility for the administration of justice and education, and to a lesser degree also over finances and local government. This process not only enhanced Poland's self-confidence and drive for complete independence, but by building an administrative apparatus and an experienced civil service an infrastructure was formed which facilitated the orderly transition to full independence in the chaotic November days of 1918 following the withdrawal of the occupying armies.

The interest of the Central Powers in Poland was immediate and of a specifically military nature. Their task was to win the war, and the Polish question was subordinated to this central goal. Their long-range plans vis-à-vis Poland contained many self-contradictory elements and were therefore left vague. Polish interests, on the other hand, were political rather than military and long-range rather than immediate. The principal aim of Polish policy was to work for a favorable peace settlement that would guarantee full independence, which she was beginning to recover in stages. Relations became particularly tense after the first

Treaty of Brest–Litovsk, ceding to the Ukraine the district of Cholm, which was included among Poland's historical claims. This action led to a formal protest by the Regency Council and the resignation of the Kucharzewski Cabinet. Despite these frictions, the Brest–Litovsk treaty enhanced the prospects of a favorable outcome of the war for Germany and thereby increased Poland's perceived need to come to a *modus vivendi* with the Central Powers. In March of that year, a group of political figures from Warsaw came to a private understanding with the leaders of the majority parties in the German *Reichstag*. Under the terms of the agreement, Poland was given a free hand to expand her territory in the north-easterly direction and both sides accepted Germany's eastern border of 1914 as the future boundary between Germany and Poland.[2] The latter provision was to protect Germany against any eventual demands for the recovery of historical Polish lands and Poland against an eastern frontier revision which was then being considered in Germany.[3] This private understanding was followed by a formal offer of alliance which the new Steczkowski government directed to the Central Powers on April 29, 1918. The proposal included the above provisions which were to be expanded to give Poland free navigation on the Vistula and to allow a revision of the frontier at Cholm. The Polish request to clarify her relations with the Central Powers through this alliance agreement came to nothing, partly because of other preoccupations by the Central

[2] Conze, *Polnische Nation*, p. 350.

[3] A detailed account of the border revision as a factor in German-Polish relations during World War I appears in Imanuel Geiss, *Der Polnische Grenzstreifen 1914–1918* (Hamburg, 1960). As the prospects for a separate peace with Russia were waning, after 1915, the idea of establishing an independent Poland as a bulwark between Germany and Russia began to gain greater currency in Germany. Doubts as to Poland's ability to shield Germany against a Russian attack fathered the plan for a strategically improved German eastern boundary that would be drawn at Poland's expense. Numerous proposals of this kind were considered during the war. The label of a border adjustment, which these bore, is somewhat euphemistic in view of the large territory and population that would have been affected. If these plans had come to fruition, it would have entailed a new partition of Poland.

While the military, under General Ludendorff, took the strongest initiative on this point, Germany's civilian authorities were also involved. Geiss exposes the myth that these plans for territorial expansion were forced on a reluctant civilian government by its General Staff. As early as December 1914, the *Reichskanzlei* consulted with various authorities about improving Germany's eastern boundary and colonizing the newly acquired districts. Chancellor Bethmann–Hollweg did not wish to publicize these plans lest they run into opposition with the Catholic *Zentrum* and the Social Democrats. This silence has often led to the mistaken impression that he opposed the annexation plans.

Powers, partly because of Germany's reluctance to guarantee the 1914 border.

Polish suspicions about German war aims and the deterioration of Germany's military posture accelerated the estrangement between the Central Powers and Warsaw. The full extent of the cleavage was demonstrated when, on October 26, 1918, without consulting Berlin or Vienna, the Regency Council appointed Głąbiński, a member of the anti-German National Democratic party, minister of foreign affairs and thus formalized the existence of a Foreign Office which had existed in nucleus form since January of that year.[4]

The anticipated military co-operation, which had been the principal rationale for the Poland policy of the Central Powers, never materialized. The hope which Ludendorff and his colleagues had nourished that the Proclamation of 1916 would produce an enthusiastic Polish response in the form of a voluntary recruitment proved entirely illusory. Piłsudski and his supporters refused to engage in any voluntary recruitment or conscription before the aims of the Central Powers had been clarified and before there existed a Polish government under whose direction such an army could serve. These reservations erupted into open dispute over the question of the loyalty oath which the Polish troops were to swear to the Emperors of Germany and Austria–Hungary. The Polish refusal to comply led to Piłsudski's imprisonment in the fortress of Magdeburg and the internment of the legionnaires from Congress Poland. In protest over the first Brest–Litovsk treaty, some 1,500 Galician members of the dissolved Legion, under the command of Colonel Józef Haller, crossed into Ukranian territory. About half of these eventually reached France where they became the core of the Polish army in France.

The Ulyssian wanderings of Haller's men symbolized the remarkable diplomatic metamorphosis of a country whose major military and political efforts had been on the side of the Central Powers but which surfaced from the debacle of the war on the side of the victorious Entente.

Three principal factors conspired to bring about this successful *volte face*. In the first place, people like Piłsudski and the Warsaw authorities under the Regency Council had pursued strictly Polish national goals. This had temporarily produced certain forms of collaboration with the Central Powers, but it had given way to growing frustration,

[4] Roman Debicki, *The Foreign Policy of Poland 1919–1939* (New York, 1962), p. 11.

estrangement, and open conflict. Poland's aloof and negative attitude toward Germany tended to deter any subsequent Allied attempts to accuse her of war-time collusion with the enemy, even though a certain amount of Allied suspicion of apparent pro-German sympathies among some Poles lingered for several years and earned Piłsudski a bad press in the West. Second, there was the firm patronage of France, as part of the French concept of a new European order in which Poland was to function as a major partner. Finally, one should not ignore the role which was played by those Polish representatives who had been active in seeking a solution in conjunction with the Entente Powers.

The key figure among this latter group was Roman Dmowski. Before the war, Dmowski had been active in Polish politics as editor of the *Przegląd Wszechpolski*, as principal founder of the National Democratic party, and also, later, as delegate to the St. Petersburg *Duma*. Dmowski's policies represented a liberal-bourgeois version of those which had been pursued by the great Prince Adam Czartoryski a century earlier. Like his predecessor, Dmowski was skeptical about the prospects of gaining complete independence for Poland and therefore supported the concept of a united and autonomous Poland as part of a territorially enlarged and politically liberalized Russian Empire. His role in the *Duma* and his war-time activities in St. Petersburg were aimed in this direction. But Russia's military defeat and political intransigence frustrated progress, and in 1916 Dmowski and his supporters, like Czartoryski before, decided to shift the focus of their diplomatic activities from St. Petersburg to Paris and London.

The Lausanne Conference of National Democratic politicians and affiliated groups, in August 1917, saw the creation of the National Committee (*Komitet Narodowy Polski*) under Dmowski's chairmanship. The National Committee created an intricate network of contacts in the Western capitals and maintained envoys in Paris, London, Washington, and Rome. The Allied governments, on their part, dealt with the committee as if it were the legitimate Polish government in exile, even though official diplomatic recognition was withheld.

Thanks to the advocacy of the National Committee, the Polish question was kept alive in the discussions of Allied statesmen. The signing of the Treaty of Brest–Litovsk freed the Allied Powers from any remaining commitments to Russia and thereby acted as a catalyst in preparing the way for the Declaration of June 3, 1918, by the Prime Ministers of Britain, France, and Italy, in which the signatories committed themselves to the restoration of a united Poland with free access to the sea.

By linking the cause of Poland's restoration with the Allied war aims, Poland had scored a major success. This success can, to a large extent, be attributed to the diplomatic efforts of the National Committee, reinforced by a Polish military contribution to the Allied war effort. On June 4, 1917, the French government issued a decree that announced the creation of an autonomous Polish army in France. The degree of autonomy which this army was to enjoy remained unspecified, and it remained under French over-all command and direction almost until the end of the war when, on September 28, 1918, the National Committee assumed supreme control over the Polish army in France and appointed Józef Haller as its commander-in-chief. At the time of the November armistice, approximately 108,000 officers and men were serving in the Polish army in France, some 24,000 of whom had been recruited in the United States.[5] During the war, this Polish army never engaged in combat as an army, although some of its smaller units at the battalion and regimental level were sent to the front as replacements for Allied troops in order to get combat experience.

The Haller Army, as this force was called, achieved military significance not so much during World War I but in the post-armistice period, when the arrival of these troops in Poland considerably reinforced the military posture of that country. Its main contribution during the war lay in the diplomatic rather than the military sphere, for the existence of the Polish army in France led to its recognition as "an autonomous, Allied and cobelligerent army,"[6] and thereby assured Poland's admission to the peace negotiations on the side of the Allied Powers.

Despite this recognition of its allied status, Polish representatives neither participated in the armistice negotiations nor was there any mention made of Poland in the terms of the armistice. Moreover, the Allies had refused the Polish request to have the eastern armistice line correspond to the 1772 boundary and thereby lay the basis for the reincorporation of Poland's historical western provinces. Instead, they sought to maintain a modicum of order in the east and to halt the advance of

---

[5] Stanley Pliska, "The 'Polish–American Army' 1917–1921," *Polish Review* 10 (1965): 55.

[6] France was the first Allied power to extend such recognition in its military convention with the Polish National Committee on September 28, 1918. Britain followed suit on October 11 and the United States on November 1.

Bolshevism. With this in mind, the Allies allowed the German occupying forces to retain their advanced position in the east until a later Allied withdrawal order.

A DIPLOMATIC INTERLUDE

In view of Poland's gravitation toward the Allied camp at the conclusion of the war, it is interesting to examine a brief interlude of renewed German–Polish diplomatic activities that was associated with the mission of Count Harry Kessler to Warsaw in November 1918. Kessler, a wealthy aristocrat who played an influential role in the cultural and literary life of Germany during the Weimar period, had met Piłsudski during the Volhynian campaign of 1915. Acting on the instruction of the German government, Kessler had visited the Polish leader in his Magdeburg prison on October 31, 1918, in order to get an up-to-date impression of the latter's views on Polish–German relations after the impending armistice. In this particular conversation, Piłsudski gave Kessler to understand that he would require only a few months to build up a Polish army that could cope domestically with the Bolshevist threat. But in the estimate of the Polish leader it would take several years to lay the political and military foundations which would allow Poland to wage a foreign war. Consequently, the present generation of Poles would not be disposed to fight a war with Germany for the recovery of Poznań and West Prussia, although they would naturally accept these provinces as a gift of the Entente.[7]

Kessler saw Piłsudski soon afterward when he accompanied him from Magdeburg to Berlin on the latter's return to Warsaw on November 9. When the new Polish government under the leadership of Piłsudski invited the Allied Powers and Germany to give it recognition and to establish diplomatic relations,[8] Germany responded almost instantly by dispatching Count Kessler as envoy to Warsaw. The Count seemed doubly suited for this delicate task because of his recent contacts with Piłsudski and his support for the new republican regime in Germany. Much like Brockdorff–Rantzau, Kessler had come to endorse the socialist

[7] Letter, Count Kessler to Chancellor Prince Max of Baden, November 1, 1918, Deutsches Zentralarchiv (Potsdam), Reichsamt des Inneren, IAO Polen Gen. No. 36, vol. 4, pp. 228–32; cited in Jerzy Holzer, "Rozmowa Piłsudskiego z Hrabią Kesslerem," *Kwartalnik Historyczny*, vol. 68 (1961): 447–50.

[8] Zdzisław Wroniak, "Nawiązanie stosunków dyplomatycznych przez Polskę z Niemcami w 1918 roku," *Historia* 6 (1964): 233.

government in Germany from an inner conviction of the political and spiritual decadence of the Hohenzollern monarchy.

Piłsudski's motive for seeking diplomatic recognition from the Allies is self-evident. This was the victorious coalition on whose good graces at the forthcoming peace conference depended much of Poland's future. More immediately, such a step would have greatly enhanced his position in the contest with the National Democrats and its foreign organ, the National Committee. Futhermore, the invitation to the Allied Powers, which significantly by-passed the National Committee and appealed directly to the former, had been preceded by the request that the Polish army in France be transferred to Poland in order to defend the homeland in its fight against Bolshevism.

It is somewhat more difficult to appraise Piłsudski's real motives for extending the same invitation to his defeated German neighbor, all the more as such a step was bound to prick the central nerve of Allied sensitivity. The most pressing need for dealing with Germany was the problem of negotiating an agreement for the orderly evacuation of some 400,000 German soldiers who were stationed in the Ukraine and in eastern Poland under the *Ober-Ost* command of the German army. The continued presence of these German forces who kept part of Poland under occupation was a violation of Polish sovereignty. It also posed an additional danger, for the growing Communist sympathies in this rapidly disintegrating army threatened to spread the germs of Bolshevism throughout Poland. Piłsudski's initiative toward Germany might also have been dictated by the wish to underscore the fact that he was contemplating foreign policy options other than alignment with the victorious coalition, and thereby to put pressure on the Allies to recognize his government. Finally, the move might in fact already have foreshadowed Piłsudski's subsequent attempts to regularize relations with Germany, especially while Poland was engaged in a conflict with Russia, in order to give Poland a more independent foreign policy role and to safeguard her against an unbalanced reliance on the Allied Powers.

Germany welcomed the opportunity to establish diplomatic relations with Warsaw. She, too, was interested in arranging for the evacuation of her armed forces from eastern Poland and the Ukraine. It was clear that the days of imperial politics were over, and the continued stay of these troops in that region only exposed them to the influence of Bolshevism. Their presence in Germany, on the other hand, might add to the credibility of her threat to resume fighting rather than accept a draconian peace. At the same time, it was hoped in Berlin that by opening diplomatic relations with Warsaw, Poland might be discredited in the eyes of the Allies and persuaded to adopt a neutral stand.

The situation which confronted Kessler on his arrival in Warsaw on November 21 would have confounded even a seasoned diplomat. He had to represent a defeated power and an internally unconsolidated regime in a hostile country which itself was experiencing internal turmoil. To complicate his task, he had to wage his diplomatic battle on two fronts: against the Warsaw government and against OHL Ost (*Ober-Heereslei-tung Ost*), the German eastern army command, which bitterly complained that Kessler represented Polish rather than German interests.[9] The German envoy was concerned that unless an early agreement for the orderly evacuation of German troops was concluded, the semi-rebellious German soldiers would march through Poland at their own will and thus give France a pretext to cancel the armistice.[10]

His task was facilitated by Piłsudski's friendly and co-operative behavior throughout his brief mission. On several occasions the Polish leader referred to their joint task in leading the two countries from their traditional hostility to a new friendship.[11] Despite the friendly reception from Piłsudski and the tolerable working climate which Kessler had established with most Polish officials, his position in Warsaw became increasingly tenuous because of Allied pressure and the open hostility of the general public, in particular of the National Democrats. These pressures were sufficient to prompt the Polish Foreign Ministry to demand Kessler's immediate departure from Poland on December 15, a request with which he complied that same day.[12]

Kessler's diplomatic mission, brief and turbulent as it had been, was an event of key importance for the newly installed regime in Warsaw. In the first place, during his short tenure as German representative in Warsaw, Kessler had been able to conclude a preliminary agreement with the Polish government and the Ober-Ost command which was finalized on February 5, 1919. The agreement regulated the orderly evacuation of the 400,000 German soldiers from Polish and Ukranian territory by way of Kowel–Białystok–Grajewo–East Prussia. In addition, the agreement

---

[9] Graf Harry Kessler, *Aus den Tagebüchern, 1918–1937* (Munich, 1965), p. 24.
[10] *Ibid.*
[11] *Ibid.*, p. 17.
[12] Ostensibly, the reasons which were given to justify the demanded rupture were the activities of the *Ostmarkenverein* in Poland's western provinces and the Bolshevist propaganda which the German army was spreading in Poland. On December 17, Niemojewski, the Polish envoy in Berlin, was recalled.

made provision for Polish purchase of arms from the withdrawing German forces and arranged for the transport of some 50,000 Russian prisoners-of-war through Polish territory, in the process of which persons of Polish nationality were filtered out.

Second, his mission represented the regime's first formal diplomatic relations with a foreign power. Even in its state of military defeat and political turmoil, Germany remained a Great Power and relations with it enhanced the international prestige and viability of Piłsudski and his government, and thereby made the Allied Powers and the National Committee more amenable to the idea of coming to terms with him.

THE CREATION OF A NEW POLISH GOVERNMENT
AND ITS INTERNATIONAL CONSEQUENCES

The failure of the National Committee to gain recognition from the Allies, except from France, as the de facto government of Poland made that body more receptive to the idea of an arrangement with Piłsudski. A week before Kessler's expulsion, Grabski was dispatched to Warsaw to start discussions with Piłsudski. Although some progress was made during these talks, the final breakthrough had to wait the patriotic compromise between Piłsudski and Paderewski which on January 16, 1919, culminated in the formation of a non-partisan government of specialists.[13]

In the new government Piłsudski retained his position as chief of state (*Naczelnik Pánstwa*) with wide authority in the military field, while Paderewski combined the portfolios of prime minister and foreign minister. Dmowski was confirmed in his position as chief of the Polish delegation to the Paris Peace Conference, and within a few days of this event the new government was accorded official recognition by the Allied Powers. Dmowski thus at long last represented a government that enjoyed international recognition.

The Paderewski–Piłsudski truce, which brought together strongly contrasting personalities and political groups of very different orientation, constituted a patriotic feat which was of immense service to their nation, for it stabilized the internal political situation in Poland and considerably improved Polish chances of Allied support for her territorial claims at the forthcoming peace conference. More immediate was Poland's concern

[13] A detailed account of the circumstances which led to the formation of the Paderewski–Piłsudski government is given by Z. Wroniak, "Geneza Rządów Paderewskiego," *Historia* 4 (1959): 129–64.

with Allied assistance in the form of food, war materiel, and possibly direct military aid in her fight against Bolshevism. Such aid seemed all the more imperative because of the perceived fear of a common German–Bolshevist front against Poland. Writing to his friend Dłuski in Paris, a day after the formation of the Paderewski government, Piłsudski commented on the disciplined evacuation of the German army, its impressive military potential, and the threat of a German–Russian military alliance against Poland.[14]

The inclusion of two different factions in the new government was also singularly opportune with respect to the immediate political tasks which confronted the Polish Republic. Dmowski and his National Democratic colleagues, who in historical terms might be associated with the western orientation of Poland under the Piast dynasty, had their strongest home base in the western provinces of Poland, especially in Poznań. They were the most forceful advocates of a Polish western expansion and of close alliance ties with the Entente Powers. Their intimate diplomatic contacts in Allied capitals and their negotiating skills, no less than their basic political orientation, made them ideally suited to represent Poland at the forthcoming peace conference and to gain maximum concessions for Poland's western territorial aspirations. If a favorable outcome for Poland's territorial aspirations in the west could best be achieved by stiff bargaining at the diplomatic tables in Paris, her territorial claims in the east largely had to be carved by the sword. Piłsudski and many of his followers were "Easterners," i.e., advocates of the Jagellonian tradition of a confederate multinational commonwealth, which found its cultural and political role in an eastward advance and acted as an independent force in European politics. Given this different regional orientation in their respective policies, it was natural for the former group to view Germany as Poland's principal adversary and obstacle to the realization of their ambitions, and for the latter to see Russia cast into this adversary role. In the same manner, both sides tended to emphasize to the point of exaggeration their own achievements in reconstructing Poland's frontiers, while belittling those of their competitors.[15]

[14] Cited in Komarnicki, *Rebirth of Poland*, pp. 261–62.

[15] Leon Wasilewski, in *Józef Piłsudski, jakim go znałem* (Warsaw, 1935), p. 171, cited in Harald Laeuen, *Polnische Tragödie* (Stuttgart, 1955), p. 287, reports how Piłsudski told him in February 1919 that all Polish gains on her western frontier were merely gifts of the Entente, while he himself was going to carve the Polish empire in the east.

The Poznań Uprising and the Armistice Convention

Paderewski's arrival in Poland was another event of considerable consequence for the future of German–Polish relations. The appearance of this brilliant artist and dynamic figure amidst the tense atmosphere in Poznań on December 27, 1918, produced a spontaneous mass demonstration, and when this led to repressive countermeasures by the German authorities, the situation escalated to open hostilities. Fighting spilled from the city of Poznań to the rest of the province, and the German army in its state of demoralization and partial dissolution failed to nip the movement in its bud. As was later to be repeated in the case of the Upper Silesian uprisings, the Allies viewed these spontaneous local events with some misgivings, for while the Polish cause enjoyed considerable Allied sympathy, they distrusted such unsanctioned military initiatives which challenged their own authority and intensified their difficulties in dealing with Germany.

When the fighting in Poznań did not subside, the Allies abandoned their original passivity and forced Germany to sign the Trier Armistice Convention on February 16, 1919. In this convention Germany agreed to suspend hostilities in the province of Poznań and to accept a demarcation line across which her forces were not to move, thereby leaving the greater part of that province under de facto Polish control.

The German military reacted with shock and consternation when it became known that Erzberger had signed the Trier Armistice Convention. Realists like General von Seeckt, the commander of the *AOK Nord* (*Armee Ober-Kommando Nord*—Army Supreme Command North) drew the necessary conclusions which rejected the idea of a military recovery of the province of Poznań after the official recognition of the demarcation line.[16] Others were less willing to accept this fact. In a Cabinet session on April 24, 1919, during which the discussion centered on Germany's eastern security problem, General Groener reported on the measures which had been taken to strengthen the defense along the Poznań demarcation line and to prepare for the military recovery of that province.[17] Groener admitted that the task of recovering Poznań by military

---

[16] *General Hans von Seeckt Nachlass* [hereafter called Seeckt Papers] (Bundesarchiv, Coblenz), microfilm reel 26.

[17] *General Wilhelm Groener Nachlass* [hereafter called Groener Papers] (Bundesarchiv, Coblenz), microfilm reel 22.

means was becoming increasingly difficult with the arrival of the disciplined Haller Army which reinforced existing Polish forces.[18] But it was still feasible, provided Germany substantially weakened her other fronts. In this report, Groener merely presented the recovery plan as an available military option but did not urge its adoption because, as he himself admitted, he could not judge whether the military recapture of Poznań was politically acceptable under these circumstances.[19]

The agreement on the Poznań demarcation line only mildly reduced the military anxieties that had existed in Germany as well as in Poland ever since the November armistice. Poland feared a German military offensive which sought to recover the entire province of Poznań, while Germany regarded Danzig, Upper Silesia, and to a lesser extent also, East Prussia as potential targets of a Polish-inspired insurrection, following the Poznań precedent. The internal revolutionary situation in East Prussia and Upper Silesia tended to increase German anxieties, as it rendered these regions more vulnerable to foreign pressure and intervention. This uncertainty was intensified by the experience of a militarily oriented society like Germany suddenly finding itself in the nudity of virtual disarmament. While some of these security obsessions were exaggerated, the unsettled political situation in East Europe, the concentration of Polish troops along the German frontier, as well as the romantic national fervor of the new-born Republic, made Poland an uneasy neighbor for any power. "The situation in the east," writes the long-time minister of defense of the Weimar period, Otto Gessler, "intensified by the unpredictable aggressive desires of the Poles, created an object of constant and most acute concern for the *Reichsregierung* during the first years after the conclusion of the war."[20]

The demobilization of the German army had proceeded so rapidly even before the formal demobilization decree of December 31, 1918, that Marshal von Hindenburg on November 23 appealed to army units to create a voluntary border guard for the purpose of maintaining internal

---

[18] After the November armistice, the Polish government pressed for the immediate return of the Haller Army from France and insisted that they use the sea route via Danzig. Germany feared that Poland might exploit the presence of these forces in Danzig to stage a coup. The dispute centered on Article 16 of the armistice which raised the question whether Poland was permitted to transport military goods through Danzig. After some hesitation the Allies supported the German stand and the Haller Army returned by land.

[19] *Groener Papers*, reel 22.

[20] Otto Gessler, *Reichswehrpolitik in der Weimarer Zeit* (Stuttgart, 1958), p. 142.

order and for defending the threatened eastern provinces. Concurrently, and acting on their own initiative, former army officers established the first *Freikorps* or Free Corps. Thus the clandestine border defense system [*Grenzschutz*] was formed which vegetated—half tolerated by the government, half resented—along the German–Polish frontier during the entire period of the Weimar Republic.

After February the German military viewed the strategic situation on the Polish frontier with somewhat greater confidence, despite the continued influx of alarmist reports from private and official sources in the border districts. By mid-February Groener believed the danger of a Polish or Czech invasion of Upper Silesia to have receded; what remained was mainly the threat of a Bolshevist uprising.[21] On April 14 the military situation report of the German army command noted with satisfaction that Poland had reduced her forces on the Upper Silesian border and had shifted them to her eastern front. The report speculated that most of the returning Haller forces would also be deployed in the east.[22]

In the above-mentioned Cabinet briefing of April 24, 1919, General Groener painted a relatively confident picture of the military situation in the east. He felt that Germany could cope with the military problems in that area if she maintained her present strength. The Cabinet followed his advice to retain the *Grenzschutz* until the internal and external situation in the east had become somewhat stabilized. Opposition to this decision did not come from the Social Democrats or the Prussian government, as might be expected, but from Erzberger of the *Zentrum*.

While German fears temporarily diminished, Polish apprehensions about possible German military actions came to a rapid crescendo in May of that year. Poland feared that Germany might reject the Allied peace proposals and renew military operations by launching an offensive campaign in the east, while engaging in a defensive strategy against the superior forces of the Allies in the west. On the eve of receiving the Allied draft proposals, Germany mobilized her military units on the Polish frontier in a show of determination and as a means of deterring any possible pre-emptive Polish moves.[23] Shortly before Germany submitted her

---

[21] *Groener Papers*, reel 1, p. 664.

[22] *Ibid.*, reel 22. The strength of AOK Nord was 103,000 men, that of AOK Süd 106,000. The total strength of the Polish army at that time, including Haller's forces, was estimated at 440,000, but the major portion of this was deployed on Poland's eastern front.

[23] Paderewski to Foreign Minister Pichon of France, May 6, 1919, *Archiwum Ignacego Paderewskiego* [hereafter referred to as Paderewski Papers] (Archiwum Akt Nowych, Warsaw) [hereafter called AAN], folder 711.

answer to the draft proposal, Polish fears reached war scare dimensions. The Warsaw government was bombarded with disquieting reports from the army command and local authorities in frontier districts which announced German military activities close to the border and speculated about aggressive moves by Germany. These anxieties were particularly acute as Poland was ill-prepared to engage in military activities on her western frontier because her striking power was then concentrated in eastern Galicia, where Haller had just launched his May offensive.

On May 22 the Chief of the Polish Army Command informed Prime Minister Paderewski of intelligence reports which indicated that a German attack was imminent and therefore asked that the military detachments in Poznań be integrated with the rest of the Polish army. The report also spoke of the existence of a German–Soviet alliance which would be made public in a few days. It was speculated that under this alliance agreement German officers would go to Russia as instructors and unemployed German workers would find work in Russian factories, while German troops would be withdrawn from the Baltic and redeployed in Silesia.[24] Paderewski received an even gloomier report on the following day which seemed to confirm that Germany would attack Poland if she decided to reject the treaty proposals. In view of this critical situation, the army command urged the government to come to an immediate agreement with Czechoslovakia that would secure the latter's co-operation in such an event.[25] On the same day, the Council of Ministers took note of a letter of the War Ministry which listed several preparatory orders that had been drawn up in the event of war with Germany.[26] On May 27 the minister of interior, Wojciechowski, reported to the Cabinet about the panic which had broken out in several border districts as civilians were trying to take refuge from the expected German invasion. Apparently the panic had been precipitated by nervous orders which had been issued by the local civilian and military authorities. As a means of calming the situation, it was resolved that ministers instruct their respective departments that there would be no evacuation under any circumstances.[27]

---

[24] *Ibid.* It is interesting to see that the Polish impression that German officers were going to Russia as military instructors was to be realized, although some three years later.

[25] *Ibid.*

[26] *Protokoły Posiedzeń Rady Ministrów Rzeczypospolitej Polskiej* [Protocols of the Council of Ministers of the Polish Republic; hereafter referred to as PPRM] (AAN), May 23, 1919, VI, p. 436.

[27] *Ibid.*, May 27, 1919, p. 479.

It was only when Germany had signed and ratified the peace treaty that Polish military apprehensions somewhat subsided.

The Versailles Peace Treaty

By the time the official peace negotiation unfolded, Poland had reached the advantageous position of having established a unified government which enjoyed international recognition by the victorious powers that determined the proceedings and outcome of the conference. Only a few months before, in September 1918, when Dmowski visited President Wilson, he found him unwilling to concede the Polish demand of establishing a direct territorial access to the sea. Wilson stuck to his earlier version of access that was to be achieved by making Danzig a free port and by neutralizing the Vistula. But the cumulation of such major events as the savage terminal months of fighting, the military and political collapse of Germany, the armistice, and the creation of a unified and internationally recognized government in Poland, had gradually made the Allied and Associated Powers more amenable to the ambitious demands of Poland.

The members of the Polish delegation arrived at the Paris Peace Conference well prepared with historical, economic, political, and strategic arguments and equipped with suitcases full of maps, documents, and memoranda to substantiate and support an entire catalogue of claims. The Polish demands, as proposed by Dmowski to the Council of Ten on February 25, 1919, covered most of Upper Silesia, parts of Central Silesia, Poznań, West Prussia, the eastern part of Pomerania, Danzig, the district of the Mazures, Ermland, and the Memel region. Dmowski also asked for the creation of an independent East Prussian state in order to separate that province from the rest of Germany and thus prevent the creation of a Polish "corridor" through the territory of the German *Reich*, for he "had realized the incompatability of the Polish and German territorial claims and hoped that such a solution could prevent German attempts for a border revision in the future."[28]

The Commission on Poland in its recommendation of March 19, 1919, adopted most of these Polish demands, although it modified them with respect to East Prussia and urged that in the Allenstein district a plebiscite be held to determine the wishes of the people. Even though the British and the French delegates to this commission had been in

[28] Hans Roos, *Geschichte der Polnischen Nation 1916–1960* (Stuttgart, 1961), p. 58.

broad agreement on this report, Lloyd George voiced strong criticism when Cambon presented it to the Supreme Council. Lloyd George's objections were set forth in a memorandum of March 25.

> The proposal of the Polish Commission that we should place 2,100,000 Germans under the control of a people which is of a different religion and which has never proved its capacity for stable self-government throughout its history, must, in my judgment, lead sooner or later to a new war in the east of Europe.[29]

Lloyd George's position at the peace conference and later at Spa has made him something of a *bête noire* among Polish historians. But it would probably be an exaggeration to ascribe to him particularly strong anti-Polish sentiments beyond the somewhat imperious and impatient Great Power approach that he displayed in dealing with all smaller East European states. In the case of Poland there was the added concern that an overly harsh territorial settlement at the expense of Germany might drive the latter into the hands of the Bolshevists or would impair Germany's economic capacity and, with it, her ability to resume full trade relations with Britain and to make reparations payments. But more than anything else, the British Prime Minister feared that if the boundaries of the restored Polish state were to violate the self-determination aspirations of different ethnic groups, a dangerous trap would be laid for a future conflict between Poland and her more powerful neighbors, thus again risking a general European conflagration. It was from this long-term security preoccupation and not from any intrinsic anti-Polish sentiment that Lloyd George became the principal obstacle within the Allied camp to the full realization of Poland's historical claims. As a result of his protests, a plebiscite solution was agreed upon for the districts of Allenstein and Marienwerder, and a compromise was reached on the Danzig question which envisaged the creation of a Free City under the protection of the League. In a note of May 7, 1919, the Allied and Associated Powers communicated this solution to the German government.

In her answer of May 29 to the Allies, Germany categorically rejected the territorial solution in the east; instead, she proposed a plan that would give Poland free port facilities in Danzig, Königsberg, and Memel, free shipping facilities on the Vistula, and special railroad treaties under international guarantee. This line of argument which would have secured for Poland free access to the sea, without, however, getting the "Corridor," represented the principal theme of Germany's

[29] Great Britain, *Parliamentary Papers*, XXIII (1922), Cmd. 1614.

subsequent revisionist proposals. The German protests strengthened Lloyd George's position vis-à-vis Clemenceau and Wilson and helped him to extort from his reluctant colleagues an additional compromise in the form of the Upper Silesian plebiscite. The latter was the most significant concession which the German peace delegation was able to gain from its counterproposals.

The territorial issue was thus resolved in a manner which both Germany and Poland had desperately tried to avoid. German objections, which met with virtually unanimous popular backing, found their principal target in the loss of West Prussia and Danzig and the resulting insular status of East Prussia, as well as the uncertainty of the Upper Silesian boundary drawing. Poland, on the other hand, felt that her historical claims had not been equitably satisfied by the Danzig and Upper Silesian solution of the treaty and feared that her security considerations had been ignored by the creation of a narrow land corridor which was enclosed by German territory and "corked" by the hostile Free City of Danzig. The "Corridor" solution exposed Poland to German military pressure and kept alive the spirit of revisionism and revanchism in Germany.

In addition to the territorial clauses, the Treaty of Versailles also contained numerous other provisions in the realm of economics, finance, citizenship, transport, and public administration that specifically related to Germany and Poland. How these affected German–Polish relations will be discussed in subsequent chapters. The fact that such a large portion of the items which touched on German–Polish relations could be traced directly to this international treaty stimulated to no small degree the interest and involvement of the European powers in almost all facets of German–Polish relations. Finally, even those general military, economic, and reparations provisions of the treaty which did not directly involve Poland, imposed general economic and security constraints on Germany and thus had the effect of weakening Germany's over-all bargaining position vis-à-vis Poland in the postwar years.

During the entire inter-war period the Versailles treaty acted as a rallying point for German public opinion, which transcended class lines, regional diversities, and different political party affiliations, and thus provided the inner dynamics for a course of revanchism, revisionism, and spiritual defiance against what was regarded as a hostile and treacherous international environment. It was a case of political alienation on a grand scale. The focus of popular resistance fell particularly on the war guilt clause, the reparations demands, and on the territorial losses. As the chief beneficiary of Germany's territorial losses, Poland, next to France (the principal architect of the whole settlement), became the chief target of German hostility. And since Poland was weaker than either France or Germany and a former subject state, there was a special note of contempt and derision added to Germany's hostility toward Poland.

When the Versailles treaty came into effect on January 10, 1920, the final territorial settlement of the East Prussian and Upper Silesian plebiscite districts remained uncertain. On that date Germany had to surrender the area and city of Danzig, which was reconstituted as a Free City, and to cede to Poland outright the provinces of Poznań and West Prussia (Pomorze). The surrender of Danzig represented a loss of some 1,914 sq. kilometers, with a population of 331,000, of which 315,000 were German speaking.[30] The transfer of Poznań and West Prussia brought Germany a loss of 42,927 sq. km. which, according to the Prussian census of 1910, had a total population of 2,962,000. Of this population 1,714,000 in the same census gave Polish as their mother tongue; 1,080,000 listed German; while 105,000 belonged to the Cashubian and 9,000 to the Mazurian language groups.[31]

With the exception of the commercial importance of Danzig, the lost territory in West Prussia and Poznań constituted a relatively sparsely populated agricultural region which was of no particular importance to Germany as an area of major industrial, commercial, scientific, or educational activity. But it was an area of great strategic importance for Germany, as its loss insulated East Prussia, making it militarily vulnerable, and as it changed the geostrategic position of Berlin from the center of an empire to something of a "frontier" city within a 100 mile radius of the Polish border. What was perceived most strongly, however, was the emotional impact brought about by the loss of an area with which Germany had established intimate historical and cultural ties over several centuries. It can, therefore, not seem surprising that in the highly emotionally charged atmosphere of that time, German public opinion at large and all her political parties should have rejected the territorial provisions of the peace treaty as they applied to Germany's eastern frontier.[32]

[30] F. W. Putzgers, *Historischer Schulatlas* (Leipzig, 1935), p. 118.

[31] Werner Markert, ed., *Osteuropa Handbuch—Polen* (Cologne, 1959), p. 22.

[32] Germany, *Verhandlungen der Verfassungsgebenden Deutschen Nationalversammlung* [Debates of the German Constituent National Assembly], *Stenographische Berichte*, vol. 326, May 12, 1919. After the adoption of the Weimar Constitution on

The Polish reaction was more ambivalent. Public opinion, which had been driven to a state of high emotional fervor and great expectations, reacted critically to the territorial settlement which did not fully recover the historical claims of Poland's western frontier of 1772. In addition, the Minorities Treaty which Poland had been forced to sign with the Allied Powers met with considerable resentment, as a slight on Polish sovereignty, and with real political concern, for it appeared to be a built-in mechanism for international intervention, of which Poland had experienced so much in her tragic history. The humiliation was all the more acute because Germany was not required to adhere to a similar international minorities convention, which made Poland appear as a culturally degraded country.

Several leading Polish historians of the inter-war period expressed their reservations about the Versailles settlement.[33] Stanisław Głąbiński, who had acted as *Sejm rapporteur* for the ratification of the Versailles treaty, mentions in his memoirs that parliamentary ratification in Poland was given only because Poland thereby became an independent state, but that the treaty was viewed as a *Diktat* which the victorious Poland had been forced to accept just like the defeated Germany.[34]

Despite these reservations, the Polish government of the day and its successors made faithful adherence to the Versailles treaty the cornerstone of Poland's foreign policy. The treaty was viewed as the instrument which had restored her full independence and as the best guarantee for her survival as an independent state.[35] Throughout the inter-war period Poland acted as champion of the territorial status quo in Europe, and her diplomatic energy was fully engaged in resisting all those revisionist strivings which originated in Germany or elsewhere. This adherence to

---

July 31, 1919, the National Assembly returned to Berlin and resumed the name of *Reichstag*.

[33] See M. Bobrzyński, *Wskrzeszenie państwa polskiego* (Cracow, 1920); R. Dmowski, *Polityka polska*. Dmowski, who was otherwise strongly pro-Entente in his opinions, notes critically how at this first international conference of democratic powers, a few individuals exercised far greater power in deciding the fates of millions than any autocrat in history (*ibid.*, p. 359). Contemporary Polish historians are even more critical in their evaluation of the Versailles treaty. For a summary of contemporary Polish opinion, see Henryk Zieliński, "Znaczenie Traktatu Wersalskiego dla rozwoju stosunków polsko-niemieckich po I Wojnie Światowej," *Kwartalnik Historyczny*, vol. 70 (1963): 23–33.

[34] S. Glabiński, *Wsponienia polityczne* (Pelplin, 1939), p. 427; cited in Laeuen, *Polnische Tragödie*, p. 288.

[35] Aleksander Skrzyński, *Polska i pokoy* (Warsaw, 1923); cited in Laeuen *Polnische Tragödie*, p. 84.

the peace settlement in no small way restricted Poland's own freedom of action, as it bound her to respect its provisions even if these should clash with her short-term interests. This attitude was reflected in the official stand which the Polish government took against Korfanty's insurrection in Upper Silesia in May 1921, despite the strong echo of support which the revolt found in Polish public opinion. A Foreign Ministry memorandum which formed the basis for Prime Minister Witos' explanation to the *Sejm* advanced the argument that the Versailles treaty provisions had to be upheld, even as they applied to Poland, for in the application of the treaty terms Poland found her best security guarantee.[36]

[36] *PPRM*, 14 (1921): 322.

II

A Period of Uncertainty:
From Versailles to Geneva

In the interval between the coming into effect of the Versailles treaty and the Geneva Convention on Upper Silesia in May 1922, German–Polish relations were manifested by uncertainty, extreme tension, and occasional attempts at organized violence. The key elements of conflict during this period were the problems of putting into effect the different clauses of the peace treaty, the uncertainty of the final territorial delineation in East Prussia and Upper Silesia, and the international crisis produced by the Polish–Soviet War of 1920.

In view of this hostile climate, it is all the more remarkable that the two countries were able to reach a series of complex agreements on a number of technical, economic, and political matters, most of which arose in connection with the implementation of the peace treaty terms. Despite the official breach of diplomatic relations on the eve of the peace conference, bilateral contacts between the two governments never ceased entirely. These contacts were broadened toward the end of 1919 and in 1920, concomitant with the need to cope with the growing number of issues that arose from the Versailles treaty.

At the very outset, Germany's Foreign Minister Müller, of the Social Democrats [SPD], made an eloquent plea for establishing sound working relations with the new Polish Republic so that the detrimental aspects of the imposed treaty might be reduced:

> The Versailles Treaty has not given us the frontiers in the east to which Germany had been entitled if self-determination of the population had been the guiding factor. . . . Thus, the dictated peace has not respected

the vital interests of either state. Nevertheless, we will seriously attempt to create good-neighborly relations between both parties. We are eager to alleviate, as far as possible, the damages of the Peace Treaty by direct negotiations.[1]

In this pursuit Müller received the backing of his own party and of the Erzberger wing of the *Zentrum* party. Even some moderate Nationalists agreed that for the sake of aiding the German minority group in Poland one should work for a tolerable relationship.[2] Müller's immediate successors in the rapidly changing portfolio of the Foreign Ministry, notably Dr. Simons, had similar goals. In December 1920 Dr. Simons noted that both nations depended more than ever "not only on a mere peaceful coexistence but on industrious co-operation."[3]

In July 1919 bilateral discussions were held in Toruń and later in Danzig. These German–Polish talks were resumed in Berlin toward the end of September, after they had been temporarily interrupted by the first Upper Silesian insurrection in August of that year. The first in a series of agreements was reached on October 1, 1919, when both parties promised to release persons who had been interned for political reasons, most of them in connection with the recent Upper Silesian insurrection.[4] In the course of the next few months, Stockhammern, the German delegate, and his Polish counterpart, Diamand, reached agreement on a number of points. These included provisions for the smooth administrative transfer of sovereignty on January 10, 1920, in those regions that were to be ceded to Poland. Both sides shared the desire to avoid military clashes or disorder. At that particular time Poland suffered from an acute shortage of trained civil servants. To help meet this deficiency,

---

[1] Nationalversammlung, *Sten. Berichte*, 328, July 23, 1919, p. 1856.

[2] Reichstag, *Sten. Berichte*, 330, October 23, 1919, p. 3375; speech by Schultz (DNVP).

[3] Note by Simons, December 19, 1920. *Aken des Auswärtigen Amtes* [Records of the German Foreign Ministry], (Archiv des Auswärtigen Amtes, Bonn. A microfilmed copy of these documents is deposited in the National Archives, Washington, D.C.); files of the Foreign Minister, reel 1424, serial 2945H, frames D570 294–297. For the microfilmed records of the German Foreign Ministry the following sequence will be used hereafter: AA, standing for *Auswärtiges Amt*, to be followed by the origin of the file, i.e., RAM [*Reichsminister des Äusseren*] indicating that it originated from the files of the Foreign Minister; while StS [*Staatssekretär*] denotes the files of the Undersecretary; GA [*Geheimakten*] marks the secret files, and D,M,T, and W refer to the documents from the files of the directors of the Eastern Division of the Foreign Ministry, von Dirksen, von Moltke, Trautmann, and Wallroth respectively. The same sequence of reel, serial, and frame numbers will be kept. Under this abbreviated form, the above document would be cited as AA, RAM/1424/2945H/D570 294–97.

[4] Reichstag, *Anlagen zu den Sten. Berichten*, 339, Nr. 1180.

Germany promised to persuade her civil servants to remain at their posts for at least two months after the transfer of sovereignty. In return, Poland agreed to forego her treaty rights to liquidate the mobile property of these particular civil servants. Also included was the provision under which Poland temporarily accorded to Germany the right of free navigation on the Vistula, while Germany permitted the transit ot material for the Polish army. Finally, the agreement included a number of stipulations for the reciprocal exchange of goods. Germany agreed to lend Poland 100 locomotives and rolling stock and promised to supply Poland with certain quantities of seeds and fertilizer. In return, Poland agreed to furnish Germany with certain quantities of foodstuffs.[5]

While these agreements promised economic gains to both signatories, and in the case of Poland also helped her consolidate her administrative authority in the newly gained territories, the transactions were not without risk to Poland, since Germany tried to exploit her superior bargaining position by attaching some far-reaching political conditions to the provisional agreements. If the German tactics had succeeded, they would, in part at least have revised some of the terms of the Versailles treaty. Count von Lerchenfeld, a counsellor in the German Foreign Ministry, had quite openly told the *Reichstag* that the German government should encourage German civil servants and teachers to remain in the ceded territory in order to strengthen the German character of the area and to use this provision as a lever to revise the Versailles treaty terms on the question of optants and liquidations.[6] Foreign Minister Müller echoed the same idea when he expressed considerable confidence that Poland would be forced to rely on the continued service of German administrators and would thus seek to extend their sojourn of two months. Germany, on her part, would be happy to comply if her other demands met with a satisfactory solution.[7]

For Poland this posed an acute predicament, for while these provisional agreements were of benefit in her precarious economic and administrative situation, they threatened to place her in a position of dependence on Germany. Moreover, these bilateral negotiations aroused the suspicion of the Allies who protested against the attempt to modify the liquidation provisions of the Versailles treaty. Consequently, Poland was put under considerable international pressure to break off her

[5] *Records of the U.S. State Department* (National Archives, Washington, D.C.), 760c.62/1. Hereafter referred to as *SD*, 760c. 62/1.
[6] Reichstag, *Sten. Berichte*, 330, October 24, 1919, p. 3388.
[7] *Ibid.*, 331, December 13, 1919, p. 4040.

bilateral Berlin talks and to transfer them to Paris, where they could be held on a multilateral basis under the watchful eyes of Poland's international sponsors.

The question of bilateral negotiations with Germany also produced a vigorous domestic controversy in Poland. Piłsudski and the Socialists favored direct negotiations with Germany, while the National Democrats, spurned by Polish representatives in Allied capitals, urged a rupture of the Berlin talks and adherence to Allied wishes. Already, on November 1, 1919, Prince Sapieha, the Polish minister in London, had sent a nervous warning that the economic negotiations with Germany created much concern in London and Paris banking circles.[8] Wielowieycki, a member of the Polish delegation in Paris, in a letter to a friend complained bitterly about the disastrous lack of skill and diplomatic finesse of the Polish negotiators in Berlin. Their behavior had left the unfortunate impression among the Allies that Poland was acting in bad faith and was disassociating herself from the war-time coalition. What had made a particularly negative impression had been the provisional agreement under which Poland accorded Germany freedom of navigation on the Vistula, which amounted to an internationalization of that river, precisely what Poland had refused to the Allies.[9] Wielowieycki's wish that negotiations be transferred to Paris was reiterated in a memorandum by Patek on November 24, shortly before he became foreign minister.[10]

Four days later, Clemenceau informed the Polish delegation of the opinion of the Supreme Council, which held that negotiations ought to be shifted to Paris and that no further bilateral agreements of this kind should be signed with Germany. The Polish government capitulated in the face of these pressure tactics, recalled Diamond and Korfanty from Berlin, and moved negotiations to Paris. In January 1920 it also revoked the economic agreements which had been concluded with Germany in the previous October. This unilateral cancellation prompted Germany to retaliate by imposing a hidden economic blockade on Poland which reached full dimensions with her declaration of neutrality during the Polish–Soviet War. Negotiations were resumed in Paris, where they were held under the chairmanship of General Le Rond who represented the Allied Powers. Soon thereafter, on January 9, 1920, agreement was reached, in fact or in principle, on a number of issues. These covered matters of social insurance in the ceded areas, pensions, the return of

[8] *Paderewski Papers*, folder 713, p. 1.
[9] *Ibid.*, pp. 3–4, November 17, 1919.
[10] *Ibid.*, p. 6.

documents and archival material to Poland, and restitutions to Poland for goods and money confiscated by the German military occupation during World War I.[11]

THE POLISH–SOVIET WAR

In March of that year diplomatic relations, which had remained severed since the expulsion of Kessler, were resumed when Szebeko came to Berlin as *chargé d'affaires* and Count Oberndorff went to Warsaw in the same capacity. Despite this formal step toward normalization and the continuation of the Paris talks, no other agreement of consequence was concluded for some time because of the international crisis produced by the Polish–Soviet War.

Ever since February 1919, when the Polish army had engaged the Soviet forces which had advanced on the heels of the withdrawing German army, there had been intermittent combat between Poles and Soviets. By May of that year Wilno and Minsk were in Polish hands and Piłsudski's dream of reviving the Jagellonian tradition of a multinational East European commonwealth under Polish leadership appeared to gain real substance. What precise format this commonwealth was to take remained rather vague. Piłsudski's federal plans extended mainly to Lithuania, while relations with the Ukraine, Byelorussia, and the Baltic States would probably fall into the category of alliances and thus create a heavy frontier belt of allies and satellites between Poland and the Soviet Union.[12] The scheme was not without grandeur but the restoration of this historical formation did not fully take into account the relative decline of Polish power vis-à-vis her two neighbors and the frenzy of nationalism which had swept over all of Europe and would have brought Piłsudski's supranational solution into immediate conflict with the national aspirations of the different ethnic groups.

Between December 1919 and March 1920 both Poles and Soviets engaged in delicate bargaining maneuvers on the question of armistice talks. Neither side seems to have acted in good faith and feverish military preparations accompanied these diplomatic exchanges. The Soviets were probably serious in their desire for peace at that particular time,

---

[11] Jerzy Krasuski, *Stosunki polsko-niemieckie 1919–1925* (Poznań, 1962), vol. I, pp. 202–3.

[12] Konstantin Symmons-Symonolewicz, "Polish Political Thought of the Eastern Borderlands of Poland, 1918–1930," *Polish Review* 4, nos. 1–2 (1959): 67–68. M. K. Dziewanowski, *Joseph Piłsudski: European Federalist* (Stanford, 1969).

but they also hoped to exploit the armistice talks to discredit Poland in the eyes of the Allies and to flood her with revolutionary propaganda. The Poles, in turn, inserted a "joker" when they insisted that armistice talks be held at Borisov and that fighting be suspended only in that sector, precisely where the Soviet army had concentrated most of its forces. Under the Polish proposal, military operations would have continued along the rest of the front where Russia was weakest. When these maneuvers failed to open the way for armistice negotiations, Piłsudski moved with great rapidity and resolution. He concluded a political treaty and a military convention with the Ukrainian leader Petlura. A few days later, on April 26, Piłsudski launched a spectacular offensive which was crowned with the capture of Kiev on May 8.

Under the brilliant leadership of the young ex-Guards officer Tukhachevsky, the Russians struck a quick counterblow which brought the Soviet army to the gates of Warsaw by August. Under the shadow of the Soviet advance, Prime Minister Grabski made a Canossa-like trip to the Allied conference at Spa early in July. At Spa, where Lloyd George and Lord Curzon virtually dominated proceedings, Poland was forced to accede to a number of humiliating conditions, which seemed to dissolve the very foundations on which the new Poland had so laboriously been reconstituted. Chief among them was the acceptance of the so-called Curzon Line as the future Polish–Soviet boundary in return for an Allied pledge for mediation and assistance.

The real settlement, however, was not brought about by Allied intervention but by a Polish victory in the Battle of the Vistula. Lord D'Abernon refers to this so-called miracle on the Vistula as the eighteenth decisive battle of the world. It was the result of a counteroffensive which Piłsudski launched from the south on August 16 and which threatened to cut off Tukhachevsky's forces and thus forced their rapid retreat.[13] Armistice talks were initiated soon thereafter in Minsk, and on October 12, 1920, some six months after the initiation of full-scale hostilities, the two adversaries signed an armistice and a provisional peace treaty at Riga.

[13] Piotr Wandycz, in "General Weygand and the Battle of Warsaw 1920," *Journal of Central European Affairs* 19 (1960): 357–65, exposes the faulty legend according to which it was the French General Weygand, rather than Piłsudski, who was the master-mind behind the *ordre de bataille* which brought the Victory on the Vistula. The Weygand legend, which was initially circulated by Piłsudski's domestic opponents and was eagerly taken up in France, offended the Marshal's *amour propre* and contributed to the reserve and suspicion which he subsequently demonstrated toward his French ally.

The dramatic and traumatic events of the 1920 summer campaign also formed a vital tangent for German–Polish relations. The rapid advance of the Red Army during the summer months mesmerized German opinion, as it was widely believed that the chance for a massive roll-back of the whole structure of the peace settlement had come within grasp with the anticipated defeat and collapse of Poland. German labor openly sympathized with the Bolshevist cause in the Polish–Soviet War, the SPD signed an official appeal not to transport any war materiel to Poland, and in Danzig dock workers went on strike and refused to unload war materiel that was destined for Poland.[14] Certain Rightist circles were in favor of German military intervention or of starting an insurrection in Pomorze in order to prepare the way for the collapse of Poland and the restoration of the 1914 German–Russian frontier.[15] One has to realize the massive emotional appeal which the prospect of a revision of the Versailles treaty held for the German people in order to explain the relative lack of concern that was shown for the foreign and domestic political consequences of a Soviet defeat of Poland. The ardent desire for the former seemed to stifle any real concern for the latter. The German government and leading bourgeois circles, however, were more fully aware of the threat of a Soviet victory and therefore viewed the Soviet military advance with more ambivalent feelings. The concern of the government at the time seemed to be less with the foreign political or strategic consequences of a Soviet victory than with its domestic impact on the latent revolutionary situation in Germany. The German government, as Morawski, the head of the German desk in the Polish

---

[14] Even if the German government had not prevented the transit of war materiel to Poland as the result of its neutrality declaration, a threatened strike of German railroad workers would have made it impossible to send war goods to Poland.

The decision of the Danzig Constituent Assembly to adopt a neutral position in the Polish–Soviet War and the strike of Danzig dock workers were viewed as demonstrations of hostility toward Poland. This particular experience prompted the subsequent League decision allowing Poland to construct a munitions depot on the Westerplatte and to guard it with an armed detachment. Moreover, it exercised great weight in the Polish decision to construct the rival harbor at Gdynia.

[15] On August 26, 1920, the Turkish military hero, Enver Pasha, reported to his close friend and confidant, General von Seeckt, the content of a conversation with Trotsky's assistant, Slansky. The latter had suggested that in order to strengthen the Trotsky faction in the Kremlin which desired an understanding with Germany and recognition of the 1914 frontiers, it would be useful if Germany would unofficially aid the Red army in the present war. This could be done by providing the Red army with intelligence information and by secretly selling them arms. Enver Pasha strongly supported the offer and urged Seeckt that Germany create an army of volunteers in the "Corridor" or organize an insurrection in that area (*Seeckt Papers*, reel 24).

Foreign Ministry correctly concluded, "found it impossible to reconcile its foreign policy, which demanded the annihilation of Poland, with its domestic policy, which was very largely directed by the fear of a Spartacist revolution."[16]

Without prior consultation with the *Reichstag*, the German government decided on July 20 to adhere to a policy of strict neutrality and to prohibit the transit of arms to either belligerent. All German political parties, including the Communists, accepted this decision without objection. Dr. Simons justified the government's policy of neutrality in the following terms: "Germany's responsibility in participating in any way in support of Poland would be enormously great, but we no more desire that as a result of our participation Poland will disappear from the scene."[17]

Talleyrand's dictum that nonintervention is something very complex which basically means the same as intervention, also found its application in this case, for the apparently nonpartisan German declaration worked to Poland's disadvantage as it terminated the sale and transit of war materiel to Poland. Since the Soviet Union had not benefited from such transactions, this ban meant little to her. Poland, on the other hand, was thereby largely cut off from Western arms supplies, for Czechoslovakia pursued the same neutrality and transit prohibition policy as Germany, and shipments through Danzig were temporarily blocked. During the height of the military crisis, Poland was therefore severely curtailed in her supplies of foreign arms, since the only other remaining route by way of Rumania was slow and tortuous.

The course of nonintervention was also sanctioned by one of Poland's most irreconcilable enemies, Germany's recently named commander of the *Reichswehr*, General Hans von Seeckt. In the history of Weimar Germany the name Seeckt has almost become synonymous with German–Soviet military collusion and collaboration for the forceful overthrow of the Versailles treaty. Similarly, Seeckt has become known as the implacable enemy of Poland who worked for a new elimination of that country from the map of Europe. Indeed, the image of Seeckt and the *Reichswehr* as the sepulchre of anti-Polish feeling in Germany was so pronounced that Hitler and Field Marshal von Blomberg, during Beck's visit to Berlin in 1935, made definite attempts to contrast it with

    [16] Sir Horace Rumbold to Lord Curzon, September 3, 1920, *Records of the British Foreign Office*, Public Record Office, London; Foreign Office series 371, vol. 4827, p. 6. Hereafter referred to as *FO*, 371/4827.
    [17] Reichstag, *Sten. Berichte*, 344, July 26, 1920, p. 264.

the newly emerging friendly sentiments within the ranks of the army. "Von Blomberg, ainsi qu'Hitler," wrote Beck, "répéta à plusieurs reprises qu'il ne demandait pas mieux que de voir disparaître les vieux préjugés de la Reichswehr à l'égard de la Pologne grâce à des contacts directs entre les deux armées."[18]

Seeckt left no doubt of his intentions regarding Poland and of the role which he had assigned to Russia in executing this policy. Answering Brockdorff-Rantzau's *Pro Memoria* of 1922 on the future of German–Soviet relations, Seeckt wrote:

> Poland is the crux of the Eastern problem. The existence of Poland is unbearable and incompatible with the vital interests of Germany. She must vanish and shall vanish through her own internal weakness and through Russia—with our assistance. Poland is even more unbearable for Russia than for us; no Russian government can ever reach a settlement with Poland. With Poland falls one of the strongest pillars of the Versailles Peace, the power out-post of France. To achieve this goal must be one of the most fundamental drives of German policy since it can be achieved. But it can be achieved only through Russia or through her help. Poland can never offer any advantage to Germany; not economic, as she is not capable of development, nor political, as she is France's vassal.[19]

In his pamphlet *Deutschland zwischen West und Ost*, Seeckt pointed out that "there cannot be any reconcilation between equal and equal; there remains only the subjection of Germany. But if a reconciliation is impossible and a subjugation excluded, only struggle remains."[20] Seeckt's aim went beyond the mere reduction of Poland to her ethnographic frontiers, instead, it envisaged her complete disappearance from the map of Europe. Any settlement along ethnographic lines, even if favorable to Germany, could be regarded as no more than a truce.[21]

Yet in appraising Seeckt's Poland policy we must distinguish sharply between his broader aims for the future and his actual behavior under the circumstances in which he found himself. Seeckt, in contrast to wide circles of other *Reichswehr* officers, possessed the stern self-discipline of subjecting his long-term goals to the scrutinizing test of present reality. He was not a general who would blindly lead his country into an ad-

---

[18] Józef Beck, *Dernier Rapport, Politique Polonaise 1926–1939* (Neuchâtel, 1951), p. 100.

[19] *Seeckt Papers*, reel 24.

[20] Hans von Seeckt, *Deutschland zwischen West und Ost* (Hamburg, 1930), pp. 30–31.

[21] *Ibid.*, p. 33.

venturous war. "The experienced and knowing soldier," he later wrote, "fears war far more than the phantast can, who, not knowing war, only speaks of peace."[22] As a result, there appears a very definite variance between his grand design for the future and his actual tactical conduct. This, indeed, may have been one of the riddles which he presented to his subordinates and which earned him the name of the "sphinx." Consequently, while his strategy ought to have launched him onto the road of a German–Soviet military collaboration during the Polish–Soviet War, Seeckt in a realistic appraisal of Germany's extremely limited military capabilities rejected a German participation, even though his sympathies clearly lay with the Red Army.

Already, in February 1920, in a memorandum to President Ebert and Defense Minister Noske, Seeckt had correctly predicted that Polish–Soviet hostilities would break out during the summer and that France, Britain, and the United States would assist Poland with military advisers, money, and materiel but not with troops. Seeckt had categorically rejected any assistance to Poland under such circumstances, regardless of British promises and French threats, for apart from the necessity to work for a rapprochement with Russia, it was Germany's "pressing duty to welcome every sign which promised a weakening or even destruction of our intolerable neighbor." A joint German–Polish military effort was thus entirely unthinkable and would not be tolerated by German public opinion.[23] Seeckt admitted that a Soviet advance into Poland posed certain threats to Germany, but these would have to be met by Germany alone—the Allies would probably restore Germany's military freedom of action in such a case—and not by an alliance with Poland.[24] At the height of the Soviet military penetration into Poland, Seeckt wrote another memorandum in which he urged that Germany appeal to the Red Army to spare the former German areas the horrors of war because of the German population in those regions. In this way she would demonstrate to the whole world her close cultural ties to these lost areas and would thus take the first step for their eventual restoration to Germany. However, a direct intervention on the side of the Soviet Union was out of the question, as it would produce an immediate Allied invasion of Germany and might even embroil her with Soviet Russia, for such a move would pre-empt a Soviet occupation of Polish territory.[25]

[22] Hans von Seeckt, *Gedanken eines Soldaten* (Berlin, 1929), p. 12.
[23] Memorandum, February 26, 1920, *Seeckt Papers*, reel 21.
[24] *Ibid.*
[25] Memorandum, July 31, 1920, *ibid.*

Seeckt's belief that a German military intervention would prompt an immediate Allied military response was well founded in the realities of the situation. On August 13, that is at the height of the crisis, the French minister of war, Lefèvre, spoke with the Polish military attaché to inform him that France could not mobilize for the purpose of dispatching an expeditionary army to aid Poland. Such a move would be intolerable to the war-weary French public. But the Minister gave his assurance that in the event of a German intervention against Poland, France would immediately mobilize and march against Germany. Lefèvre let it be understood that France had already made full preparations for this contingency.[26]

While the government pursued a neutral course and certain extremist elements favored intervention on the side of Soviet Russia, still other elements in Germany envisaged an Allied mandate for German participation in a joint action by the Western powers in aid of Poland. As payoff for their participation they expected not only the repulsion of the Communist advance but also Polish and Allied consent to some territorial revisions.

The threads to enlist German support on the side of Poland were spun in various places. At the height of the Polish crisis Lord D'Abernon, writing from Warsaw where he was serving on the Allied mission, stressed the "importance of obtaining German cooperation against the Soviets."[27] The American minister in Warsaw, Hugh Gibson, in his confidential report of September 9, 1920, confirms the fact that on arriving in Warsaw D'Abernon had urged the Poles to solicit German assistance to help repel the Red Army. Subsequently he had abandoned the idea when the Polish authorities had convinced him that such a step was unthinkable, for not only would it prompt the Allies to abandon Poland but it would probably also entail the return of Danzig and Upper Silesia to Germany, as well as German control over internal Polish affairs that might be impossible to shake off.[28]

Lord D'Abernon's original position was upheld in certain German circles desiring an Allied mandate to join the war on the side of Poland. Chief among them was the German diplomatic representative in War-

---

[26] *Archiwum Ministerstwa Spraw Zagranicznych* [Records of the Ministry of Foreign Affairs], (Archiwum Akt Nowych, Warsaw), P. II (Political Division II, i.e., Western Europe), folder 4477. Hereafter referred to as AMSZ, P. II, fol. 4477.

[27] Viscount Edgar D'Abernon, *The Eighteenth Decisive Battle in the World, Warsaw 1920* (London, 1931), p. 72.

[28] SD, 769c.62/6.

saw, Count Oberndorff, who actively, but unsuccessfully, exerted himself in that direction. This German diplomat suffered from an almost physical aversion to Bolshevism and hoped for a favorable reaction from the Polish government and the Allied diplomats in Warsaw to his plan of including Germany in an anti-Communist front. At the height of the crisis, Oberndorff warned against any German attempts to align herself with Soviet Russia in the destruction of Poland. His report also contained a veiled argument for collaboration with Poland, even though no open request for aid was made.

> I will not here decide the difficult question whether and under what circumstances we should help the Poles in their extreme calamity: We are disarmed, under the tutelage of the Entente, and our weakness can force us into neutrality. But *we must wish that Poland remains intact:* certainly she is in many ways our adversary but also the wall which separates us from the Red peril, and it would be a crime against our country and against all of humanity if we should *contribute but in the smallest to a victory of the Soviets.*[29]

Nothing came of these overtures, however, for not only did they fail to get the stamp of official German approval but they also met with French and Polish rejection. "The representatives of the Western powers," notes Dirksen, "let themselves be drawn into friendly, yet noncommittal conversations. The Polish government had no intention of including the hated and still feared German neighbor in a combination of any sort."[30] To the French, such a mandate would once again have evoked the unpopular specter of a Polish–German alliance, while its price, a revision of the German–Polish boundary, was entirely unacceptable to Poland. In Warsaw it was feared that the German government might follow a strategy which sought to embroil Poland with France by drawing her into discussions on the removal of transit restrictions on war materiel. On July 28 Prince Sapieha, the Polish foreign minister, therefore instructed the head of the legation in Berlin to treat with reserve any attempt by Foreign Minister Simons to draw him into a discussion of these issues. Instead, he should take soundings among labor organizations and political groups to try to stop the sabotage of the transit of war materiel through the "Corridor."[31]

[29] Secret Report, Oberndorff, July 1, 1920, AA, GA/3723/K170/K023 969–73.
[30] Herbert von Dirksen, *Moskau, Tokio, London* (Stuttgart, 1949), p. 36.
[31] AMSZ, files of the Berlin Legation, Wiązka [bundle] 19, teczka [folder] 1 (hereafter referred to as AMSZ, Berlin Legation, W. 19, t. 1); cited in Krasuski, *Stosunki polsko-niemieckie,* I, p. 92.

Despite Warsaw's caution about discussions with Germany, rumors of Polish initiatives to make a deal with Germany continued to circulate in Poland and abroad. Much of this speculation seems to have been planted by the National Democrats who sought to discredit Piłsudski and the PPS for their apparent Germanophile sentiments. In its sitting of August 30, the Cabinet unanimously denied the rumor that a proposal of alliance with Germany had ever been made or discussed in Cabinet.[32] But various writers have revived these allegations and made them the basis of their interpretations. Laeuen states that when the Red Army was at the gates of Warsaw, Piłsudski had confidentially proposed that in return for German economic and financial aid Poland renounce the Upper Silesian plebiscite.[33] Francesco Tommasini, the Italian envoy to Warsaw, goes even further and asserts that the Polish proposal not only included Upper Silesia but also the "Corridor."[34]

The validity of either proposal is highly questionable. The German diplomatic records show no trace of such a proposal.[35] The Polish official position, as we have seen, clearly opposed such a move, which would also have met with a robust rebuff by the entire Polish population. More proudly nationalistic and militant than ever, as a consequence of their present crisis, the Poles betrayed no sign that they would voluntarily evacuate at anyone's request—much less on their own initiative—the areas which they considered their lawful property. If any overtures were made at all by Piłsudski, as appears to be the case, these came later in the year when he feared a renewed Soviet attack; however, in the latter case the offer was not for territorial compensation but for improved relations, especially in the economic field.

Throughout the war, when Poland was forced to concentrate her efforts in the east and consequently left her western flank partially exposed, she lived under the oppressive cloud of an imminent German attack or a German-inspired insurrection in the western provinces. The

---

[32] *PPRM*, 11 (1920), p. 463.

[33] Harald Laeuen, *Polnisches Zwischenspiel. Eine Episode der Ostpolitik* (Berlin, 1940), pp. 64–66.

[34] Francesco Tommasini, *La Risurrezione della Polonia* (Milan, 1925); cited in Christian Höltje, *Die Weimarer Republik und das Ost-Locarno Problem, 1919–1934* (Würzburg, 1958), p. 27. In a letter which Dirksen wrote to Höltje in April 1955, he called Tommasini's allegation "entirely improbable."

[35] Wipert von Blücher, who served in the *Ostabteilung* of the *Auswärtiges Amt* at that time, wrote to Höltje in May 1955 that he had never heard of such a proposal. In view of his close association with Maltzan, it was impossible that a proposal of this kind would not have come to his ears. Cited in Höltje, *Ost–Locarno*, p. 27.

attention of the Inter-Allied Military Control Commission was drawn to the build-up of war materiel on the Polish border and German reconnaissance flights over Poland to aid the Red Army.[36] The Polish General Staff suspected that some of the heavy military equipment in East Prussia was intended to supply the Red Army.[37] The general uncertainty of the situation gave rise to wildly exaggerated rumors of large German military units crossing the German boundary and joining the Soviet and Lithuanian armies in order to conduct operations against Poland.[38]

Another complicating factor was suddenly added to the already tense situation when late in August some 70,000 Soviet soldiers evaded capture by the advancing Polish army by taking refuge in East Prussia, where, in accordance with the duties of a neutral power, the German authorities were obliged to intern them. The Allies rejected the German request to let the army and the paramilitary *Grenzwehr* enter the area in order to help cope with this unexpected emergency. Germany was thus hardpressed to protect the life and property of its local population and to discharge its international obligations as a neutral power. The Allies, in turn, were concerned that by disarming the interned Soviet soldiers, the German arms reservoir might exceed the treaty limits and therefore insisted that the Allied Military Control Commission supervise these disarmament procedures. Viktor Kopp, the unofficial Soviet representative in Berlin, in turn, protested against this action as a violation of Germany's neutral status. In Soviet eyes the violation was all the more reprehensible, as the disarmament activities were conducted precisely by those powers who were aiding Poland against the Soviet Union.[39] Finally, Poland launched several protests in which she accused Germany of both negligence and collusion in letting interned Soviet soldiers escape to Lithuania, from where they made their way home to Russia.[40] This multiple emergency was not resolved until September 6, when the Conference of Ambassadors agreed to the shipment of the Soviet internees

---

[36] AMSZ, Berlin Legation, W.4, t.1; cited in Krasuski, *Stosunki polsko-niemieckie*, I, p. 86.

[37] General Staff Report, August 14, 1920, AMSZ, P. II, fol. 4477.

[38] General Staff Reports of June 4, and August 20, 1920, *ibid*. The conservative *Königsberger Zeitung* of August 10, 1920, admitted that whole groups of Germans were going over to fight on the Soviet side. The individuals concerned consisted largely of Leftist sympathizers, Free Corps members, and other disenchanted adventurists. But this eastward drift of German mercenaries was sporadic, unorganized, and infinitely smaller than the nervous Polish speculations at the time made it out to be.

[39] Report, Lord Kilmarnock, September 2, 1920, FO, 371/4826, p. 176.

[40] Report, Sir Horace Rumbold, September 4, 1920, *ibid.*, p. 200.

from the exposed area of East Prussia to the more tranquil environment of the interior of the *Reich*. On the same day, Poland and Germany reached agreement on the method of transporting these units through the "Corridor." Then the movement was completed without further incident.

After the preliminary Peace Treaty of Riga in October, the Polish government undertook fresh initiatives to improve relations with Germany, which had plunged to such perilous depths during the Polish–Soviet War. The principal Polish motive seems to have been an assurance of peace on its western front in the possible event of renewed Soviet hostilities. In addition, having escaped military defeat, Poland was now on the verge of an economic collapse and was therefore interested in ending Germany's de facto economic blockade.

Vice Premier Daszyński tried to promote semi-official contacts with various German groups and Consul Karol Rose and Stanisław Wachowiak, undersecretary in the Ministry of former Prussian Territories, came to Berlin, where they held discussions with German officials. The Germans promised to terminate their economic blockade and to provide long-term credits in return for Poland's renunciation of the practice of liquidating the property of German nationals.[41] The Polish negotiators showed interest in the proposal. But under French pressure, Poland was forced to declare such a *quid pro quo* to be a violation of the Versailles treaty and to disavow the official nature of the Rose–Wachowiak talks.[42]

What had seemed like a propitious beginning to some far-reaching economic and technical agreements was thus interrupted by outside pressure. Negotiations were once again shifted to Paris, where they were held under the chairmanship of Seydoux, who acted as delegate of the

[41] Memorandum, Kessler, of his discussions with Consul Rose, December 16, 1920, AA, RAM/1424/2945H/D570 313–20.

[42] Krasuski, *Stosunki polski-niemieckie*, I, pp. 215–16. Some of the ambivalence in the direction of Polish foreign policy at that time can be attributed to internal cleavages. Piłsudski relied heavily on his former PPS party colleague Ignacy Daszyński whose planned appointment to the post of foreign minister had apparently been blocked by French opposition, but who, in his capacity as vice premier, exercised a general supervisory role over foreign affairs. (Report Gibson, October 20, 1920, SD, 860c. 00/72). Daszyński kept his own men in the different European capitals—Diamond in Berlin and Biliński in Vienna—and worked toward improved relations with Germany. At the same time, the official direction of foreign policy was in the hands of Prince Sapieha who followed a pro-Allied course and strove for a rapprochement with Russia. Sapieha was one of Poland's great magnates and had avoided involvement in partisan politics. His political strength rested precisely on his nonpartisanship.

Supreme Council. The only concrete achievement of these Paris talks was the signing of the "Corridor" Transit Convention on April 21, 1921. This particular accord settled one of the most important issues in German–Polish relations, in what even Germany's Foreign Minister Köster had to admit was a "satisfactory manner."[43] The agreement assigned six railroad lines for connecting East Prussia with the rest of Germany. Daily twenty-four "privileged trains," i.e., trains exempt from all passport and visa formalities, commuted on these lines. All neutral observers and even objective Germans admitted that, despite certain inevitable minor obstacles and irritations, the constant flow of traffic through the "Corridor" was uninterrupted and smooth throughout the entire interwar period, regardless of tensions and crises, until the very outbreak of World War II. Warsaw was well aware of the political realities and implications. The "Corridor" was not only the danger spot in German–Polish relations but the weakest link in the whole chain of the new territorial settlement in Europe. Any interference by Poland in the traffic movement in the "Corridor" would not only have provoked an immediate international crisis but would also have placed in German hands the most powerful propaganda weapon in support of her revisionist strivings. As long as the tug-of-war between the German policy of revisionism and Poland's preservation of the status quo continued to be the dominant theme in German–Polish relations, the traffic through the "Corridor" was assured unhindered transit.

Together with the initial attempt to improve economic relations through direct negotiations there was an effort by some Polish circles to approach German Catholic groups who might be more amenable to harmonized relations with their Catholic neighbors in view of certain common spiritual and cultural traditions and because of the jointly perceived Communist threat. In November 1920 Archbishop Kakowski of Warsaw (who in 1917 had headed the Regency Council) visited Germany to sound out Chancellor Fehrenbach of the Catholic Center party on the prospects of improved German–Polish relations.[44] In December the Polish Consul in Munich in conversations with Bavarian authorities repeatedly emphasized the Polish desire for a reconciliation and the need

[43] Reichstag, *Sten Berichte*, 349, April 28, 1921, p. 3478. For a complete text of the transit convention see "Korridorvertrag," Reichstag, *Sten. Berichte, Anlagen*, 367, No. 2191 of Jan. 21, 1921

[44] Z. Gąsiorowski, "Stresemann and Poland Before Locarno," *Journal of Central European Affairs* 18 (1958): 27.

for making common arrangements to keep the advance of Bolshevism in check.[45]

The Plebiscite Decisions and the Upper Silesian Insurrection

Next to the Polish–Soviet War, the uncertainty about the final territorial solution that was to be determined by plebiscites was the major issue poisoning German–Polish relations at the time and preventing any normalization. The East Prussian plebiscite, which was held on July 11, 1920, produced considerable friction but no major incidents. From the Polish point of view it occurred at the most unfortunate time, when her economy was in a state of upheaval and the very survival of the Polish state was placed in jeopardy by the advance of the Red Army. In addition, Germany had provided transportation for former residents of the plebiscite area so that they could cast their vote for Germany. She also had the advantage of controlling the economy and news media of the area. The only Polish paper in the region, the *Gazeta Olsztyńska*, was owned by a Pole with pro-German sympathies and thus gave no support to the Polish position.[46] In the months preceding the plebiscite, the Polish Consul in Allenstein (Olsztyn) had sent a series of bleak reports which portended no good for the coming event. The Polish or Slavic population of the area was impoverished, passive, and intimidated and lacked a fully developed Polish national consciousness. This was particularly true of the Mazurians who were Protestants, but to a lesser degree also of the Polish-

---

[45] Letter, von Kahr to Foreign Minister, December 25, 1920, AA, RAM/1424/ 2945H/D570 332–34. In 1920 the French had tried to mobilize latent separatist trends in Bavaria. But by November Lord D'Abernon was able to report that France had realized the futility of this move and had abandoned her support for Bavarian separatism (FO, 371/4758, pp. 197–98). For a brief while the Polish consulate in Munich had imitated the French policy of promoting separatism and for this purpose had asked the Papal Nuncio Pacelli (later Pope Pius XII) to intervene with the Bavarian Premier von Kahr about raising its office to full legation status. Kahr had rejected this request, and in line with the French change of policy, Poland, too, abandoned the scheme of fostering an independent Bavarian state. The Polish commitment to Bavarian separatism had been ambiguous from the start. Her interest had been with getting certain Bavarian economic products and to have Bavaria support the cancellation of the scheduled Upper Silesian plebiscite rather than with promoting separatism for its own sake. In fact, the separation of Bavaria would have removed from German politics that sector that was least hostile to Poland and most inclined to exert a moderating influence on Germany's policy toward Poland.

[46] Report, Polish Consulate in Allenstein (Olsztyn), April 15, 1920, AMSZ, P. II, fol. 4611, pp. 120–22.

speaking Catholic population of Ermland (Warmia), of whom only one third did eventually vote for Poland. The Polish diplomatic officers in the area lacked time, money, contacts, and access to the newspapers, and by the admission of some of their own officers they had alienated the Inter-Allied Plebiscite Commission because of their tactlessness and lack of command of French.[47]

In the final vote 7,980 or 2.2 per cent in the Allenstein district voted for Poland; in the Marienwerder district the figure was 7,947 or 7.6 per cent, against 363,209 and 105,004 respectively who opted for Germany.[48] The outcome was a great disappointment for Poland and entirely contradicted Dmowski's Paris thesis about the Polish national consciousness of the population in the area.

The Polish vote would certainly have scored somewhat better under more favorable circumstances, but there can be little doubt that the overwhelming popular sentiment, regardless of religious or linguistic background, was for continued membership in the *Reich*. The Conference of Ambassadors interpreted the mandate in this manner and assigned the whole area to Germany with the exception of some eight villages.

Compared to East Prussia, the Upper Silesian plebiscite was a decision of a much greater magnitude, both in terms of its economic importance and the size of the population concerned. Also, the pattern of cultural and political affiliations and loyalties in Upper Silesia constituted a mozaic of much greater complexity. Even before the actual plebiscite, the Polish element in the area had staged two armed uprisings. The first of these, which occurred in August 1919, had been organized by the POW but had quickly been brought under control by units of the *Reichswehr*. The Warsaw authorities had watched it with mixed feelings. On the one hand, their sympathy lay with the insurgents and they viewed the movement as a tool for awakening Polish national consciousness among the Upper Silesian population. On the other hand, they feared that its anarchical and revolutionary tendencies might also catch fire in Poland. In the opinion of the Vice Minister of Foreign Affairs, Skrzyński, the chief danger inherent in the Silesian situation was that of a social revolution.[49] Moreover, the Polish government was nervous lest the in-

[47] Report of April 8, 1920, *ibid.*, p. 50.
[48] Werner Markert, ed., *Polen: Osteuropa Handbuch* (Cologne, 1959), p. 22. A full account of the East Prussian plebiscite is given in M. Worgitzki, *Geschichte der Abstimmung in Ostpreussen* (Leipzig, 1921).
[49] Letter, Skrzyński to Paderewski, September 12, 1920, in Tadeusz Jędruszcak, *Polityka Polski w sprawie Górnego Śląska 1918–1922* (Warsaw, 1958), p. 157.

surrection prompt the Allies to dispose of the explosive situation by neutralizing the entire Upper Silesian area, which, according to Skrzyński, would have been the worst possible outcome for Poland.[50]

The appearance of Allied troops and the arrival of the governing commission for the plebiscite district early in 1920 did not adequately stabilize the situation and renewed fighting erupted in August of that year. The signal for the second uprising was given by the Polish plebiscite commissar, Korfanty, who called on Polish political parties and trade unions to organize for the defense of Polish property and life in the face of discrimination by German administrative authorities. The uprising had also been propelled by the desire to avoid a repetition of the unfortunate outcome of the East Prussian plebiscite. Furthermore, it may have been fired by the rumors which fed on the critical military situation in the Polish–Soviet War. Some spoke of a German *fait accompli;* others feared that the hard-pressed Witos government might bargain for German military assistance in return for sacrificing Polish interests in Upper Silesia. The main target of the second insurrection had been the purely German character of the police in the area, and order was re-established on the basis of a compromise which created a new police force, half of which was composed of Germans and half of Poles.

The actual Upper Silesian plebiscite, on March 20, 1921, was conducted in an atmosphere of considerable tension but without major incident. The plebiscite results showed 60 per cent favoring a continued adherence to Germany, while 40 per cent expressed themselves in favor of joining Poland.[51] In Germany the majority vote was widely hailed as a German victory and as a mandate for the continued affiliation of the whole area with Germany.[52] This interpretation was in contradiction to the Versailles treaty, which had stipulated that the decision would be made by a majority vote by communes and not by a majority vote of the entire region. Because of these treaty terms and because of the nature of

---

[50] Letter, Skrzyński to Korfanty, September 9, 1919, *Paderewski Papers,* fol. 2147. The question of Upper Silesian separatism during that period is discussed in Henryk Zieliński, "La Question de 'L'Etat Indépendant de Haute-Silésie' après la Première Guerre Mondiale (1919–1921)," *Acta Poloniae Historica* 4 (1961): 34–57.

[51] The exact plebiscite figures gave Germany 54 per cent by communes and Poland 42.5 per cent by communes. In terms of votes, 707,605 (or 59.6 per cent) cast their vote for Germany and 479,359 (or 40.3 per cent) voted for Poland. (Sara Wambaugh, *Plebiscites Since the World War,* I [Washington, 1933], p. 250). The German vote had been composed of 408,000 persons who were German-speaking and 300,000 who were Polish-speaking. Of those who had voted for Poland, all but 5,000 had listed Polish as their mother language (Markert, *Polen,* p. 26).

[52] Reichstag, *Sten. Berichte,* 349, April 20, 1921, pp. 3324ff.

the plebiscite outcome, the latter was not in itself a definite settlement but only the guideline to a subsequent international decision.

The state of uncertainty and tension was, therefore, prolonged beyond the plebiscite date. The Plebiscite Commission was unable to agree on a boundary line. When news leaked out that Percival and de Marinis, the British and Italian representatives on the commission, had proposed a line that would have assigned the entire Upper Silesian industrial complex to Germany, the Poles in Upper Silesia felt that their interests would be betrayed by an Allied compromise and sought to pre-empt an unfavorable international verdict by staging a *fait accompli*. On May 2 they called for a general strike in the coal mines. A few hours later the movement had reached the proportion of a full-scale insurrection. Within a few days the insurgents had gained control of the entire region which Korfanty had claimed for Poland, which included almost two-thirds of the plebiscite area and all the important industrial and mining districts.

This spontaneous eruption of Polish national sentiment in Upper Silesia, which found a fervent echo throughout Poland, threw the Warsaw government into an acute dilemma. Both their sympathies and popular Polish pressure would have propelled them toward an open declaration of support for the insurgent movement and direct economic and military assistance. On the other hand, the danger of military entanglements with Germany and of a negative Allied reaction dictated a policy of caution and nonintervention. Knowing how difficult it would be to maintain Polish neutrality once violence had broken out, the Polish government had made a desperate last-minute attempt to stem the insurrectionist tide. In a secret session on May 2, the Cabinet categorically decided against the use of force in Upper Silesia and asked Korfanty to use every means at his disposal to stop all military activities.[53]

However, military activities in Upper Silesia overtook these restraining resolutions. Once the insurrection was underway, the concern of the Polish authorities was with liquidating it as quickly and advantageously as possible without being pushed into open intervention. To accomplish these ends the Cabinet in a series of sessions between May 3 and May 5 decided to recall Korfanty for having transgressed his authority and instructions, to seal the Polish–German frontier in order to prevent Polish military units from crossing over into Upper Silesia, and to close the recruitment offices of the NPR [*Narodowa Partia Robotnicza*—National Workers party] which was engaged in a program of recruiting Polish

[53] *PPRM*, 14 (1921), p. 262.

volunteers to fight in Upper Silesia. These restraining measures were highly unpopular in Poland and widened the cleavages within the government, as was witnessed by the threat of the resignation of Jankowski, the minister of labor and member of the pro-interventionist NPR.[54]

In making the unpopular choice to refrain from intervention and to liquidate the insurrection, the Polish government had been motivated primarily by the realization that it was unable to provide the necessary materiel and food supplies in order to guarantee the success of the insurrection. Also, there was the concern of the military that the Polish forces might be confronted by a full counterattack of the German Free Corps and *Orgesch* units and perhaps even by units of the *Reichswehr* which they could not withstand. In addition, the Polish government was afraid that the insurrection might provide a dangerous example for anarchical and lawless behavior within Poland itself. Finally, after consultation with the Allied representatives it became clear that on the whole the Allies opposed the insurrectionist movement and that any failure to comply with their wish for a cease-fire in Upper Silesia might negatively influence their stand in determining the final settlement. Thus caught by their own inability to impose a unilateral decision and dependent on the good will of the Allies, the Polish government was impelled to opt for the unpopular course of nonintervention.

Despite this official policy, it would be difficult to absolve the Polish government entirely of responsibility for and involvement in the Upper Silesian violence of 1921. While prudence had dictated a policy of nonintervention, the government's clear sympathy for a unilateral de facto solution, if it could only have been made to succeed, had been evident and had communicated itself to those elements which started the insurrection. Before the insurrection the Warsaw authorities had made no attempt to restrain the violent press campaign that advocated a solution by force. Moreover, by overtly attacking the justice of the final solution, even before the Conference of Ambassadors had actually pronounced itself on the matter, the government had indirectly invited a *fait accompli* by force.[55] More specifically, for a few days Korfanty had been allowed to direct his insurgent movement from Polish soil and his dismissal as plebi-

---

[54] *Ibid.*, pp. 265–70.
[55] Report, Gibson, May 13, 1921, *SD*, 760c.6215/84. The American Minister, who otherwise absolved the Polish government of complicity or improper support of the insurrection, criticized the Warsaw authorities for having failed to exercise a moderating influence on the hysterical press and for ignoring the fact that Poland was bound to respect the decision of the Supreme Council.

scite commissar was little more than a façade, as the government remained in daily contact with him and let him recommend his own successor. Also, toward the end of the insurrection the closing of the border
between Poland and Upper Silesia seemed to be less firmly enforced and
increasing amounts of arms and supplies from private Polish sources
found their way to Upper Silesia.[56] On May 28 the Cabinet agreed to
supply Korfanty with money and food supplies, but this assistance was
designed to help liquidate the whole insurrectionist movement as rapidly
as possible without losing control or face and not as a means to continue
hostilities.[57]

Among the Western Powers the reaction to the Upper Silesian insurrection was generally negative, as they reiterated their demand for a
restoration of order and for a final decision by the Supreme Council.
Lloyd George gave a blistering address to Parliament on May 13 in which
he accused Poland of breaking the Versailles treaty, challenged the validity of Poland's historical claims to Upper Silesia, and threatened to have
the *Reichswehr* sent into the troubled area unless the Allied plebiscite
troops restored order. The Italians were incensed because twenty soldiers
from their plebiscite contingent in Upper Silesia had been killed when
they offered resistance to the Polish insurgents.

The French position is more difficult to assess. The French government, press, and business groups, some of the latter having recently
been invited by Poland to establish themselves in the industrial district
of Upper Silesia, were all solidly in favor of a boundary demarcation in
Upper Silesia which would satisfy Polish economic and strategic needs.
But the insurrection itself was viewed in Paris with considerable dismay
and alarm. To be sure, General Niessel, the head of the French military
mission to Warsaw, had publicly applauded the action of the insurgents;[58] the French military contingent in Upper Silesia had made no
effort to hinder or disarm the Polish insurgents; and the chairman of the
Plebiscite Commission, General Le Rond, had maintained intimate contacts with Korfanty.[59] But the behavior of the French government was
more cautious than that of its representatives in Upper Silesia and Warsaw, whose immediate exposure to the Polish point of view might ex-

---

[56] Report, Gibson, June 8, 1921, SD, 760c.6215/141.
[57] *PPRM*, 14 (1921), p. 479.
[58] Report, Gibson, May 13, 1921, SD, 760c.6215/84, p. 12.
[59] When the Polish government asked Korfanty to liquidate the insurrection,
he had stated that he would first have to consult with General Le Rond before com-
plying with the demand. (*PPRM*, May 6, 1921, 14, p. 273).

plain their inclination to over-respond in this particular situation. At the *Quai d'Orsay* a cooler logic prevailed. It was felt that French influence on the Supreme Council was sufficient to guarantee a favorable settlement for Poland. The insurrection merely complicated this task by sharpening British and Italian objections. Furthermore, it might lead to a humiliating Polish defeat in Upper Silesia, or worse, to a full-scale conflict between Poland and Germany. Panafieu, the French minister, "intervened at the Polish Ministry of Foreign Affairs to insist that the insurrection be halted and Polish methods drastically altered."[60] When Prime Minister Witos justified his government's stand on the insurrection issue, he presented to the *Sejm* a note from the French government in which the latter called on the insurgents to lay down their arms on the full assurance that the Upper Silesian question would be settled strictly in accordance with the Versailles treaty and that all Germans who entered Upper Silesia would be disarmed.[61]

On the German side, the reaction to the military activities of the Polish insurgents was rapid and generally effective and thereby justified the Polish General Staff's firm skepticism toward the whole insurrectionist venture.[62] The German government had anticipated military complications over the plebiscite results and had made some preparations to meet this emergency. As early as December 11, 1920, General von Seeckt had warned Foreign Minister Simons of the concentration of Polish troops on the German frontier which, according to Seeckt, merited the tentative conclusion that Poland sought "to rectify an unfavorable plebiscite result by force of arms."[63] Seeckt repeated these concerns in a discussion he had with Simons a few weeks later and urged the Foreign Minister to suspend the export of locomotives and other strategic goods to Poland as long as Germany had "to expect to meet this State with arms in hand in the near future."[64] In response to these urgings, the German Cabinet decided on January 25, 1921, to resist "a Polish assault with force of arms."[65]

When Korfanty staged his uprising it was resisted by local civilian

---

[60] Piotr Wandycz, *France and Her Eastern Allies 1919–1925* (Minneapolis, 1962).

[61] *PPRM*, 14, p. 443.

[62] Report, Farman, a member of the U.S. military staff in Warsaw, to the U.S. War Department, May 27, 1921, *SD*, 760c.6215/91.

[63] AA, GA/3724/K170/K024 028.

[64] Simons's memorandum of his conversation with Seeckt, January 11, 1921, AA, RAM/1424/2945H/D570 345.

[65] Friedrich von Rabenau, *Seeckt—Aus seinem Leben* (Leipzig, 1940), p. 298.

self-defense [*Selbstschutz*] units, who were soon reinforced by veterans from the rest of Germany, by Free Corps units and other paramilitary formations, and, toward the end of the fighting, also by student volunteer groups. These units assembled in Breslau, where they were quickly organized and armed. The German government actively, though secretly, supported these voluntary defense units in Upper Silesia. The *Reichswehr* had been put on a state of alert and was prepared to act if the necessity arose, although, as Chancellor Fehrenbach assured the *Reichstag*, the latter would be consulted before the government gave an order to send the army into action.[66] The army secretly provided the voluntary defense units with arms, and Seeckt had provided active staff officers to advise them professionally. In order to avoid charges of *Reichswehr* collusion, these officers appeared in civilian dress and all support and communications ran through the channels of the Upper Silesian civilian authorities.[67]

The German government carefully avoided a more direct form of military involvement for fear of inviting the entry of regular Polish armed forces and with it those of France, for Briand had informed the French press that "la France n'acceptera pas une intervention armée de l'Allemagne."[68] This elaborate caution on the part of the German government was supported by the German military leadership. General von Seeckt, a noncorruptible realist, had assessed the situation similarly and his views no doubt exercised great weight in the corresponding decision of the German Cabinet. Over a decade later, in defending the policies of Chancellor Wirth during the Upper Silesian insurrection, Seeckt explained to Count Westarp his and the government's motives for nonintervention in the 1921 crisis:

> The German defense of Upper Silesia had to be carried out by volunteers whose organization and equipment could not be prepared openly. I had rejected the use of the *Reichswehr*. This would have precipitated a clash with the regular Polish troops that were standing by and would thereby have provided the *casus foederis* which the French General [meaning Le Rond] always hoped for and anticipated. I was unable to assume the responsibility for the consequences thereof.[69]

The military climax of the insurrection occurred during the last

---

[66] Reichstag, *Sten. Berichte*, 349, May 6, 1921, pp. 3624–26. Fehrenbach's Cabinet had resigned two days earlier, and he was acting as a caretaker chancellor until his *Zentrum* party colleague Wirth formed a new government on May 10.
[67] Rabenau, *Seeckt*, p. 300.
[68] G. Suarez, *Briand* (Paris, 1941), p. 195.
[69] Rabenau, *Seeckt*, p. 299.

days of May in the vicinity of the towns of Annaberg and Rosenberg. On the German side, the chief military thrust was provided by members of the Free Corps and units of *Orgesch* whose home base was Bavaria. At that time there were some 25,000 to 30,000 men fighting on the German side and 60,000 to 70,000 in the ranks of the Polish insurgents. Despite this sizable military effort on both sides, peace was restored by June 18, partly because of the mediatory role of the Inter-Allied Plebiscite Commission and the creation of a neutral zone by the commission's forces, partly because the Polish government worked toward the liquidation of the insurgency movement and the Berlin authorities were unwilling to exploit their military victory at Annaberg.

It is by no means certain whether the military activities of members of the Free Corps and *Orgesch* did in any substantial way contribute to making the outcome of the final decision on Upper Silesia any more favorable to Germany. Their intervention did prevent more territory from falling into the hands of Korfanty's insurgents. But here it would be dangerous to draw the analogy with the Poznań uprising of 1919, where all land won by the insurgents could be treated as a permanent acquisition by Poland, as all Allies supported Poland's claims to the province of Poznań. But this unanimity of Allied opinion no longer applied with respect to Upper Silesia.

THE GENEVA CONVENTION ON UPPER SILESIA

The final verdict on the plebiscite was neither given by the Polish insurgents nor by their German counterparts. The events in Upper Silesia had demonstrated the necessity of a rapid decision on this explosive issue. But the Conference of Ambassadors was unable to reach a conclusion and shifted the main burden onto the shoulders of the League of Nations by requesting an opinion from the League Council. The Council appointed a German–Polish commission to recommend a demarcation line in accordance with the wishes of the people, as expressed in their vote by communes, and with due regard for economic and geographical considerations. In the deliberations of the commission and the Council the question of the boundary delineation became a disputed issue which involved strictly political pressures as well as the real desire for an equitable settlement that would express the wishes of the Upper Silesian population. Even if the Council had been motivated purely by the latter sentiment, the mixed distribution of the population groups made this a complex riddle which no slide-rule techniques could unravel.

Accepting the advice of the Council, the Conference of Ambassadors in its note of October 20, 1921, announced its decision to partition the area under dispute. As a result of the division, Poland received one-quarter of the area (3,213 sq. km. out of a total of 12,969 sq. km.) and 44 per cent of the population (980,000 out of a total of 2,300,000). In terms of the over-all population distribution the partition therefore corresponded exactly to the plebiscite results. But in Germany the basic principle of partition was rejected, just as the particular manner in which the frontier was finally drawn was bitterly criticized.[70] On the latter point, the principal criticism centered on the argument that 44.2 per cent of the population in the Polish sector had voted for Germany (as against 22.8 per cent in the German sector who had voted for Poland). More important even, the Polish sector included almost the entire Upper Silesian industrial area and the principal resource basin: four-fifths of the entire Upper Silesian coal mines, four-fifths of the coal production (about one-quarter of the entire German coal production by 1913 figures), two-thirds of the iron industry, and the entire zinc mines of Upper Silesia, which constituted 80 per cent of the entire German zinc production.[71]

In order to alleviate the disruptive effects to human and economic relations that would otherwise have followed the partition of this highly integrated community, the Conference of Ambassadors in its final decision stipulated that Germany and Poland were to enter into a convention on Upper Silesia that would create a temporary status for fifteen years, during which special provisions for the maintenance of the economic life and for the protection of minorities were to apply. In November 1921 Germany and Poland appointed plenipotentiaries to negotiate the proposed convention under the chairmanship of the former President of the Swiss Confederation, Calonder, whom the League of Nations had appointed to this mediatory role. Despite the enormously complex and lengthy subject matter and the sensitivity of the issue, agreement was

---

[70] All political parties in Germany, from the Communists (KPD) on the extreme Left to the Nationalists (DNVP) on the extreme Right, rejected the decision of the Conference of Ambassadors as unjust in itself, and as a violation of the otherwise much maligned Treaty of Versailles. (Reichstag, *Sten. Berichte*, 351, October 26, 1921, pp. 4733–72). It is interesting to note that Dr. Breitscheid of the Independent Socialists attributed the relatively poor German performance in the plebiscite not only to Prussia's chauvinistic Poland policy of the last fifty years but also to the fact that in the plebiscite campaign Germany had emphasized national issues at the expense of those social issues which were of particular concern to the Silesian working classes (*ibid.*, pp. 4754–55).

[71] Wilhelm Volz, "Und Oberschlesien?," *Deutsche Rundschau*, vol. 191 (1922): 52.

reached quickly and on May 15, 1922, the Upper Silesian Convention was signed at Geneva.[72]

The Geneva Convention on Upper Silesia provided the last of the major agreements between Poland and Germany on questions arising out of the terms of the Versailles treaty. With its 606 articles the Convention was a more voluminous and in all probability a more complex document than the Versailles treaty. Its preamble stressed the common interest of preserving the economic life of the entire Upper Silesian area and in securing protection for the minority groups. It was hoped that after the expiration of the Convention in fifteen years the economics of both countries would have adjusted to the new situation.

On the matter of liquidation of property, the Geneva Convention (Arts. 6 to 23) provided a much more restrictive pattern than the Versailles treaty. Liquidation was restricted to large industries employing more than 600 persons annually (but only if the Mixed Commission determined that this would be indispensable for the maintenance of the business concerned) and to large agrarian estates, i.e., estates of over 100 hectares, but no more than one-third of the total area of such estates could be liquidated. Also questions of citizenship and option (Arts. 25–55) were treated in a far more liberal spirit than was provided by the Versailles treaty.

The protection of the cultural, religious, political, and economic life of the minorities (Arts. 65–157) occupied a particularly prominent position in the clauses of the Convention. Never in an international treaty had so much attention been paid to the human element involved. "Never before did the attempt go so far to secure individual rights and protect them individually."[73] For a period of fifteen years Germany also agreed to accept the provisions in respect to German Upper Silesia which Poland had accepted for all of her minorities in the Minority Treaty she had signed with the Allied and Associated Powers on June 28, 1919. The minority provisions of the Geneva Protocol for once established an equal basis for the treatment of both German and Polish minorities, which was otherwise absent because Germany was not subject to the international treaty on minorities. The success of the minority protection provisions of the Geneva Convention can be measured by the fact that even during the ruthless Hitler regime, Jews who were persecuted in the rest of Ger-

[72] A complete text of the Convention is found in G. Kaeckenbeeck, *The International Experiment of Upper Silesia. A Study of the Working of the Upper Silesian Settlement, 1922–1937* (London, 1942), pp. 572–859.
[73] *Ibid.*, p. 24.

many were sheltered in Upper Silesia until the expiration of the convention in 1937.

The provisions of the Geneva Convention for the protection of minorities were not only more numerous and complex than those contained in the Minority Treaty of 1919 but also contained a substantial improvement in the technique of supervising the execution of these terms. While the latter treaty left the execution of the terms entirely within the hands of the country concerned, though permitting petitions from the minority groups to the League, the Geneva Convention installed a local machinery with competence to deal on the spot with most of the routine minority disputes. Each state was required to establish in its part of the plebiscite area a Minorities Office (Art. 148) to which the minority could address petitions (Art. 149). If this office failed to satisfy the petitioner, the petition was to be forwarded to the President of the Mixed Commission for the purpose of soliciting the latter's opinion. The President's opinion was then communicated to the proper administrative authorities. The Minorities Office and the President of the Mixed Commission, by virtue of their local residence and expertise, were far better equipped to settle routine minority problems quickly and effectively than the distant and procrastinating machinery of the League. The result was a greatly improved system of protection of minority rights.

The second part of the Convention set up an extremely detailed list of economic provisions which sought to ensure the continued economic functioning of the area and to reduce the destructive impact of the partition. For a period of fifteen years all raw materials (agricultural goods, timber, and industrial raw materials) having their origin in one of the two partings and being destined to be consumed or manufactured in the other were to be exempt from all tariffs (Art. 218). Also, in accordance with Art. 268 of the Versailles treaty, all raw materials and manufactured goods having their origin in the Polish part of Upper Silesia were to be imported into Germany exempt from tariffs for a period of three years. Poland on her part, by Article 330 was obliged to permit the export of coal, iron ores, lead, and zinc from Polish Upper Silesia to Germany for a period of fifteen years. Germany assumed a similar guarantee. Detailed provisions were made to facilitate border crossing and work on the other side for persons living within a five-kilometer radius of the border. Indeed, these detailed provisions assumed such a degree of intricate refinement that stipulations were made for farmers to take their lunch to the other side (Art. 240) and midwives the instruments they required for the execution of their delicate and vital profession (Art. 247). Furthermore, detailed arrangements were made for questions relating to transit, currency, banks, the regulation of the water and electricity supplies, as well as the administration of the railroad system and the communications network.

As requested by the initial decision of the Conference of Ambassadors, two bodies, the Arbitral Tribunal and the Mixed Commission, were set up to supervise the execution of the terms of the Convention. The Arbitral Tribunal, consisting of one Polish and one German arbitrator and a president who was appointed by the League, "was entrusted with the duty of settling any private disputes which may result from the application of the Convention."[74] Its decision was binding on the court or authority concerned. There was no appeal or revision of its decision. The Arbitral Tribunal was not just a deciding agency, but also a law-creating and law-defining agency. Its jurisdiction applied to cases involving the suppression or diminution of rights vested before the partition (Art. 5); questions of nationality, option, and the right of residence (Arts. 56 and 58); matters concerning circulation permits (Arts. 296–298 and 300); rights of banks (Art. 313), and the settlement of disputes concerning water supplies (Arts. 368 and 369).[75] The function of the Mixed Commission was more diplomatic in character and was primarily concerned with the settlement of administrative and economic disputes.

The Geneva Convention settled the last major unresolved issue between Germany and Poland that arose from the peace treaty without, however, inaugurating a distinct improvement of relations. The Convention, which had come into existence largely as the result of international prescription and mediation, represented a remarkably enlightened and progressive document in its treatment of minorities and economic questions and thus helped to alleviate the human and economic ills caused by the partition of an integrated industrial community. As such it might in itself have served as a catalyst for guiding German–Polish relations at large onto the road of peaceful and conciliatory accommodation. In application, however, the Geneva Convention failed to accomplish the broader task of harmonizing German–Polish relations and the execution of its terms in relation to Upper Silesia gave rise to innumerable disputes and continued friction.

[74] *Ibid.*, p. 27.
[75] *Ibid.*, pp. 28–29.

III

The Eviction of Optants, 1922–1925

THE ISSUES WHICH APPEARED most frequently in German–Polish relations in the decade after the Geneva Convention fall into two principal categories. The first was composed of the major political questions such as the territorial dispute, the fate of the minority groups, and security issues such as the Locarno treaty. These matters either did not reach the stage of negotiations at all, like the issue of territorial revision, or, like the Locarno security arrangements, they were treated in a wider international context rather than bilaterally.

The second category of issues, consisting of eviction of citizens, liquidation of property, and the creation of trade barriers was subject to prolonged and almost continuous negotiations between Germany and Poland. These talks were often conducted in an atmosphere of considerable hostility and ill will, but at the same time with remarkable perseverance. The persistence with which the same problems kept reappearing on the agenda of German–Polish negotiations gives the somewhat erroneous impression of a totally static situation in the relations of the two countries. This interpretation tends to ignore fluctuations in the climate of their relations and the very tangible progress which was in fact made between 1922 and 1930 in settling a wide range of issues.

It will be recalled from the preceding chapter that toward the end of 1919, in response to Allied pressure, Poland had broken off the bilateral negotiations which she had conducted with Germany on a number of technical and economic issues and had shifted negotiations to Paris, where they were conducted under the chairmanship of a delegate of the Conference of Ambassadors. Very little tangible headway was made in

52

these multilateral talks beyond the Paris Declaration of January 9, 1920, and after 1922 both Germany and Poland preferred to revert to bilateral negotiations on these specific points.

Poland's major incentive to resume negotiations was provided by the negative effects of the German economic blockade which had commenced in January 1920 and had been intensified as a result of the Polish–Soviet War of 1920. Germany, for her part, was willing to revoke her policy of economic boycott if this would compensate in other areas where she had priority interests, namely the questions of optants, liquidation, German colonists, and transit to the Soviet Union. Moreover, her policy of economic boycott turned out to be a two-sided sword. While it injured Poland economically, it met with criticism from many German industrialists who feared the loss of the Polish market to foreign competitors and who had therefore begun to circumvent the boycott by exporting to Poland by way of Austria, Czechoslovakia, and Scandinavia. Foreign Minister Rathenau himself opposed the boycott. In part, this might have been a reflection of the intimate personal and professional ties which he had with German industrial circles. More important, the policy of boycott reduced the credibility of Germany's *Erfüllungspolitik* [policy of satisfaction] which Rathenau and Chancellor Wirth had inaugurated vis-à-vis the West. Germany's interest in getting guaranteed transit rights through Poland had become acute as the result of the recent signing of the German–Soviet Treaty of Rapallo in April 1922, one of the most important and dramatic events in the diplomacy of the inter-war period.[1] In Germany the Rapallo treaty created high hopes of significant economic, and possibly also military, co-operation with the Soviet Union and thus highlighted her dependence on transit facilities through Poland. It is not devoid of a certain historical irony that a treaty which was at least tacitly directed against Poland should have heightened the importance of her geographic location and thereby have enhanced her bargaining position with Germany in the current round of negotia-

---

[1] There exists a voluminous literature on the Rapallo treaty. The following are some of the principal works on the subject: Wipert on Blücher, *Deutschlands Weg nach Rapallo* (Wiesbaden, 1951); F. H. Carr, *The Bolshevik Revolution, 1919–1923* (New York, 1953), vol. 3, pp. 339–82; Gerald Freund, *Unholy Alliance* (London, 1957); Gustav Hilger and A. G. Meyer, *The Incompatible Allies: German–Soviet Relations, 1918–1941* (New York, 1953); Kurt Rosenbaum, *Community of Fate: German–Soviet Diplomatic Relations, 1922–1928* (Syracuse, 1965); a recent East German study using archival material from the DDR is provided by Günther Rosenfeld, *Sowjetrussland und Deutschland, 1917–1922* (Berlin, 1960). A contemporary Polish interpretation is found in Jerzy Krasuski, "Wpływ Traktatu w Rapallo na stosunki polsko-niemieckie," *Przegląd Zachodni* 17 (1961): 53–65.

tions. In fact, this was the key issue which brought Germany to the bargaining table in the first place.

Poland had gained proof of Germany's particular interest in transit facilities by having procured a German document which stressed that without such transit rights trade with Russia could not profitably develop and that considerable concessions would therefore be necessary to procure this privilege.[2] In April 1922, Foreign Ministers Rathenau and Skirmunt met at the abortive Genoa Conference, whose only real achievement had been its backlash in the form of the Rapallo treaty. Rathenau promised his Polish colleague that Germany's economic boycott would soon end, thereby admitting officially that such a blockade had in fact existed.

In the Warsaw Declaration of July 20, 1922, both sides agreed that in September of that year negotiations would resume on a number of outstanding issues. At the same time, Poland also informally conceded to Germany transit facilities for nonmilitary goods. Two days after the Declaration, Germany fulfilled her side of the agreement when her Commissar for Export and Import notified the concerned industries that all export restrictions on trade with Poland were invalid and that henceforth such trade would follow normal administrative practices without requiring special export licences.

After this hurdle had been cleared, negotiations opened in Dresden, a city which represented symbolically the close historical and cultural ties that had existed between Germany and Poland. The German team was headed by Karl von Stockhammern of the *Auswärtiges Amt*, and the Polish one by Kazimierz Olszowski, a director in the Polish Foreign Ministry who had headed the delegation that had concluded the Geneva Convention on Upper Silesia. The negotiations centered on juridical and financial questions, largely an implementation and extension of the Paris convention of January 9, 1920, and dealt with matters of communications as well. Despite laborious protractions and high hopes, the results of the Dresden talks were disappointing with many problems still unsolved. On December 18, 1922, Olszowski and Stockhammern signed a sanitary convention and reached agreement on converting the so-called Kries notes (bank notes that had been issued during the German military occupation, bearing the name of the head of the German civilian administration, Wolfgang von Kries). Other minor agreements on financial

---

[2] AMSZ, *Berlin Legation*, March 17, 1922, W.53, t.3; cited in Jerzy Krasuski, *Stosunki polsko-niemieckie, 1919–1925* (Poznań, 1962), I, p. 229.

questions and on border crossing procedures followed in 1923. But the Dresden talks yielded no major results. Poland objected to the German practice of tying the agenda to progress on the question of optants and liquidations. Germany, for her part, was disappointed that the Polish negotiators refused to enter into a formal agreement on transit. As the agreement stood, Poland could interpret the restriction on military materiel with sufficient latitude to exclude almost all products, if she so desired. That the traffic through Poland did, in fact, function quite smoothly can be attributed less to any German–Polish understanding than to Article 22 of the Polish–Soviet Riga Treaty of March 1921.

Despite these ambiguous results, the governments of both powers made some effort to normalize relations. One result of this policy was the upgrading of the status of their diplomatic representatives from provisional *chargé d'affaires* to that of minister plenipotentiary. Germany had taken the initiative in May 1922 by sending Ulrich Rauscher as German minister, and Poland reciprocated in June 1923 by appointing Kazimierz Olszowski Polish minister in Berlin. Olszowski's place at the bilateral negotiations was given to Witold Prądzyński, formerly a director in the Ministry of Justice, and negotiations were shifted from Dresden to Warsaw.

In making the new appointments both governments had selected men of unusually high caliber. Olszowski was a diplomat with a quick mind, a sharp tongue, and a very candid approach, who had no compunction in pointing out to Stresemann the frequent contradictions of his hostile public policy statements and his more conciliatory private promises. His diplomatic reports from Berlin show him to have been a very shrewd observer of Germany's domestic and foreign policy. His counterpart, Ulrich Rauscher, was even more influential in shaping the course of German–Polish relations, partly because he retained his Warsaw post for over eight years, and partly because of the growing influence which he gained over Stresemann. If one examines Rauscher's role in Warsaw, especially his contribution to the completion of the liquidation agreement and trade treaty, one is led to conclude that next to Stresemann his was the most important influence in determining German–Polish relations during the Weimar period.

Rauscher was one of the postwar "newcomers" to the *Auswärtiges Amt* who did not share the aristocratic or big business background of his colleagues. His career had been made in journalism and as President Ebert's protégé he had acted as press chief of the German government between 1919–20. During the Kapp *Putsch* his press appeal for a general strike had helped save the government at that critical period. In reward, he had been appointed envoy to the Georgian Republic. When the brief interlude of Georgia's independence came to an abrupt end in 1922, Rauscher left Tiflis and returned to Berlin in search of a new post. It was not without certain symbolic overtones that his next appointment was to be Warsaw: although no more than a few hours removed from Berlin, the banks of the Vistula, as viewed from the German capital at that time, seemed as remote as the Caucasian Mountains.

Both of his predecessors in Warsaw, Count von Oberndorff and von Schoen, had favored a conciliatory course toward Poland. But they had found the political climate in the Polish capital sufficiently nonconducive to their well-being that in the fashion of today's professors they had reduced their tenure to short guest appearances, while leaving affairs in the hands of a secretary whose main duty, according to the testimony of Dirksen, consisted of daily trips by crowded streetcars—the German legation at that time did not even rate an automobile—to the *Palais Brühl* for the purpose of delivering some note of protest.[3] During the following eight years Rauscher carried out his frustrating and arduous duties as German minister to Poland with singular skill, imagination, vigor, and joviality, and if in the annals of German diplomacy during the Weimar period the bouquets of historians have gone to the *prima donnas*, Hoesch and Brockdorff-Rantzau, this was largely because Rauscher had been confined to the Warsaw "kennel" rather than enjoying the lime-light of Paris or Moscow. Rauscher's personality was an enormous aid in the performance of this arduous task. His robust optimism, combined with a dosage of wit, joviality, and courtesy, provided a valuable endowment which helped him survive the frustrations of his post and assisted in creating a personal rapport with the Poles, who found this jovial Swabian a far more sympathetic representative than the Prussian officials to whom they were accustomed. According to the testimony of Ambassador Laroche, Rauscher was well liked by the Polish Foreign Ministry and favored by Piłsudski.[4]

Rauscher came to Warsaw without a definite program. He was free from the emotional bonds under which his less flexible colleagues labored, who, once having embraced a particular strategy of action, were loath to abandon it. But from the very beginning he showed a strong interest in improving German–Polish relations, especially in the eco-

[3] Dirksen, *Moskau, Tokio, London* (Stuttgart, 1949), p. 41.
[4] Jules Laroche, *La Pologne de Pilsudski. Souvenirs d'une ambassade 1926–1935* (Paris, 1953), pp. 67, 125.

nomic sphere. In his view, normalization constituted a priority item for German foreign policy for its own sake and, even more so, a *sine qua non* for a reconciliation with France. In Rauscher's estimate the road to Paris went through Warsaw.

Rauscher's search for normal relations with Poland represented, in his own words, a policy of calculated interest and did not stem from any affection for the Poles.[5] His private letters abounded in biting sarcasm at their expense. Neither Skrzyński nor Zaleski, who after all supported Rauscher's search for normalization, escaped his criticism; in Skrzyński he saw an "extraordinarily large liability of vanity and self-exaggeration," coupled with an inner indecision and fear of responsibility,[6] and Zaleski, because of his political impotence against Piłsudski, earned the unflattering title of *Briefträger* [mail-man]. The charge of his opponents, therefore, that Rauscher had fallen victim to the charms of his "hosts" was without foundation.

During the first years of his mission one of the chief problems confronting Rauscher was the practice of evicting each other's citizens, especially those persons who had exercised their right under Article 91 of the Versailles treaty, which allowed German nationals in Poland to opt for German citizenship and to return to Germany with all their property. The same privilege applied to Polish nationals in Germany. This provision had been inserted for the protection of the German and Polish minority groups, to prevent their detention against their will in what might possibly be a hostile environment. As it was actually applied, however, it seemed to work precisely in the opposite direction, tending to evict members of the minorities against what, on second thought, seemed to be a more accurate reflection of their real will. When the option took place in 1920, many of the optants were confused about the actual meaning of their act. Others had been misled by their minority leaders into believing that by opting they merely affirmed their cultural ties to their respective nationality group without forfeiting their right of residence. In the case of the German optants, many had exercised their right of choice merely as a means to escape the draft during the Polish–Soviet War, without any desire to emigrate to Germany. Altogether some 75,000 Poles in Germany and some 150,000 Germans in Poland had exercised their right of option.[7] The great majority of these, especially

[5] Private letter Rauscher to Undersecretary von Bülow, August 13, 1930, AA, RAM/1430/2954H/D575 229.
[6] AA, GA/3729/K171/K027 502–4; April 3, 1925.
[7] SD, 760c.6215/432; September 14, 1925.

urban residents and persons without property, had left: the German optants returning to Germany and the Polish optants either moving to Poland or to the mining regions of France. But once conditions had become somewhat more settled, many of the optants, especially the Germans with immobile property, were reluctant to leave their home for the country whose citizenship they had adopted.

The process of continued evictions under various pretexts kept alive the vicious circle of inflamed press reports and retaliatory measures. Already, in May 1923, Germany had launched one of these circular aberrations by evicting 78 Polish citizens who had been indicted for crimes or were unable to make a living. This in turn had prompted Poland to expel 156 German citizens, even though no such charges could be laid against them.[8] The independent and hasty actions of the local governments of Bavaria and Mecklenburg precipitated a new round of crises. Early in November 1923, the Bavarian government announced its intention to evict some forty Polish Jews, while the Mecklenburg authorities demanded and enforced the return of all seasonal Polish farm laborers.

Fearing an undesired escalation, the German government interfered with the local authorities in order to revoke the above decrees, but while the Bavarian government agreed to retract its eviction decree in a number of cases, the expulsion in Mecklenburg had already been fully executed. In this instance the Polish government appeared as eager as the German Foreign Ministry to keep the explosive issue under control, but its Interior Minister had been forced to appease popular demand by announcing the eviction of twenty-four families from Poznań.[9] In a conversation which Schubert had with the Polish envoy on January 28, 1924, both diplomats were in agreement on the undesirability of these retaliatory eviction decrees, which made for an unbearable atmosphere in their mutual relations. In the agreement of these two diplomats there was something indicative of the whole spectrum of German–Polish relations: the diplomats of both countries, while not sharing any mutual affection, were convinced that despite the differences that drew them apart, an acceptable working relationship had to be created. This was their task as diplomats, and in fulfilling it they frequently gave the appearance of forming a clandestine professional alliance against the common enemy of a hostile press, an enraged public, and hasty actions

---

[8] AA, RAM/1425/2945H/D570 949; June 5, 1923.
[9] Ibid., D571 172; January 17, 1924.

by local authorities, which interfered in the performance of this self-imposed task of rationality. Schubert was more indignant with the behavior of the local German authorities than with the Polish retaliatory measures, when he noted that the governments of the *Länder* should be warned of the political consequences of their acts of "unprecedented folly."[10]

In March 1924 Germany and Poland came to a verbal agreement that evictions, other than in the case of optants, would be handled in a manner which conformed to international practice. This gentlemen's agreement remained in force until October 1926, when Poland declared herself no longer bound by its stipulations.

On the question of citizenship, members of the German minority in Poland were, paradoxically, in a preferred position to preserve their German charac:er if they acquired Polish citizenship. As Polish citizens they not only enjoyed greater legal protection but were also safe from eviction and exempted from the liquidation clauses of the Versailles treaty. Precisely for these reasons it was in Poland's interest to interpret the treaty in such a manner as would reduce or defer the granting of Polish citizenship to German nationals to a maximum degree. She therefore tried to construe Article 91 of the Versailles treaty so as to exclude from citizenship those persons whose domicile between 1908 and 1920 in what was now Poland had at any one time been interrupted. Similarly, persons who had a second domicile outside Poland were to be excluded. The legal dispute on citizenship and optants was further complicated by the fact that there was some deviation between Article 91 of the Versailles treaty and Articles 3 and 4 of the Minority treaty which dealt with the same subject. Germany took her stand on the former, which stipulated that optants were free ("auront la faculté") to change their residence to the state for which they had opted (Art. 91, Sect. 6). Poland, on the other hand, defended her position by relying on Article 3 of the Minority treaty, which made the withdrawal of such optants compulsory ("devront"). This Germany did not recognize, for not only had that particular section of the Minority treaty been followed by the precautionary insertion "insofar as the peace treaty shall not provide otherwise," but also because in accordance with international legal practice in a dispute over the interpretation of two conflicting treaty terms, the less exclusive interpretation applies. This discrepancy furnished Germany with

[10] Note by Schubert of his conversation with Olszowski, AA, RAM/1425/2945H/D571 194–95.

some legal ammunition; however, little support could be given to her claim that she had been assured of the right of her optants to remain in Poland. Germany had not been ignorant of the consequences of option and had therefore discouraged its use. Moreover, of the 150,000–175,000 Germans who had availed themselves of this privilege, the great majority had drawn the consequence of their choice and had left before 1924.

As early as 1920 the German government had approached Warsaw with the request for conducting negotiations to clarify this point. Poland had rejected the request on the grounds that it constituted an exclusively domestic and not an international issue. Later, the talks held in Dresden between September 1922 and June 1923 on this and other questions led to no results. The continued international friction that was being generated by the unresolved optant and citizenship question caused some concern in Geneva. In Germany this presented a welcome opportunity to shift the whole issue from its bilateral stage to a platform of international arbitration, where she was more assured of a favorable settlement. On March 3, 1924, Undersecretary von Maltzan instructed the legations in London and Stockholm to persuade Lord Parmoor and Branting to accept the idea of neutral arbitration and expressed his preference for Kaeckenbeeck as arbitrator.[11] In response to Lord Parmoor's suggestions, the League Council recommended that if the two sides had not reached agreement on the citizenship and optant issue by April 1, a mediator be appointed who would enjoy powers of arbitration over questions which still remained unresolved by June 1, 1924.[12] The two parties accepted this plan and opened negotiations in Vienna under the capable chairmanship of Kaeckenbeeck. Both sides became entrenched behind their respective interpretations, which they had proclaimed over the past years. Kaeckenbeeck resolved this impasse by arbitration on twelve basic principles which formed the core of the dispute.

On July 10 the chairman's arbitration award was announced.[13] It upheld the basic German position on all questions of citizenship, but in matters relating to optants Kaeckenbeeck supported the Polish view against that of Germany. Kaekenbeeck's award was incorporated into the draft of the convention which was signed on August 30, 1924, amidst

[11] AA, RAM/1425/2945H/D571 227.
[12] AA, RAM/1425/2945H/D571 250–51.
[13] For the terms of the award see AA, RAM/1425/2945H/D571 384–96. For the terms of the Vienna Convention see *ibid.*, 351–60; also *Actes et Documents de la Conférence polono-allemande tenue à Vienne du 30 avril au 30 août* (Vienna, 1925).

the splendid surrounding of the Vienna Hofburg. Articles 6 and 7 of the Vienna Convention stipulated that German nationals were entitled to Polish citizenship if they had been domiciled in Poland between January 1, 1908, and January 10, 1920, or if they had been born in the area of present-day Poland of parents who at that time had been domiciled there, provided this was before January 1908.

On the matter of optants, where Kaeckenbeeck's judgment had sustained Poland's right of eviction, the only concrete benefit to Germany was that it provided an orderly regulation for the removal of these persons. The day of departure for those optants without fixed property was set for August 1, 1925. Optants with fixed property which lay in the area of a fortress or within 10 km. of the boundary were to leave by November 1, 1925. The third category of optants, composed of persons with immobile property outside these special regions, was to leave by July 1, 1926. Any optant who had not received an order for departure by December 31, 1926, was to be exempted from any further eviction decree thereafter. The Convention also included the provision that those optants who left behind fixed property could annually return for a period of twenty-one days to look after their property.

The Vienna Convention, even if it did not settle the question of the optants in the manner sought by Germany, nevertheless, constituted a definite gain for her foreign and minority policy. The achievement could in no small way be attributed to her skillful maneuver of a step-by-step withdrawal from the level of fruitless bilateral negotiations to the forum of international conciliation and arbitration. This attempt at internationalizing disputes between herself and Poland represented a marked tactical reversal from Germany's original preference during the 1918–22 period for bilateral negotiations with Poland. The shift of policy was a clear reflection of Germany's speedy recovery in international politics and the growing international support and sympathy which she could muster on many issues. German–Polish relations were frequently of such a strained nature that agreement was unattainable through the process of bilateral negotiations and had to be sought through the conciliatory effort of international agencies. In this, as will be seen later, the League, for all its apparent and much condemned inability to resolve the German–Polish minority issues, played a significant role.

Regrettably for the relations of both countries, the Vienna Convention regulated the question of optants in orderly form but did not settle the issue. Poland's insistence on executing her legal rights in this matter not only imposed hardship upon thousands of peaceful, and in the great majority of cases useful, inhabitants but also placed a great liability on her relations with Germany, precisely at a time when she was eager to come to an economic agreement and when she had particular need for international good will to prevent her isolation under the new European constellation that was emerging in conjunction with the proposed security pact.

In January 1925, and again in June and July of that year, the German government had approached Warsaw with the proposal to arrange a mutual cancellation of the practice of evicting the remaining optants on either side.[14] While the foreign minister, Count Skrzyński, favored such an accommodation, the Polish government yielded to popular pressure and proceeded with the eviction order for the first category of optants on August 1, 1925.[15] Premier Grabski himself seems to have favored this expulsion because he feared that if the German optants remained in Poland and kept their property the danger that the newly acquired territory in the west would revert to Germany would increase.[16]

Stresemann, a master in the art of tactical bargaining, had correctly evaluated the predicament of the Polish government in face of the nationwide opposition against any concessions on the optant issue. He had, therefore, instructed Rauscher to approach the Polish government confidentially and propose a solution that would provide the latter with a sop for appeasing the agitated arena of public opinion. The offer which Rauscher proposed took into account Poland's internal situation, for which it made amends by allowing Poland to evict a small portion of the optants for which Germany promised to seek no retaliation. Poland, however, refused to grasp this olive branch and informed Rauscher that any Polish government which renounced its rights as derived from the Vienna Convention was doomed to fall.[17] The last chance for a reasonable settlement had thus been discarded. Writing indignantly and without attempt to hide his anti-Polish sentiments, Stresemann informed

---

[14] Stresemann's declaration before the Reichstag, Sten. Berichte, 387, August 6, 1925, p. 4123.

[15] By August 1925 there were approximately 30,000 German optants left in Poland, 23,000 of whom had no fixed property and were thus subject to eviction on August 1. The number of Polish optants remaining in Germany at that time was around 5,000. Hardly any of the latter owned any immobile property and therefore virtually all were subject to the early withdrawal clause of the Vienna Convention on August 1, 1925. (Statistics cited in Krasuski, Stosunki polsko-niemieckie, I, pp.258–59).

[16] Report, Pearson, September 14, 1925, SD, 760c.6215/432.

[17] Stresemann to all German Missions, August 6, 1925, AA, RAM/1426/2945H/D571 879.

all major German legations abroad—the content was meant to be transmitted in conversations—that while the Allied states had in many cases refrained from executing against Germany those Versailles treaty terms that might impair their relations with Germany, "Poland seven years after the termination of the War avails herself of a formal right in executing measures which must exert themselves most detrimentally on German–Polish relations at a time when Poland places—and in its economic position must place—priority value on the continuation of economic relations." Poland, according to Stresemann, had thereby effectively demonstrated that chauvinism and racial hatred were more potent factors for her than humanity and political prudence.[18]

A study of the *Reichstag* debates and press comments on this highly emotional issue provides us with an interesting insight into the opinions on Poland held by the various political parties in Germany. The optant issue was not only being treated as a matter of foreign policy but degenerated into a first-class party squabble. Already in March and April of that year the government of the *Reich* and the Prussian ministries concerned had undertaken preparatory measures to accommodate the stream of incoming optants and to provide work for them. While the much smaller number of Polish optants had quietly departed before August of that year, their German counterparts had hoped to the last minute that the Polish government would recant and had thus delayed their departure to the end. Their sudden and concentrated arrival—over 10,000 persons were involved—hit the German border town of Schneidemühl like a spring flood and thus increased the level of human inconvenience and suffering, and with it the political reaction which echoed throughout Germany. The evacuation and job placement of the optants proceeded efficiently and no justifiable charges of negligence could properly be laid against any authority. However, the parties of the Right, by grossly exaggerating facts and figures, made this an occasion for a massive attack against the Socialist government of Prussia, for, being represented in the government coalition of the *Reich*, they had to exercise greater restraint in attacking the federal government. A deputy for the Nationalists, von Lindeiner-Wildau, in an article for the August 5 edition of the *Deutsche Allgemeine Zeitung*, claimed that the efforts of the German Foreign Ministry in this respect stood in grotesque contrast to the inactivity of the Prussian government. He also included a jibe at Rauscher—this was probably more of a personal attack against that

[18] *Ibid.,* 878.

diplomat whose Socialist background made him the frequent target of Rightist attacks than a charge against the German government—by adding sarcastically that he hoped no damage would be done to Rausch-er's holidays on Lake Constance when he read of the suffering and misery of these persons for whom he was also responsible.

The Nazi organ, *Der Völkische Beobachter*, chanted of the in-describable suffering and misery of the German optants in Schnei-demühl.[19] The most "indescribable" of these miseries, apparently, had been the absence of flags and heroic speeches to mark the arrival of the refugees (the article's title had been "Keine Fahne, keine Begrüssung im Staate Severings")—the remedy of flags and Nazi greetings here recommended for consolation still had to await its magic application in a few years. The *Völkische Beobachter* unfolded a veritable campaign of hatred against Poland and categorically demanded retaliatory action by evicting not only the few remaining Polish optants but all Polish citizens in Germany. The chief target of such an eviction measure was to be Polish Jews, who, according to the Nazi propaganda, had "deprived the German worker and the German middle class of their bread and had reduced to filth our whole business life."[20] Ludendorff, the willing race horse in the stable of Nazi propagandists, made a tour of Schneidemühl, where he subjected his audience to one of his "heroic" speeches in which he exhorted them to settle near the Polish border in order to "provide the rampart against the mad aims of the Poles," and to reinforce Ger-many's great cultural mission in the East.[21]

During the *Reichstag* debate dealing with the expulsion of the optants, the action of Poland was condemned by all parties, yet the re-actions differed notably with the various groups and reflected their general attitude on the question of German–Polish relations. The mili-tantly nationalistic Fascists, as might be expected, made no attempt to hide their hatred for Poland, and their colleague Kube [*Deutschvölkische Freiheitspartei*] demanded that diplomatic relations be broken with this *Räuberstaat* [robber state] and advocated the expulsion of all Poles from Germany.[22] From the opposite side of the *Reichstag* benches the Com-munist deputy Rädel joined in the refrain "Poland is a robber state of the first caliber" but objected to retaliatory measures against Polish

[19] *Völkischer Beobachter*, August 5, 1925.
[20] *Ibid.*, July 29, 1925.
[21] *Ibid.*, August 13, 1925.
[22] Reichstag, *Sten. Berichte*, 387, August 6, 1925, pp. 4126–29.

optants on the ground that this would only affect workers.[23] Contrary to what might reasonably have been expected from the Nationalists, in view of their chronic anti-Polish sentiment, the speech of their deputy, Dr. von Keudell, was relatively moderate and centered on the technical details of providing for the incoming optants rather than dwelling on the more explosive political questions. Keudell himself belonged to the more moderate wing of the DNVP, and the self-imposed restraint which was echoed in his speech can, in part at least, be attributed to the membership of his party in the existing government coalition.

A moderate though objectively critical attitude characterized the position of the German Democratic party, [DDP—*Deutsche Demokratische Partei*] concerning Poland. Theirs was a pragmatic and business-like attitude that accepted the necessity of tolerable working relations with Germany's eastern neighbor but considered as illusory the more enthusiastic speculations of the SPD on the prospects of a complete reconciliation and real friendship with Poland. The DDP deputy, Dr. Haas, in referring to Kube's vitriolic outbursts, questioned the wisdom of calling Poland a robber state and somewhat sarcastically drew analogies between the anti-Semitism and morbid nationalism of the Fascists and that of Poland. Haas concluded that friendship could not develop between the two countries, as the obstacles which the Versailles treaty had imposed were too formidable, but in the interest of both countries a normal working relationship was desirable; however, even a mere normalization was extremely difficult if Poland continued her policies in the vein of these recent evictions.[24]

The Social Democrats, as part of their missionary ideology and also as the consequence of their own historical experience as an oppressed political minority, were strongly endowed with a sense of social justice which was particularly pronounced in their spontaneous support of persecuted minority groups. In this regard the SPD actively championed the cause of the German minority in Poland and never failed to condemn Poland for her behavior toward this minority group. In observance of these factors, the SPD delegate, Nowack, voiced his regret at seeing Poland ship the optants across the border like cattle. However, the Socialists' commitment to the principle of social justice never was a barren, one-sided approach—as is frequently the case—but sought justice

23 *Ibid.*, pp. 4121, 4148.
24 *Ibid.*, pp. 4142–43.

for both sides. In this respect the SPD was the only political party in Germany which consistently attempted an objective explanation of Poland's motives and behavior. In so doing, it drew heavily on the historical *Schicksalsgemeinschaft* of the era of Bismarck and Wilhelm II, when the SPD—oppressed as a political minority as the Poles were as a national minority—had strongly opposed the prevailing anti-Polish policies of the government. Consequently, whenever the Social Democrats criticized Polish behavior toward the German minority, they tried to subject Germany's own minority policy to the same rigorous scrutiny and tried to explain, if not excuse, some of Poland's more objectionable activities by interpreting them as the unfortunate fruit of Germany's former oppressive policy. That this course was in part motivated by their desire to criticize the parties of the Right for past and present sins, cannot be denied; it does not, however, detract from the validity of their case. In this vein, Nowack criticized Poland's policy of evicting optants, but at the same time he voiced regret over the poor treatment accorded to Polish farm workers in Germany who, once the harvest was in, were kicked out without further ceremony. Referring to Germany's oppressive policy toward Poland before 1918, Nowack concluded that "the policy which is presently followed by Poland is the consequence of the policy which you gentlemen [turning to the Right] have conducted before the War in the eastern provinces."[25]

Going beyond the specific question of the minorities, the idealistic concept of international co-operation and friendship was still a lively issue in the Socialists' creed and was pursued with missionary zeal. Under their *Weltanschauung* the pragmatic concept of a mere tolerable working relationship between Germany and Poland, as was frequently advocated by Germany's other bourgeois parties, was transferred into the search for a genuine reconciliation and real friendship. Nowack concluded his speech by expressing hope that a German–Polish understanding would soon be found not only on the question of optants but also regarding the tariff war which in the interest of both countries ought to be ended soon.[26] His Socialist colleague Landsberg added: "The Polish people should not believe that the German people entertain hostile attitudes. . . . I believe I can declare in the name of the German people that we wish to live in peace with Poland. [Loud approval from the ranks

[25] *Ibid.*, p. 4133.
[26] *Ibid.*, p. 4134.

of the Social Democrats] There is room on this earth for both Poland and Germany. I know Polish culture and I value it."[27]

In the impassionate and emotionally charged atmosphere of the *Reichstag*, Stresemann's collected, factual speech had a soothing effect. The Foreign Minister recalled at length the terms of the Vienna Convention, the course of the German–Polish negotiations in which the former had tried to reach an agreement that would end the unfortunate optant question, and the measures which the government had undertaken in preparing to meet the flood of refugees. Only in his concluding remarks did Stresemann strike some accompanying chords of indignation and anti-Polish sentiment. "It is not for the first time that Poland acts in a manner which cannot be found in the conduct of other nations of its kind." Referring to a recent article in the London *Times* which had urged Poland to win the friendship of Germany with a *beau geste*, Stresemann added that the *geste* which Poland had offered was "nothing other than a *geste* of force. . . . The spirit of Polish policy, which speaks from the eviction of Germans, is not the spirit of Europe's pacification, but the spirit of hate and selfishness. . . . [and] an injustice against the spirit of civilization."[28]

The negative reaction to Poland's policy of evicting optants extended beyond Germany. Britain had been particularly disturbed by it, and Briand in a private conversation with Ambassador von Hoesch expressed his disapproval.[29] The French press tried to minimize Polish responsibility but could not entirely absolve their ally,[30] and Maltzan reported from Washington that the American press tended to support the German position on the evictions.[31] Even in the Polish press some voices expressed concern and the PPS [Polish Socialist party] deputy Diamand, writing in the Socialist party organ *Robotnik*, called such deportations "appropriate measures for semi-wild natives and conditions as they prevail in the Balkans, where this might be required to avoid a massive slaughter," but not suitable for civilized countries such as Germany and Poland. The German optants, as Diamand pointed out, had lived peacefully without causing any harm, but would now spread anti-

[27] *Ibid.*, p. 4152.
[28] *Ibid.*, pp.4123–26.
[29] Telegram, Hoesch to Stresemann, August 6, 1925, AA, RAM/1426/2945H/ D571 874.
[30] AA, StS/2301/4556H/E149 292.
[31] *Ibid.*, 289.

Polish sentiments among groups that previously were not motivated by hostile feelings toward Poland. If Poland had made any concessions in this matter she would have succeeded in getting a trade treaty signed and 250,000 tons of coal would have flowed into Germany monthly, giving bread to Polish workers.[32]

In accordance with the Vienna Convention, the second category of optants would have become subject to expulsion on November 1, 1925. In order to avoid a repetition of this harrowing spectacle and to prevent a further deterioration of German–Polish relations, also to strengthen Germany's parliamentary support for the ratification of the Locarno treaties, the British foreign secretary, Austen Chamberlain, twisted the arm of his Polish colleague at Locarno to get Poland to abstain from further expulsions. Chamberlain had asked Skrzyński for permission to speak to him candidly and as a friend. When the latter consented, the Foreign Secretary pointed out to him that while nobody disputed Poland's legal right to expel the remaining German optants—some 17,000 were involved—he appealed to Skrzyński to act with the same magnanimity that Briand had shown and to ask his government to use the same conciliatory spirit on the optant issue. "Such an act . . . would be an act of the highest statesmanship, the one thing most capable of producing a marked improvement in their relations with Germany and certain to be appreciated in every country in the world." Skrzyński replied that little could be done with respect to those optants living in fortress zones, "but that he would do his utmost to secure the revocation of the order of expulsion in respect of as large a number as possible of them, and that he believed that he would be successful."[33] In fact, even before Chamberlain's intervention, Skrzyński had already dispatched a telegram to Prime Minister Grabski, on October 13, in which he asked the government to take the necessary administrative measures so that German–Polish relations would not be endangered by further evictions of German optants.[34]

On his return from Locarno and only a few days before the due-date for the eviction of the next category of optants, Skrzyński told Rauscher that in view of the new situation and the friendly atmosphere

---

[32] Cited in *Kölnische Zeitung*, August 12, 1925.

[33] W. N. Medlicott, D. Dakin, and M. E. Lambert, eds., *Documents on British Foreign Policy 1919–1939* [hereafter referred to as DBFP], Series IA, vol. 1, pp. 21–23; memorandum by Chamberlain, October 17, 1925.

[34] AMSZ, P I, W.168, t. 78k; cited in Krasuski, *Stosunki polsko-niemieckie*, I, p. 257.

brought about by Locarno, the question of the optants ought to be resolved in a conciliatory spirit; consequently, Poland was willing to comply with Germany's wishes and to renounce her right to evict those optants whose departure would otherwise be required in November. Rauscher expressed his gratitude for this last-minute change of heart by the Polish government.[35] On the following day, in a conversation with Bader, the director of the political department of the Polish Foreign Ministry, the latter pointed out the great internal difficulties which had confronted the government in taking this important step; apparently only Skrzyński's threat to resign had overcome this opposition. Bader added that while Poland considered herself bound by this pledge and would consequently refrain from the practice of evictions, this did not imply a renunciation of her actual right to do so. In his report Rauscher praised the courageous stand of the Polish Foreign Minister and considered these assurances as satisfactory, and since Skrzyński was likely to retain his portfolio even in a new cabinet, any fears of renewed evictions were unjustified.[36]

The Polish concession constituted a remarkable reversal of her previously intransigent attitude and implied a token gesture of appeasement to German public opinion. We have already seen the role which Skrzyński and Chamberlain played in this development. Others, especially economic interest groups, were also involved. According to a letter by Professor Hirsch [undersecretary in the Economic Ministry] to *Reichsbankpräsident* Schacht of December 14, 1925, "Dr. Diamand, who is very eager to establish normal economic relations with Germany, [had] played a decisive role in settling the optant dispute."[37]

Both Britain and France were pleased with this result. But the expectations of a considerable improvement in German–Polish relations which this event aroused in London, Paris, and Warsaw did not materialize. Once the concession had been made, German diplomacy immediately belittled its consequences and treated the whole matter merely as a further evil avoided rather than a starting point for a more positive policy. In a conversation with Lord D'Abernon a few months later, Schubert already tried to minimize the nature of Poland's concession. While he willingly conceded that Poland's *beau geste* after Locarno had come as a welcome surprise to Berlin, it was after all no more than just

---

35 Telegram, Rauscher, October 23, 1925, AA, RAM/1426/2945H/D571 926.
36 Telegram, Rauscher, October 24, 1925, AA, StS/2301/4556H/E149 685.
37 AA, RAM/1426/2945H/D571 975.

this, a *beau geste* with a minimal content.[38] Stresemann followed a similar course of reducing to insignificance the Polish concession which might otherwise have been utilized as the starting point for a distinct improvement in relations with Poland. When Olszowski complained that Poland had received no German recognition for this very tangible move to establish a more friendly attitude toward Germany after Locarno, Stresemann passed it off lightly and commented that he had, indeed, at one time contemplated thanking Skrzyński for the favor but had been dissuaded as Poland had only postponed the eviction decree but had not legally renounced it; furthermore, Skrzyński's behavior toward him in Locarno had been an open affront.[39] Even the favorable outcome of the optant question had thus failed to be utilized as the *cause célèbre* for the improvement of relations.

[38] Note by Schubert, February 26, 1926, AA, D/2768/5462H/E 368 699.
[39] Note by Stresemann, February 2, 1926, AA, RAM/1426/2945H/D572 000–2.

IV

German–Soviet Interlude on the Polish Question

THE BASIC DIRECTION of Poland's foreign policy in the postwar period had already become crystallized at the peace conference when Poland aligned herself with the victorious coalition. Her alignment with the Entente Powers was reconfirmed when Poland concluded an alliance and a military convention with France in February 1921,[1] and another defensive pact with Rumania in March 1921. Subsequently, the task of Polish diplomacy was to implement this policy and to maneuver to her best advantage within its confines. In the immediate postwar years the course of German foreign policy remained much more undeclared and unresolved. The international catastrophe which had befallen her and her internal cleavages delayed any decisive charting of a new foreign policy course. Even Rapallo was more of a spontaneous reaction to the danger of an understanding between the Western Powers and the Soviet Union than a definite commitment to a pro-Russian and anti-Western course of action. Similarly, the backstage battle which was then raging between Germany's "Easterners"—Seeckt, Brockdorff-Rantzau, and Maltzan—and her "Westerners"—Rathenau, Schubert, and, increas-

---

[1] For a background of the signing of the alliance and secret military convention, see Tadeusz Kuźmiński, *Polska, Francja, Niemcy 1933–1935* (Warsaw, 1963), pp. 8–15; Jules Laroche, *La Pologne de Pilsudski: Souvenirs d'une ambassade 1926–1935* (Paris, 1953), pp. 12–17; L. Noël, *L'Aggression Allemande Contre la Pologne* (Paris, 1946), pp. 93–101; Piotr Wandycz, *France and Her Eastern Allies 1919–1925: French–Czechoslovak–Polish Relations from the Paris Conference to Locarno* (Minneapolis, 1962), pp. 211–37. The full text of the secret convention appears in "Przymierze Polsko–Francuskie z roku 1921," *Najnowsze Dzieje Polski* (Warsaw, 1967), vol. 11, pp. 205–22.

ingly, Stresemann—was more a fight about future options than about an immediate commitment. At that time Germany was too weak to want to, but potentially too strong to have to, commit herself to a fundamental foreign policy course.

With the Treaty of Rapallo both powers served international notice of their common interests and their rejection of the existing international order. Both powers treated the Treaty of Rapallo and the policy which it inaugurated as an instrument for overcoming their international isolation and keeping a check on Poland. To Germany it also had the advantage of ensuring that the Soviet Union would not rejoin the victorious coalition, just as Russia hoped that the Rapallo policy would impair, if not altogether frustrate, a German reconciliation with her victors. In the estimate of men like Seeckt, the Rapallo policy of German-Soviet friendship and the secret military collusion between the *Reichswehr* and Red Army in the field of arms manufacturing and military training offered an opportunity to make Germany *bündnisfähig* [fit for an alliance] if the need arose. Also, by the mere semblance of an accompanying German–Soviet military pact, it imposed a continuous check on Poland's eastern flank and thereby deterred any possible Polish policy of military adventurism. As Seeckt styled it, it prevented the Poles "from doing with us as they please." Seeckt, according to the former German minister of defense, Otto Gessler, in many ways saw things more clearly than did Brockdorff-Rantzau. While the Count feared the consequences of having military clauses imputed to Rapallo, Seeckt regarded such suspected implications as the best guarantee for imposing restraints on Poland.[2] Seeckt was eager to preserve the option of a German–Soviet military alliance for the future, but he repeatedly turned a deaf ear to Radek's overtures in 1921, 1922 and 1923 for a joint military operation that aimed at the dissolution of the Versailles treaty by enforcing the disappearance of Poland.[3] The advantage for Germany lay in maintaining the credibility of such a policy option, not in its actual exercise. As General von Stülp-

---

[2] Otto Gessler, *Reichswehrpolitik in der Weimarer Zeit* (Stuttgart, 1958), p. 198. Following the news of the Rapallo Pact, Poland's Foreign Minister Skirmunt wrote to his envoy in Washington that the agreement hung over Poland's head like a sword of Damocles. Its only favorable aspect was that it alarmed France and might persuade the Allies to close up ranks. ("Konferencja w Genui," *Ciechanowski Deposit* [Hoover Library, Stanford]; cited in Wandycz, *France and Her Eastern Allies*, p. 261).

[3] Friedrich von Rabenau, *Seeckt. Aus seinem Leben, 1918–1936* (Leipzig, 1940), p. 319; Walter Görlitz, *Der Deutsche Generalstab* (Frankfurt, 1950), p. 339.

nagel, one of Seeckt's close collaborators, expressed it: "La possibilité pour l'Allemagne de conjuger son action avec la Russie était pour von Seeckt un atout qui ne gardait toute sa force, qu'autant qu'il n'avait pas été joué."[4] If Germany had actually made an alliance of this kind in her state of military weakness and domestic political instability, she would have exposed herself to the risks of international military reprisals and to internal Bolshevism.

THE RUHR CRISIS

Germany's Rapallo policy paid substantial political dividends during the 1923 Ruhr crisis. On January 11, 1923, France and Belgium occupied the Ruhr area in response to German defaults in her reparations payments. This action caused some concern in Germany lest Poland join these sanctionary measures by occupying Upper Silesia or East Prussia. The image of a Polish threat prompted the German and Soviet governments to establish close communication and mutual diplomatic and press support with the aim of thwarting any aggressive designs of their Polish neighbor. Already, in December, Rantzau had informed Trotsky that Germany would default on her reparations payments in January. The Commissar did not recommend German armed resistance to a possible French military sanction but promised that if "Poland, at the order of France, invade [d] Silesia, then under no circumstances would we look at it passively; we cannot permit it and we shall intervene."[5]

Following the Ruhr occupation, anti-Allied demonstrations were staged in Moscow, and *Pravda's* editorial of January 19, entitled "A Warning to Poland," announced that if Poland followed the example of her French patron and invaded Germany, this would create a war in Europe—the implication of a Soviet retaliation was obvious even though it was not directly spelled out—which would clip the wings of the greedy Polish eagle.[6] The visit of Marshal Foch to Warsaw and of General Le Rond to Upper Silesia triggered another round of machine-gun fire in the Soviet press. *Izvestiya* of May 4 referred to these visits as military preparations against Germany. A gratified Rantzau reported that behind this article he suspected Radek's vitriolic pen, for he had recently asked Radek

---

[4] Georges Castellan, "Reichswehr et Armée Rouge," in Jean B. Duroselle, ed., *Les Relations Germano–Soviétiques de 1933 à 1939* (Paris, 1954), p. 162.
[5] AA, RAM/1405/2860/E552 734.
[6] AA, GA/3724/K170/K024 409.

"to tell those gentlemen [Poles] the plain truth from here." Radek had promised to make the Polish national holiday and Foch's visit the occasion of a press attack against Poland.[7]

These Soviet warnings and hostile demonstrations caused considerable concern in Warsaw. On January 23, the Polish chargé d'affaires, Madejski, called on State Secretary von Maltzan and confessed his concern over Soviet intentions and the possible implications of Rantzau's present visit in Berlin. Maltzan took this opportunity to deliver a veiled warning to his Polish colleague when he predicted in Delphic terms that "the Russians will remain as calm as the Poles."[8]

While the Soviet demonstrations considerably helped to reduce German anxieties about Polish intentions, it is doubtful whether they actually changed Polish behavior during the Ruhr crisis. There is no indication that the Warsaw government had at any time contemplated using the Ruhr situation as a pretext for a military intervention in Germany. The French had no interest in seeing an escalation of the crisis as a result of Poland's military participation, although they seem to have pressed their Polish ally to suspend coal shipments to Germany in order to break the back of the latter's policy of passive resistance. The Poles turned to their economic advantage the temporary paralysis of the Ruhr coal mines and therefore refused to comply with their ally's wishes.[9]

The Polish government insisted from the outset that it had no intention or alliance obligation to undertake any diplomatic steps or engage in military sanctions as a result of the Ruhr occupation. In his speech to the Sejm of February 7, Foreign Minister Skrzyński stressed that the Ruhr action had been undertaken for the sake of collecting reparations and did not involve Poland. He reaffirmed his country's loyalty to France, but at the same time expressed the wish for peaceful relations with Germany and Russia.[10] Rauscher's reports from Warsaw confirmed the veracity of the official statements of the Polish government. He believed that the Warsaw authorities were quite ill at ease with the present situation and he had found no one who spoke of active support of France's action.[11]

---

[7] AA, RAM/1425/2945H/D570 910; May 7, 1923.
[8] Ibid., 836.
[9] Letter, Severing, Prussia's minister of the interior, to Foreign Minister von Rosenberg, April 15, 1923, AA, GA/3724/K170/K024 801.
[10] FO, 371/9310, pp. 37–45.
[11] Report by Rauscher, January 10, 1923, AA, GA/3724/K170/K024 177.

The dissuasive impact of the Soviet warnings, therefore, seems to have been more apparent than real, for given the Polish government's opposition to any involvement in the Ruhr crisis, no external dissuasion was needed. Moreover, as the events of October 1923 were to indicate, Moscow's ostensibly co-operative efforts had highly sinister implications for Germany. In September and October the crisis in Germany accelerated and rapidly hurled her into a whirlpool of chaos. Germany's policy of passive resistance to the Ruhr occupation had been sustained at a heavy economic cost which produced a run-away inflation on an unprecedented scale. The French were still in the Ruhr and tried to promote separatist trends in the Rhineland; Hamburg witnessed a Communist rebellion which had been inspired and aided by Moscow's COMINTERN agents; in Saxony and Thuringia, Socialists and Communists formed coalition governments; and Munich became the scene of the grotesque beerhall *Putsch* of the Nazis.

These October events presented the Communists with the opportunity which they had long awaited. This time it was not merely Zinoviev and his COMINTERN agents who encouraged and assisted a German Communist uprising, but the Soviet government itself which undertook official diplomatic steps to prepare the stage for a take-over. The principal aims of Soviet diplomacy with respect to the revolutionary situation were two-fold. In the first place, Russia wished Poland and the Baltic States to take a position of strict neutrality and nonintervention regarding internal developments in Germany and their international repercussions. Second, she wanted to be assured of unhindered transit facilities through these states so that she might ship wheat and other goods to assist a new and fragile Communist regime in Germany.

On August 20, the Polish envoy in Moscow, Roman Knoll, informed his Foreign Minister of a conversation he had held with Karl Radek, a key figure in the COMINTERN and an expert on Germany. Radek had spoken of the possibility of a Communist revolution in Germany. Because of this eventuality, the Soviet government wanted to enter into talks with Poland with the aim of reaching agreement on the following points:

1) In case of a Communist revolution in Germany, Russia would agree to tear East Prussia from the rest of Germany and to have it annexed to Poland or let it enter into some other form of association with Poland;

2) Poland would resign all other territorial claims against Germany;
3) Poland would grant immediate transit facilities for Russian wheat shipments to Germany;
4) Poland would try to keep France neutral.[12]

Foreign Minister Seyda reacted negatively to this opening bid by the Soviets. He agreed to let these talks with Radek continue in order to explore Soviet intentions which, in the opinion of Seyda, were to embarrass Poland internationally and to make her less alert to the real danger, i.e., the Bolshevization of Germany.[13]

In October Viktor Kopp, a senior member of the Soviet Foreign Commissariat and a specialist on German affairs, visited Riga, Kaunas, and Warsaw to try to persuade these countries to declare their *désintéressement* in internal political developments in Germany; to offer unhindered transit facilities to the Soviet Union; and to sign nonaggression pacts with Moscow. In Warsaw, the real shrine and last stop on Kopp's profane pilgrimage, the Soviet emissary raised the same three points, although his tone was more conciliatory and his request for transit facilities was not backed by the type of threats which he had made in Riga.[14] The focus of the Warsaw discussions fell on the transit provisions of the Treaty of Riga. Poland wished to clarify these in the form of a commercial agreement. But Seyda firmly refused to link the execution of the Riga transit clause to internal political developments in Germany and to make an official statement of *désintéressement*, for Warsaw regarded its policy of nonintervention in German affairs as self-evident.[15] On November 5, Dmowski informed the Cabinet that negotiations were deadlocked on this issue. The Cabinet authorized the publication of a communiqué in which the government emphasized that by linking the transit problem to political conditions in Germany the Soviets had introduced a political twist to the question, while Poland wished to treat it purely as an economic matter. Consequently, no agreement had been reached.[16]

---

[12] AMSZ, Paris Embassy, W.4, t.1; cited in Jerzy Krasuski, *Stosunki polsko-niemiecki, 1919–1925* (Poznań, 1962) I, p. 109.
[13] *Ibid.*
[14] Report, Sir W. Max Muller, October 29, 1923, FO, 371/9357, pp. 146–47.
[15] *Ibid.*, p. 151; October 31, 1923.
[16] PPRM, 24 (1923), p. 508. At the time that discussions with Kopp had been in progress, Dmowski had replaced Seyda as foreign minister and the latter had been moved to the position of deputy foreign minister.

Kopp's efforts to neutralize Poland in the event of a Communist take-over in Germany and Radek's proposal to reward Warsaw for its nonintervention in such a situation with the annexation of East Prussia, expose the full duplicity of the scheme which the Soviets were pursuing. On the one hand, the Soviet government posed as the champion of German independence and territorial integrity by concentrating troops on the Polish frontier and by issuing warning declarations that a Polish invasion of East Prussia would be a *casus belli*. On the other hand, that same government not only actively plotted to incite a revolution in Germany but also sought to enlist Polish co-operation in this development by resorting to the much condemned imperialist practice of rewarding a collaborator with territory seized from a third party.

When the Polish plan failed, Moscow reverted to its original position of supporting Germany against Poland. In fact, the Kremlin even sought to get extra mileage out of Kopp's machinations by trying to leave the impression that his activities had been solely intended to assist the existing German government by pressuring Poland to adopt a neutral course.[17]

In Germany the full extent of the Kremlin's duplicity was only partially understood and no news of the Soviet proposal regarding Poland's annexation of East Prussia seems to have come to the notice of Berlin. Even with this information gap, the basic nature of Soviet double-dealing filtered down to Berlin, where it laid a firm barrier of suspicion and disillusionment which was never entirely overcome, despite diplomatic efforts on both sides.

The Polish Question in German–Soviet Relations after 1923

Brockdorff-Rantzau was aware that the Polish question was one of the most urgent problems facing Germany and the Soviet Union and a catalyst for their friendly collaboration. He therefore sought to expand this co-operation during the early stage of the Ruhr crisis and to create a more lasting arrangement for Soviet aid in the event of an attack by Poland, while stopping short of a full military alliance with the Soviet Union. The opportunity for such an arrangement seemed to have arrived in the summer of 1923 when Russia was eager for German credits and assistance for her arms production program. On July 30, 1923, a

---

[17] AA, RAM/1425/2945H/D571 090–91.

provisional agreement was secretly concluded on this matter between Chancellor Cuno and Rosengoltz (alias Rosenholz, alias Raschin, alias Lewin), a revolutionary with a most colorful *curriculum vitae* who was currently a member of the Revolutionary Military Council and chief of the central board of the Soviet air force. The Germans had been persuaded to enter into this delicate agreement after Rosengoltz had made certain promises with respect to Poland. Rantzau did not specify the degree to which Russia had accepted any commitments on the Polish question, but he informed Stresemann that "political conditions were tied to the execution of the military-technical programme, on the acceptance of which we can at any time make dependent our participation in the further development of the Russian armament industry."[18] The nature of the Soviet commitment and its subsequent rejection are revealed in a lengthy memorandum which Rantzau sent to Stresemann on February 20, 1924. In this memorandum, the Count explained how in 1923 he had won the approval of the President of the *Reichsbank* to provide credits for Russian armament industries out of German public funds in addition to the 35 million marks that had already been provided by the *Reichswehr* representatives in Moscow. Chancellor Cuno had informed Rosengoltz that "the German government would make all future financial assistance to the Russian armament industry dependent on two conditions; it demands 1) political safeguards regarding Poland; 2) a preferential position in the reconstruction of the Russian arms industry to the extent that in all factories in which German firms and workers are employed, no other foreigners would be admitted. Herr Raschin had voiced his approval to these conditions. . . ." Before returning to Moscow, Rantzau had called on President Ebert and the newly installed Foreign Minister Stresemann. Both had been nervous about the implications and had insisted that "the previous action in the matter of the armament industry be transferred exclusively to the economic field." Accordingly, when Rantzau saw Chicherin in September, he did not press him for the fulfillment of the conditions agreed upon by Rosengoltz. At that time the Soviet Commissar admitted knowledge of this particular agreement but refused to discuss it. A few days later the German ambassador had discussed the same question with Radek. The latter declared Russian willingness to enter into "military agreements"; however, Germany should not expect "that we will bind ourselves politically on a unilateral

---

[18] Brockdorff-Rantzau to Stresemann, September 10, 1923, AA, Brockdorff-Rantzau Papers/3432/9101H/H226 786–88.

basis for the scanty [*"lumpigen"*] millions which you are offering. . . ."
Rantzau was forced to conclude that "the political and economic goals,
which I had taken into view, have not materialized."[19]

It took over a year before the Polish question again assumed priority
in German-Soviet discussions. On December 4, 1924, Kopp suggested to
Rantzau that both sides would profit if Germany upheld her territorial
claims and Russia refused to guarantee the existing Polish–Soviet boundary.[20] In that way "mutual pressure" could be placed on Poland.[21] Kopp's
suggestion was highly welcome to Rantzau. Co-operation on the Polish
question not only offered prospects of neutralizing Germany's neighbor
but also of forming a lasting link in the chain of German–Soviet friendship which Rantzau had tried to hammer out. Undersecretary von Maltzan, as was to be expected of this "Easterner" in the Foreign Ministry
who acted as Rantzau's "personal ambassador" in Berlin, grasped the line
which Kopp had thrown out and authorized the ambassador to enter into
a confidential exchange of views on Poland. Rantzau was free to admit
that Germany, if she became a member of the League of Nations, would
be obliged to respect Poland's territorial integrity, but that this constituted no territorial guarantee, nor would it restrict Germany from under-
taking revisionist policies in the future. Maltzan then cautiously proceeded to chart the course along which the discussions on the Polish
question were to proceed:

> Furthermore, please mention that one of the primary causes of unrest in
> Eastern Europe is the violation of the ethnographic principle in the
> drawing of Poland's frontiers. . . . German and Russian interests here
> seem to run parallel. . . . Whether one ought to hint already now that
> for Germany and Russia the solution of the Polish question lies in the
> reduction of Poland to her ethnographic frontiers, I leave to your dis-
> cretion depending on the course of these conversations.[22]

---

[19] *Ibid.*, 805–9. It is not quite certain what "political safeguards regarding Poland" the Russians had given in these talks with Rantzau. They probably included
the promise to run a press campaign against Poland and to mobilize her forces on the
Polish border if Poland became belligerent.

[20] In March 1923 the Western Powers had recognized the existing borders of
Poland in the east and south-east in a declaration of the Conference of Ambassadors.

[21] Report, Brockdorff-Rantzau, December 5, 1924, AA, StS/2313/4562H/E154
862–65.

[22] Telegram, Maltzan to Brockdorff-Rantzau, December 13, 1924, AA, StS/
2313/4562H/E164 874–76. Maltzan's instructions almost appear to be a political
testament on German foreign policy as advocated by "Easterners" like himself and
Rantzau. Soon after, he was removed from his position as state secretary and sent to
Washington as ambassador. Symbolically for the new course of diplomacy which was

On December 20, Rantzau introduced his variation on Kopp's theme and probed Chicherin for his views on a parallel German–Soviet policy on the Polish question. At the outset of the conversation the Commissar displayed certain signs of real or affected nervousness but then altered his approach and "went into details and remarked that as far as he could see from the content of my report, Germany for her part only promised *neutrality,* while in turn she demanded from Russia *active support* on the question of Poland's western boundaries. Since the Minister insisted on this point, I considered it appropriate to hint that the solution to the Polish question probably lay in pushing Poland back to her ethnographic frontiers." [Underlining for italics in the original.] Chicherin welcomed this proposal as being of great importance.[23]

In their next all-night session that lasted until dawn of December 26—the habit of turning night into day, which drove their subordinates into despair, was one of the many common idiosyncrasies which helped form the very close personal bonds between these two diplomats—the thread of German–Soviet co-operation on the Polish question was spun further.

Chicherin made it clear that Russia would only undertake a step as consequential as the solution of the Polish problem if agreement was first reached with Germany on all other matters related to a common policy. In this vein, the Commissar proposed that any settlement on the Polish problem be preceded by an agreement in which "the German and the Russian government bind themselves on their part to enter into no political or economic alliance or understanding with third parties which are directed against the other," and that they "bind themselves to co-ordinate their activities in the course of future developments on the

---

on the rise, Maltzan was replaced by Carl von Schubert, whom Radek styled a "vulgar Anglophile." Dirksen pictured Schubert as "a Westerner by birth and education who belonged to the group that had an expressly anglophile orientation in our foreign service. But he possessed sufficient perspective and foreign political experience to realize that German foreign policy was faced with the duty to balance the influence of the West by good relations with Russia." (Herbert von Dirksen, *Moskau, Tokio, London* [Stuttgart, 1949], p. 55.)

[23] Telegram, Rantzau, December 24, 1924, AA, StS/2313/4562H/E154 904–6. It is interesting to see that Germany, as she had in the 1923 talks with Raschin, again wanted to get a commitment of active Russian assistance against a mere promise of neutrality in the event of a Polish-Soviet conflict. As in 1923, the Soviets found this an inadequate *quid pro quo*.

question of entering the League of Nations or of dispatching observers [to the League of Nations]." The best solution, according to Chicherin, would be for Germany and the Soviet Union to enter the League simultaneously.[24]

Chicherin's December proposals clearly revealed Russia's actual intentions. It was Moscow's predominant, and in view of the prospects of growing bonds between Berlin and the Western powers, desperate aim to conclude a concrete agreement with Germany and thus block the latter's access to any agreement with the West. Furthermore, Chicherin's apparently innocuous request to co-ordinate German and Soviet policy in relation to the League of Nations and to join together, in view of the fact that Moscow entertained no intentions of joining, has to be regarded as a poorly concealed attempt to perpetuate Germany's exclusion from the tables at Geneva. The short Polish prelude with which Kopp had opened the discussions was a bait which did, indeed, immediately attract the German fish. While Berlin tried to expand the Polish issue into the central theme of their discussions, Moscow advanced her real desiderata and hedged on the Polish question. In fact, there can be little doubt that Russia had no interest in bringing the Polish issue to a climax at that particular time. As Maltzan told Lord D'Abernon on December 28, the Red Army had undergone considerable deterioration and he doubted whether it would be "much good even against Poland."[25] Consequently, the particular interests of Berlin and Moscow did not run parallel but in very different directions. Russia wanted a concrete settlement that barred German access to the West, but she did not want to precipitate action on the Polish problem. Germany wanted to explore what might be achieved on the Polish question by a harmonized German–Soviet policy, while retaining a free hand to open her round of bidding with the West. Schubert, who answered for Stresemann, informed Rantzau that while Germany was naturally willing to continue the exchange of views on all general questions, she would like to follow Kopp's specific suggestion by commencing this exchange with a concrete problem that interested them both, namely Poland. In view of Russia's obvious intentions, it is not quite clear whether Schubert only assumed a naive role or really had failed to grasp Soviet motives when he ex-

[24] Telegram, Brockdorff-Rantzau to Stresemann, December 29, 1924, *ibid.*, 926–30.
[25] Edgar D'Abernon, *An Ambassador of Peace* (London, 1929–30), III, p. 120.

pressed surprise over Chicherin's refusal to follow up Kopp's proposal to confine discussions to the Polish question.[26]

Stresemann turned a deaf ear to Moscow's siren song and Rantzau's exhortations. He applied dilatory tactics in relations with the Kremlin under the pretext of a German cabinet crisis and presidential elections and opened negotiations with the West. While these Moscow conversations were in process, Lord D'Abernon had taken the wind out of their sails by suggesting that the time for a formal German security pact offer was propitious. Ambassadors Sthamer and Hoesch, in London and Paris respectively, were taken into confidence and on January 20, 1925, a formal proposal was handed to Lord D'Abernon. France received a similar proposal on February 9.[27] It was not until January 22 that Schubert informed Rantzau of the existence of certain security pact plans with the West,[28] and later revealed that London and Paris had been secretly approached on this question. However, the Undersecretary hastened to point out that this implied no change of policy toward Russia, that Germany would not acknowledge the permanency of her eastern frontiers and that Poland would, consequently, be offered a mere arbitration treaty.[29] A few days later, Schubert added that Germany retained an interest in following up the Soviet December proposal.[30]

Correctly interpreting Germany's procrastinating efforts as an indication of her concentration on a Western solution, the Kremlin made a desperate last-minute effort to halt this trend by re-channelling the German–Soviet talks to the Polish question from where they had originally started and where a favorable German response might be expected. On February 24, Rykov, the chairman of the Council of People's Commissars, proposed to the German ambassador what had to be interpreted as a veiled offer of a German–Russian military alliance. Brockdorff-Rantzau immediately rejected the offer:

> I myself have assumed the post in Moscow in order to revise the *Diktat* of Versailles but not as an "Ambassador of Revenge." I desired, if possible, to bring about a revision of the Versailles treaty by peaceful means and I am giving myself to no illusions that the Soviet government will ever be prepared, as is believed in certain circles at home, to conduct

---

[26] AA, StS/2313/4562H/E154 907–9.
[27] Ludwig Zimmermann, *Deutsche Aussenpolitik in der Ära der Weimarer Republik* (Göttingen, 1958), p. 255.
[28] AA, StS/2313/4562H/E154 942–43.
[29] Telegram, Schubert to Rantzau, February 12, 1925, *ibid.*, 966–69.
[30] Telegram, Schubert to Rantzau, February 23, 1925, *ibid.*, 979–84.

a war of liberation for Germany on the pattern of the year 1813; instead, it will be led by the ideas of a world revolution.[31]

Because a leak of Germany's security pact proposal might reach the Kremlin and place the German government in the embarrassing position of double dealing, Stresemann instructed his ambassador on March 6 to inform the Soviet government of Germany's proposal and to explain that this was merely a political move to counteract French expansionism and to wrest the Rhineland from French control. Rantzau was to emphasize that no shift of policy and no Eastern guarantees were contemplated.[32]

On June 2, Krestinski, the Soviet ambassador in Berlin, delivered Chicherin's reply. Moscow demanded that her December proposals be subjected to serious discussion rather than procrastination and indicated that if Germany entered the League, Russia might be forced to look for other arrangements. This was the veiled threat of a Soviet–French alignment or even a wider Soviet–French–Polish combination. Schubert tried to convince the Soviet Ambassador that Chicherin saw matters too darkly and reiterated Stresemann's theory—as voiced toward the Soviets—that Germany primarily sought League membership in order to liberate the Rhineland from French occupation and asked whether Chicherin could suggest any better means for accomplishing this.[33] Litvinov visited Stresemann while en route to Marienbad and voiced his fear over the fact that Germany appeared to slip into the anti-Soviet camp and warned that a Polish–Russian détente might easily occur.[34]

In a last effort to deter Germany from entering into a Western security pact, Russia resorted to the tactics of playing the Polish card. The primary motive seems to have been to dissuade Germany from proceeding any further with her security pact plans. On a more long-range basis, the Soviet government might also have calculated that if it failed to prevent the conclusion of the security pact and if Germany were thus to be drawn into closer relations with the Western Powers the Soviet Union should seek to compensate for this loss by improving its relations with Poland.

[31] Brockdorff-Rantzau, Political Report No. 2, February 24, 1925, AA, StS/ 2313/4562H/E155 006–9.

[32] Brockdorff-Rantzau, Political Report No. 4, March 9, 1925, *ibid.*, 010–13.

[33] Memorandum by Schubert, June 2, 1925, *ibid.*, 328–35.

[34] Note by Stresemann, June 13, 1925, *ibid.*, 374–84; Gustav Stresemann, *Vermächtnis* (Berlin, 1932), II, pp. 516–18.

On his return from Paris on June 12, 1925, the Polish diplomat Tennenbaum made a brief stop-over in Berlin where, on Soviet initiative, he met with Radek. During their talk Radek pointed out that a Western security pact served primarily British interests, as it would rearm Germany and thus help keep France and Russia in check. In his estimate the logical consequence of Germany signing a security pact with the Western Powers would be closer Polish–Soviet relations. To achieve this end, Radek suggested that Poland resign her financial claims against Russia as determined by the Treaty of Riga, and that both countries sign a nonaggression pact that would allow Poland to concentrate her troops in the west and Russia her troops in the east.[35]

Radek had spoken only in a private capacity, but his suggestion for a nonaggression pact was formally repeated when Foreign Minister Chicherin paid an official visit to Warsaw on his way to Berlin. The arrival of the Soviet Commissar in the Polish capital on September 27 was something of a sensation; however, the attention that such a visit created testified to the fact that Soviet–Polish relations were of such a poor nature that a positive outcome of the visit was unlikely. Earlier that year there had been several other border incidents, and in April Soviet opinion had been enraged by the killing of two Communist prisoners who were to be exchanged for Polish prisoners. *Izvestiya* of April 7 had attributed this murder to the state of anarchy in Poland, and in July the Warsaw press complained of three Soviet attacks on Polish border guards.[36] Under these circumstances existing realities provided a poor pavement for Chicherin's road to Warsaw, a fact over which the cordial reception and the toasts[37] could spread no cloak. Chicherin's apparent offer of a nonaggression pact was rejected by Poland as it did not include the Baltic States and Rumania.[38] Chicherin also spoke in general terms about improving the execution of the Treaty of Riga and the possible conclusion of a Polish–Soviet economic treaty. During his Warsaw visit Chicherin gave a statement to the press in which he made some strong

[35] Letter, Tennenbaum to Prime Minister Grabski, July 15, 1925, AAN, *Akta Stanisława Kauzika*, file 16; cited in Krasuski, *Stosunki polsko-niemieckie*, I, p. 375.

[36] *Berliner Tageblatt*, July 30, 1925.

[37] At a luncheon given in Chicherin's honor on September 28, Skrzyński made a toast in which he referred to the visit as a political act that Poland understood. Chicherin responded by saying that in the warm reception he saw an indication of Poland's desire to continue a policy of harmony. (See Rauscher's report of September 28, 1925, AA, GA/3027/6898H/H105 323–26).

[38] Zygmunt Gąsiorowski, "Stresemann and Poland before Locarno," *Journal of Central European Affairs* 18 (1958–59), pp. 44–45.

hints that were aimed more in the direction of Berlin than toward his hosts. His visit, he insisted, was not directed against Germany or Britain or any other country. In his view, the security pact was a piece of "Tory politics and an endeavor to detach Germany from us." He also issued a warning that if Germany entered the League without restrictions, it would mean that she agreed to become a member of an eventual coalition against the Soviet Union.[39]

The *Auswärtiges Amt* retained a confident and cool attitude throughout Chicherin's *tour de valse* on Warsaw's diplomatic parquet. Rauscher, in an expert analysis of the situation that confronted Russia and Poland, had come to the conclusion that existing conditions virtually precluded a Polish–Soviet reconciliation, even if both governments sought it for tactical reasons. Rauscher predicted that if Germany entered into a Western pact "then it is of high probability that we will approach an era of Russian–Polish reconciliatory attempts, which, however, will hardly be manifested other than through speeches and articles. . . . *But a real conciliation between the two nations would pre-suppose a revision of the Riga Treaty*, as Viktor Kopp has openly declared during his Warsaw visit 1½ years ago." A reconciliation might be agreed upon on paper, "*but the real and the emotional resistance between both countries* is so strong that one *cannot think of a lasting power-political alignment.*" Instead, realities were more potent than any possible tactical plans on the part of the two governments. Rauscher concluded that Poland and Russia would remain in a latent state of war "which eventually must find its military discharge."[40] The Warsaw correspondent of the *Vossische Zeitung* confidently reported that Chicherin's visit had led to no "positive outcome" other than a verbal repetition of generalities.[41] The *Deutsche Allgemeine Zeitung* styled the optimistic speculations in the Polish press empty fantasies and pointed out that informed circles in Warsaw had admittedly voiced their disappointment over the absence of any real results from Chicherin's visit.[42]

Chicherin's stop-over for "lunch" in Warsaw had not impressed the German Foreign Ministry and, if anything, had only revealed the weakness of the Soviet bargaining position: playing the Polish card had indicated that Moscow held a card, but equally that it was a no trump card

[39] Report, Stetson, October 3, 1925, *SD*, 860c.00/294.
[40] Report, Rauscher, June 30, 1925, AA, GA/3721/K166/K022 418–23. Underlining in the original text.
[41] *Vossische Zeitung*, September 30, 1925.
[42] *Deutsche Allgemeine Zeitung*, October 1, 1925.

and could not take a trick. During the conversations which Stresemann and Chicherin held on September 30 and October 2, the original December proposals on the Polish question figured prominently on the agenda and here, for the last time in the period under discussion, constituted a major issue in German–Soviet relations.[43] During their first session, the Commissar bitterly criticized Germany's foreign policy toward Russia: in December Rantzau had proposed to push Poland back to her ethnographic frontiers—a proposal that could not be interpreted as anything other than an appeal to military collaboration for the destruction of Poland—which he had considered of such importance that he had immediately called a meeting of the Council of Commissars [cabinet]. But instead of defining her proposal more specifically, Germany had then approached the West. Stresemann immediately countered the Commissar's blackmailing technique which virtually assigned to Germany the responsibility of proposing the fourth partition of Poland. Stresemann emphatically denied that Germany had ever made such an alliance offer for the purpose of a Polish partition, and to confirm this, he telephoned Schubert to supply the documentary details on this point. The Undersecretary, who had so rudely been shaken out of his slumber —by that time it was already way past midnight—correctly pointed out that the initiative had come from Kopp and not Rantzau.

For their second session both ministers had done their homework on the relevant documents. When Chicherin produced definite evidence of Maltzan's proposal to push Poland back to her ethnographic frontiers (Maltzan's telegram of December 13, 1924, AA, StS/2313/4562H/E154 874–76, which Rantzau had shown to Chicherin), Stresemann conceded the use of the phrase but minimized its importance as something marginal that had been left to the Ambassador's discretion to use or not to use. In this particular duel, Stresemann's expert juggling of facts and figures to suit his needs—even if at the occasional cost of orthodoxy— clearly outmatched the technique of his Soviet counterpart who was consequently forced to adopt a defensive strategy.

The Polish interlude in German–Soviet relations between the Ruhr crisis and Locarno provided German diplomacy with a valuable experience from which Stresemann's realistic appraisal did not fail to abstract the relevant conclusions. By adhering to the symbols of the Rapallo

---

[43] For Stresemann's note of the September 30 talk see AA, GA/3035/6898H/ H111 047–58; for the October 2 conversation see *ibid.*, 037–44; also the *Vermächtnis*, II, pp. 523–25. The latter, significantly makes no reference to the question of pushing Poland back to her ethnographic frontiers.

policy, the countries could impose restraints on Poland's foreign policy ambitions. A co-operative effort of Germany and Russia, which mobilized against Poland the weapons of diplomatic warnings and which resorted to pin-pricking press articles, was in their common interest, and Germany eagerly continued to exploit this channel of diplomacy. On the other hand, on the issue of a joint revisionist policy, Germany was confronted with the Kremlin's entirely different approach. Germany, because of her disarmed condition and exposed strategic location—if not also for moral reasons—had been dissuaded from using military force to bring about a revision. But Russia's proposal implied a course that entailed a military alliance for the purpose of a forceful elimination of their neighbor. Through actual experience German diplomacy had become aware how the Soviet Union had invoked the Polish issue primarily for the purpose of curtailing Germany's access to the Western Powers. Furthermore, the example of Kopp's clandestine efforts during the Ruhr crisis, in preparing the diplomatic framework for a Communist take-over in Germany, served as a constant reminder that the Communist aim lay not in waging a war of liberation against the Versailles treaty on behalf of Germany but in exploiting any favorable events in Germany for the purpose of staging a Communist take-over.

In the meantime, it was in Russia's interest to obstruct an amiable settlement of German–Polish conflicts and to retain tension between the two states. In this regard, the Polish question became an area of conflicting rather than concurrent interests between Germany and the Soviet Union. An analysis of the nature of Moscow's December proposals indicated that a German–Soviet revisionist policy along the lines envisaged by Moscow would proceed by the road of war. Stresemann was as apprehensive as Brockdorff-Rantzau of the dangers of a German–Soviet military alliance and after a conversation with the Count in July 1925 he warned: "To enter into a marriage [enter into alliance] with Communist Russia would mean to lay onself in bed with the murderer of one's own nation."[44] Stresemann might in all sincerity have denied that Locarno and Germany's entry into the League entailed an option for either West or East.[45] But in the German estimate Locarno did pave the way for a reconciliation with the West and thereby seemed to open the prospects for a territorial revision by peaceful means and with international consent rather than by force. It must, of course, remain a matter

[44] Cited in Annelise Thimme, *Gustav Stresemann. Eine politische Biographie zur Geschichte der Weimarer-Zeit* (Hannover and Frankfurt, 1957), pp. 108–9.
[45] Stresemann, *Vermächtnis*, II, p. 554.

of unresolved historical speculation whether Germany would have abided by her commitment to a policy of peaceful revision if the Locarno policy of conciliation had been allowed to continue for long without bringing the expected revisionist fruits in the east. But by the assessment that was given to the Locarno settlement at its inception by Germany's foreign policy decision-makers, Locarno did constitute an option for a policy of peaceful revision of her eastern frontiers against a solution that envisaged the use of force. As such it was an option for a revisionist policy in conjunction with the collaboration of the Western Powers and against the forceful means that were involved in the Russian proposal. There is evidence that in 1925 neither Stresemann nor the officials in the Foreign Ministry were fully aware of the extent to which circumstances excluded the possibility of a German–Soviet collaboration on a peaceful revision of Poland's frontiers, and, consequently, the extent to which the expressed commitment to a revision solely by peaceful means had fixed Germany on a Western course. In 1925 Stresemann was still convinced that Russia, by raising the whole issue of her boundaries with Poland, might provide the opportunity for a general peaceful revision, probably by preparing the way for an international conference. Writing anonymously in the *Hamburger Fremdenblatt* of April 10, 1925, Stresemann noted:

> Against the *status quo* in the West . . . there stands, on the other hand, the clearly expressed non-guarantee of Germany's eastern frontiers. In this, Poland finds herself in the same position vis-à-vis Germany as toward Russia, since also the Russian Empire does not give *de facto* recognition to its borders with Poland. Matters in the east have not been settled. At the moment when Russia makes the decision whether she wants to operate permanently behind these boundaries or whether to roll up the question of the Baltic States and of Poland, at that moment begins a new chapter in European history. Still, in this regard we don't have to think in terms of a new World War or an execution by arms. Instead, one can imagine that all of these questions will form the subject of a great international conference which on this point will create a new law for the real self-determination of nations.[46]

During subsequent years, however, the German Foreign Office saw with greater clarity that a policy of peaceful revisionism was a one-way road that proceeded by way of the Western capitals and that no avenue to Moscow existed for this approach. Looking at the whole question in retrospect, the present generation might be inclined to view Weimar

[46] *Ibid.*, II, p. 93.

Germany's entire policy of peaceful revisionism toward Poland as a dead-end road or irreconcilable paradox: there might be peace, in which case her revisionist territorial aspirations would have to be sacrificed; or there might be a revision, but it would not be by peaceful means. Hitler chose the latter course. Significantly, his policy led him to put into brutal practice the tentative and furtive explorations that had been conducted between Berlin and Moscow in 1924 and 1925.

V

The Polish Question at Locarno

VIEWED IN RETROSPECT, Stresemann's security pact offer in 1925 was neither the sacrificial *Erfüllungs—und Verzichtspolitik* on the altar of European conciliation, an interpretation given by his contemporary admirers whose account shed more warmth than light on Stresemann's policies, nor was it the conscious and sinister Machiavellian grand strategy of deception and the blueprint for aggression, according to the later rendition which became popular during World War II and which induced some historians to brand Stresemann as the spiritual forefather of Hitler. Instead, it was a reflection of very sober *Realpolitik*.[1] By 1925 it had become evident that Germany would neither be relieved of the threat of further Allied sanctions on the pattern of the Ruhr occupation, nor win the early evacuation of the Rhineland as well as relief from other onerous burdens of the peace treaty, nor would she be assured of further international loans, unless she herself contributed her share toward satisfying France's deeply ingrained craving for security. It appeared that no other realistic avenue existed for the satisfaction of these German aspirations. The secret discussions which had been held with the Soviet Union between 1923 and 1925 on the subject of revising the existing treaty system had done their share in hastening this realization.

By her proposal Germany could make a magnanimous gesture without, however, being compelled to forego those aspirations which seemed

---

[1] For recent interpretations of Stresemann's foreign policy, see Henry L. Bretton, *Stresemann and the Revision of Versailles. A Fight for Reason* (Stanford, 1953); Hans Gatzke, *Stresemann and the Rearmament of Germany* (Baltimore, 1956); Annelise Thimme, *Gustav Stresemann* (Hanover, 1957).

to lie within the realm of eventual fulfillment. When one considers the cool calculations which underlay the German offer, Locarno loses some of its more sentimental overtones. Viewed in its proper perspective, including the freedom which it left to Germany to work for a revision of her eastern frontiers, Locarno can at best be regarded as an experiment. Whether it could really have become the instrument for a European peace, for which it was then hailed, depended on whether the acceptance of the status quo and her conciliation in the west might eventually have produced a similar orientation in her eastern policy.

As the legal ancestors of the German proposal, one should consider Chancellor Cuno's abortive nonaggression pact offer of December 1922 and the so-called Geneva Protocol—the planned system of compulsory arbitration accompanied by collective sanctions in the case of violation —that had been agreed to by the League of Nations in October 1924 in an attempt to "put teeth" into the somewhat defective Covenant. The Geneva Protocol had been backed by France and had met with a particularly enthusiastic response from Poland and Czechoslovakia. The British Labour government accorded it similar support. But when the Conservatives came into office after the October election, Britain's traditional caution against accepting too extensive an international commitment reasserted itself and the protocol was not ratified. Having thus lost one of its principal sponsors, the Geneva Protocol quickly became a non-negotiable instrument on the international security market. In order to compensate France for having thus thwarted one of her major security schemes, the new British government and especially its Francophile foreign secretary, Austen Chamberlain, contemplated the idea of offering France a defense pact. Lord D'Abernon welcomed a British defense commitment on the Continent but feared the anti-German bias inherent in a purely bilateral British–French security pact. He, therefore, advocated the idea of a multilateral pact that would also include Germany and thus supplement his patient labors in bringing about Germany's reconciliation with the Western Powers. His idea fell on fertile ground in Berlin and bore fruit in discussions with Schubert and Stresemann late in 1924.

Neither the memorandum which was presented to London on January 20, 1925, nor the one which was received in Paris on February 9, had made any reference to Poland or Czechoslovakia. But in anticipation of the French demand to expand the offer to include her eastern allies, Germany adopted a pre-emptive strategy and proposed to sign arbitration treaties with all her neighbors, not just the members of the proposed Rhine pact.[2] While the latter part of the proposal clearly attempted to circumnavigate the anticipated Polish obstacle, Germany had made the proposal as innocuous as possible by refraining from a direct offer to Warsaw and, furthermore, by diluting it to a strategy that extended this offer to all her neighbors. The question of the eastern boundaries was first mentioned specifically by Ambassador Hoesch in his talk with Herriot on February 17, when he suggested that some quieting assurance might be given to Poland and Czechoslovakia.[3]

The French reaction to Germany's security offer was noncommittal. On February 20, the *Quai d'Orsay* informed Ambassador Hoesch that before France could give any reply she would have to consult with her allies on the creation of a system of security "within the framework of the Treaty of Versailles."[4] In turning first to her eastern allies, France behaved in accordance with Germany's pessimistic predictions.

French interests in Poland's security had already been demonstrated during the Paris peace conference and the Upper Silesian plebiscite. This had taken more formal and reciprocal form with the signing of a treaty of alliance and a secret military convention during Piłsudski's visit to Paris in February 1921.[5] For France this alliance was the anchor of her East European policy; for Poland it was the very foundation of her foreign and security policy. Despite the importance attributed to it by both sides, a certain amount of friction and resentment accompanied the alliance from its inception, and it would be inaccurate to view it as an unqualified success, only later disturbed by France's Locarno policy and by Piłsudski's return to power. The French–Polish alliance might have been a marriage of love, but it was not always a marriage of convenience. On

---

[2] Already, in March 1924, Stresemann had pointed out that in order to settle the major issues with France it might be necessary to conclude some form of agreement with Poland. Since a guarantee of the eastern frontier was out of the question, Stresemann was giving thought to proposing to conclude an arbitration treaty with Poland, possibly following the model of the Bryan Treaties of 1913 and 1914. (AA, StS/2299/4556H/E148 361–68). Hoesch's reply from Paris had been cautious but positive (*ibid.*, 345), but Rauscher had considered the timing for such an offer psychologically unadvisable, as he feared that Poland would insist on a guarantee pact with French participation (*ibid.*, 354–56). In 1924 Rauscher's negative view had prevailed and Germany refrained from taking the initiative on this sensitive issue.

[3] Piotr S. Wandycz, *France and Her Eastern Allies 1919–1925* (Minneapolis, 1962), p. 329.

[4] Gustav Stresemann, *Vermächtnis* (Berlin, 1932), II, p. 62.

[5] A text of the alliance treaty appears in League of Nations, *Treaty Series* 18 (1923): 12. The text of the secret military convention is found in *Najnowsze Dzieje Polski 1919–1939* 11 (1967): 212–17.

the Polish side, the economic treaty which had been tied to the military agreements and which had granted far-reaching economic concessions to French interest groups was viewed as unfair and disadvantageous. Poland also resented the French refusal to guarantee the Polish–Soviet border and the very limited and somewhat vague commitments to aid Poland in the event of a Polish–Soviet war. For the latter eventuality, France merely pledged to try to keep Germany neutral, to keep the communication lines to Poland open, and to assist Poland with war materiel and technical personnel. In France there was some skepticism about tying one's fortunes to a country whose future role and very survival were still in doubt and which, according to Marshal Foch, had "ni frontières, ni gouvernement, ni armée."[6] Underlying the French misgivings was the gnawing suspicion that in opting for Poland, one had drawn a losing card. While Germany remained weak and disarmed, Warsaw might serve as an acceptable *Ersatz*, but against a recovered and rearmed Germany the winning card was the renewal of the prewar French–Russian alliance, an option that now seemed foreclosed by her alliance with Warsaw.

When the news of Germany's security pact offer broke in Warsaw, it was greeted with stormy protests from all quarters. Herriot informed Hoesch of the "enormous excitement" that it had caused in Polish circles.[7] The Polish press occupied itself with the question more than with any other foreign political issue. Early in March, *Czas* ran a series of articles in which it accused Germany of trying to disrupt the Polish–French alliance.[8] *Kurjer Polski* of March 2 warned that a security pact which excluded Poland would constitute a revision of the Versailles treaty, and *Gazeta Warszawska* of March 5 compared the Western security pact to a new partition of Poland by diplomatic means. Two days later, the same paper warned that if France joined such a pact, this would mean the end of the French–Polish alliance. In Warsaw and other cities mass demonstrations of protest were staged. These were not directed against Germany alone, but also against Britain and Italy.

That the German proposal would meet with Polish objections was natural and had been anticipated in Berlin. The security proposal was a clear attempt to differentiate between the status of the western and

[6] Léon Noël, *L'Aggression allemande contre la Pologne* (Paris, 1946), p. 100.
[7] Telegram, Hoesch to Schubert, March 6, 1925, AA, RAM/1425/2945H/ D571 499.
[8] Cited in Wandycz, *France and Her Eastern Allies*, p. 332.

eastern boundaries. By offering France security on the Rhine, Germany might succeed in reversing the French policy of seeking security beyond her immediate boundaries through international pacts.

What Germany had not expected, however, was that the very instrument by which French and Polish fears were to be allayed, namely the proposed conciliation and arbitration treaties, should become the center of Polish concern. On March 7, in a conversation with Dirksen, Olszowski betrayed considerable anxiety lest the proposed arbitration treaty include a territorial clause that would enable Germany to realize her revisionist claims by international arbitration.[9] Two days later, at a luncheon in the Polish legation, Olszowski again raised the same issue with Dirksen and was reassured by the latter that Germany envisaged an arbitration formula which would settle legal disputes by a process binding arbitration while reserving disputes of a political nature for settlement by a conciliation commission.[10] Gaus, the legal adviser of the German Foreign Ministry, repeated this formula, which he had designed, and gave Olszowski his word of honor that Germany did not intend to use the proposed arbitration agreement to bring about a territorial revision.[11]

Stresemann was rather irked that such sinister significance was now being attributed to what in fact was little more than a token gesture of conciliation toward Poland, and he fired off a telegram to the German consulate in Geneva where the League of Nations was currently in session. Stresemann rejected as utterly false Warsaw's speculations that Germany intended to use the eastern arbitration treaties for settling the question of her eastern frontiers. The security pact applied exclusively to the west, but knowing that "from the French point of view also the eastern problem plays a role, we have proposed the idea of concluding a far-reaching arbitration treaty with all states, thus also with the eastern neighbors, in order to meet the French position and to demonstrate our peaceful intentions toward the east."[12]

Schubert echoed the same sentiments in a telegram to Hoesch on March 10, where he concluded that "whatever one might think of the German arbitration proposal, it is a sign of Germany's desire to reach a peaceful understanding and not an indication of aggressive aims."[13]

[9] Memorandum, Dirksen, AA, GA/3729/K171/K027 478–79.

[10] *Ibid.*, 491.

[11] Report, Olszowski, March 13, 1925, AMSZ, Berlin Legation, W.167, t.139k; cited in Wiesław Balcerak, *Polityka Zagraniczna Polski w dobie Locarna* (Warsaw, 1967), p. 88.

[12] AA, RAM/1425/2945H/D571 512.

[13] *Ibid.*, 519.

Talking to Lord D'Abernon a week later, Schubert disclaimed any German desire to modify the Polish frontier by arbitration. Germany envisaged binding arbitration only for legal disputes and conciliatory and nonbinding awards on political questions. Frontier disputes belonged to the second category, and, if Poland desired, Germany would specifically agree to exclude territorial questions from arbitration procedures. On March 28, after having checked this point with Chancellor Luther and Stresemann, Schubert informed the British Ambassador that the German government categorically renounced bringing an alteration to the German–Polish frontier by other than peaceful means.[14]

With respect to the arbitration treaties, this explanation was an accurate version of Germany's position. Throughout the negotiations which preceded Locarno, Germany insisted on restricting arbitration procedure to legal disputes. There was no thought of making it an instrument of revisionism. The shortcoming of the eastern arbitration treaties was not that they offered Germany a back door for bringing up the territorial issue by legal means but that they were an inadequate substitute for the kind of agreement that would have imposed barriers against pursuing the issue by other means.

Apart from that, Germany had no intention of starting to reap the harvest of her eastern revisionist policy before the western security pact was safely under lock and key. When Dirksen spoke with Sahm, the President of the Danzig Senate, he was surprised to hear that the latter wanted to raise the eastern territorial question at this particular time. Such an attempt at this stage, explained Dirksen, would not only entail the collapse of the security pact negotiations, but under the present power constellation it was doomed to failure.[15] Dirksen made this conversation the occasion for a lengthy memorandum which warned that an introduction of the revisionist issue at this time would have a fatal effect on the progress of the security pact and would prompt the Entente Powers to demand a German guarantee of the territorial status quo in the east.[16] Writing to his friend and neighboring landowner in Silesia, Detz von Reinersdorff, Dirksen urged his Rightist friends in the border regions to refrain from any movement that might pressure the German government to invoke the revisionist issue at present. World opinion was not yet prepared for such a step, even though in Britain and the United States the

---

[14] Letter, Chamberlain to Max Muller, April 3, 1925, *FO*, 371/10730, p. 109.
[15] Memorandum, Dirksen, March 18, 1925, AA, D/2771/5462H/E368 442–43.
[16] AA, StS/2267/4509H/E125 752–53; March 20, 1925.

realization of the untenability of the German–Polish frontier was gradually winning ground. While silence and restraint were necessary for the time being, Dirksen assured his friends that Upper Silesia would not be forgotten when the hour for a revisionist solution had arrived.[17]

FOREIGN MINISTER SKRZYŃSKI'S TRAVELS

In order to frustrate the German security proposal or to turn it into a more comprehensive security system that included a guarantee for Poland's boundaries, Foreign Minister Skrzyński went abroad after making a soothing announcement to the *Sejm* Foreign Affairs Committee. Paris was the key target of his mission and he visited the French capital before and after attending the League session in Geneva.

In the period before Piłsudski's return to power, Skrzyński was the most important person in the Foreign Ministry and probably the only person holding that portfolio who exerted any real influence in shaping the course of foreign policy. His predecessors had held the post for too brief an interval and lacked diplomatic experience or domestic political support to make any real impact. They were little more than caretakers of an existing apparatus whose routine functions they supervised with varying degrees of efficiency and interest.

Count Aleksander Skrzyński was the scion of an aristocratic and wealthy family from southern Poland. He had gained his early diplomatic training and experience as a member of the Austro–Hungarian diplomatic corps, and after the restitution of Poland he had served as Polish minister in Bucharest. In addition to these respectable diplomatic credentials, he enjoyed good political connections both with the Left, because of his progressive orientation, and with the more conservative groups through his personal and family links with the land-owning aristocracy. He had already held the foreign ministry portfolio in Sikorski's short-lived government in 1923 and had returned to that post in August of 1924 under Prime Minister Grabski, with whom he enjoyed very cordial relations. The combination of his diplomatic experience and political skills and connections that were, moreover, unencumbered by declared partisanship made it possible for him to make a real impact in shaping Polish foreign policy, especially since Prime Minister Grabski was primarily concerned with economic and financial matters and left Skrzyński a free hand in the foreign policy field.

[17] AA, D/2769/5462H/E368 070–72; April 27, 1925.

Skrzyński had a flexible and intuitive approach and was a man of good will. He was not a person of great intellect and there was nothing revolutionary in his policy. He continued to make the alliance with France the foundation of Polish foreign policy and happily identified himself with the change of French policy toward the League of Nations, which occurred under Herriot who wanted to use that body as an instrument for international conciliation and not merely as a restructured wartime coalition against Germany. This approach suited Skrzyński's preference for normalizing relations with his Russian, Czech, and German neighbors. If there was any innovation in Polish policy that can be attributed to Skrzyński, it was his attempt to create more intimate relations with Great Britain and the rest of the Anglo-Saxon world, an orientation that was continued after Piłsudski returned to power and which tried to underscore the independence and flexibility of Polish foreign policy.

Foreign diplomats were not entirely kind in their comments on Skrzyński. Rauscher often joked about his vanity and indecisiveness. Another German official, Max von Stockhausen, in a grossly biased and unfair comment, referred to Skrzyński as "a typical Polish nobleman, not very clean, not very appetizing, quite suited for the role of a lover in a second-class operetta."[18] Initial British reaction was no more favorable. In 1920 Horace Rumbold had called him "an impractical babbler," and later Max Muller commented that he and his French colleague considered Skrzyński incapable of clear thought.[19] Chamberlain's first impression was equally negative. "I must admit," he wrote, "that M. Skrzyński, who is said to pride himself on being both the handsomest and youngest Minister for Foreign Affairs, had not made an agreeable impression on me when I met him in society, and had seemed to me perfectly disagreeable in his attitude during our League of Nations Council meeting." But after talking to him later in private, Chamberlain had been "agreeably surprised" by the Foreign Minister's good English, good sense, and straightforward speech which contrasted strongly with his public utterances.[20]

There is no direct record of what was actually said during Skrzyński's Paris visit, but the absence of any comment by Herriot—he left a very detailed account of a similar talk with Beneš—and other reports seem

---

[18] Max von Stockhausen, *Sechs Jahre Reichskanzlei. Von Rapallo bis Locarno* (Bonn, 1954), p. 179.

[19] Max Muller to Lord Curzon, February 14, 1923, *FO*, 371/9310, p. 41.

[20] Chamberlain to Sir Eyre Crowe, March 14, 1925, *FO*, 371/10727, p. 34.

to confirm the impression that privately his visit occasioned some stormy sessions in which Skrzyński accused France of wanting to betray Poland, a fact which Herriot vehemently denied.[21] Departing from Paris, the Polish Foreign Minister held a press conference in which he professed to be greatly relieved by Herriot's assurances, adding that Poland really had never been nervous since she placed explicit trust in France's word. Skrzyński pointed out that Herriot had repeatedly insisted that France would seek no guarantee for herself at the expense of Poland. Hoesch added that while the Polish diplomat had been unable to hide his aversion to Germany's proposal for an arbitration treaty, he had declared, probably for tactical reasons, that "Poland would be willing to examine the German proposals, once they had taken on definite form.[22]

Almost from the beginning of the German proposal Chamberlain had taken upon himself the role of "honest broker" between the French–Polish position and the German stand, a role which by his own estimate he was conducting "perhaps even a little more honestly than the author of that well-known phrase."[23] [He was referring, of course, to Bismarck.] Chamberlain noted that he had lost no opportunity to point out to the French and Poles the magnitude of the German arbitration proposal and their assurance to refrain from force in the revision of their eastern frontiers and that he used this argument to deprecate the suspicions of Poland and France toward the German offer.[24]

At Geneva, Chamberlain engaged Skrzyński in a lengthy private conversation in which he gained a much more positive impression of his Polish colleague than he had previously held. Chamberlain had pointed out that Poland's geographic position between two powerful neighbors made it advisable that she come to terms with at least one of them, "and good sense suggests that it will be more profitable and easier to cultivate good and even friendly relations with the German Reich than with the Soviet Union." The Foreign Secretary warned his Polish colleague that Poland would bear a heavy responsibility if "the present offer to promote peace should break down through her intransigence, exaggerated fears, or inability to realize where her advantage lies."[25] When

[21] Wandycz, *France and Her Eastern Allies*, p. 334.
[22] Report, Hoesch, March 19, 1925, AA, GA/3726/K170/K025 639.
[23] Sir Charles Petrie, *The Life and Letters of the Right Hon. Sir Austen Chamberlain* (London, 1940), II, p. 275.
[24] Letter, Chamberlain to Max Muller, April 3, 1925, FO, 371/10730, p. 109.
[25] *Ibid.*

Skrzyński interjeted that a western pact might legitimize Germany's eastern revisionist aspirations, Chamberlain used the argument that just as France had never given up her claims to Alsace-Lorraine, one could not expect Germany to surrender her eastern aspirations. In view of the fact that the French revisionist aspirations had in the end materialized, it is hard to see what comfort Skrzyński was meant to derive from this argument. Nor could Chamberlain's position that an improvement of French security would also augment Poland's security have sounded very convincing to the Polish Minister.[26] Nevertheless, Skrzyński seems to have been reassured by the meeting. He later told Briand and others that he had been much touched by Chamberlain's talk, and the British Foreign Secretary himself was of the impression that the conversation had had a good effect on his Polish colleague and would henceforth prevent him from making the kind of statements he had made during his Paris visit.[27]

If Skrzyński really considered Chamberlain's somewhat naive arguments reassuring, as indeed seems to be the case, the reason must have been that he interpreted Chamberlain's position as being opposed to a revision of the German–Polish frontier. It is not quite certain, on the basis of available documents, whether such a conclusion was warranted. In the above-cited letter to Max Muller on April 3, Chamberlain mentions how he had explained the British position to Skrzyński: other than her obligations under the Covenant Britain could not undertake any security guarantees beyond the Rhineland pact. But this abstention did not mean that Britain was licensing war elsewhere, and by stabilizing conditions in the west one automatically gave an additional guarantee to the frontiers in the east. According to Chamberlain, Germany "would be most ill-advised to attempt, even by peaceful means, to precipitate a solution in the East, for which the time is not yet ripe."

The distinct impression one gets from this statement is that Chamberlain opposed an eastern revision at that time, but it does not indicate that he opposed it in principle or as a future policy. Perhaps in his attempt to overcome Polish resistance to the security pact he had presented himself as more anti-revisionist than he really was; perhaps Skryzński had fallen victim to his own wishful thinking. Probably it was a combination of both, for when he returned to Warsaw and addressed the *Sejm* Foreign

---

[26] Chamberlain to Sir Eyre Crowe, March 14, 1925, FO, 371/10728, p. 34.
[27] *Ibid.*

Affairs Committee on March 24, he stated that Herriot had convinced him of France's loyalty and that Chamberlain had assured him that Britain would not permit the revision of the Versailles treaty "and fully appreciated that no democracy could voluntarily surrender a single yard of its territory." He added that Poland would never agree to a pact that guaranteed the western boundaries but kept the Polish frontier open. According to Skrzyński's public testimony, Poland had no cause for anxiety: her security was firmly rooted in the peace treaties, her allies, her army, and in international solidarity.[28]

As was typical of Skrzyński, the optimism and confidence of his public stand contrasted sharply with the gloomy evaluation which he gave privately. A few days after this speech Max Muller found him in one of his "most uncommunicative and vague moods." According to Muller, he had returned from Paris with even stronger anti-German feelings than before. He regarded the whole proposal as a German trap to lull the Allies into a false feeling of security and to drive a wedge between Poland and France. By signing the Versailles treaty, Germany had already guaranteed the eastern and western frontiers and he could not see how a second signature would strengthen this obligation. The only real basis for a security pact was one which granted absolute equality to the eastern and western frontiers. He himself would prefer a Geneva-Protocol-type security solution. Skrzyński also insisted that if Germany got a League Council seat, Poland would have to be given one as well, otherwise her position would become impossible.[29]

Skrzyński's public pronouncement on France's unshakable loyalty was meant to calm Polish public opinion and perhaps also to shame France into observing her commitments to Poland, but this outward confidence merely masked the suspicion and tension which existed at the official level. All the anxieties about the reliability of its French ally were confirmed by the sensational news which Olszowski communicated to Skrzyński on March 28 from his Berlin post. In this letter, Olszowski recounted how he had asked Ambassador de Margerie directly to confirm the accuracy of a recent article by Koraba-Kucharski, the Paris correspondent of the *Rzeczypospolita*, which had given the content of a conversa-

[28] Report, Max Muller, March 18, 1925, *FO*, 371/10730, p. 126.
[29] Letter, Max Muller to Chamberlain, March 28, 1925, *FO*, 371/10730, p. 128. Marginal note by Chamberlain: "M. Skrzyński has had a relapse. Perhaps he exhausted himself in his speech or perhaps he has been too much talked to! I had an idea of sending him a message, but I will refrain."

tion between Stresemann and de Margerie. According to this article, Stresemann had commented on the danger of Soviet aggression. The Red Army was well equipped and the Western Powers should meet this threat by joint action. The present German government did not want a Soviet victory but the public was opposed to any co-operation with the West unless Germany's territorial claims were satisfied, for in the event of a Soviet victory the "Corridor" and Upper Silesia would automatically revert to Germany. To Olszowski's surprise de Margerie confirmed the accuracy of the article and admitted that Stresemann had spoken in this manner with only one exception. According to Stresemann, the Russians, if they were strong, would move in the direction of Rumania and Byelorussia; on the other hand, if the Soviet regime were close to a fall it would attack Rumania and Poland as a diversionary measure. De Margerie had been surprised at the extreme accuracy of Korab's information, which he attributed to a gross indiscretion by the *Quai d'Orsay*. Following this confession by de Margerie, Olszowski tried to inform his French colleague: the Soviet Union had no intention of making war against Poland or Rumania and Stresemann's perspective had been entirely wrong. His maneuver had been no more than a crude bait to get the Western Powers interested in the revision of the "Corridor" and Upper Silesia.[30]

De Margerie's confession confirmed the worst of Polish suspicions, namely that France was fully aware of Germany's revisionist policy and, quite contrary to the promises given to Skrzyński at Paris, supported or at least condoned such behavior.

April in Paris was not a good time for the Polish cause as it brought the fall of the Herriot government. In the new Painlevé government the foreign affairs portfolio fell to Aristide Briand, a consummate and dynamic politician who spoke with the tongue of angels, hypnotizing his listeners and frequently also himself. Briand had by then outgrown the narrow nationalistic phase of his earlier career and was embarked on the wider and more ambitious course of international conciliation that was to find its principal application in French–German reconciliation. The specific interests of his allies must often have seemed somewhat peripheral, if not altogether a hindrance, in Briand's pursuit of these broader and somewhat more visionary aims.

---

[30] Secret letter, Olszowski to Skrzyński, March 28, 1925, AMSZ, P I, t. 232k; cited in Jerzy Krasuski, *Stosunki polsko-niemieckie, 1919–1925* (Poznań, 1962), I, pp. 402–3.

Given Poland's hostile reaction to Germany's security proposal and the unsatisfactory trend in her discussions with France, it seemed perfectly logical for Warsaw to try to co-ordinate its security policy with Prague, where some of the same reservations toward the German proposal could be encountered.

Despite the fact that both countries were allies of France and the product of the Paris peace settlement and shared many historical and cultural attributes, their postwar relations had been determined by their mutual antagonism to a much greater degree than by that which they had in common.[31] Polish–Czech antagonism was extremely deep-rooted and the dispute over the territory of Teschen was more of a symbol of their hostile relations than its primary cause.

Periodic attempts to improve their relations had not been successful. But the German security pact proposal, which both Prague and Warsaw viewed as a dexterous move to isolate them from their French ally, seemed to provide the needed incentive for a real understanding between these estranged neighbors. Their common concerns prompted Beneš and Skrzyński to exchange visits in mid-April which culminated in the conclusion of a number of agreements, including a treaty of arbitration and conciliation for all subjects under dispute except territorial questions, a commercial treaty, and other technical conventions. This outcome set into motion a flurry of diplomatic speculation on the possibility that these agreements, like an iceberg, were merely the small visible portion of a wider accord that included a secret military alliance between Prague and Warsaw. But both Rauscher and his colleague in Prague, Koch, regarded this as highly unlikely.[32]

The cordial meeting which Skrzyński had with Beneš during the September session of the League of Nations confirmed his optimistic belief that the two countries would uphold a common front at the forthcoming security conference. These hopes were to be shattered a few days later. On September 18, Stresemann held a press conference at which he stated that neither Poland nor Czechoslovakia had approached Ger-

---

[31] For an account of Czech–Polish relations during that period, see Zygmunt Gąsiorowski, "Polish–Czechoslovak Relations 1918–1922," *Slavonic and East European Review* 35 (1956) and "Polish–Czechoslovak Relations 1922–1926," *ibid.* 35 (1957); Karol Bader, *Stosunki polsko-czeskie* (Warsaw, 1938); Alina Szklarska-Lohmannowa, *Polsko-Czechosłowackie stosunki dyplomatyczne w latach 1918–1925* (Warsaw, 1967).

[32] AA, D/2769/5462H/E368 044–45; March 25, 1925; AA, StS/2267/4509H/E125 852–53.

many for the purpose of negotiating an arbitration treaty—a statement that in view of Prague's repeated efforts in this direction in March, May, and June was not entirely true. Beneš immediately grasped the bait and instructed his envoy to enter at once into negotiations on an arbitration treaty.

The Czech move took Warsaw completely by surprise and evoked strong indignation, for only a few days previously Skrzyński had told the *Kurjer Codzienny* that on the question of the eastern arbitration treaties complete consensus existed between Warsaw and Prague.[33] Skrzyński admitted to Muller that he had known nothing about Beneš's plan to proceed separately. The Polish Foreign Minister tried to portray it as a Czech blunder, but it was obvious to Muller that Skrzyński bitterly resented the move.[34]

Relations with France continued to be problematic and far from satisfactory. At the September session of the League of Nations, Skrzyński presented Briand with a major policy memorandum in which he emphasized that the 1921 alliance was more important than ever because of the German scheme to separate the proposed Rhineland pact from eastern security matters and thereby prevent France from coming to Poland's assistance. The Polish government would be happy to collaborate with France in promoting a general relaxation, but this could only be achieved by linking the French–Polish alliance to the Rhineland pact. The memorandum added that there was no reason why Poland should not participate in the negotiations concerning the Rhineland pact, for her alliance commitments already made her a guarantor of the French borders, whereas Italy, having no such obligations, was to participate in these negotiations.[35]

Chamberlain noted that Skrzyński was in a troubled state of mind because Briand had referred to Poland as "the rheumatism of Europe."[36] On September 17, Berthelot, the secretary general of the *Quai d'Orsay* and Briand's intimate collaborator, spent two hours with Skrzyński whom he found less reasonable than he had hoped, for the Polish Foreign Minister had proposed that Poland, France, and Germany sign a tri-

---

[33] *Kölnische Zeitung*, September 22, 1925.
[34] Max Muller to Chamberlain, September 23, 1925, *FO*, 371/10740, p. 67.
[35] AMSZ, P I, W.168, t.232k; cited in Krasuski, *Stosunki polsko-niemieckie*, I, pp. 411–12; September 7, 1925.
[36] Memorandum, Chamberlain, September 15, 1925, *FO*, 371/10740, p. 2.

partite pact.[37] Sir Eric Phipps found Berthelot "rather peevish" after this conversation and concluded that Skrzyński had not received any encouragement at all from him. "I think there is no doubt," added Phipps, "that the Polish hour struck some time ago in Paris, and I expect the violent Chłapowski, on his return, will make the welkin ring with his moans."[38]

THE LOCARNO CONFERENCE

From the moment that the German security proposal was first received in Paris, the French government was primarily concerned with determining the exact role which Britain intended to play in this security scheme. Given this preoccupation, the security claims of its eastern allies received only secondary consideration. The French government delayed a formal reply to the German offer until the British position had been clarified. What worried the minds of the *Quai d'Orsay* at this stage was the prospect that the British guarantee, so tantalizing and eagerly sought, might be turned against France in the event of a conflict into which she might be drawn as the result of her alliance commitments to Poland and Czechoslovakia. The British note of May 29 set these fears at rest and thereby helped pave the way for the successful conclusion of the security pact some five months later.

In her May note Britain had once more repeated that she was unable to engage in any form of guarantees other than for Germany's western borders, while of course honoring her eastern obligations as far as these arose out of the Covenant; furthermore, she assured France that if the latter proceeded to aid her eastern allies against Germany, this would

---

[37] In making the suggestion about a tripartite Eastern pact, Skrzyński had put forward the maximum demand which the Political Committee of the Polish Cabinet had outlined on August 25, 1925. The Cabinet directive included the following three points which, it was hoped, France might be persuaded to accept:

1) A direct French guarantee of Poland's boundaries which would not be impaired by the Rhineland pact;
2) France herself, rather than the League of Nations, would decide whether Poland's boundaries were threatened;
3) Poland, France, and Germany would sign an eastern security pact similar to the Rhineland pact; if Germany refused to join, this would be a French–Polish pact which Germany would be free to enter later.

(AMSZ, P I, W. 168, t. 23K; cited in Krasuski, *Stosunki polsko-niemieckie*, I, p. 409).

[38] Letter, Sir Eric Phipps to Victor Wellesley, September 18, 1925, FO, 371/10740, p. 47. In a marginal note Chamberlain added: "The honey-moon is over and the bickering has begun. Somewhere in the FO files there is a prophetic minute of mine."

not involve her in a conflict with Britain as long as these allies had become the subject of an unprovoked aggression by Germany, a matter that could best be determined by the norms of the League Covenant and therefore necessitated Germany's entry into that body.[39]

Briand received Ambassador Hoesch on June 4, apologizing for the delay in responding to Germany's memorandum and promising a quick answer now that the British note had been accepted by the French Cabinet and a French–British accord had thus been established. Hoesch was happily surprised to encounter Briand's favorable attitude on the question of Germany's future revision. The French statesman insisted that Germany enter the League, for once she occupied a Council seat "she could calmly discuss with her Council colleagues, unhampered by press or public opinion, all sorts of *questions which depressed her, even those touching on the Eastern problem, and perhaps prepare the way for a solution.*" France would not demand that Germany accept a limited interpretation of Articles 19 and 80 of the Versailles treaty, for since she had been forced to accept so many unfavorable articles, she should not be deprived of those that were to her advantage. The French government fully understood that "*Germany at this stage did not want to prejudice the development of the Eastern questions by another expressed confirmation or guarantee of her frontier conditions in the east.*"[40] (Underlining for italics in the original text.)

In spite of these assurances from Briand, the French note to Germany of June 16 was considered entirely unsatisfactory and its skeptical tone immediately prompted Berlin wits to call it the "Lorelei Note" ("Ich weiss nicht was soll es bedeuten, dass ich so skeptisch bin").[41] Berlin objected to the French wish for a system of extensive arbitration which ran counter to the German concept and to her demand to become guarantor of the German–Polish arbitration treaty. Germany felt that this implied an approval of the Polish–French alliance. She regarded the French wish to give Poland immediate aid if, according to her own interpretation, Poland had become a subject of aggression, a violation of the League Covenant.[42]

[39] Telegram, Hoesch, May 31, 1925, AA, StS/2267/4509/E126 461–62.

[40] Telegram, Hoesch, June 4, 1925, *ibid.,* 507–10.

[41] It was found equally unsatisfactory in Warsaw because the note had been prepared without consulting or informing Poland. (W. Sikorski, *Le problème de la paix: Le jeu des forces politiques en Europe orientale et l'alliance franco–polonaise* [Paris, 1931], p. 139).

[42] Note by Schubert of his conversation with Lord D'Abernon, June 27, 1925, AA, W/2575/5265H/E320 822–25.

As these notes led to no visible progress and patience was running short on all sides, Germany welcomed the French proposal to hold a conference of legal experts so that some basic principles might be clarified and settled. At this conference, which was held in London in the first days of September and at which Poland was not represented, the question of the eastern arbitration treaties figured prominently on the agenda. Here it was Germany's policy, against the efforts of Britain and France, to give a restrictive interpretation to the planned arbitration treaties and, insofar as the Rhine pact constituted a recognition of the status quo in the west which she rejected for the east, to impose strict barriers of separation between the western pact and the eastern treaties of arbitration. Gaus rejected the Allied draft for an arbitration treaty which included both political as well as legal disputes. He insisted that it was contrary to the very concept of arbitration to submit disputes that were not of legal nature to arbitral procedure and pointed out that France and Britain themselves in recent arbitration treaties with other countries had not accepted as wide-ranging commitments as they now requested of Germany. According to the Gaus formula, binding arbitration ought to be restricted to disputes that were primarily of a judicial nature, while predominantly political disputes were to be settled by means of a non-binding conciliation procedure.

Although Britain shunned any eastern commitments for herself, she considered it expedient, in order to get a security pact at all, to support the French demand for a more comprehensive type of arbitration and for a French guarantee of the eastern arbitration treaties. When Skirmunt had seen Chamberlain a few weeks earlier, he had asked the Foreign Secretary to put British pressure on Germany to accept a French guarantee of the German–Polish treaty of arbitration. Chamberlain had told the Polish envoy that he would be happy to see France in the same guarantor role vis-à-vis the German–Polish treaty as Britain was willing to undertake with respect to the German–French pact.[43] In line with this policy, Sir Cecil Hurst, the legal expert of the British Foreign Office, advised Gaus to comply with the French proposal and thereby to extract the poisonous tooth from the present French–Polish alliance that tended to incite Poland's aggressive activities and threatened to involve France in a war with

---

[43] Report, Skirmunt to Skrzyński, July 30, 1925, AMSZ, P I, W. 168, t. 232k; cited in Krasuski, *Stosunki polsko-niemieckie*, I, p. 415. Chamberlain's analogy was not entirely correct, for France was only assuming a one-sided guarantee, while Britain, at least formally, was willing to pledge assistance to either side in the event of unprovoked aggression.

Germany. Consequently Hurst and his French colleague, Fromageot, suggested that "the eastern treaties of arbitration, similar to those of the west, be based on a renunciation of war and at the same time be guaranteed by a third power, namely France."[44]

Gaus rejected both of these proposals. To accept France as a guarantor would mean a German recognition of the French–Polish alliance and would, furthermore, give Paris a pretext for constant interference in all German–Polish disputes. The requested declaration renouncing all forms of war would exceed the obligations under the Covenant and would establish too great an affinity between the eastern and western pact. On the latter point, Gaus reiterated Germany's official position, as expressed by Schubert, that the nonaggression pact was "basically nothing more . . . than a form of recognition which we must refuse vis-à-vis Poland, even though we otherwise have no intention of bringing up the border question at this time."[45]

Despite the lack of agreement on the nature of the eastern arbitration treaties and the guarantor role of France, the jurists' conference managed to settle the question of who would decide when the *casus foederis* for the guarantors of the Rhineland pact became operative. The formula reached stipulated that in the case of flagrant aggression or the violation of the demilitarization of the Rhineland, assistance would be immediate and the decision would be made by the participants themselves; in less extreme cases the League Council would decide whether a violation had taken place and whether an intervention was justified.

The final conference took place in October amidst the romantic atmosphere of the charming Swiss town of Locarno during splendid autumn weather. Of this the preoccupied diplomats saw little, and Chancellor Luther later joked that they had enjoyed no more than an occasional glimpse of the moon.

The German strategy at Locarno intended to reduce to a minimum the content of the eastern arbitration treaties and to isolate the Rhine-

[44] Karl Erdmann, "Das Problem der Ost—oder Westrichtung in der Locarno-Politik Stresemanns," *Geschichte in Wissenschaft und Unterricht* 6 (1955): 146–47.

[45] Letter, Schubert to Hoesch, March 21, 1925, AA, RAM/1425/2945H/D571 572–74. It is interesting to see that the Foreign Ministry advanced the same argument against a German–Polish nonaggression pact when Hitler was preparing such a move in 1933. A Foreign Ministry memorandum of November 1933 warned that a nonaggression pact would tend to eliminate the difference in the status of Germany's eastern and western frontiers which had so far been preserved. A nonaggression pact, because of its affinity to the Rhineland pact, might be interpreted as a renunciation of German revisionist claims. (AA, GA/2907/6177H/E463 489–93).

land pact from the eastern agreements. In order to supply visible proof of the separation between the problems in the east and those of the west, it was in Germany's interest to see that the Polish delegation at the conference remained in virtual isolation. On the eve of Locarno, Rauscher was hopeful that Poland might be excluded altogether. This was not merely a question of prestige but one of extraordinary intrinsic value, for "the Security Pact, which I consider absolutely essential, does not offer so many advantages that we could afford to neglect a few of these. . . . Only if the differential treatment between the Eastern and the Western question finds clear expression, and only if, by means of involving the mechanics of the League, the French–Polish alliance will be devalued, will the eastern adjunct to the Rhineland pact offer any benefit to us."[46] Three days later he asked Skrzyński point-blank whether Poland had received an official invitation,[47] a question which the Polish diplomat tried to evade by arguing that Britain and France did not consider the Locarno meeting a conference in the strict meaning of the term, but a discussion by the various powers on the exchange of the German–French notes and had therefore made it known to Beneš and himself that their presence would be desirable. The western pact and the eastern arbitration treaty, according to Skrzyński, necessitated parallel negotiations, otherwise, if an arbitration agreement was reached between Germany, on the one side, and France and Belgium, on the other, which proved unacceptable to Poland, the latter might incur the unwelcome onus of disturbing the general structure of peace.[48] On the following day, the German Minister joyously informed Berlin that the Polish Foreign Minister, indeed, travelled to Locarno without a formal admission ticket and would attend, as it were, as a gate crasher.[49]

If the absence of a formal invitation had been a minor impediment to Poland, her exclusion from the actual negotiations at Locarno was tragic reality. Poland's Foreign Minister was virtually isolated and not even a close antecameral alliance between Skrzyński and his co-exile from

---

[46] Letter, Rauscher to Koepke, October 1, 1925, AA, GA/3743/K182/K034 190–91.

[47] The only invitation which Poland had received had come from Briand. At the September session of the League, Briand had asked Chamberlain to allow Polish and Czech representatives to attend the forthcoming security conference, otherwise Skrzyński's position would become untenable. Chamberlain did not object, but believed that the initial talks should be confined to the Western representatives (Memorandum, Chamberlain, September 15, 1925, FO, 371/10740, p. 2).

[48] Telegram, Rauscher, October 3, 1925, AA, GA/3743/K182/K034 186–87.

[49] Ibid., 185; October 4, 1925.

the conference table, Beneš, could be arranged. The crafty Czech had little taste for backing a losing horse and was careful to differentiate his country's position from that of Poland.

Already on the second day of the conference, on October 6, proceedings became deadlocked over the Polish question because of the French demand to assume the role of guarantor for the German–Polish treaty of arbitration. According to Briand, France could not obtain guarantees for her own boundaries without showing equal concern for those of her eastern allies. Stresemann insisted that it was impossible for France to be an impartial guarantor while at the same time retaining her alliance with Poland and argued that by her proposal to engage in an eastern treaty of arbitration and by her entry into the League, Germany had already furnished two legitimate guarantees for the east and that France could not expect a third one.[50] This impasse was not resolved until Mrs. Chamberlain's birthday provided the occasion for a pleasure cruise on Lago Maggiore, during which Briand and Stresemann were closeted in their cabin for five hours arguing their respective positions. After the first two and one-half hours on the Russian question, Briand yielded by accepting an interpretation of Article 16 of the Covenant that was acceptable to Germany, and at the end of their session he agreed, likewise, to forego the demand for a French guarantee of the German–Polish treaty.[51] After this cavalier treatment at the hands of their French ally, Poland and Czechoslovakia had no chance of getting a serious hearing on their draft arbitration treaties.[52] The two drafts which Beneš had produced envisaged a nonaggression pact with Germany, while Skrzyński's version had proposed binding arbitration for all disputes, including those that were not of legal nature, and a declaration which banned war as an international crime—a clear attempt to procure from Germany a declaration that would renounce the resort to war and thus equate the western pact with the eastern treaties.[53] Beneš accepted defeat with good grace and quickly adjusted to the situation by withdrawing his draft proposals. He thereby underscored the difference between his position and that of the Poles who tried to retain their stand.

The representatives of Poland and Czechoslovakia were not admitted to the conference table until October 15, and then only after the humiliating spectacle in which Chamberlain asked the assembled con-

[50] Stresemann, *Vermächtnis*, II, p. 189.
[51] *Ibid.*, p. 232.
[52] Wandycz, *France and Her Eastern Allies*, p. 361.
[53] *Kölnische Zeitung*, October 10, 1925.

ference whether objections existed to their presence, to which Stresemann voiced the reservation that discussions be strictly confined to the
arbitration treaties and no mention be made of the question of territorial guarantees. Under these circumstances Poland had no other
choice than to accept the German version of a restricted arbitration
treaty.

The Locarno settlement was a collective product which consisted of
several delicately intertwined agreements. The central core was composed of the Treaty of Mutual Guarantee, the so-called Rhine pact, with
France and Belgium on the one side, and Germany on the other, and
Britain and Italy acting as guarantors. Also there were four separate
treaties of arbitration which France, Belgium, Poland, and Czechoslovakia concluded with Germany.[54] Also included in the Locarno complex
were the treaties of mutual guarantee which France signed with Poland
and Czechoslovakia.[55] Finally, there was the interpretation of Article 16
of the Covenant which the Locarno participants gave to Germany, and
to link all these agrreements that had been concluded jointly or separately there was a final protocol.[56]

In the Rhineland pact, France, Belgium, and Germany agreed to
maintain the territorial status quo in the west and to observe the demilitarization of the Rhineland (Art. 1). The signatories pledged not to
resort to war against each other except: (a) in self-defense against an attack or a flagrant violation of the Rhineland demilitarization clauses; (b)
in pursuance of Article 15 (7) and Article 16 of the Covenant (Art. 2).
Disputes were to be settled by a procedure of conciliation and arbitration,
submitting legal disputes to arbitral procedure and other forms of dispute to conciliation (Art. 3). Article 4 incorporated the formula which
had been devised at the London conference of jurists.

The arbitration treaties all followed the same model in setting up
procedures for conciliation and arbitration. The two western arbitration
treaties were identical, as were their two eastern counterparts. The difference between the two agreements was rather slight. The former specifically referred to the Treaty of Mutual Guarantee which was not mentioned in the latter. In addition, the eastern arbitration treaties were
accompanied by a preamble, absent in the former, which stressed the

[54] League of Nations, *Treaty Series* 54–55 (1926–27): 329–39.
[55] *Ibid.*, pp. 354–56.
[56] *Ibid.*, pp. 296–98.

signatories' desire to resolve international disputes "without recourse to force" and recognized that "respect for the rights established by treaty or resulting from the law of nations is obligatory for international tribunals." Such rights were not to be modified save with the consent of the concerned state.

Also relating to the Eastern question, and vitally important for her relations with Russia, the Locarno signatories gave to the German delegation their interpretation of Article 16 of the Covenant. According to this interpretation each member of the League was obliged to co-operate loyally in support of the Covenant "to an extent which (was) compatible with its military situation and (took) its geographical position into account."[57] Naturally, the Locarno signatories were not authorized to alter the Covenant, but since this declaration had been given by the most powerful members of the League, Germany was virtually assured that upon her entry into the League she would not be compelled to participate in any economic sanctions or to co-operate with any military measures that might be undertaken against the Soviet Union in the name of the League of Nations. This declaration was of enormous importance to Germany's eastern policy, as it permitted her to continue friendly relations with Moscow despite the Locarno pact and entry into the League.

Equally important for her eastern policy was the fact that in her arbitration treaty with Poland, Germany had been able to defend two principal policy aims; namely, to isolate Poland from France and to avoid any territorial commitment in the east. The former had been accomplished by excluding France as guarantor of the German–Polish arbitration treaty; the latter by avoiding a territorial guarantee or a nonaggression pact with Poland—only the preamble had referred to the non-use of force in settling disputes—and by separating the eastern agreements from the Rhine pact, thus avoiding even the inference to a status quo policy in the east.

No wonder that Germany's diplomats were almost ecstatic over the results of Locarno, where their goal of weakening Warsaw's life-line with Paris had received fresh impetus. "You will share my joy," wrote Acting Undersecretary Koepke to Rauscher after the conclusion of Locarno, "over the good result, especially as it concerns the east," for the arbitration treaty "constitutes no burden for Germany and no relief for Poland."

[57] *Survey of International Affairs 1925*, II, p. 51.

Koepke also joked about the fact that the French in talking to Gaus had constantly referred to Skrzyński as "Monsieur Serinski."[58] And Stresemann, who felt no compunction in playing on anti-Polish sentiments in Germany, told the *Arbeitsgemeinschaft deutscher Landsmannschaften* during his Locarno campaign tour that "the gentlemen Beneš and Skrzyński had to sit . . . in the antechamber until we let them in. That was the situation of the states whose position had been deceptively supported because they were the servants of others, and who were dropped the moment that an understanding with Germany seemed possible."[59] It was perhaps a kind of perversion that by reconfirming the results of the Versailles treaty on her western boundaries, Germany should have weakened the over-all treaty structure. But this was precisely the result and her aim. By reconfirming the western boundaries she had introduced a new kind of security currency which, like Gresham's Law, drove out the legal currency of the initial Paris settlement. As Stresemann explained to Maltzan, the Locarno agreements would "protect the Rhineland from the consequences of France's policy of persecution, split the Entente, and open new possibilities in the east."[60] In a letter to von Keudell, he described Locarno as an armistice which "offered the possibility of recovering German territory in the east."[61]

In an effort to remodel her alliances with Poland and Czechoslovakia along the Locarno pattern and in harmony with the League, France concluded treaties of mutual guarantee with her two eastern allies on the same day that she signed the Locarno agreements. Stresemann had refused to make France's eastern guarantee pacts an integral part of the Locarno settlement, and only the final protocol of the Locarno treaties made a brief reference to these security agreements. In the Franco–Polish Treaty of Mutual Guarantee—identical to the French–Czechoslovak agreement—both parties undertook to lend each other "immediate aid and assistance" in application of Article 16 of the Covenant, if the Locarno agreements should fail to bring peace and if such failure was accompanied by "an unprovoked recourse to arms." Similarly, in circumstances where the report of the League Council was not accepted by all its members, other than the parties in the dispute, France and Poland, acting in application of Article 15 (7) of the Covenant, would "immedi-

[58] AA, GA/3743/K182/K034 215–18; October 21, 1925.
[59] Stresemann, *Vermächtnis*, II, pp. 231–44.
[60] *Ibid.*, pp. 281–82.
[61] *Ibid.*, p. 246.

ately lend aid and assistance" to each other in the event of an unprovoked attack (Art. 1). It was further stipulated (Art. 2) that this treaty would not limit the signatories' rights and obligations as members of the League and that this document was to be registered with the League (Art. 3).

Given Poland's earlier demands for a tripartite French–Polish–German security pact, or at least for a direct French guarantee of the Polish–German arbitration treaty, the bilateral guarantee pact was a rather meager consolation prize; moveover, one which created some specific problems and doubts.

The mood which accompanied the signing of the final Locarno Protocol on October 16 can only be characterized as euphoric. Not only the temperamental and fiery Briand but also the reserved Chamberlain with his icy, monocled stare, the prosaic Luther, and the rather coarse-looking Stresemann were swept away by this emotional surge of optimism and international friendship. The peace settlement which had been unilaterally imposed at Versailles by threat of arms and brute force now seemed to have been voluntarily accepted in a spirit of mutual understanding and good will. If the principal signatories of Locarno were misled, it was self-deception rather than calculated deception, for there can be no doubt that the representatives of Britain, France, and Germany at that moment were all under the genuine impression that they had laid the framework for a lasting peace in Europe. The bells of the churches in Locarno rang out in celebration of this event and communicated to the rest of Europe the "spirit of Locarno," an era of peace and conciliation.

Least affected by this feast of good will was Poland's Foreign Minister Skrzyński. If Beneš was also disappointed, he was too good an actor to let anyone know. Beneš, who left Locarno with an assumed air of satisfaction, had shown himself as a better political as well as personal actor than his aristocratic colleague from Warsaw. Skrzyński departed in a sullen mood, and when Stresemann approached him to bid farewell, he kept his hands in his pockets and ignored the German Foreign Minister. Stresemann regarded this demonstration as a personal affront and an insult to the German nation, and when he recounted the incident to Olszowski, the Polish envoy was visibly embarrassed and tried to explain it as a complete misunderstanding, for Skrzyński apparently held Stresemann in highest esteem and his curious behavior had to be attributed to one of the Count's idiosyncrasies, one of which was the fact that he frequently stared into space while talking to people, thus giving the erroneous impression of ignoring them.[62]

RATIFICATION AND ITS DISCONTENTS

It was characteristic of the viscissitudes of democratic politics that an agreement like Locarno, which more than anything undertaken since the 1918 armistice had improved Germany's international image and raised her stature, should have encountered such stormy domestic opposition. Stresemann and Luther were in a particularly difficult position because their Cabinet was a coalition of the Center and the Right, including the truculent Nationalists who were wont to brand any reasonable and conciliatory foreign political proposal as treason and a sell-out of the German national interest. Luther in particular was worried over the reaction of the Nationalist Cabinet members and had presented a rather sour face amidst the general jubilation at Locarno. A few years later, Briand still jokingly recalled to Stresemann how "Luther had sulked in Locarno like a black cloud over Lake Maggiore."[63]

The happy outcome of Locarno with respect to Germany's eastern policy, combined with Stresemann's skillful advertising campaign, basically pre-empted any objections to the eastern arbitration treaties. Criticism was largely confined to the Rhine pact and Germany's planned entry into the League. The first Cabinet meeting after the return of the German delegation from Locarno was held on October 19, with Hindenburg presiding. Stresemann glibly explained that the old French–Polish alliance had become less strong since its having been linked to the League Covenant. Under the new French–Polish agreement the guarantee came into force, not, as previously, by virtue of the independent interpretation of either signatory, but as the result of a unanimous decision by the League Council. Furthermore, Britain, though formally only a party to the Rhineland pact, had now been brought into close association with the question of eastern security. If France were to assist Poland before the League Council had officially branded Germany as an aggressor, Britain would be obliged to come to Germany's assistance.[64] Everyone

---

[62] AA, RAM/1426/2945H/D571 000–3.

[63] Erich Eyck, A History of the Weimar Republic (Cambridge, Mass., 1963), II, p. 38.

[64] Gustav Stresemann Nachlass [hereafter referred to as Stresemann Papers] (Bundesarchiv, Coblenz; microfilmed copy in the National Archives, Washington, D.C.), 3169/7319H/H160 161–62.

naturally wished to have the "angels" on his side, in this case the English, and it is amusing to observe that both Skrzyński and Stresemann availed themselves of the unrealistic argument that Britain, as the result of Locarno, would come to their assistance in a German–Polish war. Stresemann used the argument of British assistance to strengthen the domestic appeal of his Locarno policy. But privately he knew better than anybody else how unlikely it would be under any circumstances for Britain to come to the aid of Germany against France; certainly the mere absence of a decision by the League Council was not one of them.

In Germany the Locarno treaties were ratified on November 27, 1925. The vote had been 300:174 on ratification and 275:183 on the question of German entry into the League of Nations.[65] The Nationalists had left the Luther Cabinet in protest over Locarno. The remaining coalition parties had voted for the treaty. These included the *Zentrum*, the Bavarian People's party (BVP—*Bayerische Volkspartei*) and Stresemann's own German People's party (DVP—*Deutsche Volkspartei*), for once standing behind the foreign policy of its illustrious leader. The Social Democrats and Democrats, though outside the government, also voted for ratification. The extremist parties on either side voted against ratification. This voting alignment was highly representative of foreign policy decisions during the Weimar Republic. The government was generally opposed by the extreme Left and Right and received support from the bourgeois parties and the Social Democrats. The most important fluctuation was provided by the foreign policy vote of those parties who stood Right of center: the People's party and the Nationalists. The support of the former was not always guaranteed and that of the latter was rare.

In Poland Foreign Minister Skrzyński had better luck with selling the recently accepted Locarno formula domestically than he had with getting international support for his own proposals, i.e., a return to the Geneva Protocol, a tripartite pact for the east to complement the Rhineland pact, or at least a French guarantee of the German–Polish arbitration treaty. After Locarno Skrzyński fully identified his country's foreign policy and his personal career with the agreements. Already at Locarno he had written to Prime Minister Grabski, assuring the latter that there was absolutely no doubt that after Locarno the French–Polish agreement would be strengthened because it had the full backing of Britain and was now entirely legitimized in the eyes of the world.[66]

[65] Eyck, *Weimar Republic*, II, p. 41.
[66] Telegram, Skrzyński to Grabski, October 13, 1925, AMSZ, P I, W. 168, t. 78k; cited in Krasuski, *Stosunki polsko-niemieckie*, I, p. 439.

Skrzyński's letter to Grabski must strike us as somewhat enigmatic. Surely, Locarno had failed to satisfy precisely those demands which the Foreign Minister in half a year of frantic activities and travels had tried to settle: to overcome the unequal treatment of the eastern and the western security problems, to bring France into direct association with the German–Polish arbitration treaty, and to build a common Czech–Polish front. The jubilant mood of the other statesmen could hardly have dispelled Skrzyński's feelings of failure, as was attested by his gloomy appearance at the final celebrations. His subsequent identification with and defense of the Locarno settlement probably shows him as a firm realist. Poland's options were painfully limited. France's primary concern was with augmenting the security of her own eastern boundary and she felt, perhaps mistakenly, that this could best be realized by way of the regional Rhine pact. Britain supported the French position and refused any eastern commitments for herself. Czechoslovakia, as had so recently and painfully been demonstrated again, was an unreliable element, and, in the words of Chamberlain, Beneš "had always tried to get an anchor out to windward on the Russian side."[67] There remained the Russian card, and it is natural that contemporary Polish historians should castigate Polish policy of that time for having failed to secure an alliance with the Soviet Union. But in view of the extremely strained relations that then existed between Poland and the Soviet Union, because of Soviet attempts to incite irredentist strivings among the eastern minorities in Poland, her policy of supporting Poland's adversary Lithuania and of opposing Poland's ally Rumania, not to speak of her secret proposals to Germany, the prospects of achieving anything beyond a reduction of tensions between the two countries were minimal.

Tantalized by the possibility of gaining a German commitment to the status quo on the Rhine and a British guarantee, France could hardly have been deterred from concluding the Rhineland pact by Poland's refusal to be associated with the Locarno settlement. A boycott of this feast of international good will would have further isolated Poland and would have provided fuel for Germany's propaganda efforts to represent Poland as the troublemaker of Europe. Skrzyński was unwilling to run this risk. By adhering to Locarno, Poland had not offended international opinion and Skrzyński had at least been able to return with a remodeled French–Polish guarantee treaty. In addition, Locarno did raise the expectation of

[67] Note by Chamberlain, May 2, 1925, FO, 371/10731, p. 52.

a generally improved atmosphere in European relations, and Poland's Foreign Minister frequently referred to the "spirit of Locarno" in his speeches and, with respect to the optant question, also in deeds. In the absence of a more specific guarantee, there was at least some room for hope that the spirit of international conciliation might affect Germany and mellow her revisionist policies in the east.

Henceforth, Skrzyński appeared as a firm advocate of the Locarno system, both in his public declarations and, as has been seen from his private letter to Grabski, also in his private dealings. On October 19 he justified the Locarno agreements to the Cabinet. His arguments stressed the same points that had already been made in his letter to Grabski. He emphasized that the different agreements which had been concluded at Locarno constituted an integrated whole and that they would be signed together in a formal ceremony in London. He also stressed, quite accurately, that Article 2 of the Rhine pact allowed France to come to the assistance of her eastern allies. Locarno should be regarded as a general security system based on the principles of the Covenant which Poland supported. The fact that Poland had participated on an equal footing with the Great Powers would raise her international prestige and would give her the opportunity to collaborate with the other Western Powers in maintaining international peace. Finally, Skrzyński dwelled on the French–Polish guarantee pact. This was obviously the most sensitive part for Poland, and the Foreign Minister took considerable liberties of interpretation. According to his version, the new guarantee treaty covered situations where the League Council failed to make a unanimous report and where consequently no obligation for assistance existed under the Covenant. This was correct. More doubtful was his assertion that the guarantee treaty would help to clarify France's obligations to Poland and to legitimatize them in the eyes of other countries.[68] By avoiding the more unfortunate aspects of Locarno and by stressing its more favorable aspects (international conciliation, Poland's international role, the reference to the non-use of force in the preamble to the arbitration treaty with Germany), and by taking a certain poetic licence, Skrzyński managed to sound quite convincing. He would have been even more convincing if his soothing interpretation had not diverged so strongly from his own position prior to Locarno.

When the *Sejm* Foreign Affairs Committee debated the Locarno

[68] *PPRM* 31 (1925): 84–85.

agreements, Skrzyński used the same defensive technique as before. He skipped lightly over the differences between the Rhineland pact and the eastern agreements, claiming that not all matters could be regulated uniformly and that the rest of the world regarded the Locarno treaties as an entity. He rejected the criticism that the French–Polish alliance had been weakened by tying it to the League of Nations, asserting that in the event of aggression the alliance came into play automatically without consultation with the League Council. As to the interpretation of Article 16 which had been given to the German delegation, Poland would be just as happy to dispense with German aid on Polish soil in a Polish–Soviet war. Skrzyński recalled how under similar historical circumstances, Prince Golicyn, the commander of the Russian troops, had interpreted his allied mission in a way that always prevented Prince Poniatowski from going to Cracow to fight the Austrians. Above all, he underlined the greater similarity of interests that now existed between Britain and Poland and emphasized that the importance of Locarno rested less on the legal content of the treaties than on the spirit of peace which accompanied them.[69]

Skrzyński's Locarno policy met only moderate criticism in the *Sejm* and the press. His flexible and somewhat inaccurate presentation preempted much of the opposition that might have otherwise arisen. Rauscher commented that the extremely ill-informed Foreign Affairs Committee of the *Sejm* had been duped by the Foreign Minister's vague generalities.[70] As in the case of Germany, opposition was strongest in the ranks of the extreme Left and with certain conservative groups. The most articulate critic was Stanisław Stroński, editor of the paper *Warszawianka* and leader of the conservative Christian Nationalists. In the *Sejm* Foreign Affairs Committee debate, Stroński objected to the agreement which differentiated between Germany's eastern and western frontiers, whereas they had been treated alike in the Versailles treaty. He also feared that the French–Polish alliance had been weakened, for formerly the *casus foederis* was decided by the two allies alone, now it required a decision by the League Council.[71] Stroński condemned Skrzyński's policy as a "general lyricism of peace" which was entirely too vague.[72] Opposition

---

[69] *Messager Polonais*, November 28, 1925; Report, Stetson, November 6, 1925, SD, 740.0011/212.

[70] Report, Rauscher, October 24, 1925, AA, GA/3743/K182/K034 229–32.

[71] Report, Stetson, October 27, 1925, SD, 740.0011/212.

[72] *Ost-Express*, October 22, 1925.

also came from the ranks of the more radical peasants' parties like the *Wyzwolenie* (Emancipation) party and from the Leftist National Labor party and the Communists.

The Polish press which, almost without exception, had been pessimistic before the Locarno conference, took a much more favorable attitude after Skrzyński's return.[73] Stroński's *Warszawianka* kept up its barrage of criticism, but *Kurjer Poranny*—otherwise Piłsudski's favorite paper but here differing from the Marshal's anti-Locarno position—adopted a more positive attitude and welcomed the fact that for once victors and vanquished had been brought together as equals. *Rzeczpospolita*, the organ of the Christian Democrats, approved the work of the conference and *Echo Warszawskie* ridiculed those papers which claimed that Poland had been defeated at Locarno. *Robotnik*, the organ of the Polish Socialist party, regretted the different security solutions in the east and the west but favored the possibility of better German–Polish relations arising from the spirit of Locarno.[74] Dmowski's influential *Kurjer Polski*, in its October 18 issue, called Locarno the greatest Polish victory since Versailles, as it assured the continuity of the present boundaries.[75]

During the final *Sejm* debates which preceded ratification, the opposition was largely confined to the radical Leftist groups, and even the conservatives were apathetic. The National Democrats acquiesced to save Skrzyński from embarrassment, as his position at Geneva would have been jeopardized if Poland had failed to identify herself with the Locarno agreements. There existed little enthusiasm for Locarno but the general feeling was that it would be better to accept than to reject the agreements.[76] In its vote of March 3, 1926, the *Sejm* ratified the Locarno treaties by a vote of 279:104 with 41 abstentions. The negative votes had been cast by the Christian Nationalists, *Wyzwolenie*, several peasants' parties, and the National Labor party, even though the latter was represented in the government coalition. The parliamentary delegates of the German and Ukranian minorities had abstained. Although the German minority welcomed the Locarno settlement, it expressed its opposition to the government by refusing to vote with the government even on a matter which it otherwise favored. The *Sejm* ratification de-

[73] Report, Stetson, October 27, 1925, SD, 740.0011/212.
[74] Report, Max Muller, FO, 371/10744, p. 97.
[75] AA, GA/3743/K182/K034 206.
[76] Report, Stetson, February 26, 1926, SD, 740.0011/311.

cision was accompanied by a resolution which confirmed Poland's demand for a permanent seat on the League Council.

LOCARNO AND ITS AFTERMATH

In historical evaluation Locarno has either been pictured in superlatives or in extreme negatives. In the initial wave of optimism, the former version prevailed. Briand, Chamberlain, and Stresemann were hailed as the architects of peace and received the Nobel Peace Prize. More elaborate versions even represented them as the fathers of a United Europe. With the ascendance of Hitler's aggressive policy and the outbreak of World War II, the pendulum of historical opinion has swung in the other direction. Stresemann was represented as the spiritual forerunner of Hitler, and Locarno, in the judgment of Paul Reynaud, was branded as the "policy of an ostrich," which already contained the "spirit of Munich."[77]

As in many cases of extreme fluctuation, the mean temperature might provide a more reliable index of reality. The Locarno formula, i.e., the guarantee by third powers to come to the assistance of that side which suffered unprovoked aggression, was an ingenious device. It avoided the more conventional instrument of an alliance, which was directed against a specific power and thus was bound to increase tensions and reinforce existing cleavages between two sides. Instead, it offered a kind of fluctuating alliance that was not directed against a specific power but against the outbreak of war and toward the maintenance of peace, both by dissuasion and by conciliation. The British and Italian guarantee, rather than aggravating French–German tensions, as would have been the case if they had joined France in a conventional alliance, helped to bring about a general conciliation and overcame Germany's isolation. By the Locarno formula, the enemy was not so much a specific power as the explosive situation and international tensions per se, and it went to work to mediate against this. It is for this reason that the Locarno formula, quite apart from the specific agreement to which it was originally tied, still has relevance to-day and may become a model for a future European security system. Locarno also helped bring about a French–German reconciliation which was, however, prematurely interrupted by international economic and domestic political events.

[77] Paul Reynaud, *La France a sauvé l'Europe* (Paris, 1947), pp. 47–50; cited in Wandycz, *France and Her Eastern Allies*, p. 367.

The final breakdown of Locarno that occurred with the remilitarization of the Rhineland in 1936 was not due to any structural fault in the
original agreement but to the failure of the signatories to uphold the accord to which they had pledged themselves. The domestic factors which
brought Hitler to power in Germany were basically unrelated to Locarno,
and his foreign policy—remilitarization of the Rhineland and exclusion
of British influence from the Continent—was opposed to the aims of
Locarno. Certainly, after 1932, events in Europe were running on a different track than that laid at Locarno, and one must be cautious about
establishing a causal link to the Locarno settlement.

The central weakness of the Locarno settlement lay in its inability
to match the guarantees in the west with similar guarantees in the east.
This discrepancy undermined the territorial settlement of the Versailles
treaty and encouraged Germany's revisionist drive. Even though the diplomatic language between Warsaw and Berlin assimilated some of the
conciliatory phrases of the harmonious tenor which characterized the
so-called Locarno spirit among Western Powers, and even though Skrzyński had invoked this spirit when making concessions relating to the suspension of optant evictions, in the long run Locarno did not prove to be
a suitable vehicle for directing Germany and Poland toward a policy of
reconciliation. On the contrary, the western settlement of Locarno sustained and abetted Germany's revisionist aspirations in the east and
thereby kept her on an irreconcilable course vis-à-vis Poland which she
travelled with freshly instilled vigor.

Another unfavorable feature of Locarno was the negative impact it
had on the course of French–Polish relations. In the eyes of many Poles,
Locarno was a clear indication that France had opted for a direct arrangement with Germany instead of upholding the existing treaty system
through a series of collective defence agreements. Even the guarantee
which France had given to Poland at Locarno failed to overcome this
negative impression. It was feared in Warsaw that by tying the guarantee
to the League Covenant, France's willingness and ability to provide effective military assistance might suffer. In this connection the question arose
as to whether French military assistance to Poland depended on a decision of the League Council which declared Germany an aggressor. The
French were inclined to accept this particular interpretation. To many
Frenchmen the original alliance of 1921 seemed like a *carte blanche*
which might be exploited by Poland, with the result that France could be
dragged into a war against her own wishes and better judgment. The new
agreement provided Paris with ample legal ammunition to seek cover

behind the League of Nations, with all its slow-motion procedures and its inability to render a verdict, if French policy was unresolved about assisting Poland in a particular situation. On the other hand, nothing in the Locarno guarantee could have dissuaded the French from giving immediate aid to Poland before a Council decision had been taken, if this had really been their wish.

The Polish position, which incidentally was also supported by Beneš,[78] maintained that the pledge for immediate assistance meant that the signatories alone were responsible for judging whether the *casus foederis* applied, without first awaiting the decision of the League Council.[79] The Polish interpretation, which tried to make it possible to bypass the League of Nations, was further supported by the fact that the Locarno guarantee pact specifically called for military assistance under Article 15 (7) of the Covenant, that is in situations where there was no unanimous report of the Council and where consequently it was not in a position to declare one party an aggressor.

Whatever the legal merit of these arguments, Polish diplomats, and particularly her military, were critical of that aspect of the Locarno guarantee which might make French assistance dependent on a League decision. They therefore sought to add to it a protocol, similar to Article 4 of the Rhineland pact, which would specifically allow immediate assistance prior to a League Council decision in cases of flagrant aggression. But in the discussions which were held on this point, particularly in 1929 in connection with the Rhineland evacuation, the French remained vague and elusive and no agreement was reached.[80]

As a further protection against possible loop-holes in the Locarno guarantee, Poland sought to uphold the validity of the original alliance parallel to the subsequent agreement. In a memorandum of December 14, 1925, the chief of the General Staff, General Stanisław Haller, criticized the Locarno agreements for having left Germany free to continue her revisionist policy and for having left unclear the nature of France's commitments to Poland. Haller also feared that the Locarno agreements would indirectly prompt the evacuation of the Rhineland and the liquida-

[78] "Eduard Benesch und die tschechische Aussenpolitik," *Berliner Monatshefte* 16 (1938): 817.

[79] Leon Babiński, "Analiza prawna Traktatów Lokarnenskich," October 19, 1925, AMSZ, P I, W. 168, t. 78k; cited in Krasuski, *Stosunki polsko-niemieckie, I,* pp. 441–44. Babiński was legal adviser of the Polish Foreign Ministry.

[80] For a summary of these conversations, see Wacław Jędrzejewicz, ed., *Diplomat in Berlin 1933–1939. Papers and Memoirs of Józef Lipski* [hereafter referred to as Lipski Papers] (New York, 1968), pp. 13–19.

tion of the Inter-Allied Military Control Commission. He therefore urged that the military convention of 1921 be left as before and that France be made to confirm it as a condition for Poland's ratification of the Locarno arbitration treaty and mutual guarantee pact.[81] As it was unlikely that the French would formally reconfirm the 1921 military convention, Warsaw did not press Paris for a final clarification of the issue. For rather than being left with the new guarantee pact only, Poland preferred the present uncertainty which might later offer recourse to the 1921 alliance if the inactivity of the League should render the Locarno guarantee ineffectual. The French government did not officially renege on its commitments under the 1921 convention. But in 1927 Ambassador Laroche approached Lipski about bringing the 1921 convention into line with Locarno by having it attuned to the Covenant so that the *casus foederis* would be restricted to Articles 16 and 15(7). In November 1927 Marshal Franchet d'Esperey came to Warsaw with a similar request. On both occasions Piłsudski refused to enter into discussions on this delicate subject.[82]

Throughout the Locarno period the original convention of 1921 may be said to have been reduced to a state of suspended animation. When the militarization of the Rhineland in 1936 brought the collapse of the entire Locarno framework, Beck succeeded in getting France to recognize the 1921 treaty as again possessing unimpaired validity.[83] The fact that no new treaty was required on that occasion confirms the assumption that the original alliance had never ceased to have effect.

There were two other consequences of the Locarno agreements which ought to be mentioned here because of their effect on German–Polish relations. The first was the German–Soviet neutrality pact, the so-called Berlin Treaty of April 24, 1926; the second was Germany's entry into the League of Nations.

Germany had concluded a neutrality pact with Moscow for the purpose of providing an adequate counterweight to Locarno. Stresemann was hopeful that the Berlin Treaty would help maintain friendly relations with Moscow, preserve Germany's flexible balancing act between east and west, and prevent an accommodation between Russia and Poland. The treaty was accompanied by an exchange of notes in which Germany

---

[81] *Archiwum Ministerstwa Spraw Wewnętrznych* [hereafter referred to as AMSW] (AAN, Warsaw), 0.II, no. 5586/II, Inf. L.N.T.D.; cited in Tadeusz Kuźmiński, *Francja, Polska, Niemcy 1933–1935* (Warsaw, 1963), pp. 20–22.

[82] *Lipski Papers*, pp. 12–13.

[83] Hans Roos, *Geschichte der polnischen Nation 1919–1960* (Stuttgart, 1961), p. 154.

promised that she would not allow her membership in the League of Nations to conflict with her policy of friendship toward the Soviet Union and that she would oppose any anti-Soviet intrigues at Geneva.[84]

The Berlin Treaty, which followed so soon after Locarno and after her own failure to conclude a nonaggression pact with the Soviets, greatly alarmed Poland. As with Rapallo, Warsaw feared that secret military clauses might have been added to the agreement. These fears were nourished by the general feeling of doubt and uncertainty as a result of Locarno. There was also some concern that the clause referring to consultation on economic matters might lead to a common anti-Polish front in the economic sphere.[85]

Immediately preceding the signing of the Berlin Treaty, the Polish government, therefore, engaged in diplomatic activities in Paris, Rome, and London, which were designed to organize a lobby of the other Locarno powers that would force Germany, in the name of her Locarno obligations, to desist from concluding this planned agreement with Moscow. On April 12 Skrzyński instructed Skirmunt to inform the British Foreign Office that in the Polish view the proposed Berlin Pact violated Locarno as it reinforced Rapallo and because it went back to the practice of making alliances against a specific state, which was avoided at Locarno. Moreover, it was dangerous to let nonmembers of the League like Russia interpret what the Covenant obligations were in cases of nonprovoked aggression. Such an interpretation would reflect the German–Soviet position, which might not be the same as the view of the League of Nations.[86] Morawski told the Italian Minister that Germany was playing a game of bad faith and that Locarno and Rapallo were contradictory and could only be reconciled by secret clauses. The only way to halt this dangerous measure was to force Germany to choose between Rapallo and Locarno.[87] According to Chłapowski's report of April 17, France favored the Polish

[84] Harvey Dyck, *Weimar Germany and Soviet Russia 1926–1933* (New York, 1966), p. 13.
[85] Memorandum of the Director of the Economic Division, May 7, 1926, AMSZ, P II, fol. 4481.
[86] AMSZ, P II, fol. 4481. Skrzyński's arguments against the practice of concluding alliances were not very convincing in the light of Poland's own policy. At Locarno, Poland had concluded a bilateral guarantee pact with France which was quite clearly directed against Germany, and she had just renewed her alliance with Rumania.
[87] Telegram, Morawski to the Polish Legation in Rome, April 19, 1926, AMSZ, P II, fol. 4615, p. 29.

proposal to take joint measures against the proposed treaty but wanted to win time in order to influence British policy.[88]

The Polish initiative was frustrated by Chamberlain's reluctance to undertake steps that might offend the Germans and drive them into the arms of Russia. In his letter to Max Muller on April 16, Chamberlain explained why he had rejected Skrzyński's proposal to make collective representations to Germany against the conclusion of the Berlin Treaty. He himself "regretted the complications and disturbance" that had been introduced by the proposed German–Soviet treaty, but he was "convinced that it would be a mistake to call upon Germany to choose between this treaty and the Locarno treaty, as Count Skrzyński suggested."[89] Briand was somewhat surprised and bitter over Britain's passivity but felt that without British participation nothing should be undertaken along the lines of the Polish proposal.[90] Confronted with this rebuff, Skrzyński immediately backtracked and instructed his envoys abroad to deny that Poland had ever desired a collective *démarche* in Berlin that would prevent the German–Soviet treaty. According to Skrzyński's new version, Poland had merely sought clarification and assurance that the proposed treaty would not violate the League Covenant.[91] On July 21 Skrzyński's successor, Zaleski, told the *Sejm* Foreign Affairs Committee that he had become convinced of the peaceful nature of the Berlin Treaty and its compatibility with the Covenant and Locarno. But privately Polish officials continued to voice their anxieties.[92]

German Entry into the League of Nations

As the Locarno agreements were tied to the League of Nations, it had been determined that Germany would have to enter the League

[88] Telegram, Chłapowski to Skrzyński, April 20, 1926, AMSZ, P II, fol. 4481. In his conversation with Briand, Chłapowski had emphasized that only the League Council and not individual states could decide whether an attack had been unprovoked. It is interesting to see Poland take this particular position, for in her bilateral talks with France regarding the Locarno guarantee pact, the Polish position had been precisely the opposite, namely that a case of unprovoked aggression was self-explanatory and did not require a decision by the League.

[89] *DBFP*, Ser. I A, vol. I, pp. 628–29.

[90] Chłapowski to Skrzyński, April 20, 1926, AMSZ, P II, fol. 4481.

[91] Telegram, Skrzyński to the Polish legations in Paris, London, and Rome, April 19, 1926, AMSZ, P II, fol. 4615, p. 26.

[92] Memorandum of a meeting between Chłapowski and Briand, August 21, 1926, AMSZ, P II, fol. 4481.

before the agreements would become effective. Germany agreed and since three of the Locarno signatories were permanent members of the Council no major obstacle to her entry was anticipated.

Originally, Poland's attitude toward the League had been skeptical. The international body was viewed as an instrument of the Versailles treaty which had stirred up so much national resentment in Poland. It was also feared that the League might become an instrument of international intervention in Poland's domestic affairs by virtue of the Minority Treaty provision which allowed Council members to instigate international investigation procedures if they perceived a violation of the Minority Treaty. In the words of Skrzyński, Poland had viewed the League "as an unsympathetic school mistress who was always taking them to task."[93] Finally, the League was identified as an instrument of British foreign policy, which was viewed as essentially anti-Polish. This hostile attitude mellowed somewhat under Skrzyński's tenure as foreign minister, for the latter was a champion of the League and an advocate of closer Polish–British relations. In line with French policy under Herriot, Skrzyński tried to get a British guarantee through the League of Nations and enthusiastically backed such international schemes as the abortive Geneva Protocol.

Already in 1924, when German entry into the League was being considered, Poland undertook steps to secure for herself a permanent seat on the League Council. This was partly a matter of prestige, but the drive for prestige had a solid political foundation, for it was believed that Poland, encircled by two more powerful neighbors, could only survive as a Great Power, a position that has more recently been adopted by General de Gaulle, although in his case more out of domestic than from international political considerations. Furthermore, it was felt that Germany could not be tolerated on the Council if a seat was denied to Poland, because of the revisionist content of Article 19 of the Covenant and the special rights conferred on the League Council as a result of the Polish–Danzig Convention of 1920, the 1922 Geneva Convention, and the Minority Treaty. It was quite properly feared that Germany might raise the revisionist issue or interfere in Polish domestic politics on the basis of the Council's responsibilities for these matters, and Poland, therefore, desired a permanent Council seat to defend herself against

---

[93] Max Muller to Chamberlain, February 19, 1926, *DBFP*, Ser. I A, vol. I, pp. 456–57.

German machinations in Geneva. Herriot was sympathetic to the Polish position and promised to support her claims for a permanent Council seat.[94]

In 1924 Britain had opposed the idea of a Polish seat and when Skrzyński spoke of it in March 1925, Chamberlain, as we have seen, thought this a "mental relapse." Chamberlain's initial skepticism was primarily based on the fear that by raising the Polish issue at that time, Germany's entry might be jeopardized. Also the intimacy of the Council's inner circle would be disrupted by the influx of new members like Poland. Skrzyński pleaded for British support and warned Chamberlain that his entire policy of conciliation and co-operation with the League would be jeopardized unless Poland received a permanent seat. He reminded Chamberlain that he had been faithful to the Locarno accords, despite parliamentary opposition and his own inner doubts, and that failure to get a permanent seat "would certainly be the end of him and his government, as Piłsudski and the Militarists on the one side and the Communists on the other would unite against him."[95] Chamberlain was cautious lest the Germans be offended, but he was generally sympathetic to the Polish demand. When he had spoken with Briand, the latter had pointed out that "there was much that was intolerable" with the situation produced by the "Corridor" and the minorities, but he hoped that Germany and Poland might yet be brought together in "some kind of compromise. . . ." Briand had thought that a compromise solution might be arranged amicably if both Germany and Poland sat together as equals on the League Council. Chamberlain felt that there was "great force" to Briand's arguments and was disposed to "support the claim of Poland."[96]

German policy, as might be expected, was actively opposed to giving Poland a permanent seat on the Council, a measure that would have upgraded Polish prestige and reduced her international isolation. In presenting her objections to the Polish claims, Germany was careful to confine her criticism to the principle of extending the number of Council seats. But her diplomatic records leave no doubt that it was not so much a matter of principle as the direct opposition to Poland's candidature; and Schubert even admitted to his confidant, Lord

[94] Memorandum, Chłapowski, September 8, 1924, *AMSZ*, P II, fol. 4719, pp. 37–42.

[95] Chamberlain to Sir William Tyrell, March 9, 1926, *DBFP*, Ser. I A, vol. I, pp. 497–99.

[96] Memorandum, Chamberlain, February 1, 1926, *ibid.*, pp. 383–84.

D'Abernon, that the situation had become particularly aggravated by the fact that the extension was to be made to accommodate Poland, which would seem like an option by Britain in favor of Poland.[97] On February 9, 1926, Dirksen noted that Poland's admission to a permanent or even a temporary Council seat would tend to confirm Poland in the position of a Great Power and humiliate Germany, while discrediting the whole Locarno policy in the eyes of the German public. Furthermore, it would frustrate Germany's Locarno goal of loosening French–Polish ties, while diminishing the prospects of a German–British co-operation on the Polish question, especially on the question of the stabilization loan. The latter would be particularly unfortunate, for "as a recovery of the ceded areas (was) impossible by means of force in the foreseeable future, with the swerving of England the last hope of clearing the German–Polish border question would fade for a long time."[98] Zechlin did not subscribe to the British and French view that once Germany and Poland found themselves sitting together on the League Council, this would promote the peaceful settlement of disputed questions in the conciliatory atmosphere of Geneva; instead, Zechlin believed that their common presence in the Council would only promote open clashes. He advised against an open rejection of the Polish candidature but suggested that a timely whisper campaign that drew attention to Poland's economic crisis and the early promotion of another suitable candidate held out hope of success.[99]

At the Geneva session of March 1926 the now familiar horse trading, bargaining process for Council seats was conducted with infinite virtuosity. Germany listed her objections to various proposed acrobatic compromise solutions, but in the end neither Germany nor Poland received a permanent Council seat because of the adamant veto of Brazil which demanded a permanent seat for herself. Her veto also had the effect of blocking Germany's admission to the League. A special study sub-commission was convoked for the purpose of examining the impasse and to recommend a solution. The recommendation involved an increase of nonpermanent members to nine, three of which were eligible for re-election. Following this recommendation the September session of the League admitted Germany to a permanent seat and Poland to a re-eligible nonpermanent seat.

For Poland this was a meager compromise solution that fell far

[97] AA, D/2770/5462H/E368 682.
[98] *Ibid.*, 641–45.
[99] *Ibid.*, 730–32; March 26, 1926.

short of her original demands and expectations. On August 23, Piłsudski had told the Political Committee of the Cabinet that the chances for Poland to get a permanent seat on the League Council were extremely small and that he was consequently contemplating withdrawing from the League altogether. Such a move might even be appreciated in the United States, although not in Europe where it might be interpreted as a Polish–Soviet rapprochement. In its resolution, the Political Committee authorized Zaleski to announce Poland's withdrawal in case she did not get a permanent seat. However, this was merely meant as a tactical device to strengthen Zaleski's hand at Geneva by underlining the seriousness of the Polish claim, but in actual fact Zaleski was not to execute this resolution.[100]

Before the September session, officials of the German Foreign Office had hoped that if Poland could not be kept from a nonpermanent seat, with the aid of German diplomacy she should at least be deprived of the triumph of being declared re-eligible. Rauscher, in spite of his sincere efforts in promoting a German–Polish détente, revealed his lack of affection for the Poles when he hoped for their failure [*Reinfall*] at Geneva;[101] and Dirksen assured his friend in Warsaw that he had instructed all German diplomats in Geneva to spread the poisonous flowers [*Giftblumen*] contained in the former's letter.[102] As a gesture of good will Stresemann had voted for Poland's admission as a semipermanent member and in talking to Sahm, the President of the Danzig Senate, he justified this conduct on the grounds that since Germany could under no circumstances have prevented Poland's admission, her negative vote would have constituted an empty and undiplomatic gesture that would have antagonized both Poland and France. This was to be avoided, as it was necessary to resolve all western issues with France in a friendly spirit before Germany could introduce the eastern question.[103] Dirksen, who was less mobile than Stresemann in disciplining his anti-Polish sentiments for reasons of national interests, opposed Germany's vote in favor of Poland's election, even though he agreed that an open anti-Polish campaign would be inadvisable in view of the fact that "the

[100] AAN, *Protokoły Komitetu Politycznego Rady Ministrów*, No. 138; cited in Jerzy Krasuski, *Stosunki polsko-niemieckie 1926–1932* (Poznań, 1964), II, pp. 25–26.

[101] Letter, Rauscher to Dirksen, September 7, 1926, AA, D/2783/5462H/E378 300–2.

[102] Letter, Dirksen to Rauscher, September 14, 1926, *ibid.*, 311.

[103] H. Sahm, "Erinnerungen aus meinen Danziger Jahren 1919–1930" (unpublished manuscript), pp. 124 ff.

atmosphere here [at Geneva] [was] too saturated with Briand's conciliatory bacteria [*Briandschen Versöhnungsbakterien*] and with Poland's
approval for our Council seat. . . ."[104] Zechlin entirely shared Dirksen's
antipathy and, in an obvious misinterpretation of Stresemann's foreign
policy goals, saw in Germany's conduct at Geneva proof for his earlier
predictions that German eastern interests would be sacrificed on the
altar of a German–French understanding. While Zechlin was reconciling
himself to the fact that Germany had voted for Poland's admission to
the Council, he was burdened by the thought that she had indirectly
accorded Poland a distinction by approving her re-eligibility.[105]

Even though Germany had failed in enforcing the exclusion of
Poland from the League Council, she continued her original aim of
isolating Poland internationally inside and outside the League. When
Zaleski had been appointed League rapporteur in the Greek–Albanian
dispute in 1928, a matter in which Germany certainly had no direct
interests, Schubert complained to the Secretary-General that Zaleski's
appointment had been viewed with the greatest consternation in Germany, and that, in future, Germany expected to have more serious consideration given to her interests. Rather than rebuff this interference with
League functions, Drummond apologized and, promising to keep German interests at heart, admitted that he had committed a serious error in
considering Zaleski a suitable candidate just because he was *persona
grata* in Paris and in Rome.[106]

[104] Letter, Dirksen to Zechlin, September 14, 1926, AA, D/2793/5462H/
E378 313–16.
[105] Letter, Zechlin to Dirksen, September 22, 1926, *ibid.*, 352.
[106] AA, StS/2364/4587H/E184 141–43; June 8, 1928.

VI

Era of Normalization:
The Liquidation Agreement

IN THE PERIOD between 1926 and 1930 there occurred a distinct improvement in German–Polish relations to the extent that one might even speak of normalization. Incidents continued and negotiations were extremely slow, but there was no longer the fear of an immediate clash; important agreements like the liquidation settlement and the trade treaty were concluded; and the general trend in policies and attitudes became more conciliatory. This positive development was less a reflection of Locarno than the result of the considerably improved economic situation and a favorable domestic political constellation in both countries.

In Germany this period coincided with domestic tranquility and the predominance of those political forces which were committed to the democratic system of the Weimar Republic and which, incidentally, were also favorably disposed toward stabilizing relations with Poland. The latter trend was particularly evident between 1928 and 1930 when the Social Democrats constituted the key element in Chancellor Müller's government. In Poland, too, domestic conditions favored better relations with Germany, following Piłsudski's return to power in May 1926. The Marshal's own predilection toward improved relations with Germany found ready support among his former party colleagues and friends from the Polish Socialist party—people like Daszyński and Diamand were known to favor an understanding with Germany—on whom Piłsudski had initially leaned for support.

Piłsudski's return to power was essentially in response to domestic rather than foreign political needs.[1] Despite his opposition to Locarno, the Marshal had been confident about Poland's security in the near future.[2] But the Polish domestic scene had been pock-marked by an extremely grave economic crisis: spiralling inflation, depreciation of the złoty on the international exchange market, the inability to get foreign credits, unemployment, and labor unrest. Facing this situation was an unruly and irresponsible Parliament and a masquerade of impotent and changing government coalitions. But unlike the situation in France, which was also marked by parliamentary instability, Poland did not possess the kind of powerful and experienced bureaucracy which kept the French state apparatus functioning intact behind this façade of chaos.

France, Britain, Germany, and the Soviet Union were all taken by surprise by the coup—not an altogether pleasant surprise—and there is no indication of any international collusion in returning the Marshal to power. The disgruntled National Democrats voiced the opinion that the coup had been engineered with British help in order to reduce French influence in Poland, to promote a German–Polish reconciliation, and to use Poland as a spearhead for an eventual aggression against the Soviet Union. This interpretation has since been expanded by Communist historiography after World War II.[3] In actual fact, however, the initial British reaction had been one of consternation, and it was only when London had been given assurance that the coup would not bring with it the personal dictatorship of Piłsudski and that the constitutional and democratic process would remain unimpaired, that the Foreign Office breathed a sigh of relief. This assurance spared the Foreign Office "the nuisance arising from delayed recognition or debating the distinction between a de facto and a de jure Government." In a memorandum prepared by Gregory and agreed to by Tyrell and Chamberlain, the Foreign Office agreed to treat the coup indulgently, "not so much a national crime as a national disaster," and not to return to the "school-mastering"

---

[1] Joseph Rothschild's *Piłsudski's Coup d'Etat* (New York, 1966), provides an excellent account of the May coup and discusses the foreign political implications of the event (pp. 292–308).

[2] Józef Beck, *Dernier rapport. Politique polonaise 1926–1939* (Neuchâtel, 1951), p. 3.

[3] K. Lapter, "Międzynarodowe tło przewrotu majowego," *Sprawy Międzynarodowe* 9, no. 5 (May 1956): 43–60; no. 6 (June 1956): 54–71. However, another Polish historian, Leon Grosfeld, has recently rejected the theory of British involvement. ("Czy Anglicy rzeczywiście byli inspiratorami przewrotu majowego?" *Kwartalnik Historyczny* 76 (1969): 677–81.

attitude that had marked British policy toward Poland between 1919 and 1923.[4] Clearly, this attitude reflects resignation rather than the jubilation that one might have expected if Britain had really acted as the midwife of the May coup.

In Germany the reaction had been one of renewed anti-Polish propaganda which sought to demonstrate by this recent event that Poland was inherently unstable and was not meant to last as a state. Chamberlain noted that the French regarded the coup almost "as a personal injury to themselves and they were right!"[5] The Soviet reaction was one of caution and nervousness. Tukhashevsky and Yegorov left Moscow for Minsk and Kharkov respectively to be on hand in the event of hostilities with Poland, but Tass denied that there had been any troop movements.[6] The Soviet press was remarkably restrained in its comments and military maneuvers, which had been scheduled to take place in the vicinity of the Polish border, were cancelled in order to reduce Polish suspicions.[7] Neither Germany nor the Soviet Union officially took sides during the May events in Warsaw but they immediately consulted on the issue. Chicherin told Brockdorff-Rantzau that Piłsudski was anti-French and pro-British. In Chicherin's estimate it was quite possible that the Marshal would seek a rapprochement with Germany, not because he held any sympathies for that country but in order to protect his rear flank so that he might confront Russia.[8]

The British Foreign Office believed that it was "almost certain" that Skrzyński would remain as foreign minister in the new government.[9] The wish might have been the father of this thought, for both Britain and France hoped that Poland's Locarno policy would continue under his guidance. Supporting their hope was the fact that Skrzyński had been close to Piłsudski and that during his tenure as prime minister, between November 1925 and May 1926, many of the Marshal's closest supporters, among them General Żeligowski, had returned to high office in the military establishment and in other departments of the government. In this manner the infrastructure for Piłsudski's return to power had been laid, either at the personal instigation of Skrzyński or at least with his knowledge. But all these calculations were upset when Piłsudski

[4] Memorandum, Gregory, May 17, 1926, *DBFP*, Ser. I A, vol. I, pp. 756—58.
[5] Note by Chamberlain, May 17, 1926, *FO*, 371/11761, p. 68.
[6] Rothschild, *Coup d'Etat*, p. 302.
[7] Report Stetson, June 8, 1926, *SD*, 860c.00/361.
[8] AA, RAM/1426/2945H/D572 253–54; May 16, 1926.
[9] *DBFP*, Ser. I A, vol. I, p. 757.

appointed August Zaleski, instead. In making this choice Piłsudski may have been motivated by his opposition to Locarno, the treaty with which Skrzyński, for better or worse, had become identified. Also Ambassador Laroche's efforts to have Skrzyński retained might have been the kiss of death, because Piłsudski wanted to pursue a more independent policy with regard to France.[10] But foremost in the Marshal's mind was probably the wish to have as foreign minister a person who would loyally follow orders without seeking to play an independent role. The patient and somewhat colorless Zaleski fulfilled this requirement, while Skrzyński was used to act independently and enjoyed sufficiently wide domestic and foreign political support to get his own policies accepted.

August Zaleski was born in Warsaw in 1883. During World War I he had been head of the Polish Information Committee in London and had subsequently served as minister in Athens and Rome. He was essentially a person of good will and a conciliatory temperament who basically followed the policy lines that had been charted by his predecessor. Following his return to power, Piłsudski had initially taken a very keen interest in all questions of foreign policy, and even matters of minute detail required his approval. Under those circumstances Zaleski, to quote the American Minister, was just "an office boy doing the bidding of Piłsudski." But the Marshal soon lost interest in the details of foreign policy. In the opinion of Dr. Littauer, a member of the Polish Foreign Ministry, Zaleski might have come to dominate Polish foreign policy if he had just taken the necessary initiative to assert himself. But by that time he had "acquired the habit of taking orders, and continue[d] to submit for the Marshal's approval every plan in contemplation."[11]

In his speech to the *Sejm* Foreign Affairs Committee on July 21, 1926, Zaleski emphasized his desire for a reconciliation with Germany and for closer German–Polish relations in the economic field.[12] Rauscher

---

[10] SD, 860c.00/369; July 14, 1926. Apparently Piłsudski's first choice had been Prince Janusz Radziwiłł. Two factors supported Radziwiłł's candidature: he held pro-German sympathies and would have facilitated an understanding with Germany and, secondly, his nomination would have helped Piłsudski's bid for support from the conservative landowning interest groups. The Marshal sent his aide-de-camp Wieniawa-Długoszowski to sound out Laroche on the possible French reactions to Radziwiłł's nomination. Laroche stated that France would favor improved German–Polish relations but was concerned about rumors about a planned territorial revision (Jules Laroche, *La Pologne de Pilsudski. Souvenirs d'une ambassade 1926–1935* [Paris, 1953] pp. 47–48). Laroche's allusion may have confirmed the impression that by appointing Radziwiłł, Poland might go too far.

[11] Report Stetson, March 26, 1927, SD, 860c.00/401.

[12] AA, D/2768/5462H/E367 383–84.

reported that from a conversation with Jackowski he had gained the distinct impression that the latter was seriously interested in bringing about a détente with Germany, and that he enjoyed the support of Zaleski and Prime Minister Bartel.[13] But as long as Germany continued on her revisionist course, the area of maneuverability available to the negotiators on both sides was strictly limited.

The state of relations which existed between Germany and Poland from 1926 to 1929 can be characterized as being, at best, a state of tenuous normalcy. If Germany did not renounce her revisionist policy, Poland did not offer a more enlightened treatment of her German minority groups. The temporary relaxation in German–Polish tensions had its origin in the economic prosperity and relative political stability which both countries enjoyed during that period, and hence one sought to reduce to a tolerable minimum the nuisance effects of a reciprocal policy of pin-pricking and tried to settle in a business-like manner (by removing them from the political circuit) routine technical and administrative issues. This search for a workable normalcy found a reliable and capable advocate in the person of Stresemann, who had calculated the gains that such a policy promised to Germany's economy and for the protection of her minority in Poland and who, furthermore, made it a subordinate function of his *grosse Politik.* By virtue of the fact that she was defending the status quo and through her bonds of alliance with France, Poland was endowed with a superior, though waning, propaganda position in the West in comparison with Germany. A policy of continued friction and petty pin-pricking would invariably be attributed to Germany's incorrigibly hostile intentions and might have jeopardized her strategy of a peaceful offensive in the West, where she sought to bring about the evacuation of the Military Control Commission and of the Rhineland and to arrange a more advantageous reparations settlement and arms equality. In order to give testimony to her peaceful and conciliatory sentiments, Germany had to offer a semblance of consistency on all fronts by matching her friendly gestures in the West with a reasonable handling of her affairs in the East.

In this spirit a long list of agreements and conventions was concluded between the two states in the detached atmosphere of technical efficiency and objectivity, far removed from the lime-light of political discord. These included an agreement of June 16, 1926, regulating customs and passport facilities for the harbor of Kurzebrack on the

[13] AA, D/2769/5462H/E367 493; August 1, 1926.

Vistula, to which Germany had been given access;[14] an arrangement of October 27, 1926, for the transfer of civic registries for districts which had become separated by the boundary;[15] a regulation of January 22, 1927, for mines in Upper Silesia which had become partitioned;[16] a convention of January 24, 1927, for the administration of the Oder, where that river formed the common boundary;[17] on July 5, 1928, a financial revalorization agreement on securities, loans, and for the collection of private debts;[18] an agreement of December 14, 1928, for savings banks whose district of operation had been cut by the boundary;[19] and on August 28, 1929, a convention on civilian air traffic.[20]

When Jackowski saw Schubert in Berlin, in November 1927, he noted with satisfaction the progress which had been made over the past year and a half in German–Polish relations as shown by the number of agreements that had been concluded.[21] The settlement of numerous issues between Germany and Poland in the face of considerable obstacles constituted a very real triumph for the skill and self-restraint of the diplomats of the *Wilhelmstrasse* and the *Palais Brühl*. According to Prince Janusz Radziwiłł, this remarkable series of treaties and conventions on various administrative, and partly even on economic, topics demonstrated a mutual understanding of the necessity for arriving at regulated, good-neighborly relations,[22] and Toynbee notes that "it was to the credit of both sides that the strained relations between them should not have prevented steady if unspectacular progress in disposing of the exceptionally large number of questions which arose as a result of the transfer of German territory to Poland."[23] Yet as long as the decision-makers and public consensus conspired in a protracted with-

[14] "Abkommen über die gemeinsame Zoll-und Passabfertigung und den Eisenbahnverkehr in Kurzebrack," Reichstag, *Sten. Berichte, Anlagen*, 413, No. 2936.

[15] "Überleitungsabkommen über Personenstandesregister," Reichstag, *Sten. Berichte, Anlagen*, 441, No. 1902.

[16] "Abkommen über Bergwerksfelder, die durch die deutsch-polnische Grenze durchschnitten sind," Reichstag, *Sten. Berichte, Anlagen*, 413, No. 2934.

[17] "Abkommen über die Verwaltung der die Grenze bildenden Strecke der Oder," Reichstag, *Sten. Berichte, Anlagen* 413, No. 2935.

[18] "Aufwertungsabkommen," Reichstag, *Sten. Berichte, Anlagen* 436, No. 1182.

[19] "Sparkassenabkommen," *ibid.*

[20] "Abkommen über den Luftverkehr zwischen dem Deutschen Reiche und der Republik Polen," Reichstag, *Sten. Berichte, Anlagen*, 455, No. 7.

[21] Note by Schubert for Stresemann, November 21, 1927, AA, RAM/1427/2945H/D573 265–66.

[22] Prince Janusz Radziwiłł, "Polnische-Deutsche Beziehungen," *Europäische Revue*, II, no. 2 (1927): 156.

[23] *Survey of International Affairs*, 1932, p. 315.

holding of the basic essentials for a breakthrough, the mastery of diplomats on both sides was unable to penetrate beyond the narrow confines of technical agreements and could not create a general breakthrough which would project their countries toward reconciliation. Diplomacy, after all, could only furnish the method but not the substance for a foreign policy solution; as such, it could temporarily alleviate suffering but was unable to cure the disease, and only by mistake could its narcotic effects be taken for a lasting cure.

In the period between 1925 and 1930 the search for an agreement on the liquidation and trade question consumed the major portion of the diplomatic negotiations between Germany and Poland, and insofar as these questions were both an important indicator and a determinant of the current relations between the two countries, and as they provide worthy case studies for the actual foreign policy formation process, they will be treated here in some detail.

THE LIQUIDATION QUESTION

In accordance with Article 297 of the Versailles treaty, the Allies had been given the right to liquidate the property of German nationals in their respective countries. This measure had been inserted in order to provide the means to compensate Allied nationals who had suffered material losses in Germany during the war. It was also meant to insure that Germany met her reparations obligations. Sums thus liquidated were to be credited to Germany's account with the Reparations Commission. Poland's right to liquidation was restricted by Article 92, which stipulated that if the property and rights of German nationals who resided in the area which had formerly belonged to Germany were liquidated, the proceeds of this liquidation would have to be paid directly to the owner. A Mixed Arbitral Tribunal was to decide disputed cases of citizenship and to award equitable compensation in cases where the owners had received an unfair price for their liquidated property and rights.

In Poland there existed strong political incentives to enforce the liquidation provisions against German nationals in order to reduce their influence in the western provinces and thereby to blunt Germany's revisionist drive. At the same time, Poland lacked the means to pay for all the liquidation measures and felt that the constant process of litigation directed against her before the Mixed Tribunal was damaging to her international image. From the very beginning Germany had tried to get Poland to resign from her liquidation rights in return for other compensation, but talks which were held on the subject at Dresden and elsewhere led to no accord.

Closely connected with the liquidation question, though legally a separate issue, was the annulment of the rights and expropriation of the properties of the so-called *Ansiedler* [settlers] and *Domänenpächter* [long-term tenants of state domains]. These latter two categories were remnants of Germany's former colonization efforts in Poland and thus served as a natural target for Poland's subsequent de-Germanization policy. In anticipation of such a response, the German authorities in the period between the armistice and the coming into effect of the Versailles treaty had undertaken measures to fortify the position of these groups by confirming a large number of *Ansiedler* as owners of their pieces of land and by transferring into private hands rights formerly exercised by the Prussian government through its *Ansiedlungskommission*, such as the collection of annual rent and the right of repurchase [*Wiederkaufsrecht*] under certain defined circumstances.[24] As all public property of the *Reich* and the German States was to become Polish fiscal property upon the transfer of sovereignty (Art. 256), the Prussian government divested itself of much of its rights and property before that date. In July and August 1919, it concluded a number of preventive treaties with the *Deutsche Bauernbank* in Danzig in which it "sold" to the latter its rights in the *Ansiedlungskommission*, including all the mortgages held on the colonists' properties.[25]

Poland never accepted the legality of this transaction and in her annulment law of July 14, 1920, she assumed the right to confiscate without compensation all property which on November 11, 1918, according to the official registers, had been German fiscal property, regardless of its subsequent transfer into private hands. In line with this interpretation, Poland professed to have become the beneficiary of the newly acquired rights of the Danzig *Bauernbank* and evicted all settlers who had acquired their farmsteads after the November armistice. This expropriative measure was even extended to those settlers who had received their land before the armistice but whose title, because of administrative delays under the general war-time confusion, had not yet been entered into the official property registers before the target date. As a result of this decree, some 4000 settlers, with a holding of 60,000 ha. of land, suf-

---

[24] Poland claimed that the *Wiederkaufsrecht* had devolved upon her and occasionally applied it after the death of the owner of a homestead or farm, thus interrupting the course of natural succession.

[25] AA, RAM/1426/2945H/D572 278—81.

fered expropriation.[26] Similarly, 179 *Domänenpächter* with 100,000 ha. of land, notwithstanding the long-term nature of their lease (customarily eighteen years) nor the fact that these domains were models of efficient administration, were evicted under the almost classic reason given in a circular letter: "In the opinion of the Polish government you are not the legal tenant and therefore obliged . . . to evacuate the domain. In case that you should be the [legal] tenant, however, I place the domain under sequestration for disorderly administration."[27]

The expropriated settlers and tenants, the majority of whom were Polish citizens, appealed to the League of Nations. On May 17, 1923, the Council requested Poland to desist from further expropriations until the dispute had been settled, a resolution which Warsaw ignored, and requested a legal commission of five to prepare an expert opinion. The commission denied the right of Poland to expropriate settlers who had received their land grant before the armistice, even if the formal title had not been issued until later.[28] Poland rejected this opinion, and the Council charged the Hague Court with the preparation of an advisory opinion. This was announced on September 10 and adopted by a Council resolution of September 27, 1923. The advisory opinion noted that until January 10, 1920, Germany had retained sovereignty over the ceded areas and hence, until that date, she was empowered to conclude contracts with the settlers which were of binding character to Poland as the successor state.[29] As all but 400 settlers had by that time been forced to leave their homesteads, the Court's opinion had no practical value other than determining an obligation for compensation on the part of Poland. On June 17, 1924, the League Council announced that the Polish government had agreed to compensate those German colonists who had been unlawfully expelled.[30]

Before 1925 the number of properties which had been liquidated were relatively few because Poland suffered from an extremely shaky financial situation and was thus in no position to provide the required financial compensation. One major exception was the complex case involving the expropriation of the Upper Silesian nitrate works at Chorzów

---

[26] AA, D/2768/5462H/E366 804–5.
[27] Herman Rauschning, *Die Entdeutschung Westpreussens und Posens* (Berlin, 1930), pp. 91–92.
[28] Friedrich Wilhelm Heyl, *Die Tätigkeit des internationalen Gerichtshofs, 1922–1928, unter besonderer Würdigung der deutschen Minderheitenfrage in Polen* (Ochsenfurt, 1930), p. 50.
[29] *Ibid.*, pp. 51–52.
[30] League of Nations, *Journal Officiel*, V, no. 7, pp. 1020–21.

in 1922. These works had formerly been the property of the German government and had been sold to the private *Oberschlesische Stickstoff-werke* in 1919. Poland challenged the validity of this sale and insisted that Chorzów had continued to be German public property; consequently, its expropriation was not an act of liquidation but fell under Article 256 of the Versailles treaty. In its ruling of May 25, 1926, the Permanent Court of International Justice reaffirmed the position it had already taken in 1923 on the colonist issue. The Court upheld the German position that until the official transfer of sovereignty—in the case of Upper Silesia, June 15, 1922—the government had been free to dispose of state property. The expropriation of Chorzów, therefore, did not fall under Article 256.[31] As a return to the former owners was out of the question, an agreement for financial compensation was finally agreed upon on November 12, 1928, between Poland's minister of industry and trade, Eugeniusz Kwiatkowski, and the representatives of the *Oberschlesische* and the *Bayerische Stickstoffwerke*. Poland agreed to compensate the former with 25 million marks and the latter with 6 million marks. In addition, Poland agreed to admit the products of German nitrate factories on favorable terms.[32]

The initial Paris agreements of January 9, 1920, had placed Poland in a creditor position with Germany. But the unfavorable verdict on the question of the colonists and on Chorzów tended to reverse her position to that of debtor. This unfavorable trend was reinforced by another international decision. In 1926 Poland had agreed to accept the arbitral decision of the Interpretation Tribunal of the Dawes Plan, even though she herself was not a signatory to that agreement.[33] In its decision of March 24, 1926, the Tribunal ruled that Polish financial claims against Germany arising from the war or the Versailles treaty were to be paid out of the German annuities which had been fixed under the Dawes Plan and not on top of them.[34]

As a result of Germany's growing economic strength and the tenor

---

[31] Permanent Court of International Justice, Judgment 7, Series A, No. 7, May 25, 1926. The judgment held importance beyond the Chorzów issue and was particularly relevant to the claims of the *Domänenpächter*, for it stated that the transfer of property from the German to the Polish state had not taken place without any obligations, and that Poland was therefore bound to honor the rights which third parties had acquired from the government.

[32] AA, RAM/1428/2945H/D573 745–50.

[33] AMSZ, P II, fol. 4723, p. 154.

[34] J. Krasuski, "Political Significance of the Polish–German Financial Accounting in 1919–1929," *Acta Poloniae Historica* 15 (1967): 71.

of these international verdicts, the Polish position in the negotiations on the settlement of mutual financial claims gradually eroded. In November 1925 talks were resumed on the liquidation question, and the Polish Cabinet authorized its Minister for Foreign Affairs to conclude an agreement on this subject in return for proper compensation.[35] Stresemann was confident that in return for economic concessions Poland might be induced to forego further liquidations.[36] But the minister of agriculture, Count Kanitz, raised such lively protests[37] that the German Cabinet in its decision of December 22, 1925, ruled against economic concessions and, instead, merely offered to pay Poland 10 million marks if she resigned from all further liquidations.[38] This proposal led to no practical results.

The return of Piłsudski raised new hopes of breaking this deadlock, and Rauscher thought it was a good omen that the conciliatory Jackowski rather than the hard-line Winiarski was conducting the talks.[39] Rauscher's own position on the matter was clear. The whole subject ought to be settled rapidly by means of a financial compensation to Poland, in return for which the latter would resign from her liquidation rights under Articles 92 and 297 of the Versailles treaty. Whatever the verdict of the international courts and arbitration bodies, those persons who had suffered liquidation would never see a penny. The longer these futile negotiations dragged on the more property would be liquidated, and the German government would always be under the obligation to compensate the victims.[40]

The subsequent liquidation negotiations were largely confined to conversations between Jackowski and Rauscher and occasional talks by the technically less informed top-level diplomats during the frequent Geneva meetings. In December, Jackowski had inquired whether in return for Poland's renunciation of future liquidation activities, Germany would compensate those persons whose claims at that time were pending before the Paris Mixed Arbitral Commission. Rauscher immediately urged that some 12 or 13 million marks be invested for this project in

---

[35] *PPRM*, 32 (1926), pp. 3–4; January 7, 1926.
[36] Note by Stresemann, December 11, 1925, AA, RAM/1426/2945H/D571 943–44.
[37] Letter, Count Kanitz to Stresemann, December 17, 1926, *ibid.*, 952–53.
[38] AA, D/2771/5462H/E369 214–15.
[39] Note by Rauscher, August 1, 1926, AA, D/2769/5462H/E367 492–94.
[40] Letter, Rauscher to Dirksen, August 20, 1926, AA, D/2769/5462H/E367 501–7.

order to free 60,000 ha. of land from the threat of expropriation.[41] Dirksen was receptive to Rauscher's plan and found it interesting that Poland should suddenly have become so eager for a settlement of the liquidation issue. He attributed this eagerness to Polish fears lest continued litigation in Paris impair her international credit.[42]

Dirksen's analysis was not incorrect but it only partially explained Polish motives. In Warsaw it was felt that it would be dangerous to let the negative drift in German–Polish relations continue unchecked and that energetic measures should be undertaken to get a general settlement which might form the prelude to Germany's acceptance of the territorial status quo. When Jackwoski talked to Rauscher on November 9, 1926, he expressed the hope that Germany's interests in settling the liquidation question were primarily political, that is to say, to reduce tensions. An isolated agreement would not accomplish this aim. This had become plainly evident when Skrzyński had agreed to make a unilateral concession on the eviction of optants after Locarno. This gesture had done nothing to introduce the "spirit of Locarno" into German–Polish relations. If tensions were to be reduced, it would be necessary to arrange a general settlement of outstanding issues on a reciprocal basis. Poland, too, had financial claims against Germany deriving from war-time occupation measures. Germany was in a great hurry to satisfy her claims, but if Germany was thinking of reducing tensions then she would have to think of a settlement on a broader basis. After this introductory lecture to Rauscher, Jackowski expanded on his reconciliatory theme and noted that for a real relaxation of tensions it would require more than a financial settlement: what was needed was a more positive public opinion and an end to Germany's revisionist efforts. Not a day went by without some reference to the revisionist issue in the German press. Germany had apparently renounced the use of force in reclaiming her lost territory. If that was so, why not accept the inevitable and establish normal relations? Jackowski felt that the ghost of Baron von Holstein was still walking through the corridors of the German Foreign Ministry with the negative spirit which had led to the great catastrophe in 1914.[43]

[41] Letter, Rauscher to Dirksen, December 23, 1926, AA, D/2771/5462H/E369 319–21.

[42] Letter, Dirksen to Rauscher, December 27, 1926, *ibid.* 322–32.

[43] Memorandum, Jackowski, November 9, 1926, AMSZ, P II, fol. 4615, pp. 42–50. The reference is to Baron Friedrich von Holstein, an influential figure in the German Foreign Ministry in the immediate post-Bismarck period. Jackowski, like many of his contemporaries, exaggerates the sinister role of this *éminence grise* and his impact on German Foreign policy.

A few weeks later, Olszowski produced a brilliant and prophetic memorandum in which he drew attention to the dangers of Germany's revisionist policy, which was designed to recover the "Corridor," to re-establish the direct link with East Prussia, and to gain greater influence over Russia. For Poland the revisionist issue was non-negotiable, for a League of Nations' guarantee of free access to the sea was meaningless, and, in addition, Poland would have to sacrifice a population of 800,000. Since German and Polish policies were entirely irreconcilable on this point, Olszowski predicted war in five to eight years. In view of this critical situation it was imperative that Poland do everything to delay such an event as long as possible and to make the necessary preparations in the meantime. This strategy of delay could best be put into effect by settling all current issues that existed between Germany and Poland and by concluding a trade treaty. The latter would be considerably facilitated by a preceding liquidation settlement, an issue which should have been regulated long ago. For Germany the continued liquidation process was aggravating and it provided a perpetual issue of dispute; also Poland was not in a position to pay for the liquidated property. The best solution would, therefore, be a settlement under which Poland resigned from all further liquidation rights and Germany promised to meet the claims of those persons whose property had already been liquidated. Olszowski blamed his own government for not having come to terms on this basis. Once the liquidation matter had been disposed of, tension would subside considerably and the road for a trade treaty would be open. Apart from its economic gains, Poland also stood to profit from the political impact which this would have in Germany. The Social Democrats and *Zentrum* already favored an economic agreement, and, once it came into operation, German industrialists and bankers would find economic relations with Poland gainful. Finally, such an agreement was a necessity if Poland was to get any foreign loans on the international money markets.

Olszowski's long-range predictions were somewhat pessimistic. Before World War I, Germany had been restrained by two powerful neighbors: Russia and France. Now Russia was weak, France had economic problems, and Britain was preoccupied with the Commonwealth, with the result that Europe was heading for a period when German expansionism would meet with decreasing counterforce. As is customary with memoranda of this type, the emphasis rested on the analysis of problems rather than the definition of a proper solution. With respect to the latter, Olszowski stressed the need for a *modus vivendi* with Germany on current issues, so that armed conflict could at least be postponed. Given the trend of his prognosis, he might have come to the opposite conclusion; namely, that if conflict was inevitable, it would be better to have an early confrontation before Germany had regained her full strength. As an additional remedy, Olszowski proposed that since Poland could not reach agreement on the recognition of the German–Polish frontier her efforts should be directed toward getting a Soviet guarantee of the existing Polish–Soviet border.[44]

Even though Rauscher and Olszowski had taken virtually an identical position on the liquidation issue at the close of 1926, negotiations dragged on unsuccessfully for three more years. During the memorable meeting between Stresemann and Piłsudski at Geneva on December 7, 1927, Stresemann availed himself of the Marshal's good humor and friendly reception and proposed that in return for a direct German–Polish financial agreement on those cases now pending before the Paris Mixed Commission, Poland would renounce her *Wiederkaufsrecht*. The old Marshal showed himself immediately agreeable to such a proposal and optimistically proclaimed that he and Stresemann would be able to reach agreement on this point in less than six months, while it would require several years if left in the hands of their officials [*Geheimräte.*][45] The Marshal's reaction reflected his characteristic bluntness, as it also showed the disdain which he had for diplomats and government officials. While it doubtlessly signified Piłsudski's sincere desire for an improvement of the relations of his country with Germany, it also spoke volumes for the complete ignorance with which Piłsudski's soldierly nature approached the complexities and legal intricacies of technical issues. In fact, it required a far longer period than the six months suggested by Piłsudski to clear the liquidation question.

One issue of contention which considerably delayed progress arose over the fact that Germany wanted to restrict the settlement to the liquidation issue, whereas Poland wished to expand it so that it would become a general financial clearing agreement under which she would be able to recover her own financial claims.

Under the Treaty of Versailles Poland could not claim reparations from Germany.[46] Her financial claims against Germany derived from

---

[44] Memorandum, Olszowski, December 1, 1926, AMSZ, P II, fol. 4614, pp. 44–50.

[45] Note by Stresemann of his conversation with Piłsudski on December 9, 1927, AA, RAM/1428/2945H/D573 408–10.

[46] Poland's only chance to collect reparations lay in Article 116 (reparations to

Article 238 instead, which compelled Germany to pay restitutions in kind and in cash for goods and money which she had misappropriated during the war, e.g., the withholding of taxes, confiscation of goods, forced labor, and the work of Polish prisoners of war. Under the "inclusive amount principle" of the Dawes Plan, Germany's restitution obligations were to be included in the Dawes annuities. The exact portion of the Dawes payments which was to be devoted to meet these preferential restitution claims was to be decided by the creditor powers. On June 14, 1925, the latter agreed that Poland was to receive 0.02 per cent of Germany's annual payments under the Dawes Plan to meet Polish restitution claims. Germany insisted, in line with the 1926 decision of the Interpretation Tribunal, that payment for these claims was not to be made directly to Poland but was to come out of the yearly payments which she made under the Dawes Plan. In the German view, it would be a dangerous precedent vis-à-vis third powers if she started making direct payments, in accordance with Warsaw's wishes.[47] Poland, on the other hand, insisted that since she was not a party to the Dawes Plan and thus derived no protection from it, it would be to her disadvantage to accept this interpretation. She also pointed out that nothing in the Dawes Plan prohibited a mutual cancellation of claims as part of a clearinghouse arrangement which she was now proposing.[48]

Impatient of further delay, the Polish government on January 9, 1929, announced its intention of commencing liquidations under lists A and B and requested Germany to propose adequate compensation for objects falling under list C.[49] Following his instructions, Rauscher immediately intervened to prevent the execution of these measures. The well-meaning yet ineffectual Zaleski admitted his personal disapproval of the whole policy of liquidations, but his objections had been over-ruled by the opposition coming from the Interior and War ministries. He promised to make his point of view known once more, but saw little hope of success in this and attached greater prospects to Rauscher's

---

Russia). If Germany had agreed to pay reparations to Russia under this article, then Poland, as a successor state of the former Russian Empire, could demand a portion of this sum. By their Rapallo agreement, Germany and Soviet Russia cancelled any mutual reparations claims that might have existed, and Poland was thereby deprived of her only chance to collect reparations from Germany.

[47] Letter, Schubert to Olszowski, February 28, 1928, *AMSZ*, P II, fol. 4674, p. 179.

[48] Memorandum, Marchlewski, April 1928, *ibid.*, pp. 202–3.

[49] Lists A and B included property in the border districts where Poland was particularly interested in reducing the influence of German nationals.

intended direct appeal to Piłsudski, who alone was in a position to "bring his Ministry [the Ministry of War] to reason."[50] Zaleski's advice was, indeed, the confession of a troubled soul and revealed his weakness in the Cabinet and especially with Piłsudski.

Rauscher's direct appeal to Piłsudski was a move of some boldness, for the Marshal, while undisputably holding the reins of power, officially occupied no more than the portfolio of minister of war, and consequently for a foreign diplomat to appeal to the minister of war on a technical financial matter certainly violated the strict barriers of diplomatic protocol. Piłsudski, however, nourished a strong personal liking for the German envoy, whose wit and joviality satisfied the aging statesman's enormous capacity for laughter, a fact on which Rauscher correctly gambled. Piłsudski gave the German diplomat a cordial reception and promised to investigate the situation, and while he did not believe that the objections of the Minister of the Interior could be removed, he hoped to strike from the liquidation lists those properties which had been added on the recommendation of the Ministry of War. As for the *Wiederkaufsrecht*, Piłsudski feared that a formal renunciation was out of the question, but a de facto solution, restricting its application in practice, might be possible.[51] The Marshal's efforts, however, had no effect, as he was unwilling to overrule the strong opposition of his Interior Minister. Piłsudski's position and stature certainly enabled him to ignore the protests of his ministers, and this at times he did not hesitate to do; his reluctance in this particular case, in all probability, stemmed from the realization that general opinion was too hostile to the idea, and he did not wish to risk a confrontation on this issue. Consequently, Poland resumed her liquidation activities, and by April Rauscher was forced to consider his intervention as having failed.

The final settlement of the liquidation question was brought about in conjunction with the new international financial settlement, the so-called Young Plan. The Dawes Plan had merely been designed as a transitional agreement that would enable Germany to make reparations payments while her economy was in the process of recovery from the effects of the war and postwar inflation. The reparations creditors pressed for a new agreement in order to get a more permanent settlement which

[50] Telegram, Rauscher, February 12, 1929, AA, RAM/1428/2945H/D573 853–55. The Polish Ministry of War and of the Interior were most active in pressing for the execution of the liquidation process.
[51] Telegram, Rauscher, February 19, 1929, *ibid.*, 878–79.

would determine Germany's total reparations debt and the means of payments, and Germany, too, was eager for a revised status in order to eliminate the international financial control mechanism which she was forced to tolerate under the existing Dawes Plan. In addition, Germany hoped to link the premature evacuation of the Rhineland to a final reparations settlement. In February 1929, a conference of financial experts convened in Paris under the chairmanship of the American, Owen D. Young. The Experts' Report was published on June 7 and became the basis for the financial settlement, the so-called Young Plan. It established three different kinds of payments: unconditional payments, postponable payments in case of economic difficulties, and payments in kind. In addition, it set up an intricate scale of ascending payments that would reach a peak in 1966, after which they would decline and come to a halt in 1988. One's mind staggers at the optimism which must have prevailed at that time, when a continuation of reparations payments until 1988 could be conceived. In our somewhat accelerated jet age of rapid turnover such an assumption seems preposterous.

In August 1929 and in January 1930 the first and second Hague conferences met to implement and to adopt the Experts' Report and to deal with such matters as the evacuation of the Rhineland. Not all financial aspects discussed at these conferences were favorable to Poland, and she strenuously opposed the Rhineland evacuation, but she participated in the financial negotiations in order to escape international isolation. As the Young Plan sustained the principle, which had already been established under the Dawes system, that Germany would not be obliged to pay any further debts arising from the war and the Versailles treaty before she had completed her reparations payments, that is until 1988, there was little hope that Poland would receive any direct compensation from Germany. It was, therefore, to her advantage to be party to an international agreement that might help her recover at least part of her claims through the reparations mechanism. Under the Young Plan the preferential restitutions, which had already been handled as part of the reparations payments under the Dawes Plan, were merged with the general reparations payments, and Poland thus joined the ranks of the reparations creditor countries, with an annual quota of 500,000 marks for thirty-seven years. Her "promotion" to a reparations creditor was a matter of considerable prestige for Poland and, furthermore, seemed to offer a better guarantee for fulfillment than a bilateral agreement with Germany. Finally, the Young Plan acquitted Poland of her debt to the

Reparations Commission—some 2.2 billion marks were involved—for her portion of the German public debt of 1914 and for the German state assets which Poland had taken over.

In an effort to pave the way for a general reparations settlement, paragraph 143 of the Experts' Report recommended that Germany renounce all her outstanding claims, including private claims of her nationals, against her creditor powers in connection with the war, the armistice, the Versailles treaty, or any agreement made in its execution. In return, the creditor nations would make no further use of their rights to liquidate the property of German nationals. At the first Hague Conference, Germany agreed to renounce her state claims but not the private claims of her citizens.

In their mutual financial claims, Germany had a better case with respect to her private demands, while Poland's state claims were both higher and better founded than the corresponding German state claims. For this reason the Polish delegation rejected the German proposal and insisted that Germany renounce all her claims, state and private, before Poland could renounce hers.[52] The deadlock which arose over this issue was shifted to the "Commission for the Liquidation of the Past" which met in Paris later that year. Here, as at the Hague Conference, Germany met a united front of creditors who demanded the renunciation of all her claims, while Poland, furthermore, insisted that she was not included in the general liquidation sacrifice of the Allies by virtue of the fact that she alone was required to pay direct compensation for her "political" liquidations. In order to break the deadlock, the German Cabinet on October 3 decided to introduce the maneuver of settling the disputed issue in direct negotiations with the various governments involved, especially with Poland, in the hope that if Germany sacrificed all her financial claims against Poland (a plan which Rauscher had been urging for the past three years), this might in turn induce Poland to sacrifice her rights of liquidation and repurchase.[53] This proposal was favorably received by her creditors.

The Polish negotiators, Mrozowski and Adamkiewicz, were skeptical about the German proposal to conduct bilateral negotiations. They regarded this as a tactical move to isolate Poland and felt that all meas-

---

[52] Memorandum to the Reparations Commission, September 28, 1928, AMSZ, P II, fol. 4711.
[53] AA, RAM/1429/2945H/D574 328.

ures falling under the Young Plan should be discussed at the plenary meetings in Paris and The Hague.[54] In addition, the past history of four years of failure in achieving an agreement with Germany on the liquidation question and other financial issues, inspired little optimism for the future prospects of such bilateral talks.

The result, however, was achieved in less than a month—a record time for German–Polish negotiations—and was more far-reaching than expected. Rauscher made Germany's financial proposals early in October and in addition offered economic compensations in relation to the trade treaty talks. In an internal discussion of October 15, the Polish Foreign Ministry officials expressed themselves in favor of an agreement on the basis of Rauscher's proposal. Such an agreement would help overcome the customs war and would normalize relations with Germany. It would also remove the embarrassing and tedious claims of German nationals that were now pending before the Paris Mixed Tribunal. The Foreign Ministry also urged that Poland comply with the German wish to renounce her right of repurchase with respect to the colonists' homesteads. This right had rarely been used anyway, and the legal basis of its application was doubtful, as it was designed to prevent the settlers from being oriented toward Poland, a factor that was no longer relevant.[55]

The mediating role of France had also contributed significantly to the effective and rapid solution. After Locarno, France no longer pursued her pernicious Versailles policy of promoting discord between Warsaw and Berlin. She now sought to consolidate the newly gained prospects of a lasting peace with Germany by promoting an approximate détente between Germany and Poland. French diplomacy, according to Laroche, sought "to oil the frequently squeaking wheels of German–Polish relations."[56] Upon Rauscher's urgings, and after having sought permission from his government, Laroche discreetly tried to support Germany's position with the Polish government,[57] but had to proceed with extreme caution, as Poland was most sensitive on the issue, and Berthelot feared that anything but the most discreet effort of the French government would have the opposite result.[58] Laroche had been kept informed of the progress of the talks, and after their successful conclusion

---

[54] Memorandum, Adamkiewicz, October 5, 1929, AMSZ, P II, fol. 4711.
[55] Report, Lipski, October 10, 1929, *ibid.*
[56] Laroche, *Souvenirs*, p. 67.
[57] Telegram, Rauscher, October 14, 1929, AA, StS/2224/4483H/E095 595.
[58] Telegram, Hoesch, October 23, 1929, *ibid.*, 601.

both Rauscher and Lipski, the principal Polish negotiator, thanked him for his efforts in finding an acceptable solution.[59]

In the liquidation agreement of October 31, 1929, the signatories mutually cancelled all their financial and property claims, both state and private, which had arisen in connection with the war or the Versailles peace. In addition, Poland agreed to sacrifice her rights, arising under Articles 92 and 297 of the Versailles treaty, to liquidate the property, rights and interests of German nationals, which on September 1, 1929, were still in the hands of their owners.[60] The treaty was to come into effect together with the Young Plan. It was accompanied by a series of explanatory notes in the form of letters exchanged between Rauscher and the Polish Foreign Ministry. Among these, Lipski confirmed that Poland's liquidation sacrifice would apply to Upper Silesia after 1937;[61] Zaleski pledged that Poland would not exercise her right of repurchase in cases of regular inheritance; and Rauscher confirmed that no claims would be made against Poland on behalf of the Danzig *Bauernbank*.[62]

Financially, the agreement represented a sacrifice for Germany, at least on paper, for as Rauscher had long ago realized, the chances of receiving payment on these claims were extremely doubtful. In the category of mutual state claims, no agreement had ever been approximated, and as the various claims advanced in this field were extremely tenuous and offered little hope of ever being realized, their mutual cancellation represented no real sacrifice for either party.[63] In the realm of private claims (Appendixes I and II) Germany's demand for 538.7 million marks was matched by Poland's 830 million figure; however, the Polish claims, both by the nature of their composition as well as their actual amounts, were highly exaggerated and in the German estimate no more than 60 million marks could be regarded as ultimately realizable. Consequently, the financial sacrifice was on the side of Germany, in return for which she saved for her minority group in Poland a total of 900 small farms and 34 large estates, with a total area of 55,000 ha. and a total value of 55 million RM; also city properties with an estimated

---

[59] Laroche, *Souvenirs*, p. 69.

[60] Reichstag, *Sten. Berichte, Anlagen*, 439, No. 1621, p. 21.

[61] AA, RAM/1429/2945H/D574 260–61.

[62] *Ibid.*, 262–65.

[63] According to German estimates, she had a balance of 133,352,000 marks in her favor on the subject of government claims, while Poland claimed a balance of 137,788,000 million marks in her own favor. (AA, RAM/1429/2945H/D574 349–51). A compromise solution of splitting the difference, consequently, would have approximated a mutual cancellation.

value of 5 million RM were thus saved from liquidation. In addition, 12,000 *Ansiedler* farmsteads of approximately 15 ha. each and a total value of 240 million marks had been freed from the danger of enforced repurchase by Poland.[64] However, this right had only been exercised on a very few occasions.[65]

The opportunity of thus providing safeguards for the continued economic existence of her minority group in Poland presented Germany with a political gain which exceeded by far any possible financial sacrifices which she was forced to incur. Rauscher, whose far-sighted conception of political realities and skillful bargaining technique had contributed significantly in fathering the treaty, triumphantly reported the favorable outcome to his Foreign Minister, calling it the "greatest service . . . which the German government had been able to render to her minority in Poland," that realized her national-political demands without making any national concessions. "In return we have normalized our relations with Poland and thereby provided for us a free road for the economic penetration of this country. In addition we have deprived the Poles of the opportunity of posing as being threatened by us and thus have removed the basis on which they could always appeal as suppliants to the sentimentality and egotism of the former Allies."[66]

Even though Poland had agreed to hold separate negotiations and had concluded the liquidation agreement in a bilateral fashion, it had been her intention from the outset to include it under the protective wing of the Young Plan. By making the liquidation treaty part of the Young Plan she hoped to enhance her international role as one of the creditor nations and to gain better safeguards for international assistance from the other signatories of the plan if Germany should violate the agreement. As might be expected, Germany tended to view any connection between the two agreements as a dangerous way to enhance Poland's role in reparations matters and to involve the other reparations powers in German–Polish disputes. German diplomacy was therefore careful to impose strict barriers of separation between the two agreements. Just as Stresemann at Locarno had sought to avoid any connection between the German–Polish arbitration treaty and the Rhine pact, at The Hague

[64] AA, RAM/1429/2945H/D574 330–34.

[65] The deputy Jan Holyński in this report to the *Sejm* on March 11, 1931, listed a mere twenty-one cases in which the *Wiederkaufsrecht* had been practised. Cited in Krasuski, "German–Polish Financial Accounting," p. 80.

[66] Memorandum, Rauscher, November 1, 1929, AA, StS/2224/4483H/E095 627–33.

his successor Curtius now labored to keep the liquidation treaty separated from the wider reparations agreement under the Young Plan. In his memoirs, Curtius points out that the "differentiation between West and East in the liquidation of the War, which had already been fought out at Locarno, had been retained. Indeed, Poland had become, heaven knows how!—our experts have accepted that in Paris—a reparations power with an annuity of 500,000 marks, but she was not in consequence to participate in the other disputes with our great creditors."[67]

Repeated Polish attempts to integrate the two agreements came to naught because of firm German opposition and French unwillingness to let Polish demands jeopardize the adoption of the Young Plan. As had been the case at Locarno, France initially backed her ally's claims, only to retract when this threatened to compromise the chances of agreement on the principal issue. The German delegation to the second Hague Conference agreed to have the text of the liquidation agreement deposited with the rest of the conference documents, but no further legal connection between it and the Young Plan was established.

The Battle for Ratification

The German government insisted that the Young Plan and the liquidation agreement be ratified separately. This was done to underline the separation of the two agreements which she had managed to preserve at The Hague. More than that, the government did not want to endanger ratification of the Young Plan by linking it to the liquidation treaty which was highly unpopular in many German circles.

Opposition in Germany was probably less intense and less widespread than in Poland, but as the system of parliamentary democracy was still operational in Germany at that time and as one could not dispense with the parliamentary opposition in Piłsudski's cavalier manner, it required serious effort and considerable skill on the part of the German government to get the treaty ratified. Considerable opposition arose from the fear that Poland might apply indirect means, such as discriminatory land reform or tax manipulation, in order to counteract the effects of the liquidation agreement. The *Reichstag* Foreign Affairs Committee in its debates voiced similar fears, and the German government had made the precautionary arrangement of having Rauscher, with

[67] Julius Curtius, *Sechs Jahre Minister der Deutschen Republik* (Heidelberg, 1948), p. 100.

his glib tongue and detailed technical knowledge of the treaty, answer these critical questions and allay common apprehensions by affirming his confidence in Poland's "good behavior" in the future.[68] After further negotiations between Rauscher and the Polish government and between Schubert and Zaleski at Geneva, where Germany pledged concessions on the import of pork in connection with the impending trade agreement, a supplement to the liquidation treaty was arranged in the form of an exchange of letters between Rauscher and Zaleski on February 1, 1930. In it Poland pledged that she would not use the *Wiederkaufsrecht* in cases where the natural heir had originally opted for Germany or was a minor, and if a person was barred from inheritance because he had been convicted of a crime, this would only apply in the case of serious offences against the state, as for example desertion or treason.[69] It was hoped that this additional clarification would reduce domestic criticism in Germany and facilitate ratification.

The position of the various political parties in Germany corresponded to the customary ranking on questions involving German–Polish relations, as had been demonstrated during the Locarno debates and on similar occasions; only this time even members of the *Zentrum* and the *Deutsche Volkspartei* were highly suspicious. In the battle array for ratification, the SPD supported the agreement most actively. The Communists, Fascists, and Nationalists were the most outspoken opponents and vied with one another in bombarding the treaty with all possible invective. The Communist leader Thälmann claimed that the liquidation agreement concealed the sinister collaboration of German and Polish imperialistic circles against the Soviet Union.[70] His colleague Jaddasch ridiculed the German government for letting itself be trapped into a common front against the Soviet Union while being forced to foot the bill at the same time, for Germany had surrendered 2.5 billion marks of state claims[71] and 550 million marks of private claims. "One has sacri-

---

[68] A summary of the November 27, 1929, session of the *Reichstag* Foreign Affairs Committee is found in AA, RAM/1429/2945H/D574 368–87.

[69] AA, RAM/1429/2945H/D574 642; AMSZ, P II, fol. 4711.

[70] Reichstag, *Sten. Berichte*, 426, February 11, 1930, p. 3940.

[71] The sum of 2.5 billion RM—the estimates fluctuated between 2 and 2.5 billion marks—mentioned here represented the value of what had been German state property before the areas were ceded to Poland. From the outset Germany had no control over this sum which, if Poland paid for it to the Reparations Commission, was to be credited by that agency against the German total debt. In fact, Poland never made payments on this account. In connection with the Young Plan, and not in relation to the liquidation agreement, and since it was obvious that she could never press any claims on this account against Poland, Germany, in return for having the

ficed a horse," cried Jaddasch, "and let oneself be compensated with an ant." [*Man hat auf ein Pferd verzichtet und sich eine Ameise in die Hand drücken lassen.*][72]

The Nazis unfolded a veritable hate-Poland campaign in their crusade to prevent ratification of the agreement. Their arguments tried to persuade more by volume and hysterics than by a logical and truthful presentation of the facts. The *Völkische Beobachter* of November 17 called it a de facto renunciation of Germany's policy of revision, for now that she had sacrificed her financial claims she had surrendered the last possible means of inducing Poland to accept a revision of the frontier. The same paper, in an article of March 21, 1930, shouted: "With it [the liquidation agreement] the German Republic renounces the rights of German nationals which have been defended for 11 years, legalizes a robbery in the amount of 2.5 billion gold marks, and, most of all, recognizes the *Polakei* [German colloquial and derisive term for Poland] as a so-called sanctioning power." Count zu Reventlow, speaking to the *Reichstag*, called it a thinly veiled East–Locarno.[73]

Of the innumerable inaccuracies involved in these charges, probably the most absurd was the charge that the agreement sacrificed the interests of the German minority in Poland, for by no other German–Polish agreement had the minority group profited so much. Initially some doubt had been voiced by the minority leaders whether the new stabilization in the East, as brought about by the liquidation treaty, might not entail a sacrifice of German revisionist policy.[74] After Rauscher had explained the nature of the agreement to these groups he received their enthusiastic backing. In a tactical move to promote the cause of ratification by using the minority as a lever, Rauscher confidentially asked his Socialist party colleague Loebe, the capable *Reichstag* President, to arrange a secret meeting between the leaders of the German minority groups in Poland and a group of carefully selected German politicians (excepting the Communists and the Hugenberg wing of the Nationalists in order to

---

present capital value of her debt reduced from 132 to 34 billion gold marks, agreed that Poland be exempted from any obligation to the Reparations Commission for this property. The charge, therefore, that Germany had sacrificed over 2 billion RM was totally meaningless; yet it was constantly used by the opponents of the liquidation agreement.

72 Reichstag, *Sten. Berichte*, 427, March 8, 1930, pp. 4242–43.

73 *Ibid.*, 426, December 13, 1929, p. 3959.

74 Letter, Graebe to Curtius, November 29, 1929, AA, RAM/1429/2945H/ D574 398–404.

avoid the risk of indiscretion) before the opening of the *Reichstag* debates. Rauscher hoped that the minority leaders would help sway the German politicians in favor of the agreement.[75] Loebe immediately pledged full support for this plan and offered the use of his home for the meeting to promote the cause "in which we all have an interest." A date was set for the first days of February.[76] The meeting itself was held in complete secrecy and no records of it can be found in the files of the Foreign Ministry.

The polemics of the Nationalists did not lag far behind those of the Nazis. They were especially apprehensive lest the liquidation agreement open the way for a trade treaty, which the DNVP violently opposed.[77] Rauscher, whose Socialist background and policy of promoting a conciliation with Poland made him the *bête noire* of the Nationalists, came under particularly severe attack, and Count zu Eulenburg told the *Reichstag* that "if it were true that . . . Herr Rauscher was supposed to render his so-to-speak masterpiece with this treaty in the pursuit of high dignities, then nobody could be of the opinion that he has passed a master's examination."[78] Dr. Quaatz condemned the agreement for legalizing Poland's robbery,[79] and Hugenberg criticized it for sacrificing over 2 billion marks which could be used to alleviate the great economic sufferings in the German East.[80] The patriotic *Ostmarken-Verein* staged a massive protest rally in Berlin's celebrated *Wintergarten*, in which the *Reichstag* member Professor Preyer, referring to Bismarck's constant awareness of the Polish threat, asserted that "anyone who sought or even considered possible an understanding and a reconciliation between the two countries that was also acceptable to Germany had learned nothing from history."[81]

The *Deutsche Volkspartei*, on the whole, was favorably disposed and saw in the liquidation agreement a safeguard for the protection of the minority but felt that Poland's financial position had improved as a

[75] Letter, Rauscher to Loebe, January 23, 1930, AA, StS/2225/4483H/E095 912–15.
[76] Letter, Loebe to Rauscher, January 25, 1930, *ibid.*, 915–16.
[77] Schiele warned that if the liquidation agreement was complemented by a trade treaty with Poland, Germany's economic and political fate would be sealed (Reichstag, *Sten. Berichte*, 427, March 10, 1930, p. 4309).
[78] Reichstag, *Sten. Berichte*, 427, March 8, 1930, p. 4310.
[79] *Ibid.*, 426, December 13, 1929, p. 3555.
[80] *Unsere Partei*, VIII, no. 3, February 1, 1930, p. 17. (*Unsere Partei* was the party organ of the DNVP).
[81] *Kreuz-Zeitung*, February 11, 1930.

result of the agreement.[82] The majority of the DVP voted in favor of ratification which, according to Rheinbaben, was for once a real achievement in aiding the minorities and not mere talk or the writing of articles and books;[83] yet Rheinbaben himself could not repress a certain skepticism about Poland's future behavior, fearing that land reform and taxation measures might be manipulated to counteract the treaty promises.[84] The position of the *Zentrum* largely coincided with that of the DVP. Brüning spoke favorably on behalf of the agreement but, in view of Poland's psyche, voiced some concerns over the prospect of the loyal execution of its terms.[85] The *Zentrum* paper *Germania* considered it a generous and far-sighted gesture on the part of the German government which placed national-political over financial considerations; however, in view of Germany's present precarious financial situation, the additional economic burden could not be treated as a bagatelle.[86]

The Democratic party warmly greeted the liquidation treaty, not only for its service to the German minority but also for the opportunity it offered of promoting a trade treaty and creating normal relations with Poland.[87] The Democrats' *Berliner Tageblatt* called it "a very important act in Germany's *Ostpolitik* and an extremely significant step toward the fortification of peace in Europe" and hoped that it would inaugurate a policy of economic and political understanding with Poland.[88]

Dr. Breitscheid, the foreign affairs expert of the Social Democrats, enthusiastically supported the liquidation treaty as a means of coming to an understanding with Poland. Such an understanding would help the German minority in Poland and it would aid Germany's economic interests. He, therefore, hoped that it would soon be followed by an economic agreement. These two agreements would "form the cornerstone for the creation of a *modus vivendi* with our eastern neighbor."[89]

The *Reichstag* ratified the liquidation treaty on March 12, 1930, with the extremely narrow margin of 236:217 and 8 abstentions. Less support had thus been given to this agreement than to the controversial

---

[82] *Kölnische Zeitung*, January 28, 1930.
[83] Reichstag, *Sten. Berichte*, 427, March 7, 1930, pp. 4184–86.
[84] *Ibid.*, 426, February 11, 1930, p. 3946.
[85] *Ibid.*, p. 3928.
[86] *Germania*, November 12, 1929.
[87] Speech by Dr. Dernburg, Reichstag, *Sten. Berichte*, 426, February 12, 1930, p. 3970.
[88] *Berliner Tageblatt*, November 2, 1929.
[89] Reichstag, *Sten. Berichte*, 426, February 11, 1930, p. 3914.

Young Plan which was ratified with a vote of 265:192.[90] In the last minutes of lobbying before the final vote, the *Bayerische Volkspartei* had gone over to the ranks of the opposition—their protest had been over domestic financial reforms—and had thus threatened to bring about the defeat of the agreement with Poland and the Young Plan. This disaster had been avoided when several *Zentrum* and DVP members, who had previously abstained, made a last-minute rescue effort by voting for the two settlements.[91]

There was another incident of last-minute suspense when President Hindenburg delayed his signature of the liquidation treaty, even after he had already given his assent to the Young Plan. The delay attempted to underscore Germany's official position of keeping the two treaties formally separated, but it also reflected the President's reluctance and distaste for the whole Polish agreement. Already, on December 4, 1929, Hindenburg had expressed his reservations over the agreement in a letter to Curtius, for apart from his general doubts about Poland's faithfulness to the treaty, he was concerned that the latter might find indirect means, such as land-reform, to overcome the obstacles of the treaty. He found Zaleski's verbal assurances to the contrary quite insufficient.[92] Hindenburg also feared that the treaty might involve a violation of the Weimar Constitution, and a long legal memorandum had to be prepared by Professor Carl Schmitt that absolved the liquidation treaty of all possible charges of violating constitutional provisions.[93] On March 18, after a week's delay, the President grudgingly affixed his signature to the treaty and accompanied this act by a memorandum to the government, urging it to step up its program of *Osthilfe*, a program of aid to the economically depressed agricultural areas of East Germany, and in particular to East Prussia, to which the old soldier was bound by so many sentimental ties.

In Poland opposition to the liquidation treaty was strongest among the Rightist and nationalistic groups, precisely those sectors which also mounted the trenches of resistance in Germany. The sacrifices which Germany had made under the agreement were largely financial. For Poland the implications were more political in nature and, therefore, even more controversial, for by giving protection to the economic base of the German minority in her western provinces, Poland might be

[90] *Schulthess' Europäischer Geschichtskalender* 71 (1930): 74.
[91] *Vorwärts*, March 13, 1930.
[92] AA, RAM/1429/2945H/D574 418–19.
[93] *Ibid.*, 288–307.

said to have indirectly provided sustenance to Germany's revisionist drive.

The agreement was welcomed by the PPS and the national minority groups which sought a reconciliation with Germany. Also the government parties and the government press gave it a favorable reception.[94] The National Democrats' vitriolic *Kurjer Poznański* of November 6 lamented that the decision to forego right of liquidation and repurchase had made a terrible impression on the entire Polish population.[95] Professor Stroński declared at a conference of the patriotic *Związek Obrony Kresów Zachodnich* [Society for the Defense of the Western Frontiers] that Poland's sacrifice of her liquidation rights would be justified only if it were accompanied by a German declaration renouncing her revisionist aims.[96] The same organization, in its resolution of November 15, 1929, censored the agreement for removing the possibility of liquidating the powerful political and cultural influence of the German minority in Poland.[97] The Christian Nationalists' *Rzeczpospolita* of November 9 regretted the government's apparent renunciation of the policy of the de-Germanization of western Poland. On the same day, the moderate Rightist and clerical paper, *Kurjer Warszawski*, made the same criticism. The National Democratic *Gazeta Warszawska* in a series of scathing articles on November 3, 8, 10, and 13 tried to mobilize popular resistance to the liquidation agreement.[98]

Ratification was considerably delayed. This was done partly for tactical reasons, to put pressure on Germany to come to terms on the trade treaty negotiations which were then entering their final stage. But there were also domestic political reasons. Piłsudski's relations with the *Sejm*, problematic and strained ever since his dramatic return to power, had reached the confrontation stage in 1929 with the impeachment of the minister of finance, Czechowicz—a more convenient and softer target than a direct accusation against the Marshal—for the misappropriation of public funds and their use to subsidize Piłsudski's election campaign in 1928. Impatient with their internal squabbles and the opposition from his unruly parliamentarians, Piłsudski prorogued the *Sejm* for most of

[94] Report by Consul von Saucken, February 27, 1930, AA, T/2607/5551H/ E392 408–9.

[95] AA, RAM/1429/2945H/D574 389.

[96] *Ibid.*, 673.

[97] Jerzy Krasuski, *Stosunki polsko-niemieckie, 1926–1932* (Poznań, 1964), II, p. 205.

[98] AA, RAM/1429/2945H/D574 674.

1930 and relied more heavily on the *camarilla* of Colonels and personal favorites.

The *Sejm* had its first opportunity to debate the liquidation treaty and the Hague agreement when the Foreign Ministry budget was presented on February 7, 1930. On that occasion it was supported by the PPS spokesman, Kazimierz Czapiński, who believed that Poland should follow the French example of trying to improve her relations with Germany. The Chairman of the Foreign Affairs Committee, Prince Radziwiłł of the BBWR [Bezpartyjny Blok Współpracy z Rządem—Nonpartisan Bloc for Co-operation with the Government], the bloc of Piłsudski supporters in the *Sejm*, warned that Poland should never give the impression that she opposed a French–German understanding and considered it a threat to her alliance with France. Zygmunt Graliński (*Wyzwolenie*) also favored the agreement. Speaking against the agreement on that occasion were Zygmunt Berezowski of the conservative Christian Nationalists, who saw the liquidation treaty as an instrument of foreign intervention, and Kuryło Walnyckyj, the representative of a pro-Communist Ukrainian group, who used the same argument as Thälmann, when he branded the liquidation treaty as a German–Polish anti-Soviet front.[99]

In the elections of November 1930 the government bloc alone won an absolute majority of 247 out of the total 444 *Sejm* seats, and, as other parties also favored adoption of the liquidation treaty and the Young Plan, ratification was assured. In the final *Sejm* debates before ratification the members of the Christian Nationalists, Professors Winiarski and Stroński, emerged as the most vocal critics of the Hague agreement and the liquidation treaty, which they regarded as yet another in the long line of defeats which Polish foreign policy had suffered since Locarno. The spokesman for the government bloc, Szawleski, availed himself of the argument which Skrzyński had used to defend Locarno when he stated that Poland should proceed in the spirit of French–German reconciliation; to reject the accords would project a policy of isolation which Poland could not afford. The Hague agreement and the liquidation treaty were jointly ratified on March 11, 1931, in a vote of 188 against 90. In addition to the affirmative vote of the government bloc, support had come from the PPS and the German, Ukrainian, and Jewish national minority members. The negative votes had been cast by the Leftist National Labor party and the *Stronnictwo Chłopskie* [Peasant Agrarian

[99] Krasuski, *Stosunki polsko-niemieckie*, II, pp. 205–6.

party] as well as by the more conservative Christian Nationalists, Christian Democrats, and the People's Club [Klub Ludowy].[100]

To persons like Piłsudski, Zaleski, and Rauscher, who had labored to get the liquidation treaty signed and ratified despite continued turbulence and innumerable obstacles, it meant more than a settlement of mutual financial claims. By removing this constant source of friction and irritation, they hoped to lay the basis for a more positive and fruitful form of German–Polish relations in the future. The Polish negotiators appear to have attached somewhat higher priority to these more far-reaching political aims, for they supported the conclusion of the agreement, even though the direct political gains which Poland derived from the liquidation settlement in no way matched the political advantages which Germany reaped with respect to her nationals in Poland.

The liquidation agreement represented the most positive achievement in German–Polish relations during the Weimar period—the subsequent commercial treaty was never ratified—and constituted the high-water mark in the gradual improvement of relations between 1926 and 1929. Unfortunately, the hope that the liquidation treaty would promote a German–Polish détente, a view which Rauscher and other sympathizers of a policy of understanding held, never materialized. Whatever positive effects the agreement could have had were soon drowned in the massive undercurrent of the subsequent economic and political disintegration of Germany and the growth of extremist groups which sabotaged all constructive plans for improved relations.

[100] *Ibid.*, pp. 207–9.

VII

The Locarno Era: German–Polish
Trade Treaty Negotiations

BY THE ELEMENTARY FACTORS of geography and the natural complement in their respective resources and outputs, Germany and Poland appeared predestined for an intimate economic partnership. The existence of an integrated transportation network stood witness to the traditionally close economic links between the two countries and seemed to invite a continuation of this situation. After World War I, Germany was Poland's principal trading partner, a major source of capital, and the most important middle-man in terms of banking, services, and contacts for Poland's international economic transactions. Poland's economic relations with the outside world, like the principal factors of her history in general, proceeded on a predominantly East–West axis, and, given the limited scope for activities with the newly formed Communist régime in Russia, an intensification in Poland's economic relations with Germany would have seemed logical.

The wide complement of economic products invited a far-reaching exchange of goods between the two nations. As a predominantly agrarian country with 61 per cent of her population engaged in farming, forestry, and fishing,[1] Poland's exports were composed of agrarian and raw material products that found a ready market in the highly industrialized German economy, while Germany supplied Poland with finished consumer goods and industrial products. "Germany happens to remain the most important market for our natural products"; wrote the Polish consul, Karol Rose, in 1926 in an effort to promote better relations between

[1] Leopold Wellisz, *Foreign Capital in Poland* (London, 1938), pp. 25–26.

the two countries after Locarno, "this argument is almost banal, but one cannot rape geography: our neighbor offers the natural market, and the exports which go further can only be a poor substitute or a necessary evil."[2] As Poland industrialized her economy, trade in industrial products could have been increased and would thus have been on a more reciprocal basis than before, following the pattern that already existed between Germany and Czechoslovakia. Historically, Germany had been Poland's creditor, and her credits, mainly in the form of short-term bank and commercial loans to facilitate Poland's foreign purchases, as late as 1930 constituted 28 per cent of the total short-term credits that had been granted to Poland.[3] Germany's capital investment in Polish enterprises showed a figure of 541 million złotys in 1930, or 20 per cent of the total foreign capital invested in Polish companies. It was concentrated in the formerly German areas, and mainly in Upper Silesia mining and iron industries.[4]

Even under the most favorable political circumstances the economic relations of two countries are bound to be somewhat problematic if their mutual dependence is too lopsided. The German economy was not only more powerful and more highly developed industrially than that of Poland, but it was also much less dependent on Poland than was true for the latter. In 1924 Germany's exports to Poland constituted a mere 6 per cent of her total exports, and her imports from that country made up only 5 per cent of her total imports. Poland ranked in fourth and sixth place, respectively, as Germany's export and import partner. But on the other hand, Germany was by far the most important trading partner which Poland had, both for her exports and imports. In that same year, 43.2 per cent of Polish goods were exported to Germany and 34.5 per cent of her total imports came from that country.[5]

This discrepancy achieved a special significance because of the strained political relations. Not only did common economic interests fail to mitigate their political disputes, but their economic relations became a cause as well as an instrument of the political tug-of-war. Nevertheless, the high level of economic transactions which continued in the

---

[2] Karol Rose, "Deutschland und Polen," *Europäische Gespräche* 4 (1926): 614.

[3] P. H. Seraphim, "Die Kapitalverflechtung zwischen Deutschland und Polen," *Osteuropa* 7 (1931–32): 201–2.

[4] *Ibid.*

[5] Statistics compiled from Reichstag, *Sten. Berichte, Anlagen*, 442, No. 2138, pp. 85–88.

face of most rigorous restrictions attested to the existence of significant mutual interests.

Originally, economic relations between Germany and Poland had largely been regulated by the provisions of the Versailles treaty and the Geneva Convention on Upper Silesia, which reduced Germany's freedom to impose measures which discriminated against Poland. Articles 264–267 of the Versailles treaty compelled Germany to admit the goods of the Allies on a most-favored-nation basis without receiving any reciprocal concessions in return. At the same time, Germany was forbidden to impose against the Allies discriminatory trade and transit measures which did not apply to all other foreign powers. By Article 268 she was committed to import from Poland for five years, free of all duties, that amount of goods which immediately before the War she had annually purchased from the areas which had now been ceded to Poland. By virtue of Article 224 of the Geneva Convention, the same provision also applied for three years to goods coming from Polish Upper Silesia.

These protective devices had not deterred Germany from using hidden discriminatory practices in her economic dealings with Poland which, as has already been seen, took the form of an undeclared economic boycott between July 1920 and July 1922. After the Warsaw declaration of July 1922, economic relations began to evolve in a more normal fashion. Germany profited from this trade and sought stable economic relations with Poland in order to enjoy transit facilities to the Soviet Union. At the same time, she followed a strategy that was designed to exert a predominant influence over the Polish economy by flooding the Polish market with German goods, technicians, experts, and entrepreneurs whose influence over Polish affairs was calculated to extend beyond the economic sector.

Between 1922 and 1924, the Polish government, which considered itself sufficiently fortified by the protective screen provided by the Versailles treaty and the Geneva Convention, treated Germany's repeated proposals for an economic agreement with reserve.[6] The problem was compounded by domestic economic crises and by the German habit of flooding the agenda of their sporadic economic talks with extraneous issues, such as the question of optants, the settlement of German nationals in Poland, and the controversy over liquidation.

---

[6] Resumé of German–Polish economic talks between 1922 and 1927, December 6, 1927, AA, GA/3788/K202/K048 871.

THE START OF ECONOMIC WARFARE IN 1925

In 1925 the situation altered drastically, for now with the lapsing of the economic provisions of the Versailles treaty and the Geneva Convention, Warsaw became vulnerable to the threat of unrestricted retaliatory measures by Germany. Under these circumstances the Polish authorities became more amenable to entering into negotiations, and preliminary talks opened in Berlin between Lewald, representing the German government, and Karlowski, the Polish delegate. On January 13, both sides came to a preliminary agreement to avoid repressive economic measures while negotiations for a trade treaty were in process, and Germany consented to extend the protective clauses of the Versailles treaty until April 30, in the hope that a more permanent settlement could be arranged in the meantime.[7]

When negotiations resumed in March, the chief stumbling block was Poland's insistence on the extension of Article 224 of the Geneva Convention, which would give her continued access to the German market for the natural products of Upper Silesia, of which the 500,000 ton monthly contingent of coal was the most important commodity. As the April deadline was approaching rapidly and no agreement was yet in sight, Lewald proposed a prolongation of the provisional agreement for another three months.[8] In its meeting of April 1, the Polish Cabinet decided to reject Berlin's proposal for a renewed provisional agreement which, it was felt, was merely designed to protect Germany until she regained full freedom of action when Article 224 of the Geneva Convention ceased to apply after June 15. The Cabinet decided that any economic agreement with Germany would have to include provisions for the export of coal and other products from Polish Upper Silesia. At the same time and in order to put a halt to Germany's dilatory tactics, the Cabinet contemplated the imposition of specific import restrictions on German goods in the hope that these would make the other side more amenable to the conclusion of an early agreement.[9]

In Berlin these threats were viewed with relative equanimity, for Warsaw's Achilles heel—its dependence on an export contingent of Upper Silesian coal—was crystal clear. An unsigned note of March 1925 in the files of the German Foreign Ministry pointed out that if Poland

---

[7] *Paderewski Papers*, fol. 2847, p. 1.
[8] *Ibid.*, p. 3.
[9] PPRM, 29 (1925), pp. 13–14.

lost her coal exports to Germany, 40,000 of her coal miners would face unemployment. "Thus, the possibility exists for exchanging significant political advantages for the conclusion of a trade treaty. The renunciation of the *Wiederkaufsrecht* is a basic demand which Germany must see fulfilled before making any concessions in the economic sphere."[10]

As negotiations dragged on unsuccessfully—Germany had purposely introduced such unacceptable and unrelated issues as the liquidation question and *Wiederkaufsrecht* to slow the pace still further—the June 15 deadline was passed, with the result that Germany's Coal Commissar immediately put the thumb screws on the Polish negotiators by reducing the import of coal from Polish Upper Silesia from a 500,000-ton to a 250,-000-ton monthly quota. At this stage, the German negotiators held out for customs reductions, MFN (most-favored-nation) treatment and an agreement allowing German nationals to settle in Poland. Poland seemed amenable to most of these wishes, provided she received a coal contingent of 350,000 tons and permission to export live pigs, cattle, and fresh meat. In its session on June 30, the Berlin Cabinet rejected the Polish proposal for the import of live animals and limited its concessions to a 100,000-ton coal contingent and the status quo on the import of fresh meat, subject to proper veterinary regulations.[11]

On June 17, 1925, while negotiations were still in process, Poland, in a miscalculated effort to press Germany into accepting her list of demands, adopted a series of import prohibitions on goods, including such items as tea, furs, furniture, textiles, automobiles, and typewriters. While this was to have general application, in practice it was exclusively directed against goods of German origin.[12] As in other such abortive warnings which Poland was to emit subsequently, the outcome mocked the intentions. Instead of yielding, Germany countered by adopting prohibitive tariffs on a number of agricultural and forestry products of Polish origin, which prompted Poland to put a long list of manufactured goods of German origin on the prohibited list. The result was a protracted cold war in the economic sphere. Surprisingly, and acting as the most persuasive argument for the need of continued economic co-operation between the two countries, despite these choking restrictions the volume of trade

[10] AA, D/2768/5462H/E367 218–19.
[11] *Paderewski Papers*, fol. 2847, pp. 3–4; AA, GA/3788/K202/K048 872–74. In this instance the Polish and the German version of events is remarkably similar.
[12] Berthold Puchert, *Der Wirtschaftskrieg des Deutschen Imperialismus Gegen Polen, 1925–1934* (East Berlin, 1963), p. 57.

soon recovered as loopholes were discovered by which these unnatural barriers could be outmaneuvered. (For figures on the value of German–Polish trade see Appendix III.)

With these retaliatory measures, Poland and Germany quickly escalated their economic dispute to the level of a trade war which, despite almost continuous negotiations and occasional reprieves, was to last until 1934. The losses of this protracted conflict were both material and political and affected both sides. It is not easy to apportion the responsibility for the outbreak of this unfortunate situation in 1925. Poland's hostile measures which were specifically directed against German goods had acted as the fuse which led to the explosion of the entire framework of rational economic bargaining. Diamand, who had been a member of the Polish economic delegation at that time, writing in the *Kurjer Warszawski* of January 9, 1930, stressed Poland's responsibility in the trade war: "We have unfolded it. I was witness. I had the government's promise that it would not take place, but I had hardly left for Berlin, when they started it by telegraph."[13]

If Poland's discriminatory economic measures had acted as a fuse, Germany's refusal to make adequate concessions on coal and meat and the addition of extraneous political issues to the economic agenda may be said to have provided the dynamite. Not only in Poland but also abroad there was the general impression that Germany was primarily responsible for the rupture, and Stresemann instructed all German legations to do their utmost to counteract this negative image. Stresemann believed that "it would be a most powerful support in our economic warfare if foreign banks answered Poland on her credit petitions that they could not grant credits as long as her economic situation had not become consolidated and regulated through trade treaties."[14]

From the wider perspective of German–Polish relations, the question of responsibility in the breakdown of the trade negotiations must be attributed not so much to any direct move or countermove by either party, but to the general failure of enlisting in their mutual relations those forces of good will that are essential for the achievement of a workable compromise solution. Nor can Puchert's Communist analysis, which views the collapse as the well-defined move of German imperialists and revanchists, satisfy the critical observer. The remarkable factor was the notorious absence of any prevalent plan or consistent policy on this issue

13 Cited in *ibid.*, p. 61.
14 AA, RAM/1426/2945H/D571 799, July 19, 1925.

within the German Foreign Ministry, and, from the impressions left by Diamand's above-listed complaint, from Stresemann's conversations with Korfanty, and from Twardowski's later summary of negotiations a similar confusion reigned in the Polish government.[15] In 1925 the German Foreign Ministry in its economic relations with Poland completely failed to gain mastery over the extreme complexities of rival economic interests, of economic as against political considerations, and of immediate gains pitted against long-term goals. As a result, it was unable to formulate a policy that would have set Germany on a clearly charted course. In the absence of a clear-cut policy, therefore, and not as the result of a definite plan, Germany drifted into the economic war.

During the 1920–22 economic war, Germany had tried to inflict crippling losses on the Polish economy by withholding the shipment of vital goods that were required by Polish industries. Now that Poland had improved her own resource basis and had become accustomed to import goods from other countries, Germany changed her approach and tried to inflict maximum economic damage by refusing to import Polish products. In the *Auswärtiges Amt* the impression prevailed that by inflicting sufficient suffering on Poland's economy, Germany would succeed in lowering her neighbor's economic demands, while at the same time arriving at a satisfactory conclusion of some of the current political issues.

Despite his commitment to the conclusion of a trade agreement, Rauscher had not been averse to the idea of a temporary rupture of negotiations for tactical reasons, provided it was the Poles who were responsible for the rupture.[16] When the trade war had come into effect, Rauscher advised that it be continued until its negative consequences had made a full impression on Poland, who was already beginning to feel the pinch of the economic war in the form of unemployment and falling prices and, once the potato crop was in, would become fully aware of the blessings of economic peace with her neighbor.[17] A memorandum of September 15, which bears the signatures of Dirksen and Zechlin, expressed the view that since Poland was unable to grant sufficient economic concessions, Germany would have to seek compensation in the political sphere. Should Poland be unwilling to comply with this, it might be advisable to postpone the opening of the trade negotiations until the ad-

[15] Stresemann diary entry, August 7, 1925, *Vermächtnis* (Berlin, 1932), II, p. 547. *Akta Juliusza Twardowskiego* [hereafter referred to as Twardowski Papers], AAN, especially his resumé of the trade negotiations in folders 59, 60, and 65.
[16] AA, D/2768/5462H/E367 208–14.
[17] *Ibid.*, E366 769–72; August 28, 1925.

verse effects of the economic war had made Poland more malleable.[18] Others in the Foreign Office, especially those who had contacts with German industrial interest groups, were of the opinion that Poland constituted too important a market for her industrial products to permit Germany to reject an opportunity for a favorable trade treaty, even if this could not be linked with any political concessions.

For the rest of 1925 and 1926, negotiations on the termination of the economic war and the conclusion of a trade agreement were sporadic and they were handled in a dilatory and vague fashion by both parties. The first talks after the rupture resumed in September of 1925. Lewald informed the Polish delegation, not without arrogance, that since Germany regarded herself as the victor in this trade war, she was no longer interested in a mere provisional agreement but wanted a full treaty.[19] But talks were soon interrupted and when Skrzyński returned from the formal signing of the Locarno agreements in London, he cornered Schubert on the ferry to Ostende and complained that he could not escape the impression that both trade delegations engaged in extremely vague conversations which avoided the central issues, with the result that Poland was still uncertain what Germany's real demands were.[20] Rauscher himself was becoming increasingly critical of the trend of developments in Berlin and when, within a month's interval, the *Auswärtiges Amt* had changed its platform from seeking a provisional agreement to that of a full treaty on a small list of desired tariff changes and then again to a more extensive list, all without consulting its Warsaw legation, he complained to Schubert that "this procedure seems to indicate to me that in the negotiations *the determining influence of a uniform will cannot be felt.*" [Underlining of italics in the original.] Instead, it appeared to Rauscher that the central interest groups of Germany's economy, instead of functioning as agencies for the collection of data, had become policymaking bodies; however, as soon as something misfired it was the Foreign Ministry that was held responsible. This state of affairs, Rauscher believed, was intolerable.[21] On the following day, Rauscher addressed a letter to a certain Strom, who apparently was in close contact with Schubert, and requested him to convince the State Secretary of the seriousness of his criticism on the previous day, which was based on very real

[18] *Ibid.*, E367 322–29; September 15, 1925.
[19] *Paderewski Papers*, fol. 2847, pp. 4–5.
[20] AA, D/2768/5462H/E367 336; December 4, 1925.
[21] Letter, Rauscher to Schubert, December 29, 1925, *ibid.*, 341–48.

concern and not merely a momentary irritation.[22] In answering the letter of his irate envoy, Schubert assured Rauscher that he was in total agreement that negotiations should not be held in a dilatory fashion merely for the sake of appearance. "Indeed, it would be erroneous to play a speculation *à la baisse* and to await the unfavorable development in Poland's economic position; such speculations always fail."[23]

REAPPRAISAL OF OBJECTIVES IN 1926

No visible progress was made during the sporadic trade negotiations which were being held in 1926. Much of the energy was directed toward a subsidiary issue, namely, the right of entry and settlement of German nationals in Poland. At that time Stresemann did little to promote a successful solution of the economic negotiations with Poland. On at least one occasion Olszowski complained that Stresemann was obstructing progress and that he was purposely misleading the *Reichstag* Foreign Affairs Committee on the state of negotiations in order to maintain a free and strong hand in his dealings with Poland.[24]

Even though no visible progress was made in the economic negotiations during 1926, the fruitless interval provided enough time for a basic reappraisal of objectives in Germany. The persuasive force of events soon brought an end to those optimistic predictions that had foreseen a rapid collapse of the Polish economy. The Polish population had shown remarkable resilience in the face of economic adversity. The British coal strike in 1926 helped Polish coal get access to the international market and thus partially compensated Poland for the loss of the German market. After Piłsudski's return to power the Polish economy experienced a remarkable upswing.

These effects did not go unnoticed in Germany. Already, in November 1925, an unsigned secret memorandum in the files of the German Foreign Ministry, probably from Dirksen's pen, had warned against the mistaken notion that if Germany continued her economic warfare, Poland would collapse and thus enable Germany to extract political concessions, including the recovery of the lost territories. The Polish population, with its East European mentality and agrarian composition, was

[22] AA, StS/2339/4569H, E168 373–74; December 30, 1925.
[23] Letter, Schubert to Rauscher, January 6, 1926, AA, D/2768/5462H/E367 349–55.
[24] Report, Olszowski, December 17, 1926, AMSZ, P II, fol. 4614, p. 12.

extremely modest in its demands and could sustain the greatest material deprivations without lapsing into anarchy. Also, after Poland's *beau geste* in the question of the optants, Germany ran the risk of incurring an international reputation as the disturber of peace, if she continued her economic war, while Poland could pose as the angel of peace.[25]

In addition, by promoting, or at least by avoiding positive action in preventing the economic warfare, the German government had not only underestimated the resilience of the Polish economy but it had also overestimated its own strength in resisting the pressures of its business interests. In February of 1926, in a long memorandum signed by Stresemann, Schubert, Ritter, Wallroth, Dirksen, and Zechlin, the discrepancy between Germany's political and economic interests was noted: a trade treaty was desirable at that time because it served the interests of the economy; a protracted trade war held out the possibility of political gains in the future.[26] The petitions of industrial and commercial interest groups, especially those of Silesia, which had suffered most from the loss of the Polish market, flowed into the Foreign Ministry in torrents, and on June 16, 1926, the presidium of the *Reichsverband der Deutschen Industrie* [National Association of German Industry] informed the Foreign Ministry that all industries unanimously desired the rapid conclusion of a trade agreement with Poland. They considered this no less valuable than a similar accord with France, for Poland, with a population of 30 million, promised to be an important market in the future; moreover, one where Germany enjoyed an edge over other competitors because of proximity and her former trade connections.[27]

Rauscher, notwithstanding his temporary endorsement of an economic warfare in 1925, had become convinced of the futility of such a policy and henceforth acted as the most consistent and persuasive advocate of an economic settlement, which to him not only represented an economic necessity but also offered the most promising method of introducing into the affairs of the two countries a normal working relationship. Rauscher was of the opinion that Germany should not enter into an economic agreement which was not favorable to her; on the other hand, if the opportunity for an advantageous settlement presented itself, he

[25] AA, StS/2339/4569H/E168 400–1. If Dirksen was the author of this memorandum, it shows that he was already moving away from the more hardline approach of his joint memorandum with Zechlin in September of that year.

[26] Deutsches Zentralarchiv Potsdam, AA, File No. 67118, pp. 178–85; cited in Puchert, *Wirtschaftskrieg*, pp. 103–4.

[27] AA, D/2768/5462H/E367 363–66.

saw no way of justifying its rejection.[28] Dirksen agreed that both for internal as well as for foreign political reasons, Germany could not afford to wage a tariff war with Poland for the sake of forcing her to her knees; "apart from the fact that it would be futile to expect of a tariff war that it would make Poland pliable to our wishes."[29] A while later, Dirksen confessed that he had never been an advocate of the school of thought which expected considerable political gains to result from the negation of a trade treaty.[30]

Wallroth and Zechlin retained a certain ambivalence in their appraisal of the situation. Insofar as "the most noble goal of Germany's Eastern policy [was] the revision of her borders," and since this policy could be aided by Poland's continued economic crisis, the failure to conclude a trade treaty was not to be regretted from the revisionist point of view. On the other hand, if Poland extended an economically favorable offer, Germany, for reasons of general policy as much as for her economic interests, could not afford to sabotage it. But even if Germany adopted the second approach and concluded an early commercial agreement, this could still be considered as a legitimate revisionist pursuit by indirect means, for a trade treaty might be secured with additional political concessions in the field of liquidations and the *Wiederkaufsrecht*. These would safeguard the continued economic existence of her minority in Poland, which in itself was necessary "in order to facilitate the introduction of the revisionist question later."[31]

During the Geneva session of September 1926, Zaleski had invited Schubert and the other members of the German delegation to a pleasure cruise on Lake Geneva. Both sides assured one another of their sincere desire to terminate the economic conflict. Schubert even predicted the economic collapse of Europe in a few years unless some kind of economic unity could be formed by means of industrial and agrarian agreements. But the cruise was not crowned by any concrete agreement.[32] The lake cruising recipe which had been tested with such great success on the "Orange Blossom" during the Locarno Conference failed in this instance; perhaps it was all in the magic name of the craft, and the conciliatory

---

[28] Letter, Rauscher to Dirksen, June 11, 1926, AA, StS/2339/4569H/E168 771–78.

[29] Letter, Dirksen to Graebe, July 27, 1926, AA, D/2768/5462H/E367 395.

[30] Letter, Dirksen to Rauscher, December 27, 1926, AA, D/2771/5462H/E369 328.

[31] Memorandum for Stresemann, signed by Wallroth and Zechlin, October 5, 1926, AA, RAM/1426/2945H/D572 394–98.

[32] Note by Schubert, September 17, 1926, AA, StS/2362/4587H/E182 362–67.

spirits which hovered over the "Orange Blossom" shunned the "Zig-Zag" [name of the boat used at this occasion].

THE STRESEMANN–JACKOWSKI PROTOCOL OF 1927

The year 1927 started inauspiciously for progress on the trade question. In January the Polish authorities evicted four German citizens who held executive positions with the Upper Silesian railroad and electricity company.[33] Insofar as the trade treaty was also meant to regulate questions of entry and settlement of German nationals in Poland, the German government interpreted this move as a deliberate provocation and broke off negotiations. This precipitate action met with strong criticism abroad, especially in Britain, and Germany's own industrial interest groups viewed it with considerable reservations.

On Chamberlain's initiative, Stresemann and Zaleski met at Geneva early in March, and agreed to hold preliminary diplomatic talks to resolve some underlying basic questions, such as the matter of settlement, before resuming actual economic negotiations. They also agreed to suspend all further evictions for the next three months in order to prevent any poisoning of the atmosphere.[34] In line wth this Geneva guideline, Lipski and Rauscher entered into discussions which culminated in the signing of a protocol on July 21, 1927, in which both parties pledged to accord to each others' nationals most-favored-nation treatment for entry, travel, and visits. Furthermore, the protocol made provisions for the settlement of merchants and businessmen, as well as employees holding positions which required special trust or high professional competence, but it excluded artisans, unlicensed tradesmen, and peddlers. These regulations for entry and settlement were to go into effect as part of a trade treaty that was to be concluded at the earliest possible opportunity.[35]

Following this accord, Rauscher pressed the Berlin authorities to fulfill their side of the Geneva bargain and to propose conditions for a trade treaty, now that the preliminary hurdle of entry and citizenship had been mastered. In his estimate, such a treaty would offer Germany an annual export market of over 500 million marks. Even though this represented less than 6 per cent of her total trade, it would significantly

---

[33] Telegram by Consul Grünau (Bytom), January 21, 1927, AA, RAM/1427/2945H/D572 527. Technically it was not an act of eviction but rather the refusal to extend the residence permit of the persons concerned.

[34] Note by Stresemann, March 10, 1927, AA, StS/2363/4587H/E182 229–30.

[35] AA, D/2768/5462H/E367 301–4; July 21, 1927.

aid in reducing unemployment and was of greater value than Germany's much advertised trade with the Soviet Union. Rauscher stressed the necessity for conducting a realistic foreign policy concerning Poland, which was not a mere function of the fantastic plans which were being hatched on the Bydgoszcz estates of the various minority leaders, who wanted to make the trade treaty dependent on innumerable political concessions.[36] Curtius, then minister of economics, adopted a similarly realistic stand. He believed in the necessity of regaining the key to the vast and untapped Polish market. Curtius realized that if Germany wanted to resume her economic leadership in Poland and conclude a trade treaty, then she would have to adopt more realistic bargaining tactics and refrain from sinking the trade treaty by attaching to it the lead weights of her ambitious political demands.[37]

But the divisions within the German government prevented any concrete offer being made to Poland. On July 14 the Cabinet had decided to furnish Poland with a proper reply as to the German position on a number of basic questions relating to the planned trade treaty. But Schiele, the Nationalist minister of agriculture, began to have second thoughts about this decision. In a letter to Stresemann, who was on holiday on the North Sea, he rejected the idea of making any economic promises to Poland before the formal resumption of talks.[38] Stresemann wanted to avoid an open breach with Schiele and the agrarian interest groups and therefore called another Cabinet meeting on August 30, but no agreement could be reached on the exact quotas which he was to offer to Zaleski at Geneva. Stresemann consequently left for Geneva without any clear instructions and only the absence of the Polish Foreign Minister, who was taking a cure elsewhere, rescued him from his predicament.

When by the middle of October, Germany had still not given her promised reply, the Polish negotiators became increasingly impatient and Piłsudski inquired on several occasions why Jackowski, who had been charged with the task of soliciting the German answer, had not yet left for Berlin. Rauscher considered further dilatory tactics inexcusable and pressured Stresemann to receive Jackowski as Piłsudski's special envoy for preliminary economic discussions. In his opinion once talks had been

[36] Note dating from approximately June 1927, AA D/2769/5462H/E367 679–86.

[37] Memorandum by Curtius, May 5, 1927, AA, RAM/1427/2945H/D572 805–36.

[38] Letter, Schiele to Stresemann, August 15, 1927, *ibid.*, 986–88.

opened with full pomp and circumstance—Jackowski held the rank of an undersecretary—it would be difficult to retract subsequently. Rauscher was relatively optimistic about the chances of a satisfactory agreement, if they could only "get over those fateful pigs."[39]

The Cabinet decided, on November 5, in view of the declining agricultural prices and economic plight of East Prussia, concessions would have to be limited to a monthly quota of 200,000 tons of coal and an annual 100,000 C.T.W. of pork for meat packing plants. It was realized that these contingents were insufficient to get a full-scale trade treaty but adequate to secure a *modus vivendi* and a normalization of trade relations, while holding out the possibility for a more extensive future agreement once economic conditions had improved.[40]

Jackowski was invited to Berlin and on November 23 he and Stresemann completed a protocol along the lines of the German Cabinet resolution. In it both sides accepted the desirability of concluding an extensive trade treaty in the future, but at present they agreed to restrict themselves to a *modus vivendi*. The latter would serve the purpose of removing the retaliatory trade measures that had been imposed in 1925 and would thereby normalize economic relations. To this effect Germany proposed those concessions which she had adopted in the Cabinet session of November 5, while Poland listed her request for a 350,000-ton coal quota and nonrestricted access for beef and pork, a fixed quota for living pigs, and free transit through Germany for Polish meat and animal products.[41] In addition, an agreement was concluded to regulate the trade of forestry products, in which Germany granted a quota for Polish cut lumber, while Poland agreed to eliminate her export restrictions for round timber and granted Germany an additional contingent for various manufactured products.[42]

The Jackowski–Stresemann Protocol at last put the economic negotiations into forward-gear after they had been virtually stalled since the 1925 trade war. The two lists of demands contained in the protocol already reflected the cleavages that were to occupy negotiators in the arduous task that lay ahead. Germany desired more extensive tariff con-

---

[39] Letter, Rauscher to Stresemann, October 30, 1927, *ibid.*, D573 161–62. Stresemann assured his envoy that he was doing everything in his power to facilitate the resumption of trade negotiations (*ibid.*, 157; October 25, 1927).

[40] *Ibid.*, 189–91.

[41] *Ibid.*, 302–7.

[42] *Ibid.*, 308–12.

cessions from Poland; Poland wished to expand the coal and fresh meat contingents which Berlin was offering and to get some access for live pigs. In addition, Poland was eager to conclude a veterinary convention that would protect her from German discrimination against Polish meat products on the grounds that these failed to satisfy her standard sanitary regulations. Apart from its negative economic effects, this particular practice was also humiliating to Poland, as it quite unfairly presented her as a semi-barbaric country that lacked adequate veterinary controls.

These principal issues remained fixed on the negotiation agenda, although the particular details were continuously reshuffled, depending on the prevailing political and economic conditions. Playing a game of musical chairs, the negotiators constantly shifted positions from aiming for a *modus vivendi* (removing the hostile supertariffs and offering quotas for products such as coal and meat), to seeking a "small" trade treaty (the former, plus a mutual reduction of tariffs), and to planning for a "big" trade treaty (the former, plus a more extensive reduction of customs duties and MFN treatment in tariffs). Frequently the negotiators shifted so rapidly that the other side was unaware of it, and often their own governments failed to keep pace with these instant changes. It was not unusual for either side to ask for a "big" trade treaty but to offer only those concessions that were reserved for a less ambitious *modus vivendi*. The result was perplexing, irritating, and time-consuming, yet this abortive merry-go-round continued.

Negotiations on the basis of the Stresemann–Jackowski Protocol opened in Warsaw in December of 1927. Both sides had made an effort to start with a clean sheet by appointing new negotiators. The Polish delegate was Juliusz Twardowski, a refined and cultured man who had spent most of his life in Vienna, first as minister for Galicia under the Hapsburg monarchy and later as cultural attaché at the Polish legation. Through his career and life in Vienna he had developed excellent contacts with Germany which helped him during the negotiations, but at the same time his efforts on behalf of the trade treaty were hindered by his lack of influence and familiarity with the Warsaw scene.

The German choice for chief negotiator was far less fortunate. In order to pacify criticism from Rightist circles and agricultural interest groups, Stresemann's choice, Dr. Ernst, had been bypassed in favor of the DNVP candidate, Hermes, a former minister of agriculture and presently chairman of the *Bauernbund* [association of farmers]. A worse candidate could hardly have been found. Apart from his formal and unbending personal manner, which was hardly an asset during these delicate talks, Hermes saw himself primarily as a representative of Germany's agrarian lobby, whose policy was aimed at sabotaging the planned trade treaty with Poland. Hermes was thus forced into the somewhat ambivalent role of representing both the Berlin government, whose ostensible aim it was to reach an economic agreement with Warsaw, and the German farm lobby, which pursued quite contrary goals. To be fair to Hermes, it must be admitted that he sincerely believed in the reconcilability of these two diverse positions and sought an economic agreement, provided it did not damage Germany's farm interests. Nevertheless, his conference acrobatics were a distinct impediment to a settlement and he used his role increasingly for the purpose of exercising a veto over the proceedings. Stresemann was displeased with this choice and the dilatory tactics of the government and sent a bristling letter to Chancellor Marx in which he objected to recent developments which tended to reduce the Cabinet to a mere dummy for particular interest groups. He had given utmost consideration to safeguarding the interests of the agrarian sector and now demanded in return that the government loyally pursue negotiations for a *modus vivendi*, as outlined in his protocol with Jackowski. "If it is not the intention of the Cabinet to resume and continue the negotiations for a definite trade treaty immediately, and if the Cabinet should prefer a dilatory to an immediate treatment, I kindly request that a decision be taken on this and to dispense with my further co-operation in this Cabinet."[43]

CHRISTMAS CHEER AND NEW YEAR'S HANGOVER

The Warsaw talks in December started on an optimistic note. The two new negotiators tried to put their best foot forward and there was even speculation that a provisional agreement might already be initialed by Christmas.[44] This benevolent Christmas spirit was further enhanced by a conference of leading German and Polish industrialists in Berlin early in December—the first such meeting that had been held between the two countries. The meeting did not confine itself to generalities

---

[43] Stresemann, *Vermächtnis*, III, pp. 235–39; November 24, 1927. Stresemann did not carry through his threat to resign when he was given assurance of the Cabinet's serious intention of coming to an economic agreement with Poland on the basis of the Stresemann-Jackowski Protocol.

[44] *Twardowski Papers*, fol. 52, p. 28.

but realistically, and without avoiding thorny areas of dispute, explored the means by which the economic relations between the two countries could be improved. The 39 German and 22 Polish delegates to the economic conference represented every major sector of their economy and constituted the cream of the economic leadership. Despite disagreement on various individual issues, there existed almost universal consensus, even among the agrarian members, on the necessity and desirability of creating closer economic ties, thereby reaping the harvest of their natural economic complementarity. For Poland it was particularly significant that the German members conceded that the import of Polish farm products into Germany was feasible, which was frequently denied at the official level. The conference met with favorable comments on both sides.[45]

On November 24, 1927, Germany and Poland had come to terms on another irksome problem in their relations that perennially cropped up because of its seasonal character. The agreement regulated the status, social insurance, and immigration procedures of the Polish seasonal farm laborers [*Wanderarbeiter*] who traditionally came to Germany each summer to help with the harvest. Like migratory birds, they drifted back to their original Polish habitat in winter. But many of them got stranded in Germany over the winter, where they roamed through the country and had a miserable existence, uprooted, exploited, and frequently unemployed. In this wretched condition the Polish migratory laborers became a target of exploitation, but at the same time they often were a plague to their community. These persons were frequently the only kind of Poles with whom Germans were familiar and thereby helped shape the negative and distorted image of Poland that prevailed in Germany. Approximately 110,000 seasonal workers were involved, of whom 65,000 regularly returned to Poland over the winter, while the remaining 45,000 lived in Germany for the entire year. Berlin objected to their illicit residence in Germany; Warsaw was offended by their treatment and eviction.

The November agreement accorded to the entire migratory farm movement, which had previously proceeded in a totally haphazard and informal fashion, official status. The workers were given passports and recruitment was to be handled officially by the Polish State Labor Recruiting Offices and in Germany by the departments concerned. Poland

[45] AMSZ, P II, fol. 4669, pp. 217–19; AA, GA/3788/K202/K048 931–34.

agreed that this particular migration had only seasonal character. Those workers who had come to Germany before January 1919 would have the right to remain permanently. Those who had arrived between 1919 and 1925 were to return to Poland within the next six years, excepting those cases where this would impose particular personal hardship, but all were eligible for return during the summer season. In addition, the agreement made provisions for social welfare benefits which the Polish farm laborers were to receive on an equitable footing with German workers.[46]

But this Christmas spirit was not to last long. Poland sprang an unpleasant surprise with the presidential border zone decree of December 23, 1927, a security measure for a zone within 30 km. of her boundaries, which empowered the local authorities to evict persons for minor offences, such as tax evasion, and authorized the *voivode* to restrict aliens in that district from engaging in trade and commerce or from enjoying the use of their property. Germany interpreted this action as being particularly designed to suit Poland's de-Germanization process which would render illusory the Lipski–Rauscher agreement on settlement. Berlin, therefore, insisted that its offensive clauses be amended and assurance be given that it would not alter the 1927 Lipski–Rauscher Protocol on settlement, before economic negotiations could be resumed.[47] With this border decree matters seemed to have regressed precisely to where they had stood when the question of evictions had formed a stumbling block early in 1927. As in the previous case, Zaleski and Stresemann met in Geneva for the March session of the League of Nations and tried to patch up matters. The Polish Foreign Minister expressed his regrets over the recent border decree, which had been adopted when he had been absent on account of illness. He informed Stresemann that he had already issued instructions to have certain of its offensive clauses amended.[48]

Those most immediately concerned with the trade negotiations began to show increasing signs of nervous strain. Rauscher confessed to Schubert that his efforts to get a suitable alteration of the border decree had left him virtually ill and sufficiently frustrated to make him

[46] Zaleski's explanation to the Cabinet, February 24, 1928, *PPRM*, 42 (1928): 256–58. Zaleski supported the agreement not only because it would aid the Polish seasonal farm workers but also because of its positive impact on Polish-German relations in general.

[47] Telegram, Ritter to Schubert, March 3, 1928, AA, RAM/1428/2945H/D573 469–70.

[48] Note by Schubert of the Stresemann–Zaleski conversation at Geneva, March 11, 1928, AA, StS/2364/4587H/E184 011–13.

want to throw in the cards. But "with some effort [he] had found the way back to his old desolate profession" in order that the thread not be cut entirely.[49] Twardowski, too, complained that he was not getting sufficient support from the different ministers. He was no longer certain whether his own government really wanted an agreement with Germany. He could only represent the Polish government as a whole, but not this or that specific ministry.[50] Later Twardowski recalled how in the early part of 1928 the question of the border decree had consumed all his energy and had brought trade negotiations to a stand-still. The Vienna Protocol, which he and Hermes had signed on April 13 and which was meant to end the stalemate, had been rejected by his government even though it had been accepted by Germany. This disavowal had compromised his position with the German negotiators. A change of the frontier regulation had been reached only after a hard struggle with the Minister of Interior, and even then the government had for a time tried to keep this alteration secret, even from Rauscher, for fear of public criticism. All this had caused endless delay and was counterproductive to the realization of Poland's broader aims.[51]

The impasse was finally overcome after an exchange of letters between Rauscher and Zaleski, in which Poland assured Germany that the decree had neither been intended nor would it be applied in practice as a fighting measure against the nationals of any state, and consequently not against the German minority. The text for this note had already been agreed upon at Vienna, but the formal exchange was delayed until July 17 when, for the occasion of the resumption of trade negotiations, it was published in the form of a general communiqué[52]

The negotiations, which were resumed in Warsaw in September 1928, quickly ran aground on the rocky shoals of coal and hog contingents. Jackowski styled Germany's wishes for customs reductions on some 450 positions as "simply fantastic," while Rauscher did not believe that Germany could accept Warsaw's proposal for a 500,000-ton coal contingent per month and an annual quota of 600,000 hogs.[53] Hermes's

[49] Letter, Rauscher to Schubert, March 22, 1928, AA, StS/2339/4569H/E168 077–79.

[50] Twardowski to the Foreign Ministry, April 19, 1928, *Twardowski Papers*, fol. 53, pp. 14–15.

[51] *Ibid.*, fol. 65, pp. 1–5.

[52] Telegram, Rauscher, July 17, 1928, AA, StS/2223/4483H/E094 929.

[53] Memorandum, Jackowski of his conversation with Rauscher, September 18, 1928, *Twardowski Papers*, fol. 53, p. 51. In addition, Poland requested a veterinary convention, transit rights through Germany for living animals and meat products, a

loyalty to the farmers' lobby and his abrupt manner in negotiation imposed an additional liability on the talks. But as the Polish press had openly criticized him, it was difficult for the German government to have him recalled for fear of causing a storm of public protest for bowing to Polish pressure.

Following the customary decision-making process for questions of international economics, the counterproposal to Warsaw's initial position was first worked out among the members of the Eastern Division of the Foreign Ministry in consultation with foreign trade experts and was then deliberated before the *Handelspolitsche Ausschuss* [trade policy committee] that included economic experts from the Foreign Ministry, as well as the ministries of Economics, Finance, and Agriculture. In this body the Foreign Ministry's program of proposing far-reaching economic concessions was endorsed by all ministries except that of Agriculture. Ordinarily major questions of policy or those issues on which the *Handelspolitische Ausschuss* had been unable to reach agreement were submitted to the Cabinet. In this particular instance, which had sharpened into a central dispute between the industrial and the agrarian interest groups in Germany, a formal meeting was staged between the key representatives of each group, with the government acting as mediator. Without resolving the conflict, the joint session only served to underline existing cleavages. Hermes had been unsuccessful in persuading his agrarian colleagues to consent to a nonquota import of Polish pork to German meat packing plants, an offer which they categorically rejected. Germany's industrial interest groups demanded that such a nonquota import permission be granted, as it constituted a *sine qua non* for the conclusion of any agreement, which German industry viewed as "an economic necessity of the first order." If the agrarian interest groups were unable to comply with this condition, they would force industry to break the previously guarded truce and to proceed unilaterally.[54]

The agricultural-industrial split presented considerable embarrassment to the German government, both for the internal repercussions and its bargaining posture vis-à-vis Poland. The subsequent Cabinet decision, under its Socialist Chancellor Müller, sought a compromise formula

---

quota of 50,000 cattle per year, and unrestricted entry of pork, beef, and mutton. She also desired permission to import 300,000 tons of scrap iron from Germany (*ibid.*, p. 47).
[54] AA, StS/2224/4483H/E094 995–98; E095 009–23; November 7, 1928.

which would not only avoid this rift but would also satisfy Poland's demands. To comply with the former, the government refrained from granting the quota-free import of Polish pork; to satisfy the latter, the fixed import quota was to be made sufficiently large. The November Cabinet decision presented the most extensive list of concessions that Germany had yet proposed and included a monthly coal quota of 350,000 tons and the guarantee of taking a weekly contingent of 11,000 slaughtered pigs, of which 5,000 were intended for re-export. Warsaw's request for a quota of beef and cattle was rejected, but the export of scrap iron to Poland was permitted.[55] Rauscher considered this proposal the best foreign trade bargain which Poland had ever struck.[56] "One can say," he informed Schubert, "that we have never come as far as now. One can also say that we are not yet far enough."[57]

In view of subsequent developments, Rauscher's second qualifying statement was more appropriate. Warsaw saw in the favorable turn of events a means of seeking further assurances and hesitated to submit the expected long list of tariff concessions. Her reply of December 22 seemed entirely unsatisfactory to Berlin, as it was not sufficiently precise and fell short of the anticipated tariff reductions.[58]

Stresemann retained Hermes in his official post as chief negotiator as a sop to Germany's farming interests and conservative opinion but increasingly bypassed him by letting Rauscher, Ritter, and private citizens like Caro of the *Industrieverband* conduct a major share of the negotiations, sometimes even behind Hermes's back. Caro came to Warsaw in February 1929 to hold discussions with industrialists and government officials. Stresemann had wished him good luck on his trip and had hoped that his discussions would pave the way for a trade treaty between the two countries which "had to come to an understanding, not only economically but also politically."[59] In March, Ritter came to Warsaw to hear the Polish counterproposals to Germany's December offer. When the divided Warsaw Cabinet was unable to come forward with any clear proposal, Ritter withdrew his proposed concessions and left Warsaw convinced that his conciliatory negotiating tactics had been

[55] *Ibid.*, 112–20; *Twardowski Papers*, fol. 53, p. 121.
[56] Letter, Rauscher to Schubert, December 9, 1928, AA, RAM/1428/2945H/D573 769–74.
[57] Letter, Rauscher to Schubert, December 22, 1928, AA, StS/2224/4483H/E095 102–6.
[58] Note by Ritter, January 25, 1929, *ibid.*, 147–48.
[59] Letter, Stresemann to Caro, February 10, 1929, *Twardowski Papers*, fol. 54, pp. 41–42.

wrong and that Hermes's hard-line approach was the only way to deal with the Poles.[60]

Ritter's negative experience in Warsaw was largely a reflection of the internal divisions which prevailed in Poland. In November 1928, Prime Minister Bartel had met with a group of Polish industrialists to win them over to the government's policy of concluding a trade treaty with Germany. Their response had been negative. In the opinion of industrialists like Wierzbicki, the creation of new industries in Poland and the construction of the port of Gdynia were based on the policy of restricting German imports and they could not see any gains in the proposed treaty with Germany. Others were inclined to tolerate a *modus vivendi* or small trade agreement if it had political advantages and would help Polish agriculture.[61]

On January 22, 1929, the Cabinet met in a secret session to discuss the recent German proposals and to review the entire question of German–Polish trade relations. Kwiatkowski gave a detailed summary of the recent history of trade relations and negotiations with Germany. In his estimate, Germany had miscalculated when she had expected the Polish economy to collapse as the result of the trade war. Poland, too, had committed errors, such as failing to conclude an economic agreement while the economic clauses of the Versailles treaty were still in force. The trade war had not been without advantages to Poland, since it had stimulated the growth of Polish industry, diversified her markets and expanded her maritime trade. But in the net balance a trade treaty would be advantageous to Poland because it would increase her exports by some 500 million złotys. He would, therefore, urge that an agreement with Germany be concluded. Kwiatkowski was backed in this position by the ministers of Finance, Agriculture, and Foreign Affairs. Piłsudski, too, supported the treaty, although with some reservations. He insisted that the interests of Polish industry be taken into consideration in lowering tariffs and that there should be no return to the erstwhile position of complete dependence on German markets. He would prefer not to accord MFN treatment to Germany, if this could be avoided, and he reminded the Cabinet that Poland had emerged as victor in the trade war and that

---

[60] Letter, Rumbold to Sargent, April 24, 1929, FO, 371/13633, pp. 2–3.

[61] AMSZ, P II, W. 25, t. 2; cited in Jerzy Krasuski, *Stosunki polsko-niemieckie, 1926–1932* (Poznań, 1964), II, pp. 120–22. In the opinion of Sir William Erskine, Bartel himself had initially been opposed to the conclusion of a trade treaty with Germany, but he had changed his views and had brought the other ministers into line with his new approach. (Erskine to Chamberlain, March 6, 1929, FO, 371/13633, p. 181.

this position of strength should be reflected in the terms of the final agreement. Otherwise he had no objections.[62]

One of the persistent misfortunes in the German–Polish trade negotiations was their absolute inability to synchronize their respective timing, with the result that when one party offered concessions and pressed for a positive advance, the other side stalled and listed reservations. From November 1928 to April 1929 Germany had made significant concessions and had promoted a positive settlement in the face of Warsaw's dilatory tactics, but when the latter presented her counterproposals on tariff concessions in April and May, Berlin accorded them a reserved reception.

During the protracted shuffle for position, the most favorable circumstances for a far-reaching agreement had been missed. As Germany commenced her spiral fall into economic depression which made itself most noticeably felt in the agrarian sector, the initial momentum for an extensive trade treaty subsided. On July 2 the Cabinet had agreed to send Hermes to Warsaw early in August for a continuous round of negotiations for a period of four to five weeks.[63] But the agricultural situation deteriorated so drastically over the summer months that the *Reichstag* felt compelled to adopt considerable protective tariffs on agrarian products and, under the pretext of the Chancellor's illness and the absence of several ministers, negotiations were postponed for another month. When Lipski saw the counsellor of the German legation, von Rintelen, the latter had to confess that the German agrarian tariffs had upset the whole basis for a trade treaty.[64] In the meeting of the German Cabinet of September 17, it was decided that the present agrarian crisis excluded the possibility of an extensive trade agreement. But in an effort to bring the economic war to a standstill and to facilitate settlement on the liquidation issue, it was decided to propose a provisional agreement reminiscent of the 1927 Stresemann–Jackowski Protcol.[65] The Cabinet

[62] *PPRM*, 46 (1929), January 22, 1929, pp. 97–100.

[63] Note by Eisenlohr, August 2, 1929, AA, RAM/1428/2945H/D574 127–30. Earlier that year, Raucher had complained to Stresemann that talks would have to be held on a more continuous basis. Hermes's practice of confining negotiations to mere guest appearances in Warsaw, with a stop-watch in his hand, were not apt to produce any positive results, especially in Poland where time was not money (AA, StS/2224/4483H/E095 262–72; May 11, 1929).

[64] Memorandum, Lipski, July 7, 1929, *Twardowski Papers*, fol. 55, p. 4.

[65] Memorandum, Eisenlohr, September 27, 1929, AA, StS/2224/4473H/E095 447–49. The Cabinet decision to resume negotiations was in line with the promise which Stresemann had given Zaleski at Geneva earlier that month. Zaleski was sensitive to the humiliation of being kept in perpetual suspense about German intentions

also accepted Hilferding's proposal to entrust negotiations for a de facto provisional agreement to the Foreign Ministry rather than to Hermes. This decision so infuriated Hermes that he tendered his resignation to the Chancellor in a letter which bristled with accusations against the apparently treacherous behavior of the Foreign Ministry.[66]

THE TRADE TREATY OF 1930: A GENERAL ASSESSMENT

It is ironic that after five years of unsuccessful negotiations, a trade agreement was finally signed at a time when economic conditions were particularly unfavorable. This proves convincingly that despite considerable obstacles, far-reaching agreements in the economic and other spheres of activity could have been realized if the real will for such an agreement had existed. With the elimination of Hermes, one of the predominant obstacles to the cause of economic agreement had been removed, and Rauscher, who had been entrusted with the negotiations, redeemed his earlier pledge that he could arrange for an agreement within six months. Negotiations proceeded continuously and privately, thus avoiding much of the press clamor, the detrimental effects of which Rauscher, as a former journalist and press chief, knew well. By adopting a business-like bargaining technique and by applying his negotiating skills as much toward Berlin as toward Warsaw, successfully bolstering Germany's concessions while clipping Poland's demands, Rauscher made rapid progress. For once, negotiations left the façade of routine, hollow play-acting and rococo-style notes between delegation heads and assumed a realistic stance and a sincere determination to come to a positive solution. In his efforts, Rauscher not only enjoyed the confidence of the Polish government but also the backing of Stresemann and, after the latter's death, of Curtius.

On September 26, Rauscher informed Twardowski that he had been authorized to conclude a "small" trade treaty, but that this could not include a contingent for pigs, otherwise it would be a comprehensive treaty, which was unacceptable to Germany at this time. Twardowski in-

---

on the trade treaty, and at a Cabinet session on August 3 he had supported the suggestion of his envoy in Berlin, Knoll, to break off negotiations and to impose maximal tariffs against Germany. Briand, too, had told Zaleski, smilingly, that Germany would never agree to a treaty unless Poland resorted to retaliatory maximal duties (*Twardowski Papers*, fol. 55, p. 44).

[66] Letter, Hermes to Chancellor Müller, September 25, 1929, AA, StS/2224/ 4473H/E095 542–46.

sisted on the formula: "no pigs, no treaty," although the Warsaw Cabinet had resolved in favor of a mini-treaty, even if this did not include pigs.[67] But Twardowski was careful not to let Rauscher know that a treaty without a hog contingent would be acceptable.

The last hurdle was cleared at a meeting of their delegations and economic experts at Geneva in January 1930. At that meeting the *Reichsverband der Industrie*, which had a particular stake in the positive outcome of the negotiations, gave Poland a private guarantee that if the German market failed to absorb the full meat contingent as stipulated by the treaty, the *Reichsverband*, on its own, would privately purchase the difference at market prices. The guarantee had a moral-political rather than a binding legal character.[68]

The treaty itself was concluded on March 17, 1930. It represented a *modus vivendi* effort according to the principles of the Stresemann–Jackowski Protocol. It contained no tariff-binding provisions, as both sides wanted to reserve the weapon of tariff protection in face of the mounting economic crisis. The body of the treaty contained an agreement on the question of entry, sojourn, and settlement of their respective nationals; a promise to accord most-favored-nation treatment in their tariff policy and the corollary stipulation that import and export prohibitions would apply only insofar as they were applied to all nations. Furthermore, Poland granted most-favored-nation treatment for shipping Polish emigrants; also free transit of all goods, except war materiel or goods violating rules of public security and hygiene, was arranged. In the treaty annexes, Germany extended to Poland import quotas for 320,000 tons of coal per month and 275,000 pigs per year (to be increased to 350,000 over the next 30 months), either in the form of slaughtered pigs to designated meat packing plants or living pigs to seaport slaughterhousees. In addition, Germany lifted her export prohibition on scrap iron. Poland, in turn, extended to Germany a varied list of import quotas on semi-finished and manufactured goods.[69]

In Germany the treaty, to which Rauscher's labor and diligence had given belated delivery, earned the warm praise of industrialist circles and of his Socialist colleagues, who regarded it as an instrument for Ger-

---

[67] Summary of the Cabinet decision of September 25, 1929, *Twardowski Papers*, fol. 55, p. 59. Niezabytowski, the minister of agriculture, was the only member of the Cabinet who objected to this decision.

[68] AA, RAM/1429/2945H/D574 648; *Twardowski Papers*, fol. 56, pp. 3–11.

[69] For a complete text of the treaty, see Reichstag, *Sten. Berichte, Anlagen*, 442, no. 2138, pp. 1–84.

many's economic recovery and for improved relations with Poland. At
the same time it was abused and criticized by agrarian interests and political parties of the Right.[70] In Poland it elicited less controversy. Kwiatkowski held a press conference in which he underlined the benefits which
the treaty would bring to Polish commerce and to the producers of raw
materials. Commenting on the Minister's exposition, *Gazeta Polska* of
March 19, 1930, called the trade treaty a turning point in the economic
revival of Central Europe, and hoped that it would bolster international
confidence in the Polish economy and thus assist in attracting German
and other foreign credits.[71]

There is no doubt that the responsibility for the tense atmosphere
during the negotiations and the five-year delay, just as the outbreak of
the trade war itself, lay on both sides. No one could be a more qualified
judge of this than the respective negotiators, Rauscher and Twardowski,
each of whom was frequently more exasperated with the position of his
own government and national interest groups than with that of the opposing delegation. Nevertheless, the burden of responsibility was un-
evenly distributed. The agreement meant relatively less to the German
than to the Polish economy, and it is therefore not surprising that, on the
whole, Germany was less committed to the idea of an economic settlement than Poland. Moreover, too many Germans, both within and outside the government, subscribed to the misconceived idea that the Polish economy would collapse in the event of a trade war and that
Germany would then be placed in a position where she could dictate an
economic agreement and exact political concessions as well. Only around
1927, when the resilience of the Polish economy had been clearly demonstrated, did German calculations become more realistic. By that time
Stresemann had become convinced of the necessity of a trade agreement

[70] The conservative *Kreuz-Zeitung* of March 23, 1930, called the treaty a fundamental error and lamented the fact that Hermes, who had represented Germany's
interests—the agrarian interests and Germany's national interests were treated as
being synonymous—with such skill and energy, had been replaced by Rauscher, whose
only concern had been with bringing about an agreement *à tout prix* in order to secure
for himself the undersecretaryship in the Foreign Ministry. *Unsere Partei*, the DNVP
organ, in its issue of March 15, 1930, called the agreement "treason against Germany's
East" and the ruin of agriculture in East Germany.

[71] A very lucid analysis of German–Polish trade relations and a positive evaluation of the effects of the trade treaty appeared in the March 29, 1930, issue of *Polska
Gospodarcza* (pp. 551–52), the most prestigious Polish economic journal. It had
been written by M. Sokolowski, a member of the Polish delegation that had negotiated the treaty.

with Warsaw, both for its economic gains and as a means of lending credibility to his conciliatory policy in the West. As we have seen, Stresemann had threatened to resign unless the government agreed to negotiate along the lines of the protocol which he had concluded with Jackowski in November 1927. Given Stresemann's position after 1927, there was at least a firm determination in the government in favor of completing an agreement. In fact, the last document which Stresemann signed on October 2, 1929, two hours before his tragically early death, was a draft proposal for the German–Polish trade treaty.[72] Berlin continued to make mistakes after 1927 with respect to tactics, timing, the choice of concessions and, most of all, in the choice of Hermes as negotiator, but these were tactical miscalculations not a fundamental error of policy as before 1927.

Poland's principal error had been her failure to avoid the trade war in the first place, at a time when Germany was still bound to the provisions of the Versailles treaty and the Geneva Convention and was not averse to the idea of an economic treaty that would grant her reciprocity, which she was denied under the former agreements. Then most of 1927 and half of 1928 had been lost because of Poland's eviction measures and the border decree that had been instigated by the Ministries of Interior and War against the warnings of her economic negotiators. Men like Zaleski and Kwiatkowski had loyally and consistently applied themselves in favor of an economic treaty, but Piłsudski had displayed little interest in it and Bartel had initially opposed it; consequently, both Knoll and Twardowski found reason to complain of a general lack of direction and a tendency to drift on the side of their government. Knoll remonstrated with Wysocki that he was flooded with contradictory instructions and urged the government to make up its mind what it really wanted.[73] In a spirit of philosophical resignation, the gentle and sophisticated Twardowski prepared a roster of sins which his government had committed—one of his folders of critical notes he even called his "Black Book." Twardowski noted that many people had made difficulties during the negotiations, too many had tried to get their fingers into the pie, but very few had helped. Polish industry had been opposed, her farmers had been inactive, the government, until the final phase, passive and skeptical, and Polish foreign policy in general had been characterized by lack of discipline.[74]

---

[72] *Twardowski Papers*, fol. 55, p. 62.
[73] Letter, Knoll to Wysocki, May 30, 1929, *ibid.*, fol. 54, pp. 230–32.
[74] Twardowski's undated resumé of negotiations, *ibid.*, fol. 59, pp. 281–84.

All too often he had been unable to discern any united government stand
on the proposed trade treaty. There were many other smaller matters
which had impeded negotiations. Knoll had tried to be helpful, but his
intervention had been too sporadic and his behavior too erratic to be of
use. During most of the negotiations the post of commercial counsellor
in Berlin had remained vacant, which had created an unfortunate information gap. The Polish press had made matters difficult, especially
their attacks on the person of Hermes; also the renewal of liquidations
in 1929 and the arrest of the German minority leader Ulitz in Upper
Silesia had impaired progress. Just when he was negotiating a veterinary
convention, a report had been sent to the *Sejm* which depicted Polish
veterinary conditions in the worst possible light. Only by a miracle had
this report not fallen into German hands. Twardowski also complained
that when he had asked for an audience with Piłsudski, he had not even
received an answer. All these factors had made negotiations enormously
complicated and tedious, but he admitted that during the last year of
negotiations the difficulties and impediments had been an exception and
no longer the rule.[75]

Just as the burden of responsibility for the failure to reach an agreement at a much earlier date rested with both sides—but with a larger
weight falling on Germany—so also the losses created by the trade war
affected both sides. The losses were not only material but also political,
for the economic conflict constituted a missed opportunity to realize
common economic interests and to help create a bridge in the sphere of
political activities. But within this category of losses, Poland suffered less
in relative terms and might thus be regarded as the winner in this protracted conflict. As the weaker of the two economies, Poland's ability to
sustain Germany's retaliatory economic measures was in itself a considerable achievement. The partial loss of the German market for her raw
materials and agricultural products, and the consequent decline in the
role of German manufactured goods, credits and technical and entre-
preneurial know-how, forced the Polish economy in rather brutal shot-
gun style to rely more on its own skills and resources, to diversify its trade
patterns, to reorient its trade routes, and to accelerate the pace of industrialization. As a result the Polish economy was considerably better bal-
anced and less dependent on Germany at the conclusion of the trade
treaty than it had been at the outset of the trade war in 1925. (In 1924,

[75] *Ibid.*, fol. 65, pp. 2–25.

34.5 per cent of Poland's total imports had come from Germany; by 1930 this figure had declined to 27 per cent. During the same period exports to Germany had decreased from 43.2 per cent to 25.8 per cent of Poland's total exports.) The process of industrialization and the diversification of trade patterns was bound to occur under any circumstances, but it derived much of its original impetus and accelerating force from the economic conflict with Germany. In the same manner, the conscious effort of the Polish authorities to foster maritime trade preceded the economic war but found support and justification in its subsequent occurrence.

The attempt to restructure as much of Poland's trade as possible from its continental East–West pattern to a North–South axis, which would more fully exploit the possibilities for maritime commerce, was primarily designed to free the Polish economy from its dependence on Germany. The creation of a merchant fleet, the ambitious construction of the port of Gdynia, "preferential tariffs for seaports and railways, transmarine privileges, bounties on exports, rebates on customs, differential freight rates, and the like were made operative to achieve this end."[76] German and even neutral observers were quick to criticize this effort to reorient the existing trade channels and emphasized that the more profitable trade would be with Poland's industrial neighbors in the east and west and not with the less developed agrarian economies in the south. These critics also pointed out that Poland possessed 4,165 km. of continental boundaries against a maritime frontier of only 94 km. and that there were four railroad lines for an international East–West transit, as against only one such transit line on a North–South axis. Furthermore, the primary raw material sources were more closely located to the German markets than to the harbors on the Baltic Sea from where they were shipped abroad.[77]

The foliage of economic reasoning which Poland advanced to justify its maritime commerce and general trade reorientation had deep political roots. The aim was to escape economic, and with it also political, dependence on Germany. At the same time, it was realized in Warsaw that "a Poland which did not know how to utilize her access to the sea, how to harmonize foreign trade, and to free herself from the dependence on her

[76] Paul Douglass, *The Economic Independence of Poland: A Study in Trade Adjustments to Political Objectives* (Cincinnati, 1934), p. 101.

[77] Oswald Schneider, *Die Frage der wirtschaftlichen Unabhängigkeit Polens* (Königsberg, 1933), p. 15.

neighbors, would serve her enemies with the best proof that this access to the sea was of no necessity to her and that the sacrifice had been made in vain."[78]

THE ABORTIVE RATIFICATION PROCESS AND ITS CONSEQUENCES

It was extremely unfortunate for the future of German–Polish relations that the trade treaty, which had been negotiated with so much labor and to which so many expectations had been attached, was buried by an avalanche of negative economic developments. In the eyes of Poland, Germany's subsequent failure to ratify the treaty constituted a colossal monument of her neighbor's intransigence and duplicity, and it subverted the conciliatory functions of the treaty which its authors had tried to foster.

A heavy blow to the cause of ratification was dealt by the break-up of the Great Coalition under Chancellor Müller, toward the end of March. At that time unemployment in Germany had reached crisis dimensions and the Social Democratic party had forced the Chancellor and his other Socialist party colleagues to withdraw from the Cabinet in protest over a compromise plan on unemployment relief payments that seemed unacceptable to the Socialists because of the plan's orientation toward stringent economy. The withdrawal of the SPD, which was decided against the advice of Chancellor Müller, led to the fall of the government and marks the first milestone in the collapse of the Weimar Republic. Also, with the departure of Chancellor Müller and his Socialist colleagues, the government lost its strongest supporters for a trade treaty with Poland. In the new "Cabinet of personalities" under Brüning the post of minister of agriculture went to Schiele, an avowed opponent of the trade treaty with Poland.

Early in April 1930 the *Reichstag* imposed considerable tariff increases on farm products in an attempt to boost Germany's faltering agrarian sector. Zaleski instructed Knoll to inform Curtius that if these agrarian tariffs went into effect, the whole basis for the trade treaty would be upset and Poland would be unable to put it into operation.[79] In replying to Knoll's note of April 14, Curtius admitted that these emergency measures, which were inevitable under existing circumstances, would negatively affect Poland, but not to a degree where ratification would be

---

[78] F. Hilchen, *Żródła o rozwoju polskich portów* (Warsaw, 1928); cited in Jutta Rudershausen, *Die Polnische Seehandelspolitik* (Königsberg, 1936), p. 5.
[79] Telegram, Zaleski to Knoll, April 11, 1930, *Twardowski Papers*, fol. 55, p. 92.

placed in jeopardy.[80] During the May session of the League of Nations, Zaleski repeated his concern to Curtius and warned the German Foreign Minister that Poland would be forced to defer ratification until the exact effect of Germany's recent tariff measures could be clearly determined.[81]

Despite these reservations, Poland ratified the trade treaty in March 1931, together with the liquidation agreement. In Germany the *Reichsrat* approved it on May 28, 1930, by a vote of 40:25 with one abstention, and the *Reichstag* gave it first and second reading between June 25 and 27, where the treaty came under heavy fire from the parties of the Right. Brüning's miscalculated decision to dissolve the *Reichstag* made it impossible to proceed with the ratification at a time when a majority could still have been found for this purpose. The September elections were disastrous for the fate of the moderate political parties in Germany, as for the fate of democracy in general, because the gains went to the extremist groups on either side, in particular to the Nazis, who increased their membership in the *Reichstag* from an irritating presence of 12 delegates to an unruly and rowdy horde of 107 brownshirts. Despite this setback, Brüning and Curtius were still willing to submit the treaty for ratification if a suitable opportunity should present itself, but the timing had to be chosen carefully, lest the Nazi members prematurely return to the *Reichstag*.[82] But Brüning was plagued with other preoccupations and did not press for ratification with sufficient energy, and during the final agonies of the Weimar Republic the power constellation in the *Reichstag* never again produced a safe majority for the ratification of the agreement.

Not only did Germany default on the ratification of the trade treaty but she also refused to renew the timber agreement which had operated for the past three years, and in July 1931 she also withdrew from the joint rye agreement by which Germany and Poland had co-ordinated their foreign sales of rye over the past year.[83] Poland countered these moves by imposing retaliatory tariffs against German goods on December 31, 1931, a move that prompted Germany to establish supertariffs against those countries with which she had no trade treaty. This measure, which was

---

[80] Note, Curtius to Knoll, April 26, 1926, *ibid.*, p. 99.

[81] Note by Curtius, May 14, 1930, AA, RAM/1430/2945H/D575 055–58.

[82] In February, 1931, the Nazis had staged a temporary walk-out from the *Reichstag* in protest over changes of rules and procedures. On March 18, 1931, the Nazi press service announced that if the trade treaty were presented for ratification, the Nazi delegates would march into the *Reichstag*, vote against it and troop out again.

[83] P. Seraphim, *Die Handelspolitik Polens* (Berlin, 1935), p. 97.

particularly aimed against foreign dairy products, was all the more aggravating to Poland since it was Germany's failure to ratify the trade treaty
that placed Poland in this disadvantageous position in the first place.

On January 21, 1932, Helmut von Moltke, Rauscher's successor in
Warsaw, informed Zaleski that Chancellor Brüning wanted to regulate
trade relations with Poland by adjusting the terms of the trade treaty to
fit the new and less favorable economic situation. But the Polish government insisted that the treaty be ratified in its entirety, and Vice-Minister
Beck told the German diplomat that the existing economic crisis should
be resolved by mutual co-operation, not by retaliatory measures.[84] In an
attempt to prevent any further aggravation in German–Polish relations,
the Brüning government agreed to a compromise solution which was
arranged in a protocol signed by Zaleski and Moltke on March 26, 1932.
The protocol did not go all the way in putting into effect the terms of the
trade treaty, but in it Germany agreed to exempt Polish butter and eggs
and other farm products from the recent supertariffs, and Poland granted
contingents for German manufactured goods, thereby returning to the
situation which had existed in 1930.[85] Despite this ameliorating provision,
the economic deadlock was not fully broken until March 7, 1934, when
the Hitler regime and the Polish government agreed to abolish all retaliatory tariff measures and to let normal customs rates regulate their trade
relations.

The fate of the economic relations between Germany and Poland
intrinsically reflects their general relations at large. The failure in this
particular facet of their relations appears even more obvious and complete than the political failure to reach an understanding, for the concepts of economic complementarity and the desirability of economic co-
operation were more obvious and enjoyed the reinforcement of historical
precedent to a far greater degree than the broader concept of a fated
political community in Central Europe and the imperative for a political
understanding. But the most obvious failed, and the opportunity of engaging those material inducements which existed in an encompassing
economic rapprochement did not materialize. Hence, economic relations
between Germany and Poland, instead of serving as a nucleus for a more

---

[84] Deutsches Zentralarchiv Potsdam, *Auswärtiges Amt*, No. 66000; cited in
Krasuski, *Stosunki polsko-niemiecke*, II, p. 284.

[85] Seraphim, *Handelspolitik*, p. 97. In the opinion of Twardowski, Moltke
could claim the success of the agreement for himself. The Polish Foreign Ministry
favored the accord, as the export of butter and eggs would help Poland's balance of
payments situation (*Twardowski Papers*, fol. 69, pp. 1–6).

far-reaching political conciliation, joined the ranks of yet another in the long series of perpetual frictions and conflicts that separated the two countries. On both sides the idea of an extensive economic agreement was endorsed by their respective diplomatic authorities and was supported by the majority of their economic interest groups; yet economic minority opposition groups—agrarian interests in Germany and Poland's newly developing industry—successfully obstructed agreement by a strategy which interjected into the economic sphere the political animosities and thus converted their minority grievances into a majority cause. When Rauscher had effectively insulated economic negotiations from the general context of political disputes, he succeeded, where five years of negotiations had failed, in concluding an experimental economic agreement which was intended as a breakwater of peaceful accommodation within the sea of weltering animosities. Tragically, however, under the prevailing economic deterioration it was little more than an anachronism and its positive spill-over effect did not materialize. Before the economic agreement could be consummated, the brief interval which fate had allotted to Germany and Poland for accommodating themselves had elapsed. This applied equally to the total complex of their relations.

VIII

The Minority Question

NEXT TO THE REVISIONIST ISSUE, the closely related minority question was the most divisive and least negotiable factor in German–Polish relations during the Weimar period. Approximately one million persons were involved on either side. To represent these minority groups as nothing more than political pawns in an international territorial bargaining process would be a gross distortion and oversimplification of their complex structure and role. The history of these minority groups during the inter-war period provides a poignant document of the fate of people caught in the whirlpool of East European cultural diversity and by the more recent and consciously conducted policy of national assimilation and centralization that was practiced both in Warsaw and Berlin. It would go beyond the scope of this study to provide a history of the German and Polish minorities. All that is attempted here is to assess the direct effects of the minority question on German–Polish relations.[1]

Neither Germans nor Poles acquitted themselves with distinction

[1] A more detailed account of the minority question is found in the following: Richard Bahr, *Volk Jenseits der Grenzen* (Hamburg, 1933); Richard Breyer, *Das Deutsche Reich und Polen 1932–1937: Aussenpolitik und Volksgruppenfragen* (Würzburg, 1955); Theodor Bierschenk, *Die Deutsche Volksgruppe in Polen 1934–1939* (Kitzingen/Main, 1954); Mirosław Cygański, *Mniejszość niemiecka w Polsce centralnej w latach 1919–1939* (Łódź, 1962); Otto Heike, *Das Deutschtum in Polen, 1918–1939* (Bonn, 1955); Stephan Horak, *Poland and Her National Minorities, 1919–1939* (New York, 1961); Hermann Rauschning, *Die Entdeutschung West-preussens und Posens* (Berlin, 1930); Alojzy Targ, "Zarys Działalności Związku Po-laków w Niemczech," *Przegląd Zachodni* 18 (1962): 227–63; Wojciech Wrzesiń-ski, "Geneza Związku Polaków w Niemczech," *Przegląd Zachodni*, 18 (1962): 264–86. Dealing specifically with the minorities in Upper Silesia are Paul van Husen, *Das*

in the treatment of their respective minorities; tolerance, fairness, and magnanimity remained the great exceptions and not a standard measure of conduct. The exact forms of discrimination and chicaneries differed somewhat between the two sides. In Germany, where the Polish minority was not a significant domestic political factor nor a foreign policy threat, the discrimination was more unplanned and unofficial than in Poland and took the form of exploitation by employers and landlords. The initial failure of the Prussian government to provide educational and cultural facilities for the Polish minority tended to perpetuate their socially and economically deprived status. The Polish authorities pursued a more specific policy that sought to reduce the domestic influence and the international impact of the German minority by hastening the process of de-Germanization, especially in the regained territories. The key issues of dispute were over minority schools and property rights. If the German practice was one of continuing the cultural and economic deprivation of the Polish minority group, Poland's policy was one of dispossessing the German minority. The Versailles treaty with its liquidation, citizenship, and optant provisions offered a welcome opportunity to evict German nationals or to deprive them of their property and livelihood. Warsaw availed itself of this opportunity and, as we saw in the case of Chorzów and the colonists, enforced these provisions with such a rigor that it violated the treaty stipulations. The de-Germanization measures took on an even more open political note with the abolition of such political organizations as the *Deutschtumsbund* in 1923 and the trial of several of its leaders and of the head of the Upper Silesian *Volksbund* some seven years later. The de-Germanization aims were not just hatched in a clandestine manner but were openly supported by much of the Polish press and resounded in declarations by government officials. In a two-minute audience which he gave to a group of expropriated *Domänenpächter*, Prime Minister Witos admitted that this was "the first strike against the

---

Minderheitenrecht in Oberschlesien: die Stellungnahmen des Präsidenten der Gemischten Komission in der Zeit von Juni 1922 bis Juni 1929 (Berlin, 1930); Friedrich Heye, Die Tätigkeit des internationalen Gerichtshofs mit besonderer Würdigung der deutschen Minderheitenfrage in Polen (Ochsenfurt, 1930); Kurt Junckersdorff, ed., Das Schulrecht der Deutschen Minderheit in Polnisch Oberschlesien nach dem Genfer Abkommen (Berlin, 1930); and Julius Stone, Regional Guarantees of Minority Rights; A Study of Minorities Procedure in Upper Silesia (New York, 1933). For the role of the League of Nations in the minority question, see Julius Stone, International Guarantees of Minority Rights; Procedure of the Control of the League of Nations in Theory and Practice (London, 1932); F. P. Walters, A History of the League of Nations (2nd ed.; London, 1960), pp. 396–412.

German intelligentsia and that it was high time that the so-called bearers of German culture disappear."[2] In April 1923, Prime Minister Sikorski voiced similar sentiments in a speech in Poznań:

> The de-Germanization process ought to be completed in as rapid a tempo as possible and Poland's previous vascillation regarding the liquidation question should be altered radically. This action the . . . government will carry out in the course of this year. German optants will have to draw the consequence of their option.[3]

THE POLISH MINORITY IN GERMANY

The Polish minority population in Germany consisted of approximately one million persons. According to the 1925 census, 214,115 persons gave Polish as their mother language. If one included under the Polish quota the 507,721 who listed both German and Polish as their mother tongues, as well as those who spoke the Mazurian dialect, the total number in 1925 came to 802,924. The real figure was probably somewhat higher.[4] This number compares closely with the Polish estimate of 884,105 members of the German minority in Poland in 1927.[5]

This statistical similarity belies the enormous differences that existed between the two minority groups with respect to their political role and the social and economic conditions under which they lived. The Polish minority in Germany constituted little more than 1 per cent of the total population and existed in virtual isolation, as the size of the other minority groups in Germany was negligible. Its role in German domestic politics was insignificant. Until 1928 two of its representatives sat in the Prussian Assembly but even they lost their seats in the 1928 elections and it never managed to get one of its candidates elected to the *Reichstag*. Compared to this, the German minority made up over 3 per cent of the total population of Poland and formed part of a wider conglomeration of non-Polish ethnic groups which accounted for almost one-third of the total population. The German minority always succeeded in electing representatives to the *Sejm* and Senate; the highest number was reached in

---

[2] Cited in Rauschning, *Die Entdeutschung Westpreussens*, p. 60.

[3] AA, RAM/1425/2945H/D570 890.

[4] AA, RAM/1430/2945H/D575 458.

[5] Z. Stoliński, "Liczba i rozmieszczenie Niemców w Polsce," *Sprawy Narodowościowe* no. 4 (1927): 379; cited in Jerzy Krasuski, *Stosunki polsko-niemieskie, 1919–1925* (Poznań, 1962), I, p. 308.

the 1928 elections, when twenty-one of its candidates were elected to the *Sejm* (nineteen for the minority bloc and two as part of the PPS) and five to the Senate. The German delegates formed a key part of the minority bloc which held eighty-nine *Sejm* seats after the 1928 elections and thus constituted a force of some consequence in Polish domestic politics. Not only was the German minority politically more conscious and more actively engaged in domestic politics than its counterpart in Germany, but it was also a more significant factor in international politics. By virtue of Poland's adherence to the international Minority Treaty, the League of Nations was drawn into the complaints of the German minority and thus gave them international prominence. Still more important was Germany's policy of territorial revisionism in the east, which found stimulus and support in the existence of a sizable German population in Poland. Germany's revisionism found no counterpart in the foreign policy of Poland. If there was any target of Polish territorial revisionism, it was East Prussia, but here the aim was special international status rather than outright annexation.

The Polish minority also differed from the German with respect to its geographical distribution and economic and social structure. While the latter was geographically concentrated in the frontier regions which had formerly been part of the German *Reich*, the Polish minority was far more scattered throughout Germany. There was one important pocket in German Upper Silesia, another in the Berlin metropolitan area, and still another in the coal-mining region of the Ruhr. The great majority of Poles in Germany belonged to the working class and stood on a par with the poorest German workers and peasants. A high proportion of the German minority in Poland, on the other hand, consisted of landowners, rich farmers, industrialists, and skilled workers, and thus generally enjoyed an economically preferred status with their Polish neighbors despite their minority position.

The combination of political apathy, economic and cultural deprivation, and geographic fragmentation of the Polish minority made it extremely difficult to organize this group for the purpose of common political and economic action. After World War I, several regional Polish organizations emerged in Germany, the most important of which were the Committee for Poles in Berlin, which covered the east-Elbian region, the Union of Poles in East Prussia, which was located in Allenstein, and the Polish Executive Committee in Bochum which included the Polish minority in Westphalia and the Ruhr. Despite certain rivalries and regional diversities, in August 1922 these associations managed to unite into a single organization, the Union of Poles in Germany [*Związek Polaków w Niemczech*] which was headed by Count Sierakowski and after 1931 by the prelate Domański. The organization, which was in close contact with the Polish government and with private Polish organizations, strove to improve the economic conditions of the Polish minority, to win for them full rights of citizenship and unhindered legal protection, to put up candidates for German elections and to co-operate with the other minority groups in Germany—Friesians, Danes, and Lusatians. The principal activity of the *Związek Polaków* lay in the educational and cultural sphere and was designed to preserve the particular linguistic and cultural identity of the minority group by advocating the establishment of schools or classes in the Polish language and by sponsoring and co-ordinating the activities of cultural organizations, clubs, and sports associations. The Union of Poles published the monthly journal *Polak w Niemczech*. In addition, a number of daily newspapers were published in the Polish language, but few of these had a circulation of more than 3,000. The most important dailies were the *Gazeta Olstyńska* in East Prussia, the *Dziennik Berlinski* in Berlin, and *Naród* in Herne/Westphalia. In Upper Silesia there appeared the *Katolik Codzienny* (Beuthen), and *Nowiny Codzienne* (Oppeln), and *Dziennik Ratiborski*. The German Foreign Ministry found frequent occasion to complain about the hostile tone of the Polish minority press.[6]

Since Germany was not signatory to the international minorities treaties she was not obliged to make provisions for minority schools, other than in Upper Silesia. The Polish minority therefore profited greatly when the Prussian government, under Otto Braun on December 31, 1928, passed the Decree for the Regulation of the School System for the Polish Minority. The decree allowed teachers to be hired from Poland to teach Polish. It also made provision for the establishment of Polish private schools in Prussia, which were entitled to government subsidies covering up to 60 per cent of their teachers' salaries; furthermore, upon the request of the parents or guardians of at least forty children, these private Polish elementary schools might be transformed into public schools. The decree also contained the important provision that each citizen had the full right to decide on purely subjective grounds [*Minderheit ist wer will*] whether he or his children belonged to a minority, regardless of his linguistic, religious, or ethnic background, a decision

---

[6] Memorandum, January 8, 1931, AA, RAM/1430/2945H/D575 469–79.

which the authorities could neither challenge nor investigate.[7] As a result of the Prussian Minority School decree the number of students who received instruction in Polish rose sharply. Within two years, 54 Polish private minority schools had been established in Prussia, employing 74 teachers, 67 of whom were Polish citizens, and giving instruction to 1,758 students. In Upper Silesia 27 public minority schools with 27 teachers and 334 students were kept in operation and 652 Polish-speaking teachers were available to teach Polish and religion in German schools.[8] Kaspar Mayr estimated that in January 1930 a total of 5,872 children in Germany were receiving Polish language instruction in private and public schools.[9]

The Prussian government, including the Socialist Prime Minister Braun, had initially been extremely reluctant to tolerate and actively support the establishment of Polish minority schools, but they had been persuaded of its necessity in order to strengthen the Foreign Ministry's hand in protecting the rights of the German minority abroad. In a memorandum to the Cabinet on January 13, 1925, Stresemann had emphasized the necessity of pursuing an economic and propagandistic policy—power-political aid was as good as out of the question—which would give the fullest protection to the German minority groups abroad. This, however, made it imperative that Germany accord to all minorities within her own territory all those rights which she demanded for her own nationals abroad. The gradual revision of the eastern frontier provisions of the Versailles and Geneva dictates, Stresemann concluded, was the goal of Germany's foreign policy; however, the population structure in these areas was such that any revision would automatically bring foreign nationality groups under German rule. It should be evident that the resistance to a revision by international opinion would be considerably reduced, once it was known that "the fullest cultural freedom would be guaranteed and indeed allowed in practice to each national minority within the borders of the *Reich*."[10]

It was only natural that the Polish government should concern itself with the fate of its minority in Germany. In the first place, it was a per-

---

[7] Otto Braun, *Von Weimar zu Hitler* (New York, 1940), pp. 337–38. The emphasis on a purely subjective minority interpretation was doubtlessly inserted with the intention to fortify the German position in the Upper Silesian school dispute that had been raging since 1926.

[8] AA, RAM/1430/2945H/D575 479.

[9] Kaspar Mayr, *Ist die Verständigung zwischen Polen und Deutschland unmöglich?* (Vienna, 1931), p. 31.

[10] Stresemann Papers, FO, 520/7415H; cited in Christian Höltje, *Die Weimarer Republik und das Ost-Locarno Problem, 1919–1934* (Würzburg, 1958), pp. 102–4.

sonal and human concern and a feeling of responsibility for their ethnic brothers abroad. Whenever the German minority lodged a complaint with the League of Nations, Poland found a useful argument in pointing out the far from satisfactory condition of the Polish minority in Germany. In addition, the existence of a Polish minority in Germany showed that the German minority problem was not unique and thus weakened Germany's territorial claims, which rested substantially on the argument that her minority group in Poland should be rejoined with the fatherland. Finally, there was the long-range prospect of bringing about a change of status in East Prussia by means of mobilizing the local Polish and Mazurian minorities in that area.

In 1924 the head of the Western Division of the Polish Foreign Ministry, Potworowski, produced a lengthy memorandum which sheds important light on Poland's policy toward the Polish minority in Germany in the wider context of German–Polish relations. The memorandum is of particular significance, for its guidelines on relations with Germany were subsequently reflected in the foreign policy of Skrzyński and Zaleski, just as its prescriptions for dealing with the Polish minority in Germany coincided to a large extent with the policy which was adopted in actual practice. In retrospect it is difficult to disentangle the causal linkages: whether Potworowski's· views exercised a major influence on shaping foreign and minority policy, or whether he merely skillfully identified himself with the prevailing opinion in the Foreign Ministry, or whether he was just lucky in having accurately anticipated the trend of future policy.

Regarding the German minority in Poland, Potworowski distinguished between those who were Polish citizens and those who had retained their German nationality. Poland should cautiously rid herself of the latter as far as possible by liquidating their property and by evicting as many as possible whenever plausible reasons could be given. As for the former, he advised that a *modus vivendi* be reached with them which would transform them into loyal Polish subjects and reduce the influence which Berlin exerted over them. Germany's revisionist policy strove to demonstrate that co-operation between Poland and her German minority was impossible, and Berlin used this argument in order to get international control over the ceded areas, to be followed by their outright return to Germany. Her case would suffer a serious blow if it could in fact be demonstrated that collaboration between the Polish state and those members of the German minority who held Polish citizenship was feasible.

The second part of Potworowski's memorandum dealt with the

Polish minority in Germany. Here he distinguished between three different categories. First, there were those Poles who were scattered throughout Germany. These brought little advantage to their motherland. There was nothing Poland could do to help them and they would soon be entirely Germanized. In the meantime, their existence only gave rise to unfortunate incidents. It would, therefore, be wise to encourage them to return to their homeland. Second, there were the Polish settlements along the frontier and in German Upper Silesia. With respect to this category, Polish policy should be defensive: to provide the aid necessary to retain this group at its present strength. Third, there was the Polish and related Slavic element in East Prussia, and with respect to this region her policy should take an offensive character. In the long-run, the existing situation in East Prussia was untenable. Either its status would be changed—not necessarily in the form of annexation but by severing it from the rest of Germany—or Poland would lose the "Corridor." Poland should, therefore, seek to organize and aid the Polish population in Warmia. A different policy would have to be adopted toward the Mazurians who were ethnically Polish but spiritually German. The Mazurians should, therefore, first be mobilized for separatism and only then enlisted for the Polish cause. This would take a long time but the success of this formula had been tested in Upper Silesia over the preceding 100 years.[11]

The Polish minority base in East Prussia, on which Warsaw's offensive policy centered, was not very strong, as the plebiscite had revealed. And as Potworowski realized, the support of the Mazurians for Poland's ambitious scheme had first to be won by patient and long labor. This offensive approach, which sought to increase Polish influence in East Prussia with the aim of arranging some sort of separate international status for that province, itself stemmed from a defensive conception that sought to protect the "Corridor" against revisionist attempts by Germany. The more ambitious notion of an outright annexation of East Prussia by Poland was a historical reminiscence, a colorful dream, but not part of a concrete program of any Polish government at that time.

Following the 1920 plebiscite many Poles had left East Prussia and had thus further weakened the Polish element in that region. The pronounced social and economic cleavages between the remaining Polish workers and landowners in East Prussia further complicated the task of

[11] Memorandum, Potworowski, August 6, 1924, AMSZ, P II, fol. 4613, pp. 32–46.

the Polish consular representatives in East Prussia in enlisting the Polish minority in a common front that would support Warsaw's foreign policy objectives. Despite these complications, Srokowski, the Polish consul in Königsberg, had been optimistic that the Upper Silesian plebiscite might help bring about an advantageous solution in East Prussia. No other part of Germany had as many linguistic, cultural, religious, and economic cleavages as East Prussia and, in the opinion of Srokowski, Poland could exploit these to her advantage. The solution which he envisaged was an independent East Prussian republic under international guarantee from the Entente and Poland. Such a solution would be welcomed by the Polish workers in East Prussia, since it would lower food prices, but it would meet with opposition from the ranks of the Polish landowners of the province.[12] In 1923 Srokowski praised the energy of his Vice Consul who had helped found a Mazurian bi-weekly paper which was aimed at the pro-Polish sector of the Mazurian population. But, in his own estimate, Srokowski felt that it would be a better strategy to begin by awakening the Mazurians' own national consciousness and thus to create a separatist movement in East Prussia. For this purpose the Mazurians should be persuaded to put forward their own candidate for the next *Reichstag* elections. Only in the second stage should the Mazurians be encouraged to seek intimate ties with Poland.[13] In addition to her policy of encouraging Mazurian separatism, Poland took an offensive position with regard to East Prussia by boycotting Königsberg as a harbor and by refusing to purchase East Prussian forestry products. During the Ruhr crisis, Poland had also prevented the export of coal to East Prussia. These measures were undertaken in retaliation to the violently anti-Polish sentiments in East Prussia and as a means of underlining the need for close economic ties with Poland. The result was somewhat counterproductive, for it merely intensified the anti-Polish feeling in that province, and by inflicting losses on the East Prussian economy the Polish minority also suffered.

In 1928 Staniewicz, the new consul in Königsberg, criticized the previous policy of economic strangulation of East Prussia which had been initiated during Srokowski's tenure as consul. These hostile measures, which had been intended only for temporary application, had become

---

[12] Report, Srokowski, March 23, 1921, AMSZ, P II, fol. 4493. A Foreign Ministry marginal note questioned how the Upper Silesian plebiscite could help bring about a solution in East Prussia.

[13] Report, Srokowski, February 13, 1923, *ibid.*

frozen and had not been matched by any real political program. The result had been an increase in German economic aid to East Prussia and a decline of Polish influence in that province. Staniewicz felt that the time had come to reverse this trend. Poland should reestablish direct economic ties with East Prussia, rather than deal only through Berlin, and establish Polish business enterprises in the area.[14] But neither the strategy of boycott nor the return to more relaxed economic relations after 1928 had any impact in fostering a separatist movement in East Prussia.

The determined effort by Polish consular officials to sponsor Polish minority candidates in the 1928 elections to the *Reichstag* and the Prussian *Landtag* was also not successful. In 1928 the Polish Foreign Ministry made available 408,000 marks to finance the election campaign of Polish candidates to the *Reichstag* and the Prussian legislature and to help organize the general political activities of her minority in Germany.[15] Babiński noted that the best way to counteract Germany's revisionist claims was by drawing attention to the sizable Polish minority which still remained in Germany. The visible evidence of this would be provided if Polish minority candidates were elected to the *Reichstag* and to the Prussian assembly. Babiński was optimistic that with adequate financial backing from Poland a favorable election result could be achieved.[16] Despite these optimistic forecasts and the spirited campaign which the Polish minority leaders had launched, none of the thirteen Polish candidates for the *Reichstag* or the twelve candidates for the Prussian *Landtag* were elected. The post-mortem analysis which was conducted by the Foreign Ministry was more realistic than Babiński's optimistic predictions. It was realized that the key problem lay in the lack of political awareness by the Polish minority. Their concern was more with social and economic than with political and nationalistic issues and, consequently, their vote tended to go to the Socialists and Communists and not to the minority candidates. There was agreement that Poland had miscalculated by stressing questions of nationality and religion at the expense of economic and social problems. It was also concluded that the effort should not disperse itself but should concentrate on East Prussia and Upper Silesia and that it required continued political activity and

[14] Memorandum, Staniewicz, February 28, 1928, AMSZ, P II, fol. 4636, pp. 6–18.
[15] Memorandum, Lipski, February 16, 1928, AMSZ, P II, fol. 4513, pp. 22–26.
[16] Memorandum, Babiński, February 11, 1928, *ibid.*, pp. 27–29.

not just a spirited election campaign.[17] As a result of the 1928 election not a single delegate of the Polish minority was represented in the two parliamentary bodies in Germany that were most vital to its existence, and, henceforth, the minority had neither a voice nor a role of any significance in German domestic politics.

THE GERMAN MINORITY IN POLAND

Although numerically not much larger than its counterpart in Germany, the German minority in Poland was far more significant in its domestic and international political implications. Throughout the immediate postwar decade the German element was in a rapid decline.[18] Assessments of this decline differ substantially, partly because of the changing methods of census-taking—the 1921 census determined nationality on the basis of ethnic awareness; in 1931 nationality was established by mother tongue—and partly because the politically sensitive nature of the question invited tendentious estimates and interpretations of figures. But the trend was unmistakable, as revealed by a comparison of the figures provided by the German census of 1910 and the Polish census in 1921.

THE GERMAN POPULATION ELEMENT IN POLAND 1910–21[19]

	German census of 1910		Polish census of 1921	
	Number of Germans	German minority as % of total population	Number of Germans	German minority as % of total population
Poznań and Pomorze	1,099,321	38.6	502,967	17.3
Upper Silesia and Teschen	263,698	26.2	292,980	28.2
Galicia	90,114	1.1	39,810	0.5
Other parts of Poland	735,550	4.6	223,067	1.4
All of Poland	2,188,683	7.9	1,058,824	3.9

[17] Report from Beuthen Consulate, May 22, 1928, AMSZ, P II, fol. 4514, pp. 36–41; Memorandum, June 19, 1928, *ibid.*, pp. 212–15.

[18] For a breakdown of the different nationality groups in the population of Poland between 1921 and 1931, see Appendix IV.

[19] Wilhelm Winkler, *Statistisches Handbuch für das gesamte Deutschtum* (Berlin, 1927), p. 142.

According to estimates by Polish sources, the German minority population in 1927 was listed at 884,105, or 3 per cent of the total population,[20] while German calculations at the same time placed its strength at 1,128,000 (370,000 of these living in Poznań and Pomorze), which would have made it 3.9 per cent of the total population.[21] According to the official Polish census figures for 1931 the German minority had declined to a mere 741,000 (325,000 living in Poznań and Pomorze), or 2.3 per cent of the total population. But the minority figures of this census were generally deflated, particularly because in this instance nationality was determined on the basis of mother tongue, thus including under the Polish quota many persons whose principal language had become Polish even though they properly belonged to the ethnic minority groups. Several independent German estimates have placed the German minority figure at the outbreak of World War II in the vicinity of one million.[22] The decline of the German population was more rapid in urban communities than in rural areas, but even in the latter, the land ownership of the German minority decreased considerably as a result of voluntary sale and expropriation measures, e.g., land reform, forced liquidation, and the confiscation of the property of colonists and *Domänenpächter*.

If it is already difficult to get consensus on the exact number of Germans who left Poland, the determination of the motive for their departure poses even greater problems. No opinion polls were being conducted among the departing members that might help to enlighten us on this question, and even if opinion samples had been taken the motive for leaving was often too mixed and complex to be accurately assessed by the crude techniques of a questionaire. Rauschning, who is generally more reliable than his contemporary German commentators, for unlike the latter he presented his findings with the plea for better treatment of the German minority and not for the purpose of demanding a territorial revision, certainly exaggerates when he claims that of the 800,000 Germans who emigrated from Poznań and Pomorze only the 150,000 civil servants left voluntarily.[23] This assertion fails to take into consideration that the German population in those provinces was already dropping before World War I (hence the frantic efforts by the *Ansiedlungskommis-*

[20] Stoliński, "Liczba Niemców w Polsce," p. 379.

[21] Friedrich Heidelck, "Die Stellung des Deutschtums in Polen," *Deutsche Blätter in Polen* 2 (1929): 17.

[22] Heike (*Das Deutschtum in Polen*, p. 30) gives a figure of 1,030,000 for 1938; Bierschenk (*Deutsche Volksgruppe in Polen*, p. 10) lists 1,022,000 for 1939.

[23] Rauschning, *Die Entdeutschung Wespreussens*, p. 9.

sion), and it fails to include the War casualties suffered by residents of those areas. In addition, many Germans left voluntarily because they wanted to show their loyalty to the German *Reich* or for the more practical reason of escaping what initially seemed to be a very uncertain political and economic future under the banner of the restored Polish state.

However, a large proportion of the emigration was involuntary. It occurred either as the consequence of direct governmental eviction or expropriation measures or was forcibly induced by more informal means, e.g., insufficient provision for minority schools, personal chicanery, and discriminatory practices with respect to land reform, taxes, credits, and licences. The tactics adopted by the Poles probably did not differ radically from those exercised in Germany, with the exception that the German minority was basically a property owning group and thus constituted a more lucrative target for calculated economic discrimination.

THE POLITICAL ORGANIZATION OF THE GERMAN MINORITY

Despite their linguistic and cultural homogeneity and the common defensive orientation toward the Polish state, there were marked differences within the German minority in Poland with respect to social beliefs and revisionist attitudes.

Roughly speaking, the German minority can be divided into three basic categories. First, there was the minority group in the recently ceded regions of Poznań and Pomorze. This group was the most vocal and active of all in its revisionist demands, for it regarded its membership in the Polish state as a perverse accident of history and its present existence as a state of captivity that would soon be terminated by the reincorporation of its provinces into the German *Reich*. This particular minority sector consisted principally of small farmers and landowners, and the naturally conservative inclination of this group was reinforced by the ultranationalistic tenor of a population that had recently been torn from its motherland. It was this sector which maintained the closest connections with Berlin and from which most of the leaders of the German minority in Poland were recruited and which, consequently, was the principal target for repressive actions by the Polish authorities. While the *Deutschtumsbund* trials after 1929 showed the patent absurdity of charging the German minority leaders of this area with treasonable activities, there can be no doubt that in the eyes of Warsaw they were a disloyal element because of their political attitudes and revisionist strivings.

The second major German minority cluster was that of Polish Upper Silesia. Like the preceding group, this one had been part of the German Empire and the recent transfer of sovereignty nourished revisionist aspirations. But unlike the former, the transfer had not taken place arbitrarily but as the result of a plebiscite. Moreover, the Polish and German element in Upper Silesia had formed a much more closely integrated community, with certain traces of biculturalism and bilingualism, than had ever been reached in Poznań or Pomorze. Also the protective provisions of the Geneva Convention helped to ease relations between this German minority and the Polish authorities and thereby dissipated some of the discontent. Finally, unlike Poznań and Pomorze, Polish Upper Silesia was a predominantly industrial district and the social and economic concerns of the Polish and German workers provided common interests and cross-cutting loyalties that ameliorated the conflicts along national lines.

Third, there was the German minority in what had been Austrian Galicia and Congress Poland. The German element in these regions had roots that went back several generations and had therefore become firmly integrated in the Polish environment. In so far as persons of this background had not already become oriented to Poland, their German loyalties were a matter of cultural and linguistic affiliation with their motherland but they did not identify politically with the German *Reich*. Their activities as a minority were basically confined to preserving their German minority schools, language, and cultural institutions, but were free of the political and revisionist goals of their ethnic colleagues in Poznań, Pomorze, and Upper Silesia. The center of this particular group was the industrial city of Łódź and here, as in Upper Silesia, there existed a sphere for common interests and interactions between the German and Polish workers that cut across national cultural barriers, with the result that in the 1928 national elections two of the German minority representatives from Łódź, Kronig and Zerbe, ran on the Polish Socialist party (PPS) list and voted with that party in the *Sejm* after their election rather than adhere to the minority bloc despite much pressure from Germany to do so.[24]

Within these three regions an intricate web of political, social, and cultural organizations gradually emerged, which usually followed a

---

[24] In 1927 Rauscher had been able to prevent this "defection" to the Socialists by the two German Socialist delegates from Łódź by threatening to cut off all German subsidies for their party paper and elections in Łódź. (AA,D/2769/5462H/E367 666).

tripartite division into Socialist, Catholic-Centrist, and Rightist-National-
ist associations.²⁵ Despite considerable cleavages and various tactics
among the different parts of this nine-fold mozaic that ran along regional
and ideological lines, there existed co-operation on the broader national
issues that affected the entire German minority. Also, for the purpose of
national elections and in its voting behavior in the *Sejm* and Senate
the German minority acted as one and in close collaboration with the
other minority groups in Poland. In August 1921 a liaison office for all
German minority associations was set up in Warsaw, the *Zentralverband
der Deutschtumsbunde*. During its brief life span of less than two years
the *Zentralverband* managed to create a joint German minority bloc for
the 1922 elections which even included the Socialists and which played
a key role in establishing a wider parliamentary bloc that included the
other national minorities in Poland.

The political organizations of the German minority in Poznań and
Pomorze had come into being after the November armistice. In May
1921 the parties of the Right and Center combined in a newly formed
organization, the *Deutschtumsbund*, with headquarters in Bydgoszcz.
The Socialists remained outside this organization but co-operated with it
during elections. In August 1923 the Sikorski government abolished the
Deutschtumsbund for apparent treasonable activities. The German
minority viewed this measure, which was based on an administrative
decree rather than a court decision, as a crude denial of its constitutional
rights of association. Sikorski's abolition decree was both unwise and
unjust. It embittered the German group and was one of the contributing
factors which led to the breakdown of the brief period of co-operation
between the central government and the minority delegates in the *Sejm*,
which the Sikorski government had initially succeeded in establishing. At
the same time, the decree failed to curb the political activities of the German minorities, for in place of the *Deutschtumsbund* there appeared the
*Deutsche Vereinigung in Sejm und Senat für Posen, Netzegau und Pom-
merellen*. The latter existed ostensibly for the purpose of maintaining
a liaison between the German minority and its parliamentary members
in the *Sejm* and Senate, but it actually retained those leaders who had
headed the *Deutschtumsbund*—persons like its Secretary General
Heidelck, *Sejm* deputies Naumann and Graebe, and senators Busse and
Hasbach—and continued to pursue the same economic, financial, cul-

²⁵ A detailed summary of the German minority organizations in Poland and
their activities is contained in a memorandum of the Polish Ministry of Interior of
May 1, 1927, *AMSW*, fol. 973.

tural, and political activities as its outlawed predecessor. In the context of German–Polish relations the *Deutsche Vereinigung* in Poznań and Pomorze was the most significant of all the German minority organizations; it was militantly nationalistic and revisionist, maintained the closest contacts with the Berlin authorities, provided the most effective minority leadership in the *Sejm*, and was the most suspect one in Polish eyes. Its principal newspaper organs were the *Deutsche Rundschau* of Bydgoszcz (circulation 25,000), the *Posener Tageblatt* (circulation 15,-000), and the *Pommereller Tageblatt* (circulation 3,500).[26] The only German element in Pomorze and Poznań that did not participate in the *Deutsche Vereinigung* was the small number of Socialists who had their own organization with its seat in Bydgoszcz.

In the other regions of Poland the conservative and nationalist elements among the German minority did not enjoy the same position of predominance as in Poznań and Pomorze. In Upper Silesia the more conservative element was represented in the *Deutsch Oberschlesischer Volksbund*, which had been founded in November 1921, and in the *Deutsche Partei*. The latter was a fusion of the German Democrats, People's party and Nationalists that had been arranged in August 1922 and enjoyed particular support among the German intelligentsia, industrialists, and white-color workers in Upper Silesia. The main paper of the *Deutsche Partei* was the *Kattowitzer Zeitung* (circulation 10,000) which had originally been the paper of the German industrialists and entrepreneurs, but gradually lost its particular bias and became more representative of the whole German element in Upper Silesia. Both the *Volksbund* and the *Deutsche Partei* pursued revisionist aims. Unlike the situation in Poznań and Pomorze, in Upper Silesia the Catholic element played an active role in politics. The *Deutsche Katholische Volkspartei*, which had been founded in Katowice in December 1921, was influential among Christian workers and bourgeois groups. During the plebiscite campaign this party had advocated continued membership of all Upper Silesia in the German *Reich*. After the partition it saw its principal task in the protection of German cultural and educational institutions, but at the same time it renounced all irredentist policies and persuaded its members to become loyal citizens of the Polish state. Its newspaper, the *Oberschlesiche Kurier*, with a circulation of 30,000, was the largest German language daily in Poland. The *Katholische Volkspartei*, the *Volksbund*, and the *Deutsche Partei* together formed a single bloc in the Upper

[26] *Ibid.*

Silesian *Sejm* under the name of *Deutscher Klub*. The third element in Upper Silesia was composed of the *Deutsche Sozialistische Arbeitspartei Polens* [DSAP—German Socialist Labor party] which was supported by workers, trade unions, and the intelligentsia.

The *Sozialistische Arbeitspartei* was the only German political association which managed to create a united organization throughout Poland, with the exception of Poznań and Pomorze, where the local Socialists refused to join the central organization because of the latter's decision in 1928 to run on the PPS ticket and not for the minority bloc.[27]

The principal centers of strength of the DSAP were the industrial region of Upper Silesia and the industrial city of Łódź. As a party the DSAP had some difficulty in reconciling its national-cultural obligations to the German minority and its class loyalties to the PPS and to international Socialism. On matters of social and economic policy the DSAP delegates to the *Sejm* tended to collaborate with the PPS, but on cultural and educational questions which affected the minorities they would normally side with the minority bloc. Outside the national political arena, the *Arbeitspartei* was also active in Łódź city politics, where it was more successful in winning seats on the city council than the candidates of the German bourgeois party [*Bürgerliche Deutsche Partei*] and where it contributed substantially to the welfare and protection of the German minority of that city. The organ of the DSAP was the *Lodzer Volkszeitung* which had a circulation of 2,500. The *Bürgerliche Deutsche Partei* which was supported by property owners and Christian trade unions resembled the Catholic *Volkspartei* of Upper Silesia in its membership, ideology, and desire to establish friendly relations with the Polish population, but its functions remained restricted to Łódź city politics and never reached out to the national level. The third party of importance in central Poland was the conservative and nationalistic *Deutscher Volksverband in Polen* [German People's Association in Poland] which was very much a reflection of the *Deutschtumsbund* and its successor. The *Volksverband* had been created in 1924 by the *Sejm* deputy, Utta, to act as a conservative counterweight to the spreading influence of the DSAP throughout central Poland. The *Volksverband* consisted of the German bourgeoisie and landowners and strove for full equality for the German minority, especially in the application of the land reform. Its press organ, the *Freie Presse* and the *Volksfreund*, supported the idea of world federalism. After 1933 it acquired a distinct Nazi orientation.

27 Heike, *Das Deutschtum in Polen*, pp. 55–56.

At the official level the German minority deputies in the *Sejm* and Senate and successive Polish governments almost invariably faced each other in stark opposition. If such official actions as the discriminatory land reform practice and the abolition of the *Deutschtumsbund,* and the subsequent trial of many of its prominent members, could only discourage confidence and co-operation with the central authorities, the German minority for its part never sought to induce the central authorities to take a more conciliatory stand by abandoning its self-assigned role of a permanent opposition to whatever regime was in power in Warsaw. There were only a few exceptions to this. In December 1922 the German minority, together with the other national minorities, supported the candidature of Narutowicz for the presidency and by their vote tipped the scale in his favor, thus inadvertently prompting his tragic assassination. The national minorities also voted for his successor, Wojciechowski. Also during the initial period of Sikorski's brief tenure as prime minister some degree of co-operation between the government and the minorities was achieved. But apart from these extremely rare instances the German, as well as the other minorities, continued their opposition to the government-of-the-day on matters of procedure and protocol, no less than on matters of substance, e.g., refusal to vote for the budget and nonratification of foreign treaties. Acting partly out of necessity but also as the result of self-conditioning, the national minorities pursued a course which was aimed at embarrassing, frustrating, and restraining the government, rather than seeking to maximize their influence in decisionmaking through co-operation with the central authorities.

Piłsudski's return to power in 1926 did not reverse this trend and failed to maneuver the minority groups out of their entrenched opposition role, even though initially the German and Jewish representatives had supported his candidature for president in 1926. Although the Marshal's personal attitude toward the nationality question was more enlightened and free of the chauvinistic element that had frequently distorted the views of preceding governments, no basic change of policies took place on either side. The firmly established behavior of mutual confrontation, Piłsudski's preoccupation with other issues, and the regime's increasing reliance on the conservative-nationalistic element in Polish society, all tended to reduce the basis for an accommodation between the national minorities and the government. As the parties of the Left were most sympathetic to the wishes of the national minorities and showed more concern for the protection of minority rights, the parliamentary minority bloc became closely associated with the counter-coalition of the Left that gradually emerged in opposition to the Piłsudski government. In the case of the German minority, national-cultural considerations took precedence over social and economic issues, for most of the German parliamentary representatives belonged to the conservative rather than the Socialist camp and thus showed greater ideological affinity with the government bloc even though in their political behavior they were more closely aligned with the PPS.

Just as the Polish minority in Germany received certain financial subsidies from the Polish government, its counterpart in Poland was also financially supported from its motherland, but in the case of the latter the amount was considerably higher and came from both public and private sources. These subsidies from Germany were primarily aimed at helping to finance the election campaigns of German and other minority candidates, to help maintain the above-listed organizations, to assist in the publication of minority newspapers, and to pay for the operation of minority schools and other cultural institutions. In addition, the German government tried to offer its minority in Poland other economic benefits, such as credits to farmers and to construction projects,[28] a more lenient application of customs regulations in the case of minority products and, between 1930 and 1932, import contingents of wheat for the German minority in Pomorze.[29]

Measures of the latter category could not be privately arranged but had to be decided by the official authorities. Direct government subsidies were generally devoted to finance the election campaigns of minority candidates and their newspapers, while financial aid from private sources was more apt to be channeled into cultural and educational activities. But there existed no rigid rule on this and it is difficult to draw the lines of separation between public and private donations, as the most important private institutions for the assistance of Germans abroad, organizations like the *Deutsche Stiftung* and the *Deutsches Ausland Institut*, were heavily supported by government funds and reflected government policy aims.

Since the assistance came from various sources and was given under the cloak of secrecy, it is impossible to provide an accurate estimate of

[28] Some of these credits were handled by German banks but more often by foreign banks, especially the Buitenlandbank of The Hague, in order to preserve the anonymity of the donor. (Letter, Max Muller to Chamberlain, July 27, 1926, FO, 371/11280, pp. 28–29.)

[29] Note of a Cabinet decision of August 27, 1931, AA, GA/3720/K165/K021 923.

the financial subsidies which flowed to the German minority in Poland. In a secret memorandum of March 23, 1926, Stresemann made an eloquent plea for the assistance to these minorities, which would have to exceed the customary educational and cultural aid and make annual credits of 30 million marks available to help their economic needs; over two-thirds of this sum was to flow to the Germans living in Poland. Stresemann justified this on the grounds that the minority had more than a strictly national value, for these groups represented pillars of political influence and an economic market for German products.[30]

In a confidential letter to Rauscher dated July 5, 1927, Dirksen referred to the regular monthly $3,000 he was submitting for financing the election of German candidates and another $500 monthly for the publication of the minority journal *Natio*. Dirksen also mentioned that additional money had been granted to finance local elections; however, he had forgotten the exact sum of this, and Zechlin, who ought to know, was away on holidays.[31] On October 3, 1930, a few weeks before the Polish elections, Noebel noted in a secret memorandum that Germany had spent $91,500 for the 1928 election campaign. It is interesting to note that $60,000 of this sum had not gone to finance German minority candidates but Ukrainian and White Russian ones. Noebel urged that $21,000 be invested for the impending 1930 elections but wanted a substantial reduction in the aid to the Ukrainian and White Russian minorities. He justified this particular reduction on the grounds that the minority bloc in Poland's political life had disintegrated, and that consequently there no longer existed the same interest in financing Ukrainian candidates; however, he was prepared to recommend the sum of $1,000 for the Ukrainian cause in so far as Germany still showed a "lively interest in the Ukrainian movement."[32] Some years later the Polish Foreign

---

[30] AA,D/2773/5462H/E370 734–37.

[31] AA,D/2769/5462H/E367 698–99.

[32] AA,StS/2390/4624H/E203 099–100. These particular transactions did not escape Polish notice, and the fact that Germany financed the irredentist Ukrainian groups created particular resentment. In a private discussion with some German representatives at the Brussels conference of the League of Nations League, the Polish parliamentarian Loewenherz mentioned that Germany's regular financial support to the enemies and would-be destroyers of the Polish state (the Ukrainian separatists were meant) made a particularly bad impression in his country. (AA, D/2784/5462H/E379 542–47; February 12, 1929).

On September 11, 1931, Moltke reported that various Polish newspapers had accused the *Reichswehr* of subsidizing and aiding Ukrainian separatists and terrorists. Some articles even concluded that Germany was planning an attack against the "Corridor" and therefore wanted the Ukrainians to stab Poland in the back. (AA,

Ministry calculated that all but some 4,000,000 złotys of the Upper Silesian *Volksbund's* 17,000,000 złoty budget had come directly from Germany.[33]

Judged by present standards of foreign aid and propaganda expenses, the figures seem minimal. But this aid helped to maintain the political and cultural organizations of the German minority in Poland, and since much of this money was given for the purpose of upholding the irredentist cause among the minority and, moreover, as some of it wound up in the hands of Ukrainian separatists and terrorists, these financial subsidies made an extremely negative impression on the Poles who tended to exaggerate both the size and sinister aims of these payments.

MINORITY INCIDENTS

Incidents which involved the German minority—questions over the Polish minority in Germany rarely received international headlines —continued to mar relations between Berlin and Warsaw, even though they occurred somewhat less frequently between 1926 and 1929. One of the central minority conflicts which raged throughout this relative lull was the Upper Silesian school dispute.

Articles 74, 106, and 131 of the Geneva Convention had accorded to each Upper Silesian resident freedom to determine, according to his own conscience and at his personal responsibility, whether he belonged to a minority group and to decide what the language of his child was. This decision was not subject to challenge or investigation by the authorities. The Polish authorities had been consistently irked by the habit of many Polish-speaking families to follow the old practice of sending their children to German schools. In 1926 the Polish authorities in Upper Silesia tried to put an end to this practice which conflicted with their nationalistic aims, and imposed practical problems as well, by refusing to admit some 7,000 applications for entry into German schools on the grounds that the children spoke Polish and not German and were therefore unfit for instruction in German schools. Most of the parents

---

RAM/1430/2945H/D575 687–89). Curtius immediately responded to Moltke's report by telegraphing the following instructions to *Staatssekretär* von Bülow: "Should relations of any form still exist with Ukrainian circles, contrary to my assumptions, I request that these be broken off immediately" (*ibid.*, 694).

[33] AMSZ, P II, fol. 4698, p. 3; February 17, 1932.

who were involved in this dispute went on strike and refused to comply with the directive to send their children to Polish schools. In the German view this interference constituted a violation of the Geneva Convention, for Polish officials had neither the authority to deny a child entry into a minority school if the parents had determined that they belonged to the minority, nor could the authorities test whether a child in fact spoke the minority language. While retaining this legal stand, Stresemann accepted the compromise formula which the League Council had arranged in March 1927 and which stipulated that in cases of doubt the language of a child could be tested by a neutral examiner. This was merely a temporary solution for the 1926–27 school year designed to prevent students from being left without any schooling while the dispute remained officially unsettled.[34] In 1927 the neutral examiner, the Swiss Maurer, tested some 971 children of which 444 passed the language test and were consequently admitted to German schools.[35]

The language tests which had been agreed to by the 1927 Geneva compromise were only meant to apply during the current school year. When the Polish authorities continued them subsequently, Germany brought the whole dispute before the Hague court. The court's decision of April 26, 1928 (Judgment 12, Series A, No. 15), which was subsequently accepted by the League Council, offered a compromise solution. It upheld the German position that the declaration as to one's minority status could neither be challenged nor investigated, and that language tests for school entry would therefore have to be discontinued. At the same time, the judgment supported the Polish view that the decision whether a person belonged to a minority group was a matter of objective facts and not of purely subjective will [*de fait et non de pure volonté*]. Still, the court also admitted that under the mixed conditions which prevailed in Upper Silesia it was conceivable that a child might be fluent in both languages or in neither, and that in these doubtful cases the subjective element of will took precedence. In line with this decision and its adoption by the League Council and after a subsequent judicial opinion, both sides accepted the legality of the Polish registration commission to which parents whose children applied for entry into minority schools were to submit their language declaration. This declaration was to be made in writing rather than in person, thus saving parents the incon-

[34] Stresemann's letter to the Chancellor, March 13, 1927, AA, RAM/1427/2945H/D572 723–30.
[35] AA, M/2447/5544H/E385 874.

venience of a personal appearance and also reducing the danger of personal intimidation of the parents by the registration commission.[36] This agreement settled the principal aspect of the Upper Silesian school dispute, but bilateral negotiations on certain outstanding points continued for another three years without a definite conclusion.

In 1929 a minor incident in Oppeln became a major issue as the result of a massive campaign in the Polish press. On April 28, 1929, a visiting troup of artists and musicians from Poland gave a guest performance of a Polish national opera for the benefit of the Polish minority in Oppeln. Although some popular disturbance had been anticipated, the police protection measures had been insufficient; the performance was interrupted by stink bombs and a number of the artists were severely beaten by German youths at the railroad station. The incident had generally been regretted in the German newspapers, and the German government had immediately apologized to the Polish authorities. In addition, and in part motivated by the anticipation of a Polish complaint to the League, the German authorities had retired the police president of Oppeln and had transferred two other police officers, while instigating investigations and court proceedings against the offenders.[37]

In Poland the event was exploited to the fullest. The Polish press unfolded a vigorous anti-German campaign and anti-German demonstrations were staged in several Polish cities. In Warsaw a hostile mob surrounded the German legation so that Rauscher was forced to call off his attendance at a gala opera performance in honor of the Polish national holiday.[38] *Polska Zachodnia*, the organ of the Upper Silesian *voivode*, spoke of a "bloody carnage, a bestial attack by the German nation, [and] a disgraceful pogrom of the Huns."[39] The Oppeln incident led to the boycott of German films in Poland and thus reduced the already minimal cultural contacts between the two countries. The situation was little improved, even when the German courts condemned six of the Oppeln

---

[36] Memorandum, Moltke, May 7, 1930, AA, M/2447/5544H/E385 872–84.

[37] Letter, Koepke to Sir Eric Drummond, August 27, 1929, AA, M/2747/5544H/E385 327–52.

[38] Record of a telephone call from Rauscher, May 3, 1929, AA, RAM/1428/2945H/D573 954.

[39] *Ibid.*, D574 087–98; June 14, 1929. Not all the Polish papers subscribed to these anti-German orgies, and *Polonia* noted sarcastically that one of the injured Oppeln actors who had been seen marching in the Katowice demonstrations, heavily bandaged and the object of general pity, could be observed the next day uninjured and merry. The paper noted that when it became known that Germany intended to pay compensation to the injured actors, their state of health suddenly declined to the point where all found it necessary to stay in bed.

offenders to prison sentences ranging from three to eight months, a judgment which the *Völkische Beobachter* of October 15, 1929, styled "incomprehensibly harsh."

In turn, the Polish authorities gave the German minority good reason for complaint by staging a series of legal proceedings against several minority leaders in 1929 and 1930. Even though the Polish courts, on the whole, conducted these trials with due observance of the principles of judicial impartiality and acquitted the great majority of the accused, these show trials confirmed the feeling of insecurity in the minds of the minority, who viewed these proceedings as witchhunts inspired by political motives and disguised under the cloak of justice.

On February 13, 1929, Ulitz, the president of the Upper Silesian *Volksbund*, was arrested only a few hours after his parliamentary immunity had elapsed with the dissolution of the Upper Silesian *Sejm*. He was charged with treason in connection with aiding members of the German minority in Upper Silesia to escape the military draft. The event, which occurred so soon after Zaleski's complaint at Lugano about the *Volksbund*'s hostile and subversive behavior, caused great excitement in Germany, where it was interpreted as a prelude to the full-scale extermination of the organization. It almost embarrassed the German propaganda machine when the Katowice court dropped the charge of treason and merely passed a five-month sentence on other grounds. The court of appeal later acquitted Ulitz and thus proved that German–Polish relations did not always live up to the worst expectations.

As relations between Poland and Germany seriously deteriorated after 1930, the minority problem, as the most emotionally charged of all current issues, almost in a geometric progression began to figure more intensively and more frequently on the agenda of German–Polish conflicts. In October 1929 *Studienrat* Burchardt and three other leaders of scouting and sports groups among the German minority were arrested on the charge of espionage which was based on Polish suspicions that these youth groups received military training during their summer holidays in Germany so that they could act as armed insurgents in the event of a German–Polish conflict.[40] Similar charges were also levied in Bydgoszcz in February 1930 against a number of leaders of the former *Deutschtumsbund*, almost seven years after its dissolution. The charges included espionage, illicit contacts with a foreign power, obstruction in

[40] Report of the Consulate at Toruń, November 19, 1929, AA, GA/3786/K201/K074 242.

the execution of government decrees, and treason. The charge of treason was based on the fact that members of the *Deutschtumsbund*, including Graebe, who also became involved when his parliamentary immunity ended with the dissolution of the *Sejm*, had presented medals of the *Kyffhäuserbund*, a patriotic association of German veterans, to German veterans of the last war who were now residing in Poland. The Polish authorities saw in this action a clandestine attempt at forming military groups on Polish soil with the goal of promoting the return of that territory to Germany.[41] The totally erroneous and fantastic suspicions which were being voiced in connection with the scouting activities of German youth groups and the presentation of unofficial medals indicate how strongly certain Polish authorities labored under the apprehension that Germany's revisionist propaganda might spark a sudden armed uprising of the minority groups on Polish soil.

As was true in the Ulitz case, the actual outcome of the trials in no way justified all the investment of emotional energy and hostility. The actual sentences tended toward leniency and in no case exceeded a one-year prison term.[42] Furthermore, these sentences were never fully executed; while the accused were out on bail, the judicial process continued in tennis-match fashion, alternating between appeals and retrials. Those sentences that were not abrogated in this legal sporting exercise fell under the Polish amnesty of 1932 or were cancelled as a result of a reciprocal German–Polish agreement in 1934 to terminate legal proceedings that were still outstanding against certain persons.[43]

MINORITY COMPLAINTS OVER THE POLISH ELECTION OF 1930

The Polish general elections of November 1930 severely undermined the remnants of parliamentary democracy in Poland and at the same time precipitated a crisis in German–Polish relations over the treatment of the German minority during the election campaign. During the campaign, members of the German minority in Upper Silesia had on several occasions been subjected to acts of violence, and the minority groups in other regions, although not suffering actual physical duress, had found

41 *Ibid.*, 346–72.
42 *Kurjer Poznański*, April 18, 1930. Letter, German Consul General in Poznań, May 2, 1930, AA, GA/3786/K201/K047 549.
43 AA, GA/3787/K201 K048 454.

themselves severely curtailed in exercising their election rights. Minority candidates had frequently been prevented from campaigning freely. In Włocławek and Grudziądz the voting lists of the German bloc had been declared invalid on the fabricated grounds they did not carry the necessary number of signatures. In some 30,000 cases the right of German minority members to vote had been questioned on the grounds of undetermined citizenship,[44] and in Poznań the Concordia publishing company which printed the *Posener Tageblatt,* had been forced to cease operations during the election campaign on the trumped up charge of technical inefficiency and violation of sanitary standards.

In its indignation German opinion generally pictured the November election events as being directed purely against the German and other minority groups, while in fact the violations were part of a wider infringement of the remaining democratic foundations in Poland, as the Socialist press in Germany repeatedly tried to emphasize. By means of vigorous propaganda, police intimidation, and tampering with election results the Piłsudski regime had managed to secure a majority vote for the government bloc. The November elections in a very real sense signified the regime's repudiation of the methods of parliamentary democracy. They ended the uneasy period of tutelary democracy that had existed since Piłsudski's take-over in 1926 in the form of a compromise between the personal rule of the Marshal and his praetorian guard of "Colonels" and the constitutional authority of the parliamentary institutions. In Poland this peculiar duality had become known under the term *bartlowanie,* named after Kazimierz Bartel who had been prime minister no less than five times between 1926 and 1930 and who had wished to avoid the complete break with parliamentary practice, even though he was a close supporter of the Marshal. Already during the election campaign this system change was manifested in the most drastic and crudest form by the arbitrary arrest of a large number of deputies and political activists of the Center–Left opposition. In line with the general losses which the opposition suffered in the 1930 elections, the minority candidates fared particularly badly, and the number of German representatives in the *Sejm* shrank from 21 to 5 and from 5 to 3 in the Senate.

In Germany the outrage over these election incidents was intensified by the poor showings of German minority candidates and the government

---

[44] Speech of Curtius before the League Council, January 21, 1931, AA, GA/ 3871/K238/K069 343–44. League of Nations, *Official Journal* 12 (1931): 165–78.

was hard-pressed to take immediate retaliatory measures.[45] Despite this highly emotional climate, the government acted with restraint and submitted the whole dispute to the League of Nations, where it was to be treated as a matter of urgency at the forthcoming session of the Council. On January 6, 1931, the Upper Silesian *Volksbund*, acting on its own initiative, submitted a petition to the League and accompanied this with documentary evidence of interference with election procedure listing 255 cases of terrorism against the German minority. Sensing a distinct reaction in world opinion against the events of the November election and trying to accumulate reserves of good will for the impending showdown at Geneva, the Polish government immediately undertook conciliatory gestures. In its note to the League on January 6, 1931, Poland admitted to the occurrence of certain excesses but denied the charges of an organized campaign of terrorism. She assured the League that strict measures would be taken to punish the guilty and to prevent a recurrence in the future but emphasized that the root of these incidents had been Germany's intense anti-Polish campaign.[46]

The German–Polish problem figured prominently on the diplomatic agenda of the January Council session in Geneva. On January 21, Curtius presented the case of the German minorities in a factual and sober *plaidoyer*. The question of the protection of minority rights, Curtius argued, was a matter of grave international consequence and should be of concern to all Council members. He professed some astonishment that Germany—granted that she entertained a particular interest in the fate of the German minority—alone of all Council members should have brought this case to the attention of that body. Curtius gave a long exposition of the various incidents and emphasized the particularly destructive role played in this context by the Insurgents' Union, which could not be regarded as a private organization as it was not only supported by public funds but in its military activities was also subordinated to the official Polish military authorities. In closing, the Foreign Minister noted with satisfaction that Poland had opened legal and disciplinary proceedings against offenders and negligent government officials.[47]

[45] An interpellation by the DNVP of December 1, 1930, asked the government to renounce retroactively the ratification of the liquidation agreement (Reichstag, *Sten. Berichte, Anlagen,* 448, no. 337), and Freytagh-Loringhoven on December 5 called for an active revisionist policy on the side of the German government (Reichstag, *Sten. Berichte,* 444, pp. 332–36).

[46] *Survey of International Affairs 1932,* pp. 363–64.

[47] Speech by Curtius before the League Council, January 21, 1931, AA, GA/ 3871/K238, K069 334–51.

Zaleski's reply was also kept in moderate terms. The Polish Foreign Minister admitted that acts of violence had occurred, although he only considered 28 out of the listed 255 cases as serious. He rejected Curtius's charges against the Insurgents and their connection with the government, which he compared with that of the *Stahlhelmbund* of which Hindenburg was honorary president. The root of the whole evil, according to Zaleski, lay in Germany's incessant revisionist policy which kept alive the spirit of hatred and unrest among the minority and alone was responsible for their present predicament.[48] Curtius, in turn, felt obliged to correct Zaleski on several points of fact and rejected the analogy between *Stahlhelmbund* and Insurgents. He openly admitted Germany's adherence to a policy of revisionism; however, as she had committed herself at Locarno to pursue this policy exclusively by peaceful means, Curtius rejected the charge that her policy of peaceful revisionism could be held responsible for causing general tensions and producing the present crisis.[49]

Despite the underlying tensions there were no temperamental outbursts and when by an odd coincidence of protocol the two contestants were table partners at an official luncheon given by the President of the Council, Curtius proposed the formula *inter pocula arma silent* and thus managed to engage in a relatively friendly discussion with his Polish partner.[50]

The Council's report, which was presented on January 24 by Yoshizawa (Japan), who was acting as rapporteur, was a masterpiece of tact and diplomacy which embodied the conciliatory capacity of the League at its very best. Without being too harsh for Poland's sensibilities, the report clearly noted that evidence existed that Articles 75 and 83 of the Geneva Convention had been violated, and it supported the German view that there existed indirect responsibility on the part of the Polish authorities. The report recommended that for the May session Poland submit a detailed account of her legal proceedings against the offenders, and it urged the Polish government to take the necessary measures to sever any special connection that might exist between the public authorities and national associations such as Insurgents in order to restore the confidence of the minority, which had been profoundly shaken.[51]

Germany had hoped for a more explicit and less diplomatically

[48] *Survey of International Affairs 1932*, p. 366.
[49] Curtius, *Sechs Jahre Minister*, pp. 173–74.
[50] *Ibid.*, p. 174.
[51] *Survey of International Affairs 1932*, pp. 367–68.

formulated condemnation of Poland's activities and would have welcomed the creation of an international control commission to supervise the proceedings by which Poland restored the confidence of the minority. But the Council resolution generally met with a favorable treatment in Germany, even though the *Völkische Beobachter* called it a *Kuhhandel* [cattle trading] between Curtius and Zaleski that left Poland entirely free to pursue her de-Germanization policy.[52]

Before returning to Geneva in May, the German government utilized the services of her consulates and of the *Volksbund*, which had received an undisclosed sum of money specifically for this purpose,[53] to examine the manner in which Poland fulfilled the Council resolution in actual practice. On April 18, Consul Illgen reported from Katowice that court proceedings were under way and that adequate compensations had been awarded for material damages suffered during the election events. Still, he occasionally found the Polish courts lacking in impartiality and felt that the Polish authorities were more concerned with making a good impression in Geneva than with administering real justice.[54]

On May 23 Yoshizawa presented his report which took note of the legal proceedings by Poland. In obvious reference to Poland's failure to dissolve her ties with the Insurgents, Yoshizawa noted that the measures described in the Polish report "did not include the one which, in the opinion of certain members of the Council, would have afforded the most appropriate and effective means of severing such special bonds as might exist between the authorities and the Insurgents' Union." But immediately, he went on to add that there had been a visible improvement in the relations between the authorities and the minority. The report closed by expressing confidence that Poland would continue to take the proper measures to improve relations with her minorities.[55] The Council members were eager to accept this face-saving resolution and thus divest themselves of this embarrassing and time-consuming issue. But Curtius objected on the grounds that the late arrival of the Polish note had prevented Council members from studying it with the necessary scrutiny which this important matter deserved. The German Foreign Minister clearly sought to prolong the involvement of the League in this question in order to force Poland to continue with the legal proceedings against the offenders in the election campaign. He therefore proposed that this

[52] *Völkischer Beobachter*, January 27, 1931.
[53] AA, GA/3891/K238/K069 490; March 1931.
[54] Report by Consul Illgen, April 18, 1931, *ibid.*, 527–49.
[55] League of Nations, *Official Journal* 12 (1931): 1144–45.

issue be brought up again at the September session of the Council.[56] This motion was adopted and the matter was finally permitted to be closed at the September meeting.

The League's handling of the election issue serves as an excellent example both of the services which the international body could render in resolving an international minority dispute and of its inherent limitations. Dirksen noted with criticism that in dealing with international minority problems the League was not so much an impartial court of justice as a political body bent on arranging a compromise formula.[57] In its operations the League of Nations showed itself as an organization whose weapons were restricted to the exercise of traditional diplomatic and conciliatory techniques without commanding any executive power which could be applied in the defense of the minorities. In dealing with the Polish election case of 1930, the international body had been unable to impose an international control body on Poland, nor had the Council been able to enforce that part of its own resolution which called for the severance of ties between the Polish authorities and the Insurgents. But the mere anticipation of having the embarrassing case presented in full view of the world, induced Poland to make amends even before she made her appearance in Geneva and it exercised a general restraining influence on Polish activities against her minority groups. At the same time, the treatment of the issue by the international body provided a psychological breathing space to cool passions and, by being able to offer recourse to an alternative solution, strengthened the position of the German government in resisting the popular plea for more drastic retaliatory measures.

Germany was less appreciative of the services which the League of Nations rendered in the protection of the German minority than the League's actual performance on this matter deserved. The procedure for dealing with minority complaints had been developed before Germany became a member of the League, and in her opinion it was prejudicial to her interests, with too much emphasis on quiet diplomacy and compromise settlements of minority disputes, and not the clear-cut, dramatic judicial verdict which she desired.

At the Lugano meeting of the Council in December 1928, Stresemann and the Canadian representative, Senator Dandurand, proposed that the whole minority protection procedure of the League be reexamined at the next Council session with a view to introducing

---

[56] AA, GA/3871/K238/K069 702–8; May 23, 1931.
[57] Herbert von Dirksen, *Moskau, Tokio, London* (Stuttgart, 1959), p. 85.

changes.[58] The minority question was therefore placed on the Council's agenda for March 1929. Poland immediately tried to counteract the German initiative by demanding on her part that the international minority accords be made to apply to all League members alike, but was forced to withdraw this proposal because of French objections.[59]

The alterations in minority procedures which were agreed to at the Council meeting in Madrid in June 1929 were designed to meet some of Germany's demands but, on the whole, were minor. Most important was the provision for the expansion of the Committee of Three by two additional members if necessary.[60] The committee was also instructed to inform the other Council members of the results of its examination if the case had not been placed on the agenda of the Council.[61] Puender, the state secretary in the chancellery, telegraphed the Chancellor that, on the whole, Germany could be satisfied with these procedural improvements which allowed her to re-introduce her more extensive demands at a future date.[62] Stresemann informed the Foreign Ministry that the representatives of the German minority had thanked him for this achievement; for tactical reasons they could not emphasize this publicly but in private they agreed that the best possible solution had been found.[63]

[58] Memorandum, Schubert, March 19, 1929, AA, StS/2365/4587H/E184 913. Next to Stresemann, Senator Dandurand, a member of the French–Canadian minority, was the most active advocate of changes in the League's minority procedures. Dandurand's position was most welcome to Germany and in his Geneva speech on March 6, 1929, Stresemann urged that Dandurand's proposal, which sought to enlarge the Committee of Three so that all Council members be included, be given serious consideration (*ibid.*, 827–28). Kempff, the German Consul in Montreal, reported that Dandurand was sympathetic toward the minorities, but at the same time he was pro-French and pro-Polish. He therefore urged that efforts be made to win the Senator over to the German cause, perhaps by persuading some German university to grant him an honorary doctorate (AA,D/2784/5462H/E379 549; February 18, 1929).
[59] Memorandum, Schubert, March 19, 1929, AA, StS/2365/4587H/E184 921.
[60] The Committee of Three was a key target for German objections. The committee, consisting of the president of the Council and two other Council members, had initially acted as a screening group to investigate whether the Council ought to occupy itself with a particular minority matter. But gradually the committee not only investigated but also settled minority petitions, often without informing either the Council or the respective minority of the nature of the settlement. Germany objected to the confidential nature of the committee's proceedings, as well as to its practice of excluding the representatives of powers which had an immediate and direct interest in a particular minority dispute. In this manner Germany was automatically excluded from the Committee of Three on all matters affecting her minority in Poland.
[61] AA, StS/2366/4587H/E185 168–71.
[62] *Ibid.*, 145; June 13, 1929.
[63] *Ibid.*, 185; June 14, 1929.

Despite Germany's satisfaction over the changes in the League's minority operations, men like Walters were of the opinion that these alterations had a detrimental effect because they tended to publicize the settlement procedure and thus reduced much of the confidence which governments had held in the efficiency and impartiality of the League machinery.[64]

The new minority provisions by the League of Nations neither improved relations between the German minority and the Polish state nor promoted German–Polish collaboration in settling the recurring minority issues within the framework of the League of Nations. The minority problem, next to the revisionist issue, continued to be the major source of contention which divided the two neighbors.

[64] Walters, *League of Nations*, pp. 410–11.

IX

The Function of Revisionism

THE MOST SIGNIFICANT and the most constant single factor in the relations between Germany and Poland for the entire period under examination was the unconditional rejection by Germany of the territorial status quo in the east and the incessant diplomatic and propagandistic activities in favor of its revision. In the eyes of Poland her neighbor's revisionist claims were regarded not only as being devoid of a just foundation but also as posing a permanent threat to her national existence, which reduced to mockery any professed German intentions for a conciliation. For Germany her territorial revisionist claims against Poland were not merely a matter of policy, subject to alteration and compromise, but had been elevated to the level of a national mystique which incited its votaries to relentless zeal and whose spiritual foundations would support no modifications.

Germany's revisionist policy manifested both active and defensive attributes. Actively this involved the continuous efforts of diplomacy, publicity, and pseudo-scholarship, all pulling on the revisionist chariot. Defensively, Germany sought to frustrate Warsaw's plans for a so-called East–Locarno, i.e., an international guarantee of Poland's western frontiers.

Poland's role in rejecting these revisionist demands was somewhat more passive, partly because the Poles as the *beati possidentes* could better afford to let matters rest as they were, and partly because Poland did not have at its disposal the same publicity resources and communications channels that were available to Germany. The Polish press reacted negatively to German revisionist demands and occasionally under-

226

lined the seriousness and firmness of the Polish position by alluding to her own unsatisfied territorial claims against East Prussia. The government normally confined its official reaction and protests to those cases where revisionist pronouncements had been publicly made by official figures, such as the inflammatory speech which Treviranus, the minister of transportation, delivered in 1930. In April 1925 the Western Division of the Warsaw Foreign Ministry came to the conclusion that official policy had been somewhat too passive in counteracting Germany's revisionist tactics abroad. The Polish legation in Berlin was, therefore, instructed to abandon its previously passive stand on this particular issue and to contact different political groups in Germany, especially Socialist circles, in order to stress the economic advantages of normalization and to draw attention to the dangers and futility of Germany's revisionist policy. Germany's territorial policy was a continuation of the Prussian policy of the Hohenzollerns and should, therefore, find no sympathy in other parts of the *Reich*.[1] Skrzyński's visit to the United States later that year was in line with this particular directive as his trip was designed to spread international good will for Poland and to act as an antidote to Germany's revisionist campaign.

In his official addresses to the *Sejm* Foreign Affairs Committee, Zaleski rarely missed the opportunity to stress the need for better relations with Germany, a sentiment which he no doubt personally held. But he would usually insert a contrapuntal warning about the necessity that Germany sacrifice her revisionist strivings. In his speech to the Committee on January 4, 1927, the Foreign Minister noted that he could not remain silent in the face of certain dangerous tendencies. What these tendencies were remained unnamed, but he obviously had Germany's territorial revisionist aspirations in mind.[2]

Some time later, in his address to the *Sejm* on January 15, 1929, Foreign Minister Zaleski scanned the entire range of German–Polish relations. He noted that during World War I the German nation had demonstrated "remarkable endurance and willpower," but when she had finally lost the war, this had left a psychological compulsion to hate. Germany's hostile feelings toward the West had gradually subsided but they had not mellowed toward Poland. Nevertheless, Zaleski was hopeful that in the future the animosity toward Poland would end and that Germany's revisionist propaganda and the illusion that a revision could be achieved peacefully might be overcome by her own sense of realism

[1] AMSZ, P II, fol. 4615, pp. 1–2.
[2] *Messager Polonais*, January 4, 1927.

and the "undeniably sincere and pacific tendencies of the present government of the Reich."[3]

All Polish governments of the time treated the German demand for a territorial revision as a non-negotiable issue and in this they enjoyed the enthusiastic support of the entire Polish population regardless of party affiliation. During the Locarno debates Foreign Minister Skrzyński had proclaimed that not an inch of sacred Polish soil would ever be surrendered, and when Schubert first met Zaleski in December 1926 and rather tactlessly declared that a real German–Polish reconciliation was impossible before Danzig, the "Corridor," and Upper Silesia had returned to the Reich, Zaleski had answered with an unequivocal: "Jamais."[4]

But was the territorial question absolutely non-negotiable from the Polish point of view? Not only in Germany but also elsewhere abroad there existed the widespread belief that eventually Poland might be peacefully induced to accept some frontier alterations with Germany. Piłsudski's immediate postwar preoccupations with Poland's eastward expansion and his interest in coming to terms with Poland's western neighbor had encouraged lively speculation that during the first years of the Republic he had not been adverse to the idea of entering into a revisionist accord with Germany. Despite the absence of any evidence that he proposed or contemplated such territorial readjustment, even during the critical days of the Polish–Soviet war, these rumors persisted and were freshly circulated after his return to power in 1926. The belief that Piłsudski was the man who both could and would agree to a territorial revision of the German–Polish frontier was fairly widespread. When Diamand was in Germany on an informal mission in the summer of 1926, he told Stresemann how the Marshal had on one occasion complained to him that Poland was plagued by an excess of national minorities and that it would consequently be wiser "to sacrifice some territory in order to cement national unity more firmly."[5] Following the Piłsudski–

---

[3] *Messager Polonais*, January 17, 1929.

[4] Report, Zaleski, December 20, 1926, AMSZ, P, II, fol. 4614, p. 23. Schubert's account of the meeting diverges slightly from Zaleski's version. According to Schubert (AA, StS/2339/4569H/E168 905–9; December 10, 1926) he had, indeed, made the statement as recorded by Zaleski, but he had added that he realized that it would be premature to raise this question now, and he therefore expected no answer from Zaleski. The Polish Foreign Minister had not directly rejected Schubert's opinion and had assured the German diplomat that he was well acquainted with the frontier problem but could not provide him with an answer now, as this would provoke an enormous agitation in the Polish press.

[5] Note by Stresemann, July 28, 1926, AA, D/2771/5462H/E368 941–45.

Stresemann meeting in Geneva in December 1927, Briand had asked the Foreign Minister whether he had raised the territorial question with the Marshal. When Stresemann answered in the negative—he regarded this too sensitive an issue to be discussed during their first encounter—Briand seemed to feel that a possible opportunity for a settlement might have been missed by Stresemann's caution, because he thought the Marshal most favorably disposed to a settlement with Germany.[6] Chamberlain had been under the same impression, for on the same occasion he urged Stresemann to discuss the whole issue with Piłsudski, rather than with Zaleski, for the Marshal was the only person in Poland who could settle this problem, while Zaleski was not sufficiently influential.[7]

Zaleski himself was reputed to have been critical during the Paris Peace Conference of too extensive a westward expansion by Poland, as this would place her in perpetual conflict with Germany, and, at least according to one British report, he was less categorically opposed to a minor revision of the territorial status than his public pronouncements would imply. In the spring of 1931, Zaleski mentioned to the British Ambassador[8] a conversation which he (Zaleski) had recently held with the champion of a United Europe, Count Coudenhove-Kalergi, in which the latter had discussed Brüning's proposal for a German–Polish settlement. According to this plan, there was to be a minor frontier rectifica-

---

[6] Note by Stresemann, December 11, 1927, AA, RAM/1428/2945H/D573 425–27.

[7] Note by Stresemann, December 12, 1927, *ibid.*, 435.

[8] In October 1929 Britain and Poland raised their diplomatic missions from ministerial to ambassadorial status. Traditionally ambassadors had only been exchanged between Great Powers, but after World War I there appeared increasing "inflationary" pressure against this hard rule of protocol, as several powers clamored for Great Power recognition by receiving this ambassadorial accolade. Poland was in the forefront of this international lobby for Great Power status. Originally none of the foreign missions in Warsaw had higher than ministerial rank. In 1924 France rewarded her ally by upgrading its mission to embassy status. In its effort to isolate and deprecate Poland, German diplomacy tried to prevent other countries from following suit. Chamberlain's conservative disposition and his dislike for this inflationary trend in the diplomatic rank structure helped the German efforts. Also, Britain had been guided by Germany's extreme susceptibility on this point. But in 1929 the Foreign Office felt that in order to dispel some of Warsaw's misgivings over the Rhineland evacuation Britain ought to consent to Poland's status ambitions. (Memorandum, Selby, June 19, 1929, FO, 371/14023, p. 93.)

Rumbold noted that when informed of Britain's plan, Schubert had "made rather a wry face and it is clear that he dislikes anything which serves to exalt the horns of the Poles. He is still rather inclined to take the line that the Poles had not yet really 'made good' " (Rumbold to Sir Ronald Lindsay, June 22, 1929, *ibid.*, p. 101). In 1929 Turkey, Italy, and the United States all raised their Warsaw missions to embassies. Germany did not follow suit until 1934 as part of Hitler's good-will offensive against Poland.

tion in Upper Silesia in Germany's favor and in East Prussia in favor of Poland; Danzig was to return to Germany but Poland would continue to enjoy port facilities there; and Germany would get one railroad across the "Corridor" that would be exclusively under German supervision. Zaleski had been skeptical whether Germany would be satisfied with such a solution, and when Erskine had asked him about Poland's response, he had answered cautiously. Zaleski envisaged particular trouble if Germany asked to station soldiers to guard this railroad line. But Erskine concluded from the Minister's reaction that "personally he would raise no objections," and that this had been "the first time that Zaleski has ever mentioned to me the possibility of any concession by Poland in regard to the Corridor."[9]

Perhaps men like Piłsudski and Zaleski might have been personally inclined to consent to a minor frontier rectification if normal relations with Germany could have been achieved at that price. But their personal flexibility on this matter, in itself could not bring about a change of policy. Polish popular opinion was inclined to view the recovery of the western provinces as a matter of historical inevitability and historical right, with a tendency to ignore the practical circumstances which had produced this diplomatic feat in 1919. Given this moralistic perspective, even the most minute territorial readjustment of the Polish–German frontier took on the appearance of a dishonorable sell-out of Poland's legitimate historical claims, which would subvert the legitimacy of her existence and might serve as the prelude to a renewed partition. Piłsudski's charismatic leadership, like that of monarchs of the baroque era, rested heavily on his ability to personify the spirit and ethos of the nation. This image would have become badly tarnished if the Marshal had engaged in what would have seemed like cheap "cattle-trading," exchanging Poland's birth rights for the uncertain prospects of improved relations with Germany. Ironically, it was the German position itself which contributed toward making the territorial issue nonnegotiable. For, as in the case of Poland, German policy rested on a mystique that tolerated no diplomatic compromise. Germany's revisionist aspirations, which were publicly asserted and privately reconfirmed by Schubert's conversation with Zaleski, could not be satisfied by some minor frontier adjustments in certain districts and an improvement in transit facilities through the "Corridor." German foreign policy de-

[9] Erskine to Sir Robert (later Lord) Vansittart, April 13, 1931, FO, 371/15222, p. 155.

manded the return of Danzig, the "Corridor," and Upper Silesia, and, from the viewpoint of Poland, even more. When Zaleski came to London in December 1931, he complained to the Foreign Office that Germany did not merely object to the "Corridor" but to the very existence of Poland and that she wanted to reduce Poland to what had been Congress Poland, to block her access to the sea, and to force her into a customs union with Germany.[10]

Given this basic Polish attitude which regarded her national territorial possessions as a non-negotiable factor, Germany's relentless revisionist strivings appeared at best as an irritating and futile Quixotic habit, and at worst as a constant reminder of her neighbor's aggressive intentions.

THE REVISIONIST ELEMENT IN GERMAN AND INTERNATIONAL PUBLICITY

In Germany the revisionist campaign proceeded relentlessly through the channels of diplomacy, publicity, and scholarship. It became intensified in tone and volume during the peak seasons of crisis in German–Polish relations. Even though these activities often frustrated whatever current negotiations for a limited agreement between Berlin and Warsaw were underway, they operated not only with official tolerance but received direct and indirect government aid and encouragement. The realization that a revisionist solution could not be reached by means of direct bilateral negotiations with Poland, but only in conjunction with an international action,[11] prompted Germany to direct a steady flow of propaganda to the outside world and in particular toward France, Britain, and the United States. The aim of German publicity was to convince world opinion—German public opinion needed no persuasion—that the drawing of frontiers at Versailles had been both unjust and unwise and in their present state constituted a formidable threat to European peace, which could not be guaranteed until the territorial status quo had been subjected to a revision.

It would be extremely difficult to give even a rough approximation of the sum which the Foreign Ministry granted for this purpose from its secret funds for which it was not publicly accountable. The Foreign

---

[10] Sir John Simon to Erskine, December 10, 1931, *ibid.*, p. 281.
[11] Rheinbaben, "Deutschland und Polen—Zwölf Thesen zur Revisionspolitik," *Europäische Gespräche* 9 (1931): 97.

Ministry was by no means the only public agency which made financial contributions for revisionist writings by German and foreign authors and arranged for "guided" tours of notable foreigners to the "Corridor" area. In terms of modern investments in propaganda and public information activities, the sum was doubtless infinitesimal, yet sums were regularly appropriated for this purpose in an era that was less obsessed by publicity than ours.

In January 1929 the Foreign Ministry listed fourteen books which had been written over the preceding four years under the sponsorship of the Press Division or the Polish desk of the *Auswärtiges Amt.*[12] These included, among others, Professor Kaufmann's *Das deutsche Westpreussen,*[13] and Roth's *Die Entstehung des polnischen Staates,* and mentioned the following works by foreign authors: *Pologne, Pologne . . .* by Etchegoyen; *Le Conflit de demain; Berlin–Varsovie–Dantzig* by Tourly; *Upper Silesia, an Economic Tragedy* by Street, and René Martel's *La Pologne et nous.* Funds were also made available to foreign visitors who came to inspect conditions in the "Corridor" and Upper Silesia. In December 1925 a certain Mrs. Canivet, an assistant to the British writer Sir Robert Donald, received 1,600 marks for traveling costs during her visit of the "Corridor" and Upper Silesia, and another 1,000 marks for writing an article which favorably represented the German view.[14] In 1926 the same Mrs. Canivet was secretly put in charge of the newly organized Danzig Information Office in London, with an annual operating budget of £600,[15] for the purpose of furnishing the British press with information on Danzig and the "Corridor" and to finance trips of politically important persons to these areas.[16] In August of that year the German authorities arranged for a visit by American Ambassador

[12] Note by Roth, January 4, 1929, AA, RAM/1428/2945H/D573 799–806.
[13] Kaufmann, the director of the Danzig Archives, had tried to prove by means of the documents contained in the Danzig Archives and in West Prussian monasteries that the official and popular language in the towns and monasteries of that region had always been German. Zechlin informed the German Consul General in Danzig on November 7, 1924 (AA, GA/3725/K170/K025 463) that Kaufmann's efforts doubtlessly served a worthy cause, if they could only be directed into the right (revisionist) channels. On August 6, 1925, the Foreign Office instructed its Danzig Consulate to give to Kaufmann 6,000 marks, which was later raised to 13,200 marks, and to book them as expenses for the press division (AA, GA/3726/K170/K025 904).
[14] Letter Wallroth to the German embassy in London, December 15, 1925, AA, GA/3726/K170/K026 002.
[15] *Ibid.*, 183; March 26, 1926.
[16] Report by Thermann (German consul general in Danzig), September 1, 1926, *ibid.*, 467–69.

Schurman to Marienburg and tried to impress Sir Robert Donald and Mrs. Canivet during their visits with the favorable aspects of the German settlements in the "Corridor" as compared to the poverty and dirt of the Polish counterparts.[17]

Early in 1928 a certain Lieutenant-Colonel G. S. Hutchison, an expert in the alchemist's art of turning foreign subsidies into venomous made-to-measure propaganda, who had received propaganda commissions from the Spanish and other governments and was, moreover, acquainted with the Upper Silesian problem, had traveled to Upper Silesia and had published a pro-German account under the name of *Silesia Revisited*. For this effort he had collected £1,000 from the German Foreign Office.[18] The Foreign Ministry even entertained plans of placing Hutchison in charge of a permanent revisionist propaganda service in Britain at an annual salary c£ £2,400;[19] however, the diplomatic files do not indicate whether this appointment was ever made. In 1929 Hutchison had written to Seeckt asking him to comment on his latest work, *The W Plan*, a work of fiction dealing with espionage during World War I. Dieckhoff, the counsellor of the German embassy in London, asked Seeckt to make his comments as favorable as possible because the author had shown much sympathy and understanding for the German position.[20] In 1932 Hutchison had given free reign to his fantasy and had published a rather improbable and pro-German political novel under the title *The Governor of Kattowitz*. The novel, which attacked the behavior of the Plebiscite Commission and Polish activities during the Upper Silesian insurrections, won the approval of the German Foreign Ministry. But it was work of such doubtful literary merit that the Foreign Ministry failed in its effort to have it published in German and adapted for a film version.[21] This failure spoke more for the artistic taste of German publishers and film producers than for the persuasiveness of her diplomats. In 1932 Hutchison began to complain bitterly that his literary merits did not receive adequate financial compensation from Germany. Baron von Neurath urged Seeckt not to take these complaints too seriously. The author had, indeed, as he himself mentioned on every suitable and unsuitable occasion, been quite useful to the German cause

17 Report by the Consul in Toruń, October 4, 1926, AA, GA/3726/K170/K026 590–94.
18 AA, GA/3736/K175/K030 047.
19 *Ibid.*, 019–20; January 21, 1929.
20 Letter Dieckhoff to Seeckt, September 18, 1929, *Seeckt Papers*, reel 16.
21 *Ibid.*, reel 17; AA, GA/3736/K175/K030 113–16.

and had received more than moral support from Germany. But recently, for obvious, i.e., budgetary reasons, moral support had to prevail over financial aid.[22]

Germany's diplomats abroad were also enlisted in the cause of carrying the revisionist gospel to all nations and were periodically armed with statistical and descriptive material relating to the background of the "Corridor" problem and its present status. They were urged to utilize this material on suitable occasions in conversations with officials in the countries to which they were accredited. Their motto was not so much "to think of it constantly but never to speak of it"; rather, "to speak of it constantly but softly" and without forcing the issue to an immediate crescendo. On June 30, 1925, in connection with the security pact discussions, all German diplomatic missions abroad received numerous memoranda expounding the just nature of Germany's revisionist demands and an accompanying letter of guidance by Stresemann.[23] The Foreign Minister instructed his diplomats to avail themselves of this information at their discretion in private conversations. These need not necessarily be sought but should not be avoided if the opportunity presented itself. Stresemann urged his diplomats to emphasize categorically that the security pact offer had not been made for the purpose of rolling up the Eastern question, as such an impression would only aid the cause of her opponents. It was imperative that world opinion become convinced that the eastern frontiers, as designed by the Versailles treaty, could not survive for long. "Since military measures cannot enter into question, an alteration of the present burdensome conditions will be possible only when it becomes the common knowledge of public opinion in the determining states that a revision of Germany's eastern boundaries is required in the interest of general peace."[24] A year later, on April 27, 1926, in a top-secret memorandum to all German mission chiefs, Schubert provided statistical information on the economic decline of Polish Upper Silesia which, according to Schubert, tended to reinforce Germany's earlier predictions that Upper Silesia under Polish management would soon become a burden rather than an asset to her new owner. This information was to be treated in the same manner and with equal caution as Stresemann's instruction in his above-cited memorandum.[25]

[22] Letter, Neurath to Seeckt, May 11, 1932, *Seeckt Papers*, reel 16.
[23] AA, StS/2301/4556H/E149 417–64.
[24] *Ibid.*, 414–16.
[25] AA, GA/3810/K225/K061 588–629.

GERMANY'S PREVENTIVE DIPLOMACY AGAINST POLISH EAST–LOCARNO EFFORTS

The corollary function of Germany's revisionist policy was the prevention of Polish designs in securing an East–Locarno agreement.[26] The so-called East–Locarno agreement, as Poland envisaged it, was to duplicate the original Locarno scheme by applying it to the east. This duplication would consist of a formal German recognition of her existing boundaries with Poland, guaranteed internationally by the principal Western Powers. In due course, Poland also gave consideration to several thematic variations of less desirable substitutes, some of which dispensed with Germany's formal recognition and sought to stabilize conditions in East Europe through multilateral guarantees between Poland, on the one side, and a combination of Baltic and Scandinavian countries, and possibly Russia, on the other. All political parties in Germany categorically rejected a German participation in an East–Locarno agreement, and her diplomacy was directed toward the obstruction of such a combination. On March 22, 1927, von Rheinbaben told the *Reichstag* that "no German government which in fact concluded an East–Locarno could maintain itself for more than twenty-four hours."[27] Freytagh-Loringhoven of the DNVP concluded: "We have fortunately come so far today that the government and all parties are in agreement that there will not and that there cannot be an East–Locarno in the original sense of the word,"[28] and Chancellor Müller assured the *Reichstag* on July 5, 1928, that there would be no change in the government's policy of rejecting any East–Locarno agreement. This had been confirmed by all parties on frequent occasions, including his Socialist colleagues.[29]

Sensitive to her increasing isolation and her failure at Locarno to secure an official German recognition or an international guarantee for her western frontiers, Poland intensified her diplomatic activities in the pursuit of constructing an eastern bloc of mutual guarantee in order to contribute to a general stabilization of conditions in East Europe. Her past efforts in convoking a Baltic League had met with Finnish resist-

---

[26] For a detailed treatment of the East–Locarno problem in German–Polish relations see Christian Höltje, *Die Weimarer Republik und das Ost–Locarno Problem 1919–1934. Revision oder Garantie der deutschen Ostgrenze von 1919* (Würzburg, 1958).
[27] Reichstag, *Sten. Berichte*, 392, p. 9848.
[28] *Ibid.*, 394, January 30, 1928, p. 12509.
[29] *Ibid.*, 423, p. 92.

ance, as the latter desired the participation of her Swedish neighbor in any diplomatic constellation of this nature. In February 1926, Stresemann informed Brockdorff-Rantzau that it was beyond doubt that as recently as December 1925 Poland had approached Sweden, Finland, and Russia on the matter of concluding a mutual guarantee pact which would also include Estonia and Latvia; however, the proposal had found a negative reception in Helsinki and Stockholm.[30] After this particular failure Warsaw shifted her efforts farther east and tried to promote a similar agreement between Poland, Russia, Finland, Rumania, Estonia, and Latvia.[31] The Director of the Eastern Division of the Polish Foreign Ministry had come to Moscow for this purpose, but as Chicherin confided to Rantzau at a dinner at the Finnish legation on March 7, the Soviet government had definitely rejected the Polish pact proposal, just as on previous occasions it had refused to conclude any multilateral agreement in which it was faced by a united Baltic bloc under Warsaw's tutelage.[32]

During the League Council session of September 1927, Poland surprised the assembled powers with the draft proposal for a general nonaggression pact under which all League members would make the pledge to refrain from any form of warfare and to conclude nonaggression pacts with one another. This particular Polish proposal, which exceeded the original Covenant obligations, immediately provoked the suspicions of Germany, for the Foreign Office believed it detected in it a veiled attempt by Warsaw to procure for herself an East–Locarno agreement through the back doors of the League of Nations. In order to avoid the onus of international recalcitrance, Germany officially refrained from an outright rejection of the Polish proposal.

While publicly assuming a pose of unprejudiced neutrality to the recent Polish proposal, Stresemann adeptly engaged the service of others in shunting the unwelcome proposal. In this he found a useful ally in the person of Chamberlain, who told Stresemann that he was horrified by Poland's audacity in attacking [überfallen] the League with her plan.[33] Briand himself betrayed a certain skepticism, but was willing to consider

---

[30] Letter, Stresemann to Brockdorff-Rantzau, February 24, 1926, AA, RAM/1426/2945H/D572 083–85.

[31] Telegram, Brockdorff-Rantzau, March 6, 1926, ibid., 112. In this telegram Rantzau actually uses the term Ost–Locarno, which also appeared in other German diplomatic correspondence of that time.

[32] AA, RAM/1426/2945H/D572 113.

[33] Stresemann's note of his talk with Chamberlain, September 3, 1927, AA, StS/2363/4587H/E183 475–76.

a general resolution in which the Assembly expressed the wish that all members of the League settle their disputes peacefully and without resort to force.[34] In view of British opposition and French passivity, Sokal, the Polish delegate, agreed to having the Polish proposal diluted to a general declaration which would renounce all forms of war. But even this version proved unacceptable to Britain, as she demanded that the renunciation be confined to aggressive war only.[35] After lengthy debates between the legal experts of Poland, Britain, France, and Germany, the teeth of the resolution were pulled and it was to apply solely to wars of aggression.[36] On September 19 the Council unanimously accepted a resolution which was to be presented to the Assembly (and was subsequently adopted by that body), and which declared that it was the duty of all League members to honor and respect the principles that prohibited every war of aggression and emphasized that peaceful means had to be used for the settlement of disputes of every kind. Stresemann called this outcome a thinly veiled defeat for Poland.[37] Germany viewed the Polish proposal as an East–Locarno snare which she had tactically averted.[38] Stresemann wrote to Chancellor Marx on September 21 that the Polish proposal had amounted to an East–Locarno which the major powers—Britain, France, and Germany—had successfully thwarted, thus administering a sound defeat to Poland and deflating her prestige.[39]

In so far as the Polish proposal echoed certain aspects of the Rhineland pact provisions of the Locarno agreement, it could be said to advance her a step in the direction of a guarantee of her western boundaries. But it would be a misreading of the Polish proposal to interpret it as an explicit attempt to bring the East–Locarno question to a showdown at that particular time. The whole scheme seemed rather nebulous and Poland's own position rather uncertain and vacillating. If her motive had been to seek a definite preliminary for an East–Locarno with this particular resolution, her position under these weighty circumstances would have been more clearly defined and less easily surrendered; nor would she have proposed such measures without having first taken advance soundings in Paris and London. As it was presented, both Chamberlain

[34] Note by Stresemann of his talk with Briand, September 3, 1927, *ibid.*, 496.
[35] Telegram, Stresemann to Koepke, September 8, 1927, AA, W/2575/5265H/E321 131–33.
[36] Record of a telephone call from Geneva, September 8, 1927, *ibid.*, 129.
[37] Telegram, Stresemann to Brockdorff-Rantzau, September 10, 1927, AA, StS/2363/4587H/E183 530–35.
[38] AA, W/2575/5265H/E321 129.
[39] Stresemann, *Vermächtnis* (Berlin, 1932), III, pp. 195–96.

and Briand had been taken by complete surprise when Warsaw first submitted its proposal at Geneva, and France in particular resented not having been consulted in advance. A month later, talking to his partner Hoesch at a luncheon, Chamberlain asked the German diplomat to communicate to Stresemann that Zaleski had assured him (Chamberlain) that by submitting her latest Geneva proposal, Poland had in no way intended to force additional obligations upon Germany and that no mention had been made of Germany in the Cabinet decision of the Polish government which had introduced the resolution. The original suggestion for this resolution had come from another small power, and Chamberlain was convinced that Zaleski spoke the truth, for his answer had been spontaneous and not in response to any criticism.[40] From these facts it may be deduced that Poland's primary motives in sponsoring the League nonaggression resolution had not been to secure an East–Locarno agreement, but stemmed from a desire to promote the general prospects of peace and to enhance Poland's status as a peace-loving as well as a Great Power. That Germany could ascribe no other than East–Locarno motives to Poland's action demonstrated her fixation with the idea. For the sake of comparison it is interesting to note that Chicherin, who suffered from the perpetual fixation of seeing in every move of European diplomacy a conspiracy to isolate or attack the Soviet Union, told Brockdorff-Rantzau that he regarded the whole proposal as nothing but a Polish maneuver to isolate the Soviet Union.[41]

It was only in connection with the international diplomatic talks in 1928 on the early evacuation of the Rhineland that Poland made a definite bid to tie this action to an East–Locarno. The desire to bring to an early close the foreign military occupation of the Rhineland zone, or in the words of Stresemann's letter to the Crown Prince, "first to get the strangler off our throat,"[42] was the most immediate primary goal of German foreign policy. The fiasco of Thoiry had delayed its realization but did not deter further German efforts. In the beginning of 1928 Berlin seemed to sense Poincaré's willingness to resume the Thoiry thread, provided it was accompanied by sufficient compensation to France in the form of a final and favorable settlement of the entire reparations question. "Under no circumstances," wrote Stresemann to Schubert, "should

[40] Telegram, Hoesch to Stresemann, October 9, 1927, AA, GA/3743/K182/K034 310–14.
[41] AA, RAM/1427/2945H/D573 045–46.
[42] Stresemann, Vermächtnis, II, p. 555; September 7, 1925.

the Rhineland evacuation have the same outcome as Thoiry,"[43] and he carefully surveyed the whole range of political issues in his conversation with Poincaré when he visited Paris on August 27, 1928, on the occasion of signing the Kellogg Pact.[44] During the Geneva session of September, Germany officially proposed, what had previously been reserved to private conversations, to settle the evacuation and reparation questions, and on September 16 the Entente Powers, as well as Germany and Japan, agreed to hold negotiations on the subject of an early Rhineland evacuation and recognized the necessity of finding a final solution to the reparations question.[45]

In the face of Germany's relentless revisionist strivings, the continued presence of foreign troops in the Rhineland offered to Poland the best possible security substitute for a Locarno-type international guarantee of her frontiers with Germany. It, furthermore, served as reassurance against the realization of a complete German–French reconciliation and thus helped underline the value of the French–Polish alliance in French eyes. Warsaw, consequently, witnessed the diplomatic preliminaries concerning the evacuation with extreme anxiety, and Berthelot confessed to Ambassador Hoesch that every second week Poland registered her security demands in Paris, or rather complained that her security interests did not receive due consideration by her French ally.[46]

Already, after the Thoiry meeting, the Polish Foreign Ministry contemplated the means whereby a premature evacuation of the Rhineland, which had suddenly become a likely prospect, could be made the occasion for an eastern security agreement. The Rhineland evacuation, argued a policy memorandum of the Foreign Ministry, clearly affected Polish security, and consequently Poland should be compensated for this security loss by getting a nonaggression pact with Germany that would follow Article 2 of the Rhine pact and would be placed under the guarantee of a third power. In addition, an attempt should be made in connection with the Rhineland evacuation to tighten the meshes of the international treaty network to prevent a revision. Article 16 of the Covenant and her alliance with France protected Poland against revision by means of flagrant aggression. The alliance also had validity under condi-

---

[43] *Stresemann Papers*, 3150/7378H/H168 110–11.
[44] Ludwig Zimmerman, *Deutsche Aussenpolitik in der Ära der Weimarer Republik* (Göttingen, 1958), p. 357.
[45] *Ibid.*, p. 360.
[46] Telegram, Hoesch, September 8, 1928, AA, D/2775/5462H/E372 298–300.

tions of "legal" war as specified by Article 15 (7) of the Covenant. Similarly, the unanimity provision for a peaceful revision under Article 19 of
the Covenant seemed to offer Poland adequate protection against Germany's revisionist policy. The only possible loopholes lay in Article 17
of the German–Polish arbitration treaty of 1925, which stipulated that
in the event that the Conciliation Commission should be unable to
settle a dispute, the dispute was to be submitted for settlement by the
League Council. This provision, it was feared, might serve Germany's
revisionist aims and it would therefore be useful to get it removed from
the arbitration treaty.[47]

When the Rhineland evacuation question again became acute in
1928, the first reaction in Poland almost instinctively was to try to insist
on the prolongation of the occupation. The newspaper *Czas* of June 16,
1928, pointed out that the best security guarantee for France and Poland
lay in the continuation of the Rhineland occupation, for once foreign
troops had left German soil the whole question of reparations payments
would be placed in jeopardy. But once a premature withdrawal seemed
unavoidable, Warsaw changed its tactics and tried to capitalize on the
inevitable and to link the evacuation with an eastern security agreement.

Article 429 of the Versailles treaty laid the base for a three-step
evacuation process that was to be completed by 1935 if Germany had
faithfully fulfilled the treaty terms. It also allowed for a delayed occupation beyond that date if "the guarantees against unprovoked aggression
by Germany [were] not considered sufficient." Zaleski took his stand on
a corollary interpretation of Article 429: if the failure to get sufficient
security guarantees could be used to delay the evacuation of the Rhineland, then a premature withdrawal should be accompanied by additional
security guarantees, namely German adherence to an Eastern pact. Having put forward this position in his address to the *Sejm* Foreign Affairs
Committee on May 18 and May 25, Zaleski hastened to Paris to put his
formula into action. In an address to the French–Polish Organization in
Paris on June 11, in an interview with the *Petit Parisien* two days later,
and in subsequent interviews in Brussels, he pointed out that after discussions with Briand and Berthelot he had become convinced that
France and Poland maintained identical views on the issue: in other
words, that France backed Warsaw's demands for an East–Locarno as
compensation for the Rhineland evacuation.[48]

[47] Undated memorandum, AMSZ, P II, fol. 4615, pp. 10–39.
[48] Telegram, Schubert to German missions in London, Brussels, Rome, and
Warsaw, June 16, 1928, AA, GA/3743/K182/K034 353.

Zaleski's pronouncements naturally met with strong criticism in Germany, but critical voices were raised elsewhere, including Poland itself. The Socialist paper *Robotnik* of July 17 found fault with the Minister's attempts to meddle in the Rhineland evacuation question which, in the opinion of the paper, was of no concern to Poland as it was not connected with the eastern security problem.[49] The *Robotnik* article produced an immediate government response. Vice Minister Wysocki wrote to the PPS leader and *Sejm* Marshal Daszyński observing how absolutely crucial it was for Polish security interests to win international recognition for the connection between the Rhineland evacuation and the security of Poland's western border, especially since the French were reluctant to accept such links. It was therefore imperative that all Polish parties, including the PPS, close ranks on this particular issue and back the official policy which tried to establish this connection. Wysocki asked for Daszyński's co-operation in bringing the PPS in line with these policy aims.[50]

In Berlin, Zaleski's Paris pronouncements aroused deep concern, for it was feared that the French might, indeed, have yielded to Polish pressure, which, in the words of Schubert, would constitute "a serious turning point in the development of our entire relations with France."[51]

Having been instructed to discover the real state of affairs, Hoesch called on Briand and found the latter obviously embarrassed by Zaleski's public assertions. Although Briand refused to engage in any polemics against the Foreign Minister of his ally, he reluctantly confided to the German diplomat, upon the latter's repeated pledge of utmost secrecy, that in his conversations with Zaleski not a word had been spoken concerning Poland's right to participate in the Rhineland evacuation question, and that when in his Senate speech of last winter he (Briand) had spoken of the right of other nations to participate in the evacuation issue, he had referred to Britain, Italy, and Belgium and not to Poland, and that this still applied.[52] In conclusion, Briand revealed his personal, as well as France's national predicament of combining the apparently irreconcilable: to appear at once as advocate for the security interests of her eastern ally, while at the same time bypassing these in the pursuit of

[49] Letter, Wysocki to Daszyński, July 20, 1928, AMSZ, P II, fol. 4617, pp. 99–101.
[50] *Ibid.*
[51] AA, GA/3743/K182/K034 355; June 16, 1928.
[52] Top secret telegram by Hoesch to Stresemann, June 22, 1928, AA, D/2774/5462H/E371 538–41.

a direct conciliation with her immediate neighbor. "Briand then added," reported Hoesch, "that he did of course not make himself inaccessible to Polish security wishes, nor did he fundamentally reject to discuss these with Poland, and also with Germany, in an uncommitted manner. However, he was convinced that Germany did not want any conflict with Poland."[53]

In Britain the *Manchester Guardian* of June 21, 1928, was extremely critical of Zaleski's attempt to link the Rhineland evacuation question with the East–Locarno issue. The *Guardian* erroneously believed Zaleski's statements to have been encouraged by France. In the view of this paper, the whole talk of an East–Locarno was pure nonsense because a territorial revision of the German–Polish frontier was both necessary and just. Chamberlain, too, was displeased with Zaleski's attempt to float Polish demands on the waves of the Rhineland question and, as Berthelot confided to Hoesch, had summoned the Polish envoy to warn that if Zaleski repeated these recent assertions, he (Chamberlain) would formally disavow the Foreign Minister and declare before Parliament that Britain was under no obligation to consider any possible Polish security wishes in connection with the Rhineland evacuation.[54] Chamberlain did precisely as he had threatened without, however, calling Poland by name. Speaking to the House of Commons two weeks later, the Foreign Secretary noted that the only powers other than the direct participants of the occupation which were to be consulted on the evacuation question were the remaining members of the Conference of Ambassadors, i.e., Italy and Belgium. Chamberlain found a precedent for his view in the fact that Briand, in his capacity as president of the Conference of Ambassadors, had addressed his note of November 16, 1925, which dealt with the evacuation of the first Rhineland zone, only to the members of the Conference of Ambassadors.[55]

On February 6, 1929, the parties of the government and of the Right in the *Sejm* accepted a resolution which had been sponsored by the For-

---

[53] *Ibid.*, 540. It is unlikely that Zaleski would have made the kind of public speeches which he did after his talks with Briand and Berthelot, if the Rhineland evacuation and eastern security issue had not been discussed at all, as Briand wanted Hoesch to believe. In all likelihood Briand had already done what he told Hoesch he would be inclined to do in future, namely to engage his ally in friendly but vague discussions which committed him to nothing. Given Zaleski's determination on this issue, it is difficult to see how Briand could have avoided a discussion on it. Zaleski might have misjudged Briand's position, or he may still have believed that he could force his ally's hand, when he gave his Paris declarations.

[54] Telegram, Hoesch, July 5, 1928, *ibid.*, 545.

[55] AA, D/2774/5462H/E371 553.

eign Affairs Committee and which gave assent to the early evacuation of the Rhineland as a means to normalize international relations. However, in view of the alarming state of affairs in Germany—the *Reichstag* debates of November 1928 had called for a revision of the German frontiers in the east and had discussed the construction of battle cruisers [*Panzerkreuzer*], measures which were obviously aimed against Poland[56]—the government was requested to introduce the necessary measures in connection with the premature Rhineland evacuation that would fortify Poland's general position of security.[57]

In view of the distinctly negative reception which France and Britain accorded to Warsaw's endeavors to convert the Rhineland evacuation into an East–Locarno, Poland was compelled to withdraw temporarily, though not to abrogate, her demands for such a guarantee. In order to retain the confidence of her ally, she staged a graceful retreat in a fashion strongly reminiscent of her behavior after Locarno. On June 12, 1929, the paper *Glos Prawdy*, which stood close to the Piłsudski camp, reassured its anxious readers that there existed no reason for alarm, for Poland could entirely rely on the fact that France and the Western Powers would take care that the evacuation of the Rhineland would not invalidate the security of the Rhine and the Vistula. As she had already done after Locarno, Poland invoked the argument that France for her own protection would not surrender Poland's security interests. Her constant diplomatic interventions in Paris, however, testify that in actuality Poland attached little faith to this argument. Poland herself was excluded from the discussions on the evacuation of the Rhineland which

---

[56] In January 1929 the British journalist Wickham Steed embarrassed the German government by publishing in the *Review of Reviews* a memorandum which Groener, the German minister of defense, had submitted to the Cabinet in November 1928 and which by some indiscretion had fallen into British hands. The memorandum advocated the construction of battle cruisers, known as *Panzerkreuzer* A, for the defense of East Prussia against a possible Polish attack (AA, T/2606/5551H/E391 370–81). In February 1929 the same journal published a telegram by Zaleski in which the latter denied Groener's charges of aggressive Polish plans and stated that Poland would offer to Berlin the proposal of concluding a mutual guarantee pact on the inviolability of their common frontier. No such direct offer, however, was made to Germany; Zaleski's telegram received little attention and, following Sthamer's advice, Germany refrained from a response, which would only have served to enhance the publicity of the Zaleski telegram (telegram, Sthamer, February 16, 1929, AA, GA/2910/6193H/E465 736).

[57] *Kurjer Warszawski*, February 7, 1929. Rauscher did not attach great importance to the resolution as the *Sejm* and the general public had shown little interest in it. (See Rauscher's report of February 10, 1929, AA, GA/2910/6193H/E465 728–30.)

were held at The Hague, parallel with negotiations on the adoption of the Young Plan. Having failed to link the Rhineland evacuation with an East–Locarno agreement, Poland then fell back on the original Locarno agreements, as she tried to graft onto the French–Polish Locarno alliance an explicit guarantee for immediate military assistance in the case of flagrant aggression. The discussions at The Hague which were held on this proposal met with a seemingly friendly, but in fact evasive, French position and led to no results. When the last foreign troops left the Rhineland on June 30, 1930, amidst frantic jubilation in Germany, Poland was no closer to her East–Locarno goal and her security position had considerably deteriorated. By evacuating the Rhineland, France had substantially weakened her capacity, quite apart from the intention, to aid Poland in the event of an aggression by Germany, and had thus intensified Polish doubts about the reliability of the French–Polish alliance.

The specter of an East–Locarno continued to appear on several subsequent occasions, but having won the initial battle against its realization at the time of the original Locarno accords, German diplomacy found it progressively easier to cope with later maneuvers to revive the concept.

On May 21, 1930, as a final gesture to forestall the economic collapse of Europe and to prevent the complete evaporation of the Locarno spirit, Briand presented to the European governments his famous Memorandum which called for the establishment of a Confederation of European States within the League framework and for close economic collaboration, as well as the reduction of tariffs among them. Germany's official policy warmly supported Briand's proposal but secretly entertained strong reservations because of its implied security aspects. The idea of a United Europe itself was nothing new or revolutionary, but its official presentation by one of Europe's most respected statesmen was an act of boldness which put the idea in an entirely different perspective. It liberated that concept from the confines of university common rooms and society drawing-rooms and placed it on the active agenda of international politics. For all its boldness, imaginative scope, and the genuinely high-minded intentions of its sponsor, the plan was premature and rather vague in its conception and formulation. It was only realized after the disastrous consequences of another global war and under very different circumstances some twenty-five years later. The very vagueness and inherently wide dimensions of the proposal led some countries to pin all their hopes and ambitions to it, while others associated with it all their fearful imaginings. The sum of these calculations immediately gave the proposal a gigantic scope and thus virtually precluded any agreement. Germany belonged to the latter category, and given her state of mind, it was natural that she should have searched for, and found, certain East–Locarno implications in Briand's proposal. Briand had pointed out that in order to solicit the co-operation of the smaller European states for this plan, assurance of their independence and security would have to be furnished and in this connection mentioned the need to expand the system of arbitration and to extend to the whole European community the Locarno policy of international guarantees.[58]

Poland's immediate endorsement of the Briand plan only confirmed German fears that the proposal was intended to promote an East–Locarno, and on May 27 the Chancellor told Sir Horace Rumbold, the British ambassador, that the Briand Memorandum expected Germany to renounce her previous policy of eastern revisionism.[59] Curtius informed the *Reichstag* that Germany favored the attempt to find a common European solution, but that she did not want to accept the existing French security system as the foundation for the new Europe.[60] German opposition remained firm even after a confidant of Briand had made it clear that the French statesman had sought an economic solution for Europe rather than an East–Locarno settlement.[61] The purposely veiled intentions on the issue of eastern security mirrored Briand's perpetual dilemma: being aware of German opposition, he refrained from openly demanding an East–Locarno system for all of Europe. Taking into consideration this basic predicament and judging from the language of the Memorandum, one can assume that it was intended to extend the system of arbitration in Europe according to the pattern of the abortive Geneva Protocol of 1924. To Germany even this meant the extension of the arbitration system for the purpose of securing the status quo while at Locarno she had succeeded in signing the eastern arbitration treaties without the explicit recognition of the eastern territorial settlement. As before, Germany was able to pay lip-service to a plan which was little to her liking, while entrusting the scuttling operation to others. Both Italy and Britain had greeted the Briand proposal with open skepticism

[58] Höltje, *Das Ost–Locarno Problem*, p. 207.
[59] Zimmerman, *Deutsche Aussenpolitik*, p. 404.
[60] Reichstag, *Sten. Berichte*, 444, February 10, 1931, p. 877.
[61] Zimmermann, *Deutsche Aussenpolitik*, p. 404.

and during the 1930 autumn session at Geneva, following the British proposal, the whole plan was submitted to a League study commission, thereby providing a first-class funeral for this far-reaching and visionary plan for Europe's salvation.

In the same manner, Germany refused to assume any eastern guarantee commitments when this question was raised again in connection with the international financial crisis and the proposed remedies. In an effort to stimulate the international flow of private funds and thus help stem the tide of the deteriorating financial situation, President Hoover proposed a one-year moratorium on all international payments on reparations and war reconstruction debts. This plan, the so-called Hoover Moratorium, was formally accepted on July 6, 1931. Later in the month, Chancellor Brüning, Foreign Minister Curtius, and State Secretary von Bülow, accompanied by a host of financial advisers, visited Paris and then London in order to confer with Germany's creditor powers about a solution to the grave economic crisis. The German negotiators were particularly eager for a foreign loan from the central banks of Britain and France to help tide the Brüning government over its financial and domestic political crisis. Both France and Poland tried to make any international financial assistance to Germany dependent on some security settlement.[62]

Before the opening of the London financial conference, Ambassador Skirmunt saw Prime Minister Ramsay MacDonald and stressed that it would be unthinkable that Germany should receive financial assistance through the Hoover Moratorium and a foreign loan while she conducted a foreign policy that was aggressive in spirit and bent on changing the international order.[63] In a conversation with United States Ambassador Wiley, Deputy Minister Beck observed that the Polish government counted on French support for the Polish thesis that a political détente was essential before any plan for relief of the German financial predicament could be attempted. Beck hoped that some formula could be found that was compatible with German interests and not injurious to her national pride and that would protect Europe against German adventures and recurring surprises.[64] A few days later, Wiley reported

[62] Note of a conversation of Dr. Regendanz, a confidant of General von Schleicher, with Beneš, September 1, 1931, *General Kurt von Schleicher Nachlass* [hereafter called Schleicher Papers] (Bundesarchiv, Coblenz), fol. 34, p. 25.

[63] Copy of a memorandum by Skirmunt, July 13, 1931, FO, 371/15222, p. 219.

[64] Report, Wiley, July 17, 1931, SD, 760c.62/154.

that in Polish public opinion Germany's financial crisis was partly bluff and partly self-induced and that their own economy was immune to the effects of the German disaster. The Polish Foreign Ministry had not made any direct reference to an East–Locarno in conjunction with the financial crisis, but talked of the need for a general European détente which was based on reciprocal pledges.[65] In October 1931, Ambassador Skirmunt left a memorandum with the American Embassy in London which drew attention to the fact that "when accepting President Hoover's proposal concerning one year's moratorium for international debts and reparations, the Polish government expressed the opinion that the creation of an atmosphere of political détente and of mutual confidence is a necessary condition for overcoming the present economic crisis." The memorandum, which listed recent evidence of an intensified revisionist campaign by Germany, concluded with the expressed wish that France and the United States would accept this Polish thesis and influence Germany in the same direction. Poland would always be "ready for such a détente on the basis of the existing political order."[66]

At the London meeting, Foreign Secretary Henderson explained to Curtius and von Bülow that before agreeing to a loan to Germany, France wanted some definite guarantee that Germany would not avail herself of Article 19 to raise the issue of her eastern boundary. When Curtius demurred, claiming that German public opinion would never tolerate such a guarantee, the conciliatory Henderson looked for some compromise solution. Under the proposal which he put forward, Germany would not be required to make a formal sacrifice of her revisionist claims but would give a solemn pledge that for a specified period of time she would leave her revisionist claims in a state of suspended animation. When Bülow categorically rejected even such temporary abeyance of Germany's revisonist drive, Henderson became exasperated and compared this recalcitrant behavior to Nero's fiddling while Rome burned.[67]

The eagerly anticipated foreign loan to Germany did not materialize. Britain herself was in the throes of a financial crisis which soon led to the momentous decision to abandon the gold standard. France was in a better position to oblige, but Germany's obdurate political stand on

[65] *Ibid.*, 155; July 21, 1931.
[66] *Ibid.*, 160; October 17, 1931.
[67] Note by Henderson, *DBFP*, Ser. II, vol. II, pp. 220–21.

the revisionist issue removed whatever incentive there might have existed to help stabilize the economic situation in Germany.

SEARCH FOR A "CORRIDOR" SOLUTION

Even though Germany was successful on the defensive side of her revisionist policy, where she managed to thwart several Polish initiatives for an East–Locarno, her active search for a territorial revision did not bring her any closer to the realization of this cherished goal, despite unceasing involvement. This active search for a solution produced a whole kaleidoscopic set of plans, projects, positions, and proposals, none of which offered any real prospects for being accepted but each added to the burden of German–Polish relations.

As this irredentist controversy not only involved the two disputants but was generally regarded as the weak link in the chain of European security, all of Europe seemed to participate in the mental arithmetic of solving the revisionist riddle. The one common denominator which linked all of the diverse schemes which emerged in this process was the implausibility of ever seeing any of them adopted in actual practice. A few examples will suffice to demonstrate the mental acrobatics and lack of political realism that accompanied these proposals. In the August 1, 1930, issue of the *Revue de Paris*, the Comte Wladimir d'Ormesson, formerly French ambassador to the Holy See and a member of the Académie Française, came forth with a rather "academic" proposal under which Germany was to be given a "Corridor" within the existing "Corridor," a solution which was neither acceptable to Germany nor to Poland. Georges Roux envisaged the creation of a condominium over the "Corridor,"[68] a solution which, given the state of animosity between Germany and Poland and judged by the Danzig experiment, where Danzig and Polish authorities were at perpetual loggerheads, portended little hope for a satisfactory outcome.

Other proposals that were being considered, most frequently in Britain, stressed the virtues of annexing Danzig to the "Corridor," thus creating an enlarged autonomous region under some special régime analogous to the status that applied to Danzig. This particular "Corridor" theme appeared in several variations. Max Muller, who as British minister in Warsaw tended to favor the Polish side in this territorial dispute, suggested that German pressure for a "Corridor" revision be

---

[68] Georges Roux, *Les Alpes ou le Rhin?*, pp. 116–17. Cited in AA, StS/2390/4624H/E203 200.

eased by neutralizing East Prussia and separating it from the *Reich*.[69] His colleagues in the Foreign Office, particularly Lampson and Strang, were critical of Muller's suggestion. Strang noted that such neutralization would be possible only if Germany regarded East Prussia as something not quite the same as the *Reich*, which was not at all the case, for if it were, then the whole psychological problem of the "Corridor" would disappear and with it Muller's rationale for the neutralization of East Prussia.[70] Lord D'Abernon offered a "Corridor" version that was con-considerably more favorable to the German side than Max Muller's suggestion. Rather than neutralizing East Prussia, which D'Abernon considered to be out of the question, he thought in terms of neutralizing the "Corridor" instead. In the long run, the Ambassador thought Germany might accept such a solution—no mention was made about Poland's reaction—and he was working in this direction: "I am constantly urging a reasonable spirit of compromise and accommodation on German Ministers and remind them of the great service rendered in 1920 by Poland to Western Europe in general and to Germany in particular. But their prejudice is not easy to overcome."[71] An even more far-reaching accommodation to German interests than Lord D'Abernon's proposal was considered in a memorandum of December 17, 1925, by Huxley, a member of the Central Department of the Foreign Office. Somewhat contrary to Chamberlain's opinion, which held that it was "perhaps unwise and undesirable even to discuss the Corridor problem at the present time,"[72] Huxley suggested that the problem might eventually be resolved by transforming Danzig and the "Corridor" into two German *Länder* under German sovereignty. The "Corridor" portion, which had an overwhelmingly Polish population, was to enjoy full regional autonomy "as regards language, education, . . . local government, and administration. . . ." Both *Länder* were to be neutralized under international guarantee, with the result that they would be inviolable in the event of war and their residents would be exempt from military service.[73]

British diplomatic speculation about a final "Corridor" revision continued in its rather vague and academic fashion, but by its very existence tended to give sustenance to Germany's revisionist policy.

[69] Max Muller to Chamberlain, May 9, 1925, FO, 371/10731, p. 94.
[70] Marginal comments by Lampson and Strang, *ibid.*, p. 91. Chamberlain agreed with Strang's argument and added a brisk "Exactly" in the margin (*ibid.*, p. 93).
[71] Lord D'Abernon to Chamberlain, October 29, 1925, FO, 371/10744, p. 64.
[72] Memorandum, Huxley, December 17, 1925, DBFP, I A, vol. I, p. 262.
[73] *Ibid.*, pp. 262–65.

On the German side, Dirksen was willing to view these "Corridor" neutralization plans as constituting at least a theoretical interim solution,[74] but both he and Rauscher feared that the German element in Danzig might be threatened by the Polish majority in such an autonomous buffer state.[75] Furthermore, as Schubert told Lord D'Abernon, if the "Corridor" was formally neutralized, it presented the danger "that this solution, which is not of much use to us, might be regarded as a final one and not just as a step forward." This was a trap which Germany had to avoid at all costs.[76] In the face of Poland's categorical refusal to subject the question of territorial revision to diplomatic conversations—not to speak of negotiations—the various proposals for solutions never left the realm of pure hypothetical speculation and, as Schubert said, provided a more appropriate subject for doctoral dissertations than for actual diplomatic negotiations.

LITHUANIA AS THE TRADING OBJECT

In the search for a solution to the "Corridor" problem the question of equitable compensation to Poland in exchange for the return of the "Corridor" and Danzig occupied the fantasies of diplomatic minds. As a possible compensation object for the loss of the "Corridor," the creation of a new "Corridor" lying east of East Prussia and giving Poland the port of Memel, or perhaps even the total absorption of Lithuania by Poland, was frequently mentioned. This so-called Lithuanian solution provided a constant conversation piece, but no authority was publicly willing to admit knowledge of it. The possible territorial exchange received much attention during the Locarno negotiations, and, subsequently, whenever Polish–Lithuanian relations suffered from one of their recurrent crises.

In May of 1925 Sthamer reported that in London the plan for an exchange of the Vistula "Corridor" for a Memel "Corridor" (with the possibility of returning Wilno to Lithuania in order to make the deal more appetizing) was gaining popularity and that a prominent official of the Foreign Office had recently developed such a plan; however, the London envoys of Poland and Lithuania, when questioned on this matter, had flatly rejected such a solution.[77]

---

[74] Note by Dirksen, March 21, 1925, AA, D/2771/5462H/E369 450.

[75] Letter, Rauscher to Dirksen, December 4, 1925, AA, StS/2339/4569H/E168 439.

[76] AA, StS/2339/4569H/E168 390–91; October 23, 1925.

[77] Telegram, Sthamer, May 14, 1925, AA, GA/3726/K170/K026 864–65.

Doubtless, the Lithuanian exchange solution had been examined by the British Foreign Office, but it seems to have been rejected as infeasible and dangerous. Britain had certain obligations under the Covenant to preserve the independence of Lithuania, and if it was questionable whether Poland would agree to an exchange solution, it was certain that Lithuania would not voluntarily agree to accept its demise under this plan. Also, Britain had considerable influence in the Baltic States which would have been diminished with the disappearance of one of them. Most important, perhaps, was the danger that this particular solution might spark another war in Europe. The different "Corridor" solutions which the British Foreign Office envisaged later in 1925 focused on the idea of a neutralized "Corridor" and made no reference to Lithuania. When Schubert returned from the Geneva session in December 1926 he assured the Soviet ambassador that Chamberlain had stated most emphatically that Britain had abandoned all consideration of the Lithuanian "Corridor" exchange plan.[78]

In Chicherin's global image there existed a diabolical hierarchy of hostile foreign powers in which the role of Beelzebub unquestionably fell to Britain. Given this state of mind, it was natural for Soviet diplomacy to suspect Britain of being the prime mover behind the Lithuanian exchange plan and to view the whole concept as being directed against the Soviet Union. In this case a tightly "programmed" image certainly led to mistaken conclusions; for of the foreign powers it was France, next to Germany, which proved to be the most active supporter of this exchange solution. France had the same Covenant responsibilities toward Lithuania as Britain, but as an ally of Poland she enjoyed less sympathy and influence in Kaunas than Britain; hence, she stood to lose less than Britain if Lithuania were deprived of Memel or were to disappear altogether. Furthermore, unlike Britain, France had direct security commitments toward Poland and was thus more actively engaged in finding a permanent solution to the German–Polish problem which would remove the necessity of ever having to come to Poland's military assistance. Given this situation, it is easy to see why in the eyes of Paris the Lithuanian exchange solution appeared to be the missing part that might complete the puzzle and thus reconcile Berlin and Warsaw and free France from her predicament.

During the 1925 summer session of the League Council, Briand took Chamberlain to tea on the outskirts of Geneva, on which occasion the

[78] AA, RAM/1427/2945H/D572 502; December 22, 1926.

two statesmen were detained by a conscientious waitress who refused to accept their foreign currency. In Chamberlain's report of the meeting,

> Briand, who has a great sense of the real and practical, regrets that in the peace treaties the Poles bit off more than they can easily chew, and he appears to have some idea that eventually an arrangement may be made with Russia on the basis of some slight adjustment of territory, and with Germany at the expense of Lithuania, or so at least I suppose, for he said it was in view of these conversations that they had postponed the coming into force of the Memel Convention at the Ambassadors' Conference.[79]

Even in direct talks with the Germans the French government raised the possibility of compensating Poland at the expense of Lithuania in return for a "Corridor" revision. When Briand spoke to Hoesch soon after the memorable meeting between Piłsudski and Stresemann, he revealed his position on this delicate matter in somewhat Delphic terms. He emphasized that it was France's desire to retain the unlimited sovereignty of Lithuania, but at the same time he admitted that if he were responsible for the conduct of German foreign policy, he would find the most fruitful approach in pursuing the Lithuanian exchange solution.[80]

To Moscow the possibility of such an exchange presented a subject for uneasy contemplation. The absorption of Lithuania by Poland threatened to establish Warsaw's predominance over the Baltic States and to cut the territorial access route to Germany. Furthermore, a successful "Corridor" exchange solution might open the door for a German–Polish reconciliation. When Stresemann talked with Chicherin in December 1926, he denied that Germany had ever negotiated or even privately discussed the exchange scheme with Britain or any other power. Stresemann admitted that when the French journalist Sauerwein had introduced the exchange question, he had been told that Germany sought a solution which would grant Poland secure access to the sea by agreements similar to those which Germany had concluded with Czechoslovakia. The Lithuanian exchange solution was out of the question, if for no other reason than that Germany could never agree to have Memel, with its large German population, become a Polish port.[81]

[79] Chamberlain to Tyrell, June 11, 1925, FO, 371/10733, p. 133.
[80] Hoesch to Schubert, February 17, 1928, AA, D/2770/5462H/E368 765.
[81] Note by Schubert of the Stresemann–Chicherin talk of December 2, 1926, AA, GA/3035/6698H/H111 095–107.

In his relations with Moscow, Stresemann had been eager to represent all talk about a possible Lithuanian exchange solution as pure fiction. But the files of the German Foreign Ministry leave no doubt that at least between the years 1925 and 1928 this project was accorded more than a mere academic interest. Van Hamel reports that when, during his tenure as League High Commissioner for Danzig, he called on Stresemann, the Foreign Minister in an entirely noncommittal manner had asked for his opinion on the idea of compensating Poland with a passage through Lithuania and the port of Memel in return for her surrender of the "Corridor."[82] Dirksen, who spent a good deal of his time in 1925 and 1926 drawing up revisionist blueprints, saw some possibility in the exchange solution, even though he realized that Poland would never voluntarily submit to such a scheme, but only if she were exposed to extreme international pressure. Such pressure, Dirksen concluded, would basically have to come from Russia, for "without the co-operation of Russia and Germany a solution to the 'Corridor' [was] hardly thinkable." Dirksen was aware of the inherent difficulties and complications of this exchange scheme and regarded it only as a last resort for a revisionist settlement.[83]

Despite its own reservations on the exchange solution, the Foreign Ministry was careful not to block this prospective avenue prematurely. Schubert noted that in talking to Krestinski he had purposely refrained from describing the exchange program as being utterly unacceptable.[84] More significantly, Germany avoided a favorable response to the Lithuanian suggestion of July 1926 to conclude an arbitration and a minority protection treaty, as well as an agreement for the purpose of co-ordinating their policies in the League of Nations and their opposition to Poland's minority policy. While the Foreign Office favored the first part of the proposal, it entertained serious reservations against those stipulations which would altogether eliminate a future exchange solution, for, ac-

---

[82] Joost A. van Hamel, *Danzig and the Polish Problem* (New York, 1933), p. 152. The High Commissioner had been skeptical of this plan, as there was no indication of Lithuania's willingness to accept such a solution.

[83] Undated note by Dirksen, written approximately during the summer of 1925, AA, D/2768/5462H/E366 895–912. Dirksen was one of the primary exponents of that school of thought in the Foreign Office that considered a close German–Soviet co-operation indispensable for a successful solution of the revisionist issue. His partisanship for this approach apparently blinded him to the obvious fact that it was Russia's prime interest to sabotage the realization of a Lithuanian exchange solution and that in this particular instance, as also in other cases, German–Soviet policies on the Polish question were competitive and not parallel.

[84] Note by Schubert, November 19, 1926, AA, GA/3035/6698H/H111 137.

cording to the Lithuanian plan, the agreement was to be augmented by a so-called noncompensation treaty, adopting the formula: "No Memel 'Corridor' at Lithuania's expense, no surrender of East Prussia at Germany's expense."[85] During the period when Stresemann left the imprint of his flexible approach on German foreign policy, the idea of a Lithuanian exchange deal was secretly examined as one in a series of strategic plans for a territorial revision. After due evaluation it was stamped with reservations and marked unfit for present application, but mentally the plan was preserved for possible future use. Even Curtius, who seemed to accord stronger probability value to the Lithuanian exchange plan, considered the time premature for putting this strategy into execution. Answering a letter of Defense Minister Groener, who had voiced the opinion that Poland might be induced to return the "Corridor" if she could retain Gdynia and gain Lithuania and Memel, Curtius agreed that Groener's observations largely coincided with his own views and with the reports from German consulates. Much as the Foreign Minister supported the idea, he considered it necessary to keep the plan secret until the time when a public discussion would aid the revisionist cause.[86]

That a fantastic prospect of this kind could for so long have seriously occupied the minds of German diplomats indicates how the obdurate and total commitment to the revisionist cause dimmed their perceptiveness for existing political realities. The standards of eighteenth- and nineteenth-century diplomatic procedure, whereby carving and trading operations could be performed on smaller countries by mutual consent of the Great Powers without resort to a major war, could hardly be expected to apply under postwar conditions at a time when the belief in collective security stood at its zenith; moreover, when Lithuania enjoyed League membership. Furthermore, Russia was outspokenly hostile to the concept of ceding the Memel territory, and *a fortiori* to the entire absorption of Lithuania by Poland. While this left room for debate as to whether full credit could be given to Moscow's warnings that such action would constitute a *casus belli*, Germany could be under no misapprehension that any open promotion on her part of the Lithuanian

---

[85] AA, W/2575/5265H, E320 531–35.

[86] Letter, Curtius to Groener, January 30, 1931, AA, RAM/1430/2945H/ D575 540–41. It is somewhat doubtful whether Curtius seriously regarded an exchange solution of this kind as a realistic prospect. It might just have been a convenient argument with which to calm his foreign policy critics who clamored for an active revisionist program.

exchange scheme would seriously jeopardize her coveted position of friendship with the Soviet Union.

Finally, there was nothing in the attitude of Lithuania and Poland, the parties most concerned, that indicated that they would voluntarily submit to such a scheme. Lithuania would have lost the commercially and strategically important harbor of Memel, if not also her very existence as an independent state. The Lithuanian envoy in Berlin was much relieved when Schubert dismissed the whole exchange scheme as an infamous poisoning of the well [*Brunnenvergiftung*] by Germany's enemies.[87]

As for Poland, even from a purely commercial aspect, Memel represented a poor compensation for Danzig and Gdynia, which had better harbors and were closer to her overseas markets than Memel. An exchange on this basis would therefore have been a severe blow to Poland's campaign for increased maritime trade. Moreover, Poland had raised to political and quasi-religious doctrine the refusal to surrender an inch of her present territorial possessions, and her entire anti-revisionist campaign, which was based on the argument that she defended territories which had been rightfully restored to her, would have suffered a severe moral defeat if she herself surrendered some of these regions with a native Polish population in return for her participation in the partition of Lithuania. Whatever ambitions Warsaw might still have regarding the annexation of Lithuania—and there was evidence that the unhappy experience with her minority groups had considerably weakened Polish enthusiasm for the acquisition of yet another unruly and militant minority group—the exchange of the "Corridor," with a population that had a Polish majority, for Lithuania was politically unprofitable and morally infeasible.[88] Polish diplomacy viewed the whole Lithuanian exchange solution as a maneuver for a renewed partition of Poland and strongly objected to it. Speaking to the *Sejm* Foreign Affairs Committee on February 10, 1931, Zaleski declared that in modern times the traffic in people was unacceptable. The population in the "Corridor" was essentially Polish and would not be abandoned. Poland had no plans for conquest of anyone, and least of all Lithuania, to whom she was tied by a long history and friendship.[89]

[87] Note by Schubert, June 26, 1925, AA, W/2575/5265H/E320 647–48.
[88] Regendanz to Schleicher, May 27, 1932, *Schleicher Papers*, fol. 91, pp. 151–54.
[89] Report, Wiley, February 14, 1931, SD, 860c.021/14.

GERMAN REVISIONISM AND THE STABILIZATION LOAN

Concurrent with her confidential explorations of the Lithuanian exchange question as a possible avenue for her revisionist policy, Germany engaged herself more actively in the direction of pursuing a revisionist solution in connection with Poland's economic collapse and a consequent international economic stabilization effort. Already, in July 1925, when Skrzyński visited the United States in an effort to obtain an American loan to Poland, the German embassy in Washington undertook to frustrate Polish intentions. Maltzan had let it be known in the State Department that when a Foreign Minister left his country at a time of national crisis to betake himself to Washington in the full heat of summer, it spoke volumes for the poor economic condition of that country.[90] Upon his return to Warsaw, Skrzyński told Rauscher indignantly that in the United States, as in Europe, he had encountered Germany's anti-Polish propaganda at every step.[91]

Poland's economic crisis in 1925 and 1926 was viewed with concern in Western Europe, especially because of the assistance it offered to the advance of Communism, and it inspired plans for an international stabilization action for the rescue of the Polish economy. In view of Germany's strong economic influence and potential in Poland, even if this was not being fully exploited at the time, her participation was eagerly sought. This created widespread hopes in Germany of making her financial participation dependent on a previous redress of her territorial claims against Poland. Schubert, in a secret memorandum dating from approximately November 1925, did not share the view that Germany would succeed in making the stabilization loan dependent on a previous territorial revision, for never in history had a financial consortium managed to force a sovereign state to accept territorial sacrifices in return for financial help. "The question of the 'Corridor'," the State Secretary noted, "cannot be resolved other than by force, in conjunction with numerous favorable circumstances." The international loan, Schubert predicted correctly, would eventually be made regardless of German participation, and German intransigence would merely result in her exclusion from this business. But even if a financial consortium could

---

[90] Telegram, Maltzan to Zechlin, July 16, 1925, Deutsches Zentralarchiv Potsdam, AA, no. 67367, p. 195; cited in Berthold Puchert, *Der Wirtschaftskrieg des Deutschen Imperialismus gegen Polen, 1925–1934* (East Berlin, 1963), pp. 90–91.
[91] Telegram, Rauscher, August 22, 1925, Deutsches Zentralarchiv Potsdam, AA, no. 65215, p. 49; cited in Puchert, *Der Wirtschaftskrieg*, pp. 90–91.

not achieve a territorial revision, it might succeed in getting Poland to cut her military budget and reduce the size of her armed forces, thus terminating her assumed role as a Great Power and cutting her down to deserved Middle Power status. This would help create a desirable foundation "for a future power-political settlement" [*machtpolitische Auseinandersetzung*].[92]

Schubert's free confession that a revision could only be reached by force, even though force in the calculations of the Foreign Ministry meant diplomatic intervention or a possible occupation of the "Corridor" in the event of a Polish civil war or a renewed Polish–Soviet war rather than a surprise attack initiated by Germany, contradicted his own diplomatic efforts to normalize German–Polish relations and to reach a revisionist solution by peaceful means. In conversations with Paul-Boncour and Beneš in September 1926, Schubert had emphasized the need for improved relations with Poland and had been confident that eventually Poland would voluntarily consent to a peaceful revision for the sake of a reconciliation with Germany, which was of greater value to her than the continued possession of the "Corridor" and Upper Silesia.[93] This apparent ambivalence in the attitude of Schubert was shared by other officials of the Foreign Ministry. The impregnable resistance which Poland maintained against Germany's revisionist strivings forced German diplomats during their periodic inventory-taking of the revisionist policy to come to the painful conclusion that a peaceful revision was an illusion and that, consequently, the alternatives were limited either to the renunciation of her revisionist aims altogether or the pursuit of this goal by force. The first alternative they refused to accept, but they hesitated —furtive glances excepted—in facing the second. As the result of this dilemma, German diplomacy tended to repress the confrontation with reality and continued to pursue the mirage of a peaceful revision, hoping against hope and rational analysis that Warsaw's resistance would mellow, even though there was nothing in the present adamant position of Poland to encourage this view.

Schubert's momentary confrontation with reality had forced him to conclude correctly, in the above-cited memorandum of November 1925, that a revision could not be attained in conjunction with a stabilization loan or other peaceful methods but only by means of force. The impact of this realization seems to have been sufficiently disturbing to

[92] AA, StS/2339/4569H/E168 400–5.
[93] Notes by Schubert, September 19 and September 25, 1926, AA, StS/2362/ 4587H/E182 974–78; 986–91.

his rather gentle nature to induce the repression of his own conclusions, for a little later in talking with *Reichsbank* President Schacht, Schubert showed himself in agreement with the concept of manipulating a territorial revision in conjunction with the international stabilization loan.[94]

Dirksen's position was characterized by equal ambivalence. In a memorandum of November 16, 1925, he referred to the revisionist opportunities that arose from the impending political and economic collapse of Poland: "Out of the . . . necessity to protect her national compatriots in Poland against anarchy and in order to secure communication with East Prussia, as guaranteed in the peace treaty, [Germany] . . . might deduce far-reaching demands." This demand, according to Dirksen, would entail the occupation by Germany of those areas which she now claimed. "The preliminary measures for the purely technical execution of this action ought to be undertaken now, as the real event might already occur in a short time, and an immediate action would then be required."[95] But when the concept of the use of force came up in an exchange of letters with Rauscher in 1926, Dirksen's reaction was negative. On June 11, 1926, Rauscher had written to Dirksen: "I do not believe that one can solve territorial questions in conjunction with financial ones, and I do not believe that there can exist in Poland such a measure of impoverishment and need for stabilization that any Polish government would be in a position or willing to pay for her financial salvation with the sequestration of territories. The "Corridor" and Upper Silesia will return to the German *Reich* only as the consequence of a war[96] and the connected power-political upheaval in Poland, but never as the result of such logical and convincing economic considerations."[97] From this realistic appraisal Rauscher had come to the personal conclusion that Germany would have to suspend, if not officially cancel, her revisionist activities. But Rauscher had not explicitly outlined this train of thought, and Dirksen mistakenly and with some indignation interpreted it as constituting approval, if not encouragement, by Rauscher of the use of force.

> But even if I should lean toward your thesis and did not expect much in this conjunction, [stabilization loan] should this be a reason to abandon the experiment entirely . . . ? Should our only try for a solution in the

---

94 *AA*, StS/2339/4569H/E168 653–57.
95 *AA*, StS/2339/4569H/E168 406–15.
96 At the reference to the use of force two question marks, probably in Schubert's hand, are to be found in the margin.
97 *AA*, StS/2339/4569H/E168 778.

Polish question be confined to working for a solution by force? I am of
the opinion that in any case we ought to strive—one may judge the
chances for success as one will—to regain the "Corridor" and Upper
Silesia by peaceful means; as a peaceful solution there seems to me only
one, namely morally to force a Poland, which has been weakened and
placed under international pressure, to come to a political settlement
with Germany and [thereby] gain certain guarantees for the continued
existence of the rest of her territory.[98]

Toward the end of 1925, financial circles in New York and London,
in particular Montagu Norman, the powerful governor of the Bank of
England, began to draft plans for an international financial loan, with
Germany's participation, for the stabilization of the Polish złoty and the
reconstruction of the Polish economy. Hjalmar Schacht, Germany's
financial wizard, became the most active champion of the plan which
would combine Germany's financial participation in this venture with
the satisfaction of her territorial claims against Poland. But Schacht's
financial magic proved no more persuasive than the efforts of German
diplomacy and for once the task exceeded the wizard's capacity. The
plan was at once a miscalculation of the Polish psychology and of the
resilience of the Polish economy. Toward the end of 1925, Lord D'Abernon noted that Schacht seemed "so permeated with the conviction that
the existing 'Corridor' arrangement is unworkable . . . that he appears
considerably to underrate the difficulty of inducing any Polish Government to abandon their present position."[99] Diamand confessed to Schubert that his meeting with Schacht had left him "terribly depressed,"
for Schacht had countered all his suggestions for an economic reconciliation in the grand style by insisting on a preceding territorial revision.[100]

While Schacht set the stage in Berlin, the German embassy in London extended its feelers to sound out the British government and London financial circles. In March, Dufour-Féronce, the counsellor of the
German embassy, asked Norman whether it would not be best to com-

---

[98] Letter, Dirksen to Rauscher, June 15, 1926, AA, W/2575/5265H/E321 191.
In notes dating from the summer of 1925 and March 4, 1926 (AA, D/2768/5462H/
E366 911–12; AA, D/2770/5462H/E368 725–29), Dirksen had emphasized that
Germany did not seek a new partition of Poland and that she had no interest in her
neighbor's decline beyond the point of making her more submissive to a territorial
revision, and that after the effective completion of this revision there existed, from
the side of Germany, no objection to friendly political relations and economic co-
operation between Germany and Poland.
[99] Edgar D'Abernon, *An Ambassador of Peace* (London, 1929–1930), III, p.
221.
[100] Note by Schubert, January 9, 1926, AA, D/2768/5462H/E367 357.

bine the financial stabilization with a territorial settlement and told the Governor that Schacht had made any German participation dependent on a territorial revision. Norman at first listed several reservations, as most financial experts were disinclined to burden financial issues with political questions; however, he agreed with Dufour's suggestion that once Germany joined the League, the latter would provide the proper forum to handle the financial and territorial settlement with respect to Poland.[101] On March 19, Dufour saw Tyrell of the British Foreign Office and suggested that the border and stabilization questions would best be settled jointly within the League. Tyrell admitted the value of this suggestion, although he claimed that the idea had not occurred to him before.[102] When Dufour dined with Norman on April 8, he found the latter eager to enlist German participation for the international stabilization action in Poland. Norman had apparently been impressed by the argument that there could be no lasting peace in Europe until the German–Polish border problem had been solved. He was therefore applying his influence with American and British financial circles to dissuade them from extending loans to Poland until the "Corridor" and Upper Silesian question had been discussed.[103]

Stresemann considered the issue sufficiently important to provide Ambassador Sthamer with a lengthy directive for his conduct.[104] Stresemann noted with satisfaction that certain circles in Britain were beginning to realize "that the solution of this question [frontier revision in the east] was not only the most important issue of our policy, but perhaps the most important problem of European policy in general. The participation of England [was] an indispensable prerequisite for a solution by peaceful means and only such a solution would come into question for us." A peaceful revision, however, was possible only if the Polish economy had completely disintegrated, for "as long as that country retains any of its strength;" wrote Stresemann, "no Polish government will be in a position to engage in a peaceful understanding with us on the frontier question. Seen broadly, it will consequently have to be our goal to postpone the final and lasting stabilization of Poland until that country will be ripe for the settlement of the border question according to our wishes and until our political position of power will have been sufficiently

101 AA, StS/2339/4569H/E168 586–92.
102 Ibid., 606–14.
103 Ibid., 640–49. Norman had expressed himself similarly to Sthamer on the previous day. (AA, RAM/1426/2945H/D572 143–45).
104 Letter, Stresemann to Sthamer, April 10, 1926, AA, StS/2339/4569H/E168 435–40.

fortified." Should Britain start on a preliminary stabilization operation at once, it would still be advisable for Germany to participate in order to retain her hand in the game and to influence developments as far as possible according to her plans.[105] Stresemann opposed the idea of conducting the stabilization measure under the auspices of the League, for even if Germany should become a member of that body, she would not exercise sufficient power to influence the decision in her favor.[106] In concluding, the Foreign Minister warned that the whole question was one of extreme complexity and delicacy and that German diplomats should engage themselves in discussions on this point only if the matter had first been brought up by the other side.[107]

After some preliminary examinations, Britain reversed what had originally seemed like a positive view of the German plan to couple the revisionist issue with the stabilization loan and began to oppose this scheme. Lampson and Undersecretary Gregory of the Foreign Office had made it known that while German participation in the stabilization loan was still welcome, Germany should not commit the error of believing or even demanding that this be linked with the revisionist question. A revision was impossible at the time and it should be reserved for the future.[108] At the end of May, Schacht visited Montagu Norman in London and pointed out that no economic stabilization measures for Poland could be effective unless joined by Germany. Germany would willingly participate, once her territorial claims for the "Corridor"— Upper Silesia could be deferred to a later settlement—had been satisfied. But Norman, too, was now cool to Schacht's great schemes and informed him that after considerable study and deliberation of the question he had come to reject the idea of coupling the two issues. Strong,

---

105 This was also Rauscher's view, as expressed in a letter to Dirksen, December 4, 1925, AA, StS/2339/4569H/E168 435–40. Dirksen, on the other hand, and in this position he was supported by Schacht and Hilferding, opposed any interim participation by Germany, for whatever theoretical arguments could be made in favor of this strategy, world opinion would interpret such action as the surrender of Germany's negative attitude toward Poland and consequently as the renunciation of her revisionist demands (see Dirksen's letter to Rauscher, June 8, 1926, AA, W/2575/5265H/E321 204–9).

106 It is interesting to observe that Poland, too, opposed an international financial assistance program to Poland that would be conducted under the auspices of the League. Writing in the *Kurjer Warszawski* of April 20, 1926, Grabski noted that, unlike Austria and Hungary, Poland could not accept a League loan, for such a loan would be accompanied by international financial control measures which would lead to demands for a territorial revision.

107 AA, StS/2339/4569H/E168 435–40.

108 Telegram, Sthamer, May 21, 1926, AA, RAM/1426/2945H/D572 252.

of the Federal Reserve Bank of New York, and he were still eager to embark on an early stabilization effort and wanted Germany to join, but they could not accept her political demands.[109]

Despite this negative response, Montagu Norman did not seem to have entirely abandoned the German proposal, for when he spoke with Lampson during the summer, he referred to the plan to return the Eupen and Malmedy districts to Germany in return for financial compensation to Belgium. This, he thought, might provide a useful precedent for the return of the "Corridor" against financial compensation to Poland. Lampson immediately warned the Governor of the dangers of raising the "Corridor" issue at this time. British policy sought to promote a general accommodation between Germany and Poland, especially in the economic sphere. Once they had reached an accommodation, then "many things might be possible: perhaps not actually territorial readjustments, but something which might obviate the many drawbacks and inconveniences of the existing territorial status."[110] Chamberlain, too, had become concerned over Norman's apparent interest in raising the "Corridor" problem at this time and expressed the hope "that the Governor will ruminate no more on these dangerous and unprofitable themes."[111] In line with Chamberlain's wishes, Lampson noted on the following day: "I took the opportunity afforded by this [Norman's] visit today to say as much. He took it quite well."[112]

In the face of British opposition and because of the growing tendency of American bankers to press ahead with the loan, regardless of German participation, Berlin was forced to conclude that the scheme had failed. Shifting her tactics, Germany confined her subsequent efforts to an outright obstruction of a foreign loan to Poland. In November 1926, a certain Mr. Eberstadt, who was a partner of the New York firm of Dillon & Reed which had negotiated a 35 million dollar loan with Poland in 1925, came to Berlin. There he was warned that if his firm went through with paying Poland the second instalment of the loan, a sum of 15 million dollars, it could hardly expect that the German government would permit the Dillion & Reed Co. to participate in the new loan to Germany that was then under consideration.[113] In line with

---

[109] Note by Schacht of his conversation with Norman, May 29, 1926, AA, RAM/1426/2945H/D572 263–67.
[110] Note, Lampson, August 12, 1926, FO, 371/11280, pp. 49–50.
[111] Marginal note by Chamberlain, August 12, 1926, *ibid.*, p. 48.
[112] Note, Lampson, August 13, 1926, *ibid.*
[113] Note by Zechlin, November 18, 1926, AA, StS/2339/4569H/E168 862–63.

these blocking tactics, Schacht warned Kindersley, a confidant of Norman, that all money lent to Poland as part of a transaction that excluded Germany was practically a lost investment.[114]

In April 1927, Schacht met in Calais with the Governor of the Bank of England, the Director of the Bank of France, and Harrison, a representative of the Federal Reserve Bank. When the latter indicated strong interest in getting Germany to participate in the loan to Poland, Schacht pointed out that in view of the past conduct of the Polish government in meeting its financial obligations, he considered it quite out of the question that any reputable bank in Germany would participate in a loan to Poland.[115]

Despite Germany's obstructionist activities, Poland managed to negotiate an international stabilization loan for 64 million dollars from Bankers Trust Co., the Chase National Bank of New York, and Lazard Brothers of London. Even though she had been forced to accept it on rather unfavorable terms (issue price at 92 and a 7 per cent interest rate, as well as the appointment of Charles Dewey, Undersecretary of the U.S. Treasury and formerly Vice-President of the Northern Trust Co. of Chicago, as financial adviser to the Polish government with powers of direction and supervision over the Polish economy) the loan significantly contributed to consolidating Poland's financial position and in raising her international prestige. It, furthermore, dispelled the impression which Germany had tried to create internationally as part of her revisionist propaganda that there could be no international economic assistance to Poland without German participation. The lesson of failure in her financial scheme prompted Germany to seek other avenues for her revisionist policy than promoting Poland's economic collapse, and thus induced her to take a more positive attitude toward the conclusion of a trade treaty with Poland.

STRESEMANN'S REVISIONIST STRATEGY

Throughout the entire period when he held the reins of Germany's foreign policy, Stresemann pursued the goal of revising the German–Polish frontier with an unswerving tenacity, yet with extreme caution. His revisionist strategy flowed from a long-range conception and, consequently, exposed it to charges by the hot-spurred Nationalists who saw

114 Telegram, Wallroth to legations in Warsaw, London, and Washington, February 16, 1927, AA, StS/2339/4569H/E168 964.
115 Letter, Schacht to Stresemann, April 6, 1927, *ibid.*, 989–91.

in this approach at best too much passivity and at worst a complete renunciation for the sake of a utopian European goal. By his grand strategy the German–Polish border dispute was not treated as an exclusively German–Polish conflict but was purposely elevated to a general European problem which was to be settled within the international forum and with international backing, once it had become a widely accepted belief that the peace of Europe and the international economic and political co-operation with Germany could not be assured until the Eastern question had been resolved. In this respect Karl Erdmann, without exaggerating the issue, regards the Polish question as "the key which opens the way to the complicated alleys" of Stresemann's entire foreign policy.[116]

The vision of a Damascus-like conversion of Stresemann from an extreme German nationalist to a good European—a version which has been cherished more by journalism than by scholarship—misinterprets his pragmatic nature and practical approach to foreign affairs, where changes were made gradually as the result of empirical evidence and not as the result of abstract *a priori* principles. Also it finds no confirmation in the wide documentary evidence on Stresemann's life and work which has subsequently become available. Stresemann's European policy, of which the Polish revisionist issue was a primary function, lacked Briand's intellectual idealism, and if one would risk drawing the analogy between the ideology of Europeanism in the Weimar era with the altered conditions of present-day Europe, Briand's position would find him allied with the integrationist wing, while Stresemann could be expected to adhere to the de Gaullian concept of co-operation among sovereign national units. Stresemann's European policy was characterized neither by the utopian concepts of *Verzichtspolitik*, of which his enemies accused him during his lifetime, nor by a deceptive Machiavellian strategy, under the sheltering cloak of which Germany might advance exclusively national interests, as critics after his death suspected. Instead, it was the outcome of the practical realization that on account of the interconnecting nature of international affairs in the modern world, national goals had to be co-operatively adjusted through an international clearinghouse mechanism. Stresemann's concept and exercise of national self-interest in accordance with the principles of international adjust-

[116] Karl Erdmann, "Das Problem der Ost—oder Westorientierung in der Locarno-Politik Stresemanns," *Geschichte in Wissenschaft und Unterricht* 6 (1955): 137.

ment and accommodation incorporated elements of moderation, restraint, and practicability without the Hitlerian aspects of all-consuming destructiveness.

Laboring under the conviction that the satisfaction of Germany's revisionist demands in the long run represented a truly European and not merely a German national interest, the Foreign Minister promoted the proper functioning of the mechanism of international adjustment by which Germany's claims would eventually have to be settled. In this respect, Eyck is led to conclude that a logical bridge can be constructed between Stresemann's energetic pursuit of national goals, on the one hand, and his support of the principles of international co-operation, on the other, when he writes: "But he sought to achieve this grander German future by taking the paths of peace. He did so not merely because he saw no present prospects for military success, but primarily because he was convinced that international reconciliation offered a better opportunity for realizing the true interests of Germany."[117]

Stresemann's antipathy toward Poland was as firmly anchored, if less verbal, than that of the Nationalists, and in his image the idea of Germans living under Polish rule entailed elements of perversion, while the reverse conformed to the natural order. His anti-Polish sentiment was given visible form by his performance at the Lugano session of the League Council on December 15, 1928, when in a fit of uncontrolled rage he interrupted Zaleski's tirade against the activities of the Upper Silesian *Volksbund* by pounding his fist—not his shoe—on the conference table, while shouting that this was *unerhört*. It is inconceivable that the speech of a foreign minister of any other Great Power would have provoked him to a similar outburst.[118] Even if his personal antipathy occasionally transgressed the limits of self-restraint, in the conduct of his foreign policy Stresemann did not permit himself to become the victim of his negative sentiments. In 1924 and 1925 Stresemann had rejected the Soviet proposals for an alliance which aimed at the partition of Poland

[117] Erich Eyck, A *History of the Weimar Republic* (Cambridge, Mass., 1963), II, p. 214.

[118] See note by Schubert of December 15, 1928, and Stresemann's telegram of December 16, AA, StS/2365/4587H/E184 662–64; 692–95. Also Stresemann, *Vermächtnis* (Berlin, 1932), III, pp. 413–15. In all German official accounts of the Lugano incident and in Stresemann's own description it was considerably toned down, and while these referred to Stresemann's manly language, no reference was made to the fistpounding episode, which in retrospect obviously embarrassed the Minister.

and the restoration of the 1914 frontiers. The Foreign Minister did not hesitate to recognize the existence of the Polish State as an unalterable reality as well as an inherent right, and, in his 1925 directive to all German missions abroad, Stresemann emphasized that Germany's revisionist aims were confined to the "Corridor" and Upper Silesia, but excluded the rest of the province of Poznań, while insisting that a new partition of Poland along the precedent of 1793 and 1795 could never be the objective of German policy.[119] Indeed, the elaborate plans which the Foreign Office designed for the purpose of obtaining sufficient compensation for Poland and to guarantee her access to the sea in return for a revision, by themselves contradict the speculation that Germany was planning for the total elimination of her neighbor.

Stresemann's persistent pursuit of the revisionist goal leaves no doubt that he would have continued with this policy if death had not prematurely intervened. But the question whether Stresemann would have continued on the road of a peaceful revision once Germany's military situation had improved, cannot be answered with that same certainty. Because of his early death, this question must remain purely speculative. The historian's task is further complicated by the fact that in Stresemann one has a man who lived during an era of tremendous upheaval and who demonstrated an immense capacity for change and adaptation, a capacity that was derived from his great intelligence, pragmatism, and personal courage. It would be both unjust and unrealistic to judge the statesmanship of his final years by the standards which he himself had set only a decade earlier, when as a war-time politician of petty bourgeois origin he had tried to make his political mark in the nationalistically hysterical mood of war-time Germany. His tendency, even as a mature statesman, to relapse into the jingoistic jargon of his Wilhelminian student days, which was both a personal habit and a tactical device for appeasing his conservative opponents, also contributes to the proliferation of conflicting interpretations on Stresemann's policies and aims.

In his public statements and in private instructions, Stresemann consistently rejected the principle of using military force in the execution of Germany's revisionist aims. In March 1926 he reminded the French ambassador of their first conversation in 1923, when he had emphasized that Germany did not intend to proceed by force but hoped for a peaceful solution by persuading world opinion that the peace of Europe lay

[119] AA, StS/2301/4556H/E149 414–16.

in a timely territorial revision of the existing frontiers in the east.[120] In his anonymous article in the *Hamburger Fremdenblatt* of April 10, 1925, the Foreign Minister foresaw a solution in the event that the Soviet Union introduced the question of her frontiers with Poland, but even here Stresemann did not necessarily envisage a solution by force, rather as the result of an international conference. In the above-cited instructions to Sthamer on April 19, 1926, he emphasized that only a peaceful revision could be considered, and when the Foreign Minister gave a secret speech at Königsberg on December 16, 1927, before an assembled group of East Prussian political leaders, the Foreign Minister declared that "an elimination of the 'Corridor' by means of war [was] impossible," as Germany did not have the means of power.[121]

It cannot escape the observant reader that a significantly large number of Stresemann's declarations of peaceful intentions appeared in juxtaposition with the comment that Germany's lack of military strength prevented her from pursuing a solution by military means. To some extent this juxtaposition can be explained as a tactical device of the same genre as his famous letter to the Crown Prince, whose services Stresemann wanted to enlist for the purpose of placating the truculent Nationalists who were most easily persuaded by arguments that were explained in military terms. However, the frequent association of Germany's military weakness with her policy of peaceful revisionism naturally poses the leading question whether Stresemann practiced a peaceful policy only because, and as long as, Germany lacked sufficient military strength. Henry Bretton, whose obviously strong admiration for the person of Stresemann may unwittingly tend to impair the objectivity of his conclusions, firmly denies such speculation and insists that Stresemann was a "pacific revisionist" who was "dedicated to peaceful change rather than change by force," and who "clearly . . . was not thinking in terms of aggressive acts, nor in terms of immediate action."[122] But another contemporary American historian, H. W. Gatzke, evaluates Stresemann's peaceful professions more critically and concludes: "Whether in the fulfillment of Stresemann's long-range program the actual use of force was envisaged is impossible to say, and the historian must guard here against the dangers of hindsight. . . . There is ample

---

[120] Note by Stresemann, March 16, 1925, AA, RAM/1425/2945H/D571 548–49.

[121] AA, StS/2339/4569H/E169 065.

[122] Henry Bretton, *Stresemann and the Revision of Versailles: A Fight for Reason* (Stanford, 1953), pp. 13, 117.

evidence that, at least while Germany was still weak, he favored peaceful arbitration over a forcible showdown as a means of achieving his ends."[123]

In dismissing the use of force, Stresemann probably acted more under the influence of practical military considerations than from moral concern. Empirical exposure had been a masterful tutor in his political education and had induced the change from a monarchist to a pillar of the republican constitutional order, while transferring him from an opponent of *Verständigungspolitik* to its most respected champion. Stresemann realized the limitations imposed on German diplomacy as the result of her military posture, and in a letter from Geneva he complained that in a world where neither the Locarno nor the Kellogg treaties had succeeded in eliminating power politics, he had to represent a country behind which stood an impressive economic and cultural strength but no military might.[124] But Stresemann adjusted the course of German foreign policy to this limitation and was apprehensive and impatient when certain circles in Germany advocated a foreign policy that was irreconcilable with the realities of her present military position. At a press conference on March 7, 1925, the Foreign Minister admitted that during his brief tenure as chancellor he had requested of the chief of the *Heeresleitung* (the commander-in-chief of the *Reichswehr*) an exposition of Germany's military strength in the east, and he had been told that even in a defensive war Germany could not hold her boundaries with Poland, while an offensive war against Poland was entirely out of the question. "No German government," announced Stresemann, "could dare drive her people into such a hopeless war."[125] The Foreign Minister was not only aware of Poland's military superiority under the existing state of armaments but also of the fact that a German aggression on Poland would involve her in a new world war. When the Chief of the *Truppenamt*, the veiled German general staff, presented Stresemann with a copy of a recent war game which assumed that France, on account of her improved relations with Germany, and Russia, because of internal preoccupations, would remain neutral in a hypothetical localized war with Poland, Stresemann was prompted to make a sarcastic marginal note which reflected his pessimistic appraisal of the chances of keeping a war with Poland local: "Furthermore, it is apparently assumed that England became the victim of a seaquake and America, partly on account of

[123] Hans W. Gatzke, *Stresemann and the Rearmament of Germany* (Baltimore, 1954), p. 115.
[124] Annelise Thimme, *Gustav Stresemann* (Hannover, 1957), p. 96.
[125] Stresemann, *Vermächtnis*, III, p. 72.

tornadoes and partly because of false speculations, suffered ruin, while Czechoslovakia was totally preoccupied with the conclusion of a concordat."[126]

Stresemann's realistic rejection of any policy of military adventurism, at a time when Germany was partially disarmed, is well documented. Since he did not live to conduct the foreign policy of a fully rearmed Germany, we cannot arrive at a unanimous historical verdict as to whether his commitment to a peaceful solution was in fact a permanent feature of his policy or whether it was merely a temporary concession to the military weakness under which Germany was then operating. Perhaps a person of Stresemann's great stature deserves the benefit of the doubt. As Eyck writes, "[he] never pressed for a Polish war with unambiguous words, and so anyone who differs with the critics—as do almost all who knew him well—will let him enjoy the benefit of doubt."[127] In support of such a favorable verdict one can refer to Stresemann's moderation, capacity for growth, and his sense of realism. Moreover, he sought fulfillment of Germany's national interests through the general pacification of Europe, not apart from or contrary to this aim for harmonization. A revisionist war against Poland, as he clearly realized, could not be localized and would become a general conflagration which would have destroyed the very foundation of his European policy. Stresemann's fault was not that of conducting a consciously aggressive foreign policy but of failing to realize the futility and inherent dangers of insisting on a revision of the German–Polish frontier. In this miscalculation, which in time might have been corrected, he was supported and encouraged by the favorable response which Germany's revisionist policy found in Britain and France.

While awaiting and fostering the proper emotional and political climate in Europe, Stresemann's revisionist strategy proceeded with extreme caution. Both her diplomats abroad and the German press had been instructed to treat the revisionist issue gently, in a manner which would underline her desire to settle all neighborly disputes in a friendly manner, and to refrain from forcing it to a premature climax. When Schubert saw Zaleski at Geneva in December 1926, he had bluntly stated that only a return of Danzig, the "Corridor," and Upper Silesia would produce a real rapprochement between Germany and Poland. But otherwise Germany refrained from raising this issue in direct diplo-

[126] Stresemann Papers, *FO*, 520/190; cited in Erdmann, "Das Problem der Ost—oder Westorientierung," pp. 149–50.
[127] Eyck, *Weimar Republic*, II, p. 29.

matic talks with Warsaw, as she was aware of Polish resistance and believed that a settlement could only be arranged through international support and pressure.

The German minority in Poland played an important role in Stresemann's revisionist design. The continued existence of a sizable German element in Poland's western regions acted as a constant reminder of her former possession and was regarded as a trump card in her revisionist strategy. Stresemann strongly endorsed the liquidation agreement and trade treaty largely because of the assistance which they were meant to offer to the German minority, for the former fortified their economic position and the latter laid the basis for their numerical reinforcement through a new settlement of German nationals in Poland. Likewise, the Foreign Minister's advocacy of German membership in the League of Nations and a seat on the League Council was to a large extent motivated by the desire to step up the Council's functions with respect to the protection of the national minorities. But Stresemann wished for more than the improved protection of the German minority by the Council; in the long run, the German minority in Poland was to be used as a weight, and the Council to act as a lever, in the realization of her revisionist aims. This became quite evident during the March 1929 session of the League Council, when the extension of the Council's role in the protection of national minorities was debated. In his report to the Council on December 9, 1925, the rapporteur for minority affairs, the Brazilian diplomat, Mello Franco, had voiced the opinion that in the interest of international peace it would be desirable if the minorities were gradually assimilated, in which case the minority protection role of the Council would lapse.[128] When Stresemann addressed the League Council on March 6, 1929, he strongly opposed the above notion that the Council's duties with respect to the protection of national minorities should merely be transitory and concerned with temporary difficulties. The Foreign Minister stressed the need of making such protection a permanent function of the Council. As for the claims that the protection of minority rights had the effect of inciting irredentist movements and of disrupting the unity of established states, Stresemann took the liberty of reminding his colleagues that, in his opinion, the present situation in Europe still did not represent a permanent order, and that this factor was clearly expressed in the Covenant. Stresemann's veiled invocation of the revisionist Article 19 in conjunction with the minority question

[128] League of Nations, *Journal Officiel*, 7, no. 2, pp. 142–44.

drew an immediate and unusually sharp rebuke from Chamberlain. The Foreign Secretary emphasized that he, too, recognized the permanent character of the international minority treaties, but he hoped that as relations between the minority groups and their host countries improved, it would no longer be necessary and would no longer seem desirable to charge the League Council with this task. He very much regretted the German allusion to Article 19; this did not help in the protection of the minorities and its mention in this context could only create confusion.[129]

THE DIMINISHED ROLE OF RUSSIA IN GERMAN REVISIONIST POLICIES

Both Germany and Russia shared a common interest in having the other insist on the nonpermanence of its frontiers with Poland as a means of keeping the latter under pressure, but neither could derive comfort from a real revisionist settlement between its partner and Poland. Herein, then, lay a blueprint for conflict. Germany was opposed to the conclusion of a Polish–Soviet nonaggression pact or mutual guarantee of their boundary which would have strengthened the status quo in East Europe and might have laid the foundation for a Polish–Soviet understanding. The Soviet Union feared the realization of a revision of the German–Polish frontier, as it associated such a settlement with a joint German–Polish offensive action directed against itself or its client, Lithuania. In 1925 and 1926, Moscow had reacted with particular vigor against the rumors of an intended exchange of the "Corridor" for Lithuania, and there could be no doubt that an exchange solution of this kind would bring a permanent alienation between Germany and the Soviet Union.

Unlike Germany after Locarno, the Soviet Union continued to fear an international action that might be directed against her and that would use Poland as a springboard. The rationale for guaranteeing the status quo as defined by the Riga Treaty in order to remove Poland from the chain of such an international conspiracy of capitalist powers asserted itself with increasing force in Soviet minds. This concept was opposed to the German aim of keeping Poland under revisionist pressure from both directions. Earlier attempts to conclude a Polish–Soviet nonaggression pact had failed, largely because of the Polish demand to include the Baltic States in such an agreement. Despite this failure, German diplomacy had been unable to extort a categorical promise that

[129] *Ibid.*, 10, no. 4, pp. 515–32.

no such agreement would be concluded in the future. Berlin had to satisfy itself with the promise, made by Litvinov to Rantzau, that the Soviet Union would refuse to guarantee any Polish territory which had formerly belonged to Germany.[130]

Piłsudski's return to power intensified suspicions between Berlin and Moscow. The event prompted a renewal of the Soviet nonaggression pact offer. But in a conversation with Rauscher, Undersecretary Knoll ridiculed the Russian offer as another proof of Soviet double-crossing, for the Soviets, as Knoll had added sarcastically, only waged "defensive" wars.[131] Chicherin frequently expressed his concern over the prospects of a German–Polish détente, and he seemed much relieved when Rantzau assured him that in response to public pressure the German government would seek an economic agreement with Poland but that no political understanding was considered.[132]

Their respective approaches to the Polish question, rather than serving to cement relations, increasingly developed into a source of suspicion and contention. This estrangement was reflected by the growing realization in German official circles that a revision could only be arranged in co-operation with the Western Powers and that Russia's contribution in this process would be marginal.

Gaus echoed this new trend when he wrote to Schubert: "I believe I am in agreement with you that on the Polish question we can expect nothing without England and France. Russian support . . . in itself will not in the least suffice. Our relations with Russia and Lithuania can be of use to us on the Polish question only insofar as they serve to strengthen our general position vis-à-vis the Western Powers and to weaken the Polish position."[133]

[130] Letter, Brockdorff-Rantzau, May 1, 1926, AA, RAM/1411/2860H/D557 508–9.

[131] AA, GA/3036/6698H/H111 787.

[132] Telegram, Brockdorff-Rantzau, March 1, 1927, AA, RAM/1427/2945H/ D572 655.

[133] AA, W/2575/5265H/E320 523–30; July 6, 1926. The realization that the revisionist road led through Paris and London rather than Moscow was slow in gaining ground in Germany, and particularly outside the Foreign Ministry the opinion persisted that the revisionist key was held by the Soviet Union. On August 3, 1928, the German minority leader in Poland, Graebe, wrote to Seeckt that the "Corridor" problem could not be solved by force or purchase, nor by an exchange for Memel, for that area could not be betrayed either. But he foresaw a settlement emerging from the internal collapse of Poland. A renewed Polish–Soviet war would sharpen the differences between western and central Poland. When the rest of Poland had been reduced to chaos, Poznań and Pomorze would be reminded of their historical con-

Zechlin supported the same argument in a lengthy memorandum of November 19, 1926, in which he stressed the limited utility of Russian aid to Germany's revisionist cause. Perhaps if Russia defeated Poland and Rumania and dictated a peace, Germany could regain the "Corridor" through Soviet help, but a German intervention in such a war would inevitably provoke French military intervention. German–Soviet co-operation, noted Zechlin, had a very limited spillover effect outside the immediate sphere of direct relations, as had been demonstrated by the German–Soviet dialogue on the Polish question between 1924 and 1925. Intimate relations between the two powers by themselves would not bring Germany any closer to the realization of her revisionist aims. More-over, a possible "Corridor" exchange solution that involved Lithuania would proceed in opposition to, and not in co-operation with, the Soviet Union. A solution of this nature might produce a lasting German–Soviet antagonism. This was regrettable, but the issue ought to be faced squarely, for the situation in East Europe had been transformed too radically to permit the application of Bismarckian standards. From these observations Zechlin was led to conclude that the key to any revisionist solution lay not with Russia but with France, for France, because of her alliance with Poland and her position on Germany's western flank, exercised a preponderant influence on the entire question. "A German–French understanding on a wide basis should also lead to an understand-ing regarding our German interests in the East, . . . [as] the only secure route to a solution of the basic questions of German policy, not only in the West but also in the East, [led] through Paris."[134]

Even the minimum level of German–Soviet common interest on the Polish question, i.e., consensus on the desirability of a continued revisionist campaign by Germany, was placed in doubt by certain inner contradictions of Soviet policy. While Germany's revisionist efforts had the welcome effects of restraining Polish behavior vis-à-vis Moscow, as an undesirable by-product they also tended to make Poland more susceptible to the influence of France and other Western Powers. At a time of extreme Polish–Soviet tensions when the Soviets were par-ticularly apprehensive of possible foreign machinations in Warsaw, *Izvestiya* in an article of April 13, 1927, proposed that an attempt be

---

nections with Germany and might voluntarily rejoin the *Reich*. Graebe based his analysis on the autonomous sentiments which had been voiced in the western prov-inces at the time of Piłsudski's *coup d'état* (*Seeckt Papers*, reel 15).

[134] AA, StS/2339/4569H/E168 868–78.

made to curtail the hostile foreign influence in Poland by a Soviet–
Polish nonaggression pact and by a temporary abandonment of Germany's revisionist aspirations.[135]

The latter proposal was not raised again in public, but the Kremlin
renewed its attempt to extricate Poland from membership in an eventual
anti-Soviet international conspiracy by renewing her proposal for a nonaggression pact in conjunction with the signing of the Briand–Kellogg
Pact in 1928. On December 29, 1928, Litvinov invited Poland to conclude an agreement with the Soviet Union in which both signatories
would pledge to adopt immediately in their mutual relations the provisions of the Briand–Kellogg Pact rather than wait for the latter to
come into effect following its ratification by the original signatories. An
agreement to this effect, the so-called Litvinov Protocol, was signed on
February 9, 1929. Its signatories were not only Poland and the Soviet
Union but included Estonia, Latvia, Rumania, and subsequently
Lithuania, as well.

Moscow tried to appease Berlin by indicating that the Protocol was
primarily designed to protect Lithuania against Polish aggression, an aim
that should be in harmony with German interests, and that, at any rate,
it was a more diluted agreement than an ordinary nonaggression pact
and, furthermore, involved no territorial guarantees.[136] Some of Germany's concern was alleviated when the parent agreement, the Briand–
Kellogg Pact, was properly ratified and took effect, thereby removing
much of the significance of its improvised offspring, the Litvinov Protocol. The latter turned out to be of little beyond symbolic value and no
marked improvement of relations between Moscow and Warsaw ensued. But as a symbolic demonstration it had the effect of reducing still
further the importance which Germany assigned to Russia as a positive
factor in her revisionist policy against Poland.

THE WESTERN ROUTE OF GERMAN REVISIONISM

The gradual evolution of opinion in the German Foreign Ministry,
as exemplified by Zechlin, Gaus, and Schubert, which recognized that a
territorial revision could not be achieved in any manner other than in

---

[135] Cited in Harvey L. Dyck, *Weimar Germany and Soviet Russia, 1926–1933*
(New York, 1966), pp. 71–72.
[136] Report, Dirksen of his conversation with Litvinov, January 20, 1929, AA,
RAM/1414/2860H/D560 118–20; January 22, 1929, 125–27; February 27, 1929,
217–18.

conjunction with the Western Powers, was reinforced and accelerated by experiences like the Litvinov Protocol, and this change basically reflected Stresemann's evolving strategy. This realization was by no means shared by all German diplomats, and persons like Dirksen and other heirs of the Rantzau school of thought were unable to shed their conviction that a successful solution to the Polish question was predominantly a function of German–Soviet collaboration.[137]

It would be difficult to assign an exact date to Stresemann's gradually evolving realization that the road to the "Corridor" led through Paris and London. But there can be no doubt that Locarno constituted the official endorsement of this realization. The Foreign Minister himself admitted later that in connection with Locarno he had never given so much thought to Germany's Eastern question as when he was looking for an understanding with the West. The western orientation of his revisionist policy should not be construed as a distinct option in favor of the West as against Russia, and on numerous occasions Stresemann tried to dispel the notion that a choice of either was involved. In his pragmatic mind the dictates of flexibility and the necessity of preserving every conceivable avenue for a future revision were given precedence. Intimate relations with Moscow could support German revisionist aims on at least two counts; in the first place, it improved the German bargaining position in the West and thus constituted a definite asset in lending weight to her revisionist campaign in Paris and London; in the second place, it kept open the opportunity of sharing in the Russian spoils in the event of an East European conflagration touched off by a Polish–Soviet armed conflict.

Stresemann embarked on the revisionist route via Paris with marked caution and restraint. Even during the intimate atmosphere of Thoiry he had refrained from touching on the Eastern question. "These matters can only proceed step by step," Stresemann noted in his diary on October 7, 1926, "but when the time comes in which the Eastern questions

---

[137] When Dirksen had replaced Rantzau as ambassador in Moscow, he informed Berlin on July 20, 1929, that the Soviet government intended to register complaints in Warsaw for not having been officially informed of Danzig's intention to join the Kellogg Pact and the Litvinov Protocol. Dirksen urged the Foreign Office to undertake a similar step in Warsaw. This would not only fortify the position of Danzig but would also underscore the parallel interests of Germany and Russia vis-à-vis Poland. On July 23 Schubert curtly rejected Dirksen's proposal for not only was Poland under no obligation to inform Germany of Danzig's adherence to the pact but there was also no reason why Germany should slavishly subordinate her policy toward Poland to the wishes of Moscow. (AA, RAM/1428/2945H/D574 112–13; 114–15).

are subject of a debate in any form, then one must realize in Germany that this question can be solved only in concert with France."[138] Already, in August 1925, Briand had confided to Hoesch that once Germany sat on the League Council, opportunities might arise for a peaceful solution of the German–Polish territorial dispute, in which case France would certainly not be an obstacle. But if Germany pursued a policy of peaceful revision—here Briand revealed his deep-rooted anxiety—she would have to renounce the outdated Bismarckian phantom of intimate relations with Russia, which did not mean that France expected Germany to break off normal relations with Moscow.[139] On August 28, 1927, Poincaré agreed with Hoesch that the "Corridor" would have to go and expressed his confidence that with French mediation a settlement could be made with Warsaw that would give her Memel as a seaport in compensation

---

[138] Stresemann, *Vermächtnis*, III, p. 38. In 1931 the Foreign Office was questioning its embassy in Rome, where Schubert was then serving as ambassador, whether during the Thoiry talks the question of the "Corridor" had been brought up, for recently rumors had appeared of the existence of a secret French–Polish treaty of 1919, whereby the "Corridor" was to be given to Poland only temporarily and that France could demand its return to Germany, once she had received sufficient guarantees from Germany; apparently Briand's comments on the "Corridor" question at Thoiry were a reflection of this secret agreement (letter, Auer to Richter, February 13, 1931, AA, StS/2390/4624H/E203 611–12). Richter, answering on February 17, 1931, informed Auer that Schubert's documents of the Thoiry talks revealed no trace of any reference to the "Corridor" question; furthermore, Schubert himself could not recall any "Corridor" mention having been made at Thoiry (*ibid.*, 593).

Apart from the fact that Stresemann's and Schubert's accounts agree that at Thoiry the revisionist question was not discussed and that Briand could consequently not have made reference to this apparent secret Polish–French treaty, the idea that Poland would willingly have accepted such a commitment and that France at the time of the Peace Conference, while she was fighting for maximum Polish territorial gains at the expense of Germany, should have made preparations for returning this land to Germany is absolutely preposterous.

It is amazing that the German Foreign Office should have attached sufficient weight to this rumor to make inquiries in Rome and Leningrad (see Undersecretary von Bülow's hand-written letter to Zechlin, the German Consul General in Leningrad, February 10, AA, StS/2390/4624H/E203 606–7) on the basis of a letter of a British spy in Warsaw of February 2, 1931 (*ibid.*, 605) to his female accomplice in Berlin which, starting with the friendly invocation of "Girlie Darling" and a warning not to buy another Rolls Royce, and ending with the salutation "goodbye, my big child-girlie. Come soon," referred to the fact that neither France nor Poland expected the present "Corridor" to continue in its present form for long. "Imagine the French being cornered in such a way. I am not talking about Poland, they are used to such things. . . . They will have to surrender, France and Poland cannot possibly deny their arrangements . . . of which I hold the photostatic copies in hand."

[139] Telegram, Hoesch to Stresemann, August 6, 1925, AA, RAM/1426/2945H/D571 872–76.

for the loss of the "Corridor." "At any rate, the German government could rest assured that in the question of the 'Corridor,' the present French Cabinet would behave in a conciliatory and loyal manner and that Paris would welcome any agreement between Germany and Poland with particular joy."[140]

During the December 1927 Council session at Geneva, the feature attraction was provided by the colorful personality of Piłsudski who had unexpectedly made his appearance in connection with the current Polish–Lithuanian crisis. The Marshal's presence reverberated like a cannon shot through the ritualized and thickly "carpeted" decor of Geneva. He both horrified and fascinated the more stylized assembled statesmen with his behavior which contained elements of a soldier's bluntness and a country squire's coarse wit. At a luncheon on December 9, Piłsudski treated his diplomatic colleagues to a full display of his vibrant and colorful personality and entertained them with his amusing tales and lively reminiscences. Chamberlain later recalled that he had "seldom assisted at a more amusing gathering."[141] However, Chamberlain and Briand were not amused—Stresemann refers to their ill-concealed horror —when Piłsudski paid loud tribute to the "heroic achievements of the German army" during World War I.[142] After the luncheon the Marshal engaged Stresemann in a lengthy private conversation that was both friendly and frank. Piłsudski assured Stresemann that he was fully aware of Germany's difficult international position and that he wished for friendly relations between their countries. He expressed his disapproval of the preceding policy of pinpricking that had characterized German–Polish relations and emphasized that he carried no hostile feelings toward Germany; his wartime imprisonment in Magdeburg had been entirely justified and the treatment he had received during this incarceration deserved no complaints. As was his custom, the Marshal identified his personal views with the sentiments of his entire nation and emphasized that not only he personally harbored no hostile feelings toward Germany but that this attitude was also shared by all Poles; excepting ten madmen, nobody in Poland nourished any annexationist ambitions toward East Prussia. "Piłsudski," noted Stresemann after the interview, "gave the open impression of a man of military talents who entertained a some-

---

[140] *Schleicher Papers*, fol. 33, pp. 5–9.
[141] Charles A. Petrie, *The Life and Letters of the Right Hon. Sir Austen Chamberlain* (London, 1940), II, p. 320.
[142] Note by Stresemann, December 9, 1927, AA, RAM/1428/2945H/D573 408–10.

what friendly feeling toward Germany and apparently had the honest wish to come to an understanding with us by any means whatever."[143]

Even more pleasing than the outcome of his conversation with Piłsudski was the French reaction to it. Briand regretted that Stresemann had not availed himself of this opportunity to broach the revisionist issue, for he believed that the Marshal would show himself more favorably disposed to come to a settlement on all issues between Germany and Poland than would normally be anticipated. When Stresemann observed that one might perhaps offer Poland free ports in Danzig and Memel as compensation for the return of the "Corridor," Briand became "entirely enthusiastic at the thought that such a solution might be feasible. He said that the peace of Europe would then be assured and spoke not a word of criticism against the idea of a border change."[144]

Stresemann was so pleased with the general outcome of the Geneva talks that he rushed to Königsberg to address the political leaders of East Prussia, the greenhouse of radical Rightist opposition, in an attempt to enlist their support for his Locarno policy, now that the first fruits of this course seemed to have ripened. Both Piłsudski and Zaleski, said Stresemann, were of the opinion that Poland was already saturated with minorities and consequently objected to the annexation of East Prussia. An elimination of the "Corridor" by war was impossible, as Germany lacked the necessary armed strength—Stresemann had no scruples in availing himself of this tactical argument with the Nationalists for whom it was probably the only means of persuasion—consequently no course of action "other than improving our relations [with the West], especially with France," was open to Germany. "At first, France would have to lose her fear of the German threat, then recognize the untenability of the present frontier delineation, and finally agree to an alteration of this boundary drawing in return for certain compensations from us in the financial field." When France would be ready to accept all this, nobody could tell presently, but her politicians were no longer raising objections when Germany touched on the revisionist question. In the meantime, cooperation with France would have to start on an intellectual and cultural level and then move into the political sphere.[145]

Following the Geneva Council meeting, France continued her ef-

[143] *Ibid.*, 410.
[144] Note by Stresemann, December 11, 1927, *ibid.*, 425–27.
[145] Dirksen's note of Stresemann's Königsberg speech, December 16, 1927, AA, StS/2339/4569H/E169 061–69.

forts to promote a German–Polish reconciliation and expressed herself favorably on the prospects of an eventual peaceful revisionist solution. On December 22, Briand assured Hoesch that "Germany could do something with Piłsudski." He himself had been surprised how great the Marshal's desire for an understanding with Germany went. Moreover, this was all the more significant, since Piłsudski probably also had the power to force through a far-reaching settlement.[146] A few weeks later Berthelot complained to Hoesch of the piteous nature [" *jammervolle Regelung*"] of the territorial peace settlement for which a solution had to be found so that Germany's just grievances might be satisfied. An improvement of German–Polish relations, according to Berthelot, offered the best prospects for regulating even major disputes like the territorial issue.[147]

French public opinion was somewhat less encouraging to Germany's revisionist policy than her political leaders, but while originally the mere mention of a revision had been categorically rejected, some voices now began to be heard which spoke in favor of a peaceful revision and a few even openly decried the existence of a French–Polish alliance as an obstacle to a French–German rapprochement and a trap that might involuntarily implicate France in war with Germany. Count Oliver d'Etchegoyen's *Pologne, Pologne . . .* (Paris, 1926) gave an extremely negative account of Polish policy and her national character. Alcide Ebray, in his *La Paix malpropre*, called the border settlement in the east unjustified.[148] Robert Tourly, the editor-in-chief of the Socialist paper *Le Soir*, in his *Le Conflit de demain: Berlin-Varsovie-Dantzig* (Paris, 1929), described the "Corridor" as pure madness, for the elimination of which all diplomats should work day and night. Jacques Kayser, the vice-president of the Radical Socialist party, in his *La Paix en péril* (Paris, 1931), called for a general disarmament and for the peaceful revision of the Versailles treaty. Professor René Martel devoted a series of works to exorcize the existing "Corridor" settlement. Criticizing Poland's minority policy, which he styled inhumane, and her foreign policy, which he believed to be motivated by expansionist and adventurist considerations, Martel dismissed the tradition of French–Polish friendship as a colossal myth and condemned the French–Polish alliance because it apparently

---

[146] AA, RAM/1428/2945H/D573 454.
[147] Telegram, Hoesch to Stresemann and Schubert, February 5, 1928, AA, RAM/1428/2945H/D573 481–82.
[148] Alcide Ebray, *La Paix malpropre*; German trans., *Der unsaubere Friede* (Berlin, 1925) p. 140. Cited in Höltje, *Das Ost–Locarno Problem*, p. 149.

stood in the way of a complete rapprochement with Germany and courted ruin for the future.[149]

British attitudes toward the revisionist question seemed to proceed in precisely the reverse manner than in France. British publicity had all along been much more favorably inclined toward a revision of the German–Polish boundary than was the case in France. Foreign Office members, on the other hand, took a somewhat more reserved and cautious attitude than was displayed by *Quai d'Orsay* officials between 1926 and 1928 and never went so far as Briand in encouraging Germany to engage Poland in revisionist conversations at that time.

The British official policy shows certain elements of ambivalence, for while it was not averse to the principle of an eventual territorial adjustment in East Europe, it strongly objected on tactical grounds to the introduction of this issue at this early stage before Germany and Poland had harmonized their relations in other fields. This combination of flexibility in principle but restraint in actual current practice had, quite contrary to what was intended, the effect of hardening positions on both sides. Germany derived encouragement for her revisionist policy from the British stand, just as Poland gained comfort from it for her anti-revisionist position. Poland interpreted Britain's opposition, which was made on temporary tactical grounds, as opposition to the very principle of a revision. After Chamberlain's Geneva conversation with Skrzyński in March 1925, he wrote to Max Muller that in his view, "Germany, on her side, would be most ill-advised to attempt, even by peaceful means, to precipitate a solution in the east, for which the time is not yet ripe."[150] This particular interpretation by Chamberlain certainly did not exclude a future revision under more propitious circumstances. Yet, referring to the same meeting with Chamberlain, Skrzyński told the Foreign Affairs Committee how the British Foreign Secretary had assured him that Britain had no idea of permitting a revision of the Versailles treaty and of throwing doubt on the existing frontiers.[151]

Although Chamberlain left no doubt that Britain would have no objection to a revisionist solution by peaceful means, he seemed to fluctuate somewhat in his opinion whether such an accord would in fact

---

[149] René Martel, *La Pologne et Nous: La Légende et l'Histoire. Chimères et Réalités* (Paris, 1928). Other works by Martel on the same subject are *Les frontières orientales de l'Allemagne* (Paris, 1929); *La France et la Pologne* (Paris, 1931).

[150] Letter, Chamberlain to Max Muller, April 3, 1925, FO, 371/10730, p. 109.

[151] Max Muller to Chamberlain, March 28, 1925, *ibid.*, p. 128.

ever be reached. He expressed himself as doubtful when he related to Lord D'Abernon a recent conversation with Ambassador Sthamer. During this particular talk he had informed the Ambassador that Germany, like any other League member, had the right to avail herself of Article 19 of the Covenant, but that "he must not suppose that I intended to encourage Germany in the expectation of a change in the treaty settlement, nor did I think that those who continually stirred up this question served the interests of peace." The Foreign Secretary had suggested that the question be left to rest for a generation before bringing it up again.[152] In the same vein, Chamberlain left a marginal annotation with Max Muller's suggestion to neutralize East Prussia in which he remarked that there was "a danger of our all working on a tacit assumption that change is inevitable and that it is our business to make it."[153] After Locarno Chamberlain seems to have become somewhat more optimistic about the feasibility of a territorial alteration in East Europe. In a comment on October 10, 1926, he observed: "I do not say that the Versailles settlement will last for all time or that it necessarily should. . . . If it is to be changed eventually by agreement, then Germany must alter her whole attitude to Poland. Being an optimist, I sometimes allow myself to hope that in time she will see this."[154] After Locarno the Foreign Secretary seems to have gained the impression that if Germany played a conciliatory role in the League, her political friendship and economic support would become of such importance to Poland as to persuade her to come to a direct settlement. But this reconciliatory process would be delayed if Germany continued her anti-Polish campaign.[155]

This passive approach of waiting for more favorable circumstances for a territorial revision, while discouraging those attempts which sought to precipitate a solution on this delicate subject, was much to the liking of the conservatives who determined policy in Whitehall. When Huxley submitted his plan for a "Corridor" revision in 1925, both Tyrell and Lampson strongly objected to forcing the question at that time. "Let sleeping dogs sleep," the minute noted, "—if they don't, let us try to make them sleep. . . . If we can only keep peace between them [Germany and Poland], I hazard the view that it is a matter of time until the two

---

[152] Letter, Chamberlain to Lord D'Abernon, May 15, 1925, *ibid.*, 10731, p. 190.
[153] Marginal comment by Chamberlain, May 18, 1925, *ibid.*, p. 93.
[154] *Ibid.*, 11281, p. 125. Chamberlain's reference to "being an optimist," leaves no doubt that he would have viewed a frontier revision as a favorable outcome.
[155] Petrie, *Austen Chamberlain*, II, pp. 267–68; 273–74.

neighboring countries come to realise they *must* work more or less together. And when they have realised that & got on terms, then many
other things may follow. . . . Let us leave this question severely alone."
The authors of this minute concluded on an even more complacent note.
Lampson remarked: "This may seem like stagnation: I do not think it
is!" Tyrell seconded his colleague's judgment: "Stagnation at times may
& is preferable to earthquakes."[156] Commenting on Collier's variation
on the revisionist theme that had been raised by Huxley, Lampson noted
how Briand had told him that whenever he formed a new ministry he
always assigned one portfolio to Time. "Let us follow his example in this
question of German–Polish relations: & I may add I am less pessimistic
about the final outcome than some of the writers of the preceding minutes seem to be."[157]

On the whole, it can be said of British foreign policy of that period
that it favored the principle of an eventual peaceful revision of the German–Polish frontier which, in its present condition, was viewed as unsafe,
unsound, and, possibly for that very reason, even unjust. British objections
to Germany's revisionist policy were over matters of tactics and timing,
not over the principle. It was relatively easy for British policy to arrive at
this position, for Britain did not share the historical and sentimental ties
which linked Paris and Warsaw. Also, Britain could refer to the gloomy
predictions on the territorial settlement which her representatives had
made at the Paris conference. Furthermore, a territorial revision would
not be made at her own expense. In addition, there was some feeling that
the existing settlement discriminated against direct British interests in
the Baltic. Morel, a Member of Parliament, had called Danzig a "French
Gibraltar in the Baltic," and had accused France of wanting to transform
Danzig into a naval base for her own use.[158] After a conversation with
Undersecretary Gregory during the Danzig mail-box controversy in 1925,
Sthamer concluded that he could not escape the impression that
"Englishmen did not wish Poland to have her own Baltic seaport at
all."[159]

In British publicity, support for a territorial revision was expressed
in a much more open and less cautious manner than in the Foreign Of-

[156] *DBFP*, Ser. I A, vol. I, pp. 264–65; December 20 and 21, 1925.
[157] *Ibid.*, p. 279, January 2, 1926.
[158] Cited in AA, GA/3725/K170/K025 446–52.
[159] AA, GA/3809/K223/K060 848–50. The exact date of this report is illegi-
ble, as part of the document has been destroyed by fire.

fice, and this publicity campaign was conducted more actively and more consistently than was true for the French news media. Innumerable newspaper articles expressed this sentiment which can be summarized by quoting from Lord Rothermere's March 26, 1929, editorial in the *Daily News*: "To remain complacently content with the partial Locarno pact . . . is as foolish as to trust to a lifeline of a single strand. The nation is looking with anxiety for the British Foreign Secretary to take the lead in removing the deadly dangers which the blunders of the peace treaties have left in Europe." Also a long list of books, some of them inspired by Germany's propagandistic efforts or directly aided by German funds, appeared in Britain and advocated the need for a revision of the German–Polish boundary. The following are the most important: D. Lockhart, *Seeds of War* (London, 1926); R. B. Hansen, *Poland's Westward Trend* (London, 1927); Sir Robert Donald, *The Polish Corridor and the Consequences* (London, 1929); Graham S. Hutchison, *Silesia Revisited* (London, 1929).

A wide range of favorable opinion in the United States presented Germany with the convincing proof that her strategy of peaceful revisionism was beginning to bear fruit. In October 1931, Senator Borah, the chairman of the Senate Foreign Relations Committee, emphasized the need of revising the situation which the Paris settlement had created with respect to reparations, the "Corridor," Silesia, and Hungary, as a prerequisite for escaping the impact of the Depression.[160] A month later when Grandi paid a call on Secretary of State Stimson and Undersecretary Castle, the latter voiced pessimism over the success of the disarmament question as long as the political problems in Europe, and in particular the "Corridor," had not previously been resolved.[161]

Italy, though a victor power, out of indignation over the limited spoils which she had carried out of the war, in fact associated herself diplomatically with the legion of dissatisfied revisionist powers. Baron von Neurath, Germany's ambassador to Rome, reported to Schubert on March 10, 1925, that he had received assurance from the *Quirinal* that Italy's guarantee for Germany's western boundary would not be extended to include the German–Polish frontier as well, for Italy regarded it as unnatural.[162] Shortly after the German–Soviet Neutrality Pact of 1926,

---

[160] *Survey of International Affairs, 1932*, p. 323.
[161] Ludwig Zimmermann, *Deutsche Aussenpolitik in der Ära der Weimarer Republik* (Göttingen, 1958), p. 471.
[162] AA, RAM/1425/2945H/D571 517.

Neurath suspected that Poland would renew her earlier schemes for a Polish–Italian guarantee pact, but he was convinced that her bird-call would be in vain, for Mussolini had spoken most deprecatingly of Poland's future.[163] Despite the development of warm relations between Rome and Warsaw after 1926 and parallel interests in the Balkans, Italy retained her basically favorable attitude toward Germany's revisionist policy against Poland. In April 1928, when some exceedingly cordial toasts which had been exchanged on the occasion of Zaleski's Rome visit gave rise to speculation of a possible Italian guarantee of the "Corridor," Neurath reaffirmed his earlier conviction that such a guarantee was entirely out of the question and incompatible with Mussolini's basic attitude.[164]

There are certain parallels in the attitudes of Rome and Prague toward the issue of Germany's eastern revisionism. Both were keenly sensitive and strongly opposed to a revision that would take the form of an *Anschluss* of Austria. But they had no such reservations with respect to the "Corridor" and Danzig, which they might have been inclined to view as deflecting Germany's *Anschluss* aspirations. Although Czechoslovakia, unlike Italy, was one of the staunchest defenders of the existing international order as constituted by the Paris peace treaties, she deviated from this norm with respect to the "Corridor" problem, partly for the purpose of dissuading any German *Anschluss* attempts; partly for the sake of underlining the fact that her relations with Berlin did not fall into the same category as German–Polish relations. Perhaps there was also a measure of jealousy that the elaborate "Corridor" and Danzig scheme had been invented in order to guarantee Poland's access to the sea, instead of meeting this demand in a more modest fashion by the creation of free port facilities such as Czechoslovakia enjoyed in Germany.

The echoes which Germany's revisionist soundings produced in Prague were, on the whole, not unpleasant to German ears. A certain common empathy was provided by the fact that both Berlin and Prague had territorial disputes with Poland, and Beneš appeared to meet German revisionist strivings with understanding, and perhaps even with favor. It will be recalled that during the Security Pact discussions, the British Minister in Prague had reported that Beneš believed that "Poland would be the better for a certain amount of territorial readjust-

---

[163] AA, D/2770/5462H/E368 198; May 4, 1926.
[164] AA, D/2774/5462H/E371 518; April 23, 1928.

ment."[165] When Schubert told Beneš during the Geneva session of September 1926 that eventually Danzig, the "Corridor," and all of Upper Silesia would have to be restored to Germany, the Czech statesman seemed to agree to this insofar as it applied to Danzig and the "Corridor," but was reluctant to concede the same for Upper Silesia, which was probably too close to home base for Prague's own comfort.[166]

Beneš's views on the revision of the "Corridor" and Danzig showed certain similarity to Polish attitudes toward the *Anschluss* of Austria. In both cases there was awareness, probably stronger in Warsaw than in Prague, of the inherent dangers of tampering with the territorial provisions of the Paris peace settlement. At the same time, there was some hope that by a partial readjustment, Germany's revisionist drive might be deflected in another direction. In the calculations of Prague, this meant a revision of the "Corridor" in return for the guaranteed independence of Austria; in the minds of some Poles it gave rise to the formula of trading Vienna for the status quo on the Vistula. Already in his memorandum to Balfour on March 17, 1917, Dmowski had suggested that Germany be compensated for her territorial losses by permitting the annexation of Austria, a solution which also promised to strengthen the Catholic element in Germany as a counterweight to Prussian dominance.[167] During the peace negotiations in Paris, Poland had repeated the *Anschluss* proposal, which she regarded as inevitable in the long run.[168] Skrzyński, as we have observed in connection with Locarno, opposed the *Anschluss* formula, as it would undermine the existing order. But his refusal had not sounded entirely categorical. When Zimmermann, the League commissioner-general for Austria, conducted some inquiries on this point, he too found Polish opinion generally opposed to the notion of *Anschluss*, but discovered that certain groups of the Left and some followers of Piłsudski regarded Poland's consent for *Anschluss* as an inexpensive way of bargaining for German recognition of Poland's

---

[165] Sir George Clerk to Lampson, June 4, 1925, FO,371/10733, pp. 83–84. Beneš had voiced very similar sentiments in conversations with the U.S. *chargé* Pearson when, speaking privately rather than as foreign minister, he had indicated that he did not believe in the permanence of the present Polish frontiers. A Polish–Soviet war was not inconceivable, and in that event Germany would turn to the League with the request for a frontier rectification; Britain would support Germany's claims; and Poland would yield under severe pressure. Beneš did not think that the German action would take military form, although this might happen if Poland refused to yield (Report, Pearson, April 3, 1925, SD, 740.0011/34).
[166] AA, StS/2362/4587H/E182 990–91; September 25, 1926.
[167] Hans Roos, *Polen und Europa* (Tübingen, 1957), p. 73.
[168] Léon Noël, *L'Aggression allemande contre la Pologne* (Paris, 1946), p. 47.

western boundaries.[169] After Piłsudski's return to power, the Polish Foreign Ministry shed some of its reservations about this Austrian exchange formula. In Olszowski's political report of December 17, 1926, in which he urged that Poland conclude a liquidation agreement and other accords with Germany in order to delay what he envisaged as an inevitable drift toward war with Germany, he also touched on the *Anschluss* question. According to Olszowski, the annexation of Austria was one of the principal goals of Stresemann's policy. Its execution spelled certain dangers for Poland, as it undermined the peace settlement, but at the same time it contained certain favorable aspects, for *Anschluss* would bring its opponents—France, Italy and Czechoslovakia—closer to Poland; it would strengthen the Catholic element in Germany; and it would counterbalance the Prussian influence in German foreign policy.[170] In discussing the revisionist problem in 1931, Erskine mentioned to Zaleski "that he [Zaleski] had suggested that one of the conditions on which consent to the *Anschluss* might be granted was the recognition by Germany of her present frontiers."[171]

Germany was also given reason to believe that she was conducting her revisionist policy with the spiritual blessing of the Holy See. The population of Poland was then, as it is still, characterized by its devout adherence to the Roman Catholic faith. Given these intimate religious ties, which until Piłsudski's return to power were reciprocated by cordial church–state relations, one can hardly suspect the Vatican of holding an *a priori* bias against Poland in her territorial dispute with Germany. If the Vatican did favor a revisionist solution, as indeed one is inclined to believe, it was from a defensive and conservative viewpoint and not from any anti-Polish sentiment. In the German–Polish territorial dispute, the Holy See was primarily concerned with the dangers of a renewed European war, and, given its conservative predilection, one need hardly be surprised that it associated itself with the trend of thought which maintained that the peace would best be guaranteed if the weaker and newer (or rather, more recently reconstituted) Poland returned most of those lands which in the recent past had been under German sovereignty.

In 1925 Germany was concerned that the recently concluded concordat with Poland might impair her own revisionist chances. Two clauses, in particular, caused anxiety in Berlin. First, the provision which placed Danzig under the authority of the nuncio in Warsaw, and second,

[169] Report, Pearson, June 8, 1925, SD, 760c.6215/420.
[170] Report, Olszowski, December 17, 1926, AMSZ, P II, fol. 4614, pp. 49–50.
[171] Erskine to Vansittart, April 13, 1931, FO,371/15222, p. 155.

the stipulation that the Church could not alter the hierarchy in Poland or change the boundaries of a diocese without the permission of the Polish State. Meyer, the counsellor of the German legation at the Vatican, inquired nervously whether this meant that the Holy See would require the permission of Warsaw if, for example, the diocese of Katowice were to be reincorporated into the German Church hierarchy after the return of Upper Silesia to Germany. Monsignor Borgongini, the papal undersecretary of state, gave a reassuring answer. The Vatican would agree to insert a clause that the nuncio's authority over Danzig applied to ecclesiastical matters only, not to diplomatic questions; furthermore, Danzigers could, if they wished, always appeal directly to the Holy See. As to the diocesan boundary question, in the interpretation of the Vatican the concordat would automatically cease to be binding for those areas which were no longer under Polish sovereignty. Consequently, Poland could exercise no voice in the reorganization of those dioceses that had passed from her jurisdiction.[172] In October of that year, the Cardinal Secretary of State, Gaspari, congratulated Brentano, the German ambassador to the Vatican, on the successful outcome of the Locarno conference and added that the Holy See fully understood Germany's position regarding her eastern boundary; in fact, all foreign diplomats with whom he had discussed the issue were in agreement that the present "Corridor" situation was untenable. Even the Polish envoy had been unable to refute the German arguments entirely, although he regarded the time for a revision premature. The Cardinal himself was of the opinion that Danzig ought to be restored to Germany, but Poland should be given part of the Danzig harbor, together with railroad and river access. In view of this favorable stand, Brentano suggested that a future revisionist mediation by the Vatican be considered, for "with the high moral authority which the Holy See enjoys in Poland, it might be conceivable that the voice of the Holy See at the opportune moment could be of decisive importance and effect."[173]

The Vatican's position on the revisionist question did not escape Polish notice, and Warsaw's displeasure over it came to a climax when news of a conversation between Cardinal Gaspari and an unnamed French journalist reached Poland. In this conversation the Cardinal had dwelled on the dangers of the present territorial settlement and had complained of Poland's unreasonable attitude on this question. He

---

[172] AA, GA/3761/K192/K037 194–203; March 19, 1925.
[173] Report, Brentano, October 16, 1925, AA, GA/3726/K170/K025 974–77.

could understand that a new country like Poland was particularly susceptible to nationalistic extremism and therefore urged that France, especially Catholic groups in France, exert a moderating influence on the Poles and persuade them to re-examine the frontier question. Gaspari had styled the Polish demands as exaggerated and had mentioned that from his talk with German diplomats he had gained the impression that Germany was willing to compensate Poland with a port further east and to guarantee railroad access to it. In the opinion of the State Secretary, the whole concept of the "Corridor" made sense only in conjunction with a policy of promoting separatism in Germany, but this was now outmoded. Chłapowski, who relayed this information, thought the report close to the truth.[174]

When Skrzyński visited Rome, in January 1926, he broached this delicate question both with the Pope and Cardinal Gaspari. In his audience with the Pope, Skrzyński referred to rumors in the French Catholic press—he was unable to be more specific as Chłapowski had refused to reveal his exact source even to the Foreign Minister—about Gaspari's above-mentioned position. The Pope reacted in a strong manner, calling it utter nonsense and denying that Gaspari, who was very pro-Polish, could ever have taken such a stand. The Cardinal himself, when confronted by Skrzyński, denied that anybody in the Vatican could have endorsed such a position, but the Foreign Minister reminded his ecclesiastical colleague that as recently as October last, the Cardinal himself had spoken to him [Skrzyński] in very much the same vein, and that he might therefore have used the same argument with others. This Gaspari denied.[175]

Skrzyński refused to bicker with the Vatican on this delicate issue because of the great authority which the Holy See exercised in matters of appointments in Poland, as well as on the Lithuanian and Ukrainian questions, and the opinion of Americans of Polish extraction. But he was convinced that his gentle intervention had been useful in restraining the Vatican's revisionist enthusiasm.[176] In this prediction, Skrzyński was overly optimistic. His intervention might have made the curia more cautious about discussing the revisionist problem with third powers, but there was little indication of a change of basic attitude or of a reversal of its policy which encouraged Germany in the belief that her revisionist

174 Report, Chłapowski, December 10, 1925, AMSZ, P II, fol. 4948.
175 Memorandum, Skrzyński, January 2, 1926, ibid.
176 Ibid.

drive would meet with success and had the blessing of the Church. Some time later, Ambassador Berger noted that the Vatican's primary interest consisted of upholding the independence of Poland and of keeping her as a fortress against Communism. Nevertheless, the Holy See regarded the present German–Polish boundary as unjust and untenable and viewed Germany's revisionist policy with understanding. The Vatican looked forward to a peaceful settlement in which Poland would be called upon to make certain territorial sacrifices.[177]

GERMANY'S REVISIONIST CHANCES IN RETROSPECT

The understanding, if not also direct support, which Germany seemed to enlist for her revisionist strivings from various foreign sources during the Locarno era could not but confirm her belief in the ultimate rationale and practicability of her policy. These impressions nourished the erroneous expectation that in due time when she would press her revisionist claims she would encounter no serious objections from the Western Powers. The apparent sympathy which various European capitals accorded to her revisionist demands in the east stemmed from a mixture of guilt, opportunism, and optimistic idealism. In the public opinion of countries like Britain and the United States, the feeling that Germany had been unfairly and unwisely treated by the Versailles treaty took firm roots once the events of the war could be viewed in a less personal context and with greater historical detachment. This impression strengthened the belief that Germany was entitled to a favorable readjustment of the original verdict. During the Locarno era, when a conciliation with Germany seemed both desirable and attainable, the Western Powers, and Paris in particular, were reluctant to jeopardize the prospects of an accommodation with Germany by advertising the genuine reservations and doubts with which they viewed Germany's revisionist policy. In this dilemma they had recourse to the illusion, and the optimistic spirit of the Locarno era provided ample fuel for this trend, that the harmonious spirit would also affect German–Polish relations and allow for a peaceful settlement of the territorial dispute in a spirit of good will.

There can be no question of Briand's genuine wish to promote a German–Polish détente, and French diplomatic efforts in connection with the trade treaty and the liquidation agreement, as has been seen, were to this end. Nor should it be doubted that a peaceful settlement by

[177] AA, GA/3727/K170/K027 223–26; July 1, 1927.

Germany and Poland of their territorial dispute would have met with Briand's concurrence, although there is no evidence that France applied any direct pressure to make Poland more accommodating to Germany's irredentist wishes.[178]

Apart from Briand's general desire to build the lasting peace of Europe on the fundament of German–French and German–Polish reconciliation, more immediate considerations prompted the extreme urgency with which he tried to promote a German–Polish settlement in the years 1927 and 1928. In 1927 a series of border incidents and the assassination of Voikov, the Soviet minister to Warsaw, had reduced Polish–Soviet relations to the lowest common denominator compatible with the maintenance of peace.

In the official Soviet note of protest and in an article by Stalin himself in the July 28 issue of *Pravda*, the Voikov murder was not represented as a single unfortunate act of a demented youth but as one in a series of conspiracies—the others were the rupture of diplomatic relations by Britain, anti-Soviet demonstrations in Peking and Shanghai, and the police search of the Soviet trade mission in London—whereby the agents of the British Conservative party tried to provoke another Sarajevo incident which would involve the Soviet in war against Poland.[179] The Soviet government asked for a thorough investigation of the murder with Soviet participation and demanded stringent measures in the future to curb the terrorist and anti-Soviet activities of Russian *émigré* reactionaries who lived on Polish soil. Both sides increased their military preparations, and even after the immediate Voikov crisis had abated, Ambas-

---

[178] In 1933 von Moltke reported that Laroche had told him that he considered the "Corridor" situation untenable and believed it was in Poland's interest to come to an understanding with Germany, and for this reason the return of the "Corridor"— Poland should be allowed to keep Gdynia—was indispensable. He had repeatedly made this opinion known at the *Quai d'Orsay* but had not brought it up in conversation with the Polish authorities, all of which categorically rejected the idea of a territorial revision (AA, GA/2906/6176H/E463 397–99; February 22, 1933). Laroche's favorable view on Germany's revisionist claims, as recorded by Moltke, was not reflected in his memoirs, where he criticized German policy for failing to realize that Poland would obviously never have yielded to German demands (see Jules Laroche, *La Pologne de Pilsudski. Souvenirs d'une ambassade 1926–1935* [Paris, 1953], pp. 66–67).

[179] Cited in a report by Herbette to Briand, August 19, 1927. This and other reports by Herbette were captured by the German forces in World War II and published as anti-Soviet propaganda material by the Archivkommission des Auswärtigen Amtes, *Ein Französischer Diplomat über die Bolschewistische Gefahr. Berichte des Botschafters der Französischen Republik, Jean Herbette, aus den Jahren 1927–1931* (Berlin, 1943), pp. 38–39.

sador Herbette reported to Briand on March 21, 1928, that "the signs of preparation for a war are so numerous and open in the USSR that one cannot doubt the intentions of the Soviet government."[180] Faced by the imminent prospects of a Polish–Soviet war, it was of maximum urgency for France to protect Piłsudski's western flank from a simultaneous German invasion by arranging for a German–Polish settlement that would ensure German neutrality in such an event. With the improvement of Polish–Soviet and French–Soviet relations after 1930, an understanding between Warsaw and Berlin lost some of the urgency which it had held for Paris in 1927.

The cautious propaganda campaign with which Stresemann gained converts for Germany's revisionist position and the flexibility with which he modulated and shifted the accents, when, like Orpheus playing on the multistringed revisionist lyre, he proceeded to restore the Eurydice of Germany's lost territories from the shadows of Polish sovereignty, attest to his astute mastery of the art of diplomacy. Yet when we pose the critical question whether at the end of his diplomatic career he had come any closer to the realization of his goal of a peaceful revision, the answer will have to be negative. Stresemann had correctly deduced from the Polish attitude that a peaceful revision could not be arranged bilaterally between Germany and Poland, but had to come as the result of an international action that would persuade Poland or pressure her into submission; in consequence, Stresemann's revisionist activities were directed toward Paris and London rather than Warsaw.

The commitment of the entire Polish nation in refusing to submit to a territorial revision of any kind was total and irreversible, and if Piłsudski and a few other individuals privately held the view that Poland's security interests would best be served by a settlement with Germany, even if this entailed some minor territorial sacrifices, they were aware that the overwhelming majority of the public was unable to accept such reasoning and never gave public expression to this view. Even Poles of the caliber of Skrzyński and Zaleski, who sincerely strove for improved relations with Germany, regarded a territorial revision as an unacceptable price for a settlement with her neighbor.

The completely uncompromising Polish attitude on this matter, which became increasingly evident as Germany fortified her revisionist pressure, deprived Germany's policy of peaceful revisionism of its argumentative impact and reduced it to a paradox, for there could only be a

180 *Ibid.*, p. 77.

revision by the application of force, in which case it belied the term peaceful, or there could be a policy of peace vis-à-vis Poland, in which case there would be no revision. In the face of Warsaw's adamant posture, no international action within the confines of peaceful means held any promise of extorting a revisionist solution. With the knowledge of this it became inconceivable that the Western Powers would have attempted a *Runcimanization* of Poland on the Czech model of 1938. Even in the hypothetical case that as the result of extreme international pressure and economic boycott from the West, accompanied by threats from Russia, Poland should have submitted to a territorial revision, Western statesmen could not be ignorant of the fact that this would not inaugurate the desired and lasting peace in East Europe, as the German argument would have it; instead, a solution of this nature would merely reverse the source of tensions without eliminating them, for it would prove as unacceptable to Poland as the present situation was to Germany and thus substitute tensions caused by Polish revisionist strivings for the present German ones.

During the relative security lull of the Locarno years, conversations on the question of revision could solicit benevolent reactions in the West. But as was seen by the events after 1930, whenever Germany attempted to shift the revisionist issue from the realm of theoretical speculation into practical policy, it became an unwelcome threat to Europe's security for which Germany was held responsible. As a means of combatting the anxiety which German–Polish tensions evoked whenever Germany raised the revisionist issue, the Western Powers automatically resorted to what psychologically might be styled regression, by reverting to that position which had originally best suited their security needs, namely, the maintenance of the territorial status quo. Consequently, whenever Germany seriously raised the revisionist question, she found international pressure brought to bear to desist, rather than pressures on Poland to yield.

This crystallization of opinion against Germany's revisionist policy affected not only France but it could also be found in the British Foreign Office. In the summer of 1930, Sthamer, referring to a recent conversation of a member of the embassy with R. W. Leeper of the Foreign Office Press Division, voiced his concern lest the Foreign Office revert to the more rigid and anti-revisionist stand that had characterized its behavior during Gregory's tenure as undersecretary. Leeper had expressed his regret over Germany's recent revisionist revival. He believed that by refusing to treat Poles as equals and to conduct normal relations with them Germans only injured themselves, weakened their own position in Poland, and provoked a Polish invasion of East Prussia, just as the recalcitrant attitude of the Danzig authorities had been responsible for the construction of Gdynia and their consequent economic suffering. It would pay for Germany to reverse her present revisionist policy and to minimize her losses before it was too late. The only person who had realistically understood the nature of the German–Polish problem was Rauscher.[181]

The dilemma of the French government and in particular of Briand in desiring the pacification of Europe by satisfying German demands, while at the same time pegging their security on the continuation of the territorial status quo, became increasingly apparent. In August 1930, Laboulaye of the *Quai d'Orsay* confessed to Riesser, a member of the German embassy in Paris, that while all intelligent people could see that the territorial solution of the Versailles treaty was *peu heureuse*, no one could possibly expect Poland to surrender these areas which were inhabited by a solid Polish majority. "He was therefore unable to understand how Ministers of the German Reich—the reference was to the recent revisionist appeal made by Treviranus—could make demands which were simply unrealizable. This only created general unrest and considerably disturbed German–French relations."[182] Franklin Bouillon's speech in the National Assembly on November 6, 1930, was greeted by tumultuous applause from the Right which spread far into the Left wing when he referred to Poland's frontiers as also being those of France.[183] On March 12, 1931, Hoesch reported the outcome of a long conversation with Briand. Hoesch had referred to the eastern revisionist question as an irreversible and constant political factor of which a candid world would have to take note. In his answer Briand indicated that he now

---

[181] Report, Sthamer, June 24, 1930, AA, GA/3728/K170/K027 459–63.

[182] Telegram, Riesser, August 20, 1930, AA, RAM/1430/2945H/D575 584–86. French publicity, too, was beginning to reflect the more negative attitude toward Germany's revisionist claims. Comte d'Ormesson, who as late as 1930 had proposed a solution on the basis of creating a "Corridor" within the "Corridor," told a meeting of German and French Catholic notables, in December 1932, that it would be difficult to find ten Frenchmen who considered the present "Corridor" solution perfect. But at the same time, one would hardly find more than ten Frenchmen who would press for a territorial revision. Poland was a Great Power and needed the Upper Silesian region for her livelihood. A solution should therefore focus on improving transit through the "Corridor," trade relations, and Polish policies toward the German minority group. It was not France that blocked a territorial revision, but the reality of the existing situation. France realized and admitted this; Germany, too, was aware of these facts but refused to admit them (AMSZ, P II, fol. 4488).

[183] AA, T/2602/5551H/E388 880–81.

gave preference to a solution of the German–Polish problem on the basis of preserving the present territorial status quo.

> Briand did not reject these wishes but repeatedly pointed out how he believed that we pursued them inappropriately; in this manner we had, for example, not understood how to come to an understanding with Poland in Upper Silesia, which would by necessity have secured for us the continued control over Upper Silesian industry. The same applied to the "Corridor" question which we had made ever more difficult by the continued sharpening of our political and economic relations with Poland instead of preparing the way for a final solution by a progressive understanding.[184]

The inherent fallacy of Germany's misdirected revisionist policy could not have been formulated more precisely than in the above-cited pronouncement from the mouth of Europe's diplomatic sibyl, Briand. In 1931 Germany not only continued her revisionist course but pursued it with mounting intensity despite the growing, though belated, evidence that outside support would not be forthcoming and after a decade of empirical evidence which had made it plain that Poland would under no circumstances submit peacefully to the loss of any of her territory.

On the Polish question Stresemann's otherwise extremely sensitive and flexible policy suffered from the one central rigidity—it tolerated no alternative to revision. By the all or nothing attitude of her frontal strategy, Germany deprived herself of ample opportunity to minimize the effects of her territorial losses. A policy of political and economic accommodation with Poland would have offered substantial leverage, though no absolute guarantee, for getting improved protection of her minority in Poland, and it would also have helped to consolidate Germany's economic posture in Upper Silesia and the "Corridor," where she could have gained considerable economic influence, thereby minimizing the loss of these territories. Despite the lack of military power, Germany's foreign policy under Stresemann's direction had scored impressive achievements in the West by the exercise of skillful diplomacy and the utilization of her economic potential and cultural prestige. It is inconceivable that if Germany had permitted herself to direct these same weapons of diplomacy against Poland in an attempt to influence her from within, instead of concentrating on a frontal attack by means of her revisionist thunder, her search for far-reaching compensations for her territorial losses would have been to no avail.

[184] AA, RAM/1430/2945H/D575 584–86.

X

Elements of Reconciliation

THE RECORD OF GERMAN–POLISH RELATIONS during the inter-war period, with its pronounced negative tendencies, would be incomplete without reference to the conciliatory elements which emerged on both sides during the brief phase which may be called the Locarno era. On the whole, the history of German–Polish relations in the period under examination leaves little that can be regarded as edifying or heart-warming, and the historian must withstand the temptation to emphasize too strongly some of the more favorable aspects during the Locarno era in order to lighten this otherwise somber portrait. But the emergence of more conciliatory sentiments on both sides tends to dispel the notion of an historically predetermined and unalterable enmity between Germans and Poles, a so-called *Erbfeindschaft*. The conciliatory symptoms which emerged had more than purely symbolic significance, for they actually affected foreign policy. During the brief phase between 1925 and 1930, which coincides with the Locarno era, foreign policy decision-makers in both Germany and Poland quite consciously and laboriously strove for a *modus vivendi* in their routine relations, even though the more fundamental problems remained unresolved. In terms of concrete policy gains, this new approach yielded only a marginal payoff, but when projected against the initial level of open confrontation and unmitigated hostility, the conciliatory elements which were emerging represent a definite change. During this brief interval, official policy only gained sufficient momentum to edge from the stage of confrontation to a kind of peaceful co-existence or tenuous détente. But parallel with this improvement, various economic, cultural, and intellectual groups at the

295

unofficial level began to exert themselves in favor of expanding the uncertain détente into a more positively oriented and ambitious entente which would offer real collaboration instead of mere co-existence.

After 1925 a series of meetings were staged between private German and Polish economic and cultural groups which either explored specific questions in their mutual relations or focused on the entire range of problems. Initially these contacts had been established through the neutral medium of multi-national international conferences where the German and Polish delegates took time for a more private tête-à-tête. In 1925 and 1926 such contacts had been established during meetings sponsored by the League for Human Rights and some pacifist groups. These encounters did not get much public notice. In January 1926 they moved from the multi-national to the trilateral level when the Socialist party of Danzig invited its party colleagues from Warsaw and Berlin to participate in a joint meeting. The proposal caused serious misgivings in the Berlin Foreign Ministry, where it was feared that the meeting would give rise to overly pacifist ideas devoid of sufficient political realism that might embarrass the German government if they were to be directly applied to the border question.[1]

The attitude of the German Foreign Ministry toward the conciliatory initiatives of private groups was characterized by a general ambivalence. On the one hand, the *Auswärtiges Amt* favored these activities and tried to co-ordinate and promote them in order to exert a modifying influence on Polish public opinion, and thus, indirectly, also on Polish official policy. On the other hand, it could never quite overcome its deep suspicion that these groups might fall under the spell of "dangerous" elements, i.e., pacifist and anti-revisionist sentiments, and that they might create unwarranted expectations among the German public about the prospects of an early settlement. In addition, there was also an element of professional jealousy, for German diplomats were reluctant to assist in giving birth to negotiating bodies and pressure groups which, once operational, they could not fully control and which might eventually interfere with their own strategy of negotiations with Warsaw by dictating the pace and by setting the conditions. Stresemann himself was too astute a politician to associate himself with his subordinates' narrow professional views. He knew how to exploit these private contacts for the benefit of German foreign policy, and on

---

[1] Telegram of the German Consul General in Danzig, Thermann, January 15, 1926, AA, GA/3726/K170/K026 084.

repeated occasions he engaged the services of the Industrial Association and persons like Caro on behalf of the trade treaty. But his colleagues were less flexible, and while approving the principle of friendly contacts between private groups from Germany and Poland, in practice the over-cautious Foreign Ministry forever found grounds to object to the timing of a planned meeting or to the choice of persons who were involved. The Foreign Ministry's pessimism toward all matters relating to Poland was doubtless the result of years of unhappy experience, but by imparting the seal of skepticism and the image of frustration to the endeavors of private groups, it deprived them of the fresh initiative and momentum with which they sought to attack the German–Polish problem.

Early in 1927 a German–Polish Friendship Committee [*Verständigungskomitee*] was organized in the two countries. The driving force behind its creation in Germany was provided by Professor Wolf; Kuenzer, the editor of the Catholic newspaper *Germania*; Dr. Hasslacher, the business manager of the Silesian Chamber of Commerce [*Schlesische Städte und Handelskammern*]; and Helmut von Gerlach, a noted pacifist and one of those rare Germans with distinctly friendly sentiments toward Poland. The Polish counterpart was headed by Stanisław Thugutt, leader of the Leftist peasant party *Wyzwolenie*. Other key participants came from the ranks of the PPS, the Christian Democrats, and Witos's peasant party.

When Dirksen first talked to Wolf and Kuenzer he emphasized the Foreign Ministry's wish for a détente with Poland, but added that he regarded the Friendship Committee's present conciliatory efforts as inopportune in view of the current dispute over evictions. In Dirksen's opinion it would also be necessary that the movement expand its base from its present membership of pacifist and Leftist supporters and in-clude moderate as well as Right-wing groups. Kuenzer was not en-chanted by the Foreign Ministry's efforts at procrastination and voiced the opinion that a conciliatory beginning would have to be made some-where and that the eviction of four persons from Upper Silesia hardly justified a further delay.[2] "The gentlemen [of the Right] in Silesia, I believe, I can influence in this direction," wrote Dr. Hasslacher in an attempt to overcome the inertia and skepticism of the Foreign Ministry, "at any rate, the *Province of Lower Silesia* anticipates *with great longing the termination of the tariff war.* . . . We are all of the opinion that it is time—somewhat in contrast to your personal view—*for something new*

---

[2] Note by Dirksen, February 9, 1927, AA, StS/2339/4569H/E168 957–61.

to happen in order to escape the present situation. This conference in
Danzig [the Committee had proposed a meeting of German and Polish
parliamentarians in Danzig] could be something new."[3] [Italics were
underlined in the original text.]

In response to a Polish suggestion, the Friendship Committee invited a group of Polish parliamentarians and public figures to come to
Berlin in May to discuss the question of conciliation. *Robotnik* happily
welcomed the proposal and pledged participation by the Socialists, while
the *Gazeta Warszawska* accepted in somewhat more guarded terms.[4]
The German Foreign Ministry welcomed the plan but not without
certain reservations. Rauscher feared that a political meeting of parliamentarians under present circumstances might end in failure and thus
jeopardize the planned conference of economic leaders of both countries
in which he took particular interest.[5] Count Oberndorff, who had
championed the idea of a conciliation during his brief tenure as envoy to
Warsaw, had been invited to participate in the planned meeting of parliamentary and public figures. Oberndorff did not expect any direct practical
results from the conference but believed that if it were handled tactfully
it might provide some useful contacts.[6] Dirksen assured his former men-
tor that he followed the principle of welcoming every opportunity to
improve relations between the two countries, although he admitted
that when Kuenzer had first approached him during the preceding
winter with the organization of a Friendship Committee, he had been
pessimistic on account of the existing tensions and because of the
narrow political composition of the committee. But now that participation of various *Reichstag* members from the Socialists, Democrats,
Zentrum, and *Volkspartei*—Dirksen hoped that even the Nationalists
might be persuaded to join—had been assured, it would have a meaningful purpose.[7] Dirksen regretted that Poland had imposed the condition
that neither the territorial nor the minority question be made a subject
for discussion; one could hardly arrive at a true settlement of the
German–Polish problem if these questions were not also subjected to a

---

[3] Letter, Dr. Hasslacher to Wallroth, February 4, 1927, AA, GA/3788/K202/
K048 659–62.
[4] Telegram, Rauscher, May 18, 1927, *ibid.*, 747.
[5] Report, Rauscher, May 19, 1927, *ibid.*, 751–53; letter, Rauscher to Zechlin,
May 25, 1927, AA, GA/3727/K170/K027 101.
[6] Letter, Oberndorff to Dirksen, August 8, 1927, AA, StS/2339/4569H/E169
037–38.
[7] Letter, Dirksen to Count Oberndorff, August 13, 1927, *ibid.*, 039—43.

dispassionate treatment, and a conference of this nature was ideally suited for introducing these delicate matters.[8] The actual conference took place in Berlin during September and proceeded in a harmonious atmosphere of complete privacy, for it drew no public notice. The German participants were drawn from the SPD, DDP, *Zentrum*, and DVP, and the Polish delegates were affiliated with the PPS, the Christian Democrats, Christian Nationalists, and the *Wyzwolenie* and Witos's peasant parties. The value of the meeting was chiefly symbolic. Its importance lay in its very occurrence rather than in its having produced any specific results. The visit of the Polish parliamentarians was reciprocated a month later when Professor Wolf and Dr. Schmidt-Hirschberg of the DVP visited Warsaw. As was noted earlier, the conferences of economic leaders which were held in December 1927 in Berlin and in January 1928 in Warsaw were considered a success by both sides and helped mobilize certain economic pressures on behalf of the rapid conclusion of a trade treaty.

In 1926 two German journals, both of which concentrated on current political and cultural issues, *Europäische Gespräche* and *Europäische Revue*, sponsored a series of articles by prominent political and academic figures from the two countries which explored the possibilities of a genuine German–Polish reconciliation in the spirit of the Locarno détente. These articles featured the opinions of such figures as Baron Werner von Rheinbaben, Stresemann's colleague from the DVP; the former Polish Counsul General Karol Rose; the Polish industrialist Baron Forst de Battaglia; and Prince Janusz Radziwiłł, the chairman of the *Sejm* Foreign Affairs Committee. This friendly intellectual exchange in the two journals continued until 1930. Both sides were in agreement on the desirability of a genuine reconciliation and registered their satisfaction over the emerging normalization in the official relations between their countries. But the German demand for a border revision, whether expressed or implied, largely deprived them of the atmosphere in which they might otherwise have produced a political accord. In his contribution to these journalistic exchanges of opinion, Rheinbaben had reflected the official German view when he wrote that in the foreseeable future the boundary question would constantly loom over German–Polish relations, but that this should not be an impediment in the present effort of both countries to come to

---

[8] Note by Dirksen of his conversation with Dr. Hasslacher, July 18, 1927, *ibid.*, 026–28.

an understanding on those issues which, in contrast to the territorial question, were already ripe for a solution.[9]

In September 1927 Dr. Nossig, the secretary-general of the German–French Friendship Committee and a member of its German–Polish counterpart, proposed to Zechlin that Germany take the initiative in promoting cultural exchange activities with Poland. This was to be inaugurated by founding a German Institute in Warsaw and by publishing a bi-monthly German–Polish review which would be financed jointly and appear in both languages. The journal was to concentrate on economic and cultural questions which would exercise a unifying influence, while avoiding the explosive revisionist and minority issues. Zechlin showed himself receptive—if somewhat skeptical—to the proposal, but Nossig's plan never left the blueprint stage because of lack of adequate support and shortage of funds.[10]

In Poland the idea of fostering closer cultural relations and of stimulating an exchange of views between intellectuals from both countries found a lively echo. At the time when Nossig submitted his proposal for the foundation of a bilingual journal for German–Polish cultural and economic affairs, Professor Stanisław Stroński of the Christian Nationalists, who was otherwise not known for any pro-German sympathies, made an appeal for closer cultural relations with Germany to supplement the progress which was already being made in the economic sphere. Stroński referred to the recent Warsaw visit by Thomas Mann and suggested that this specific occasion be transformed into a general trend by sending Polish literary figures on tour to Germany. *Germania* commented favorably on Stroński's appeal for improved cultural relations but could not refrain from observing how this clashed with the warfare which the Polish authorities continued to wage against the cultural activities of the German minority.[11]

The Warsaw correspondent of the *Vossische Zeitung*, Immanuel Birnbaum, had actively exerted himself in aiding a reconciliation through the promotion of cultural contacts. Political events, however, interfered whenever a web of cultural exchange was beginning to take tangible form. In April 1930, Birnbaum approached the German legation in Warsaw with the request that Berlin lift the ban which it had imposed on the program of the Berlin *Hochschule für Politik* under which Professors Halecki, Krzyżanowski, and Brückner were scheduled to lecture in

[9] Rheinbaben, "Deutschland und Polen," *Europ. Gespräche* 6 (1926): 19.
[10] Note by Zechlin, September 29, 1927, AA, GA/3728/K170/K027 315–16.
[11] *Germania*, October 21, 1927.

Berlin. The visit of these Polish academic notables was to be followed by guest lectures of German professors in Poland.[12] The Foreign Office declined the request for the time being on the grounds that current political disputes made it an inopportune time for starting a cultural exchange program, even though it favored the idea in principle. Birnbaum's address to the Warsaw Foreign Press Club on October 16 of that year on the subject of "Poland in German Literature," which underlined the numerous references of sympathy and friendship for Poland that appeared in German literature, was warmly received by the Warsaw press. "At a time when the myopic and criminal demagogy in Poland incites hatred against Germany," wrote the Socialist paper *Robotnik* on October 19, 1930, in praising Birnbaum's approach, "it is the duty of all those persons who have not been infected by madness, and particularly of the intellectual elite of both countries, to prepare a way for a Polish–German understanding in the cultural field, so that this might eventually lead to a harmonious . . . co-existence between both countries which lies in their own interest, as also in the interest of world peace."[13]

In spite of the earnest dedication of individuals in both countries to help bridge the vast gulf of animosities and differences by way of promoting cultural contacts, these efforts, on the whole, were ineffective as instruments for reconciliation. The German Foreign Ministry tended to discourage and restrain rather than aid private initiative in the sphere of improving cultural relations and itself never even attempted to launch a cultural offensive as a conciliatory instrument. The dearth of cultural and intellectual interaction was not alone a reflection of the existing political controversy; more correctly, the current conflicts in the political sphere had been superimposed on a situation that had already suffered from the absence of a bilateral flow of cultural communication because of the almost complete lack of familiarity in Germany with the Polish language and with Polish culture. Cultural relations quite naturally suffered under this double handicap which the devoted efforts of a few individuals were unable to overcome.

The practice of holding informal meetings between parliamentarians and other public figures of the two countries, which had been inaugurated toward the end of 1927, was continued for several years. In August 1928 the Inter-Parliamentary Union staged a congress in Berlin which provided an opportunity for discussions between Polish and German parlia-

12 Letter, Rintelen, April 13, 1930, AA, GA/3728/K170/K027 453–54.
13 *Tagesbericht über die Polnische Presse*, October 21, 1930.

mentary personages. In Loebe, the President of the *Reichstag*, these meetings not only found an extremely capable chairman but also a devoted advocate of improved German–Polish relations. On both sides the participants agreed that frequent personal contacts of this nature, which had finally developed despite enormous obstacles, should not be allowed to lapse and that this newly found life-line ought not be lost. It was significant that for the first time Poland had relied on the mediating services of the German minority, thus using them as a bridge rather than a barrier to an understanding with Germany. At the Berlin conference much of the emphasis had fallen on economic questions. Prince Radziwiłł, who had long promoted the cause of German–Polish friendship, underlined the inherent dangers connected with the influx of American capital and urged that this be avoided by closer economic ties between Germany and Poland. Radziwiłł believed that in both the industrial and agricultural sector co-operation was feasible, but for this purpose it was necessary for Germany to cease regarding all goods of Polish origin as being of inferior quality and to give fair recognition to Poland's economic and cultural values. Radziwiłł's statement prompted Ulitzka to touch on the explosive issue of Poland's treatment of her German minority, thereby stirring up a heated controversy in the otherwise harmonious atmosphere and forcing Naumann and Graebe, the German minority leaders, to come out in open support of the German position rather than guard their previous neutrality.[14] In order to restore the friendly atmosphere of the conference and to prevent the loss of whatever positive influence this meeting might exert in improving German–Polish relations, it was decided to guard press silence on this particular episode. Unfortunately, this well-intentioned discretion was not kept in practice, and the Polish press used the incident to attack Germany for her obstructionism and Graebe and Naumann for their apparently disloyal attitude; whatever precarious gains might have accrued as a result of the meeting were thus offset by their negative effect on popular opinion.[15]

The meeting of the League of Nations League in Paris in November 1931 again provided the opportunity for politicians and intellectuals of both countries to engage in discussions on the prospects of a genuine reconciliation. Both sides agreed on the necessity of establishing closer economic relations but were frustrated by the perpetual revisionist obstacle. Stroński asserted that historically and economically Danzig had been so

14 AA, GA/3788/K202/K048 985–K049 009.
15 *Germania*, September 11, 1928.

closely associated with Poland that his countrymen failed to see how Germany could regard it as a German city. A territorial exchange was out of the question, but Poland should do everything to facilitate transit between Germany and the East Prussian "island." Dr. Łypacewicz, who represented the Polish Left, emphasized that there existed no Pole either on the Left or on the Right who would surrender the "Corridor" without war; the concept of a peaceful revision was consequently a dangerous illusion in which Germany indulged, and every demand for a return of the "Corridor" constituted a postulate for war. Professor Hoetzsch, speaking for Germany, insisted that the oppressive atmosphere in German–Polish relations was due to the rigid adherence to the untenable status quo and that this, not Germany's revisionist efforts, contained the seeds of war.[16] Commenting on the conference, Moltke believed that it had once again confirmed the old experience "that a relaxation of German–Polish relations is possible only in the direction of economic questions." Still, he believed that these discussions of parliamentary and political leaders paved the way for talks between German and Polish statesmen and thus served a useful purpose.[17]

The history of these unofficial conferences of political and economic leaders from the two countries served to clarify certain aspects of German–Polish relations. For one thing, it established that among the decision-making elite groups there existed a distinct awareness that conditions of proximity presented a challenge for economic and political gains that could only be exploited by a policy of co-operation. Awareness of common interests in the economic field was more obvious and agreement in this sector more easily attainable than was true for the political field, so much so that before the Great Depression had exerted its paralyzing grip, it appeared that a political reconciliation might come as a result of the growing economic interrelation.

These private conferences had demonstrated that political leaders of both countries could assemble in a spirit of good will to examine some of the obstacles in their present relations. Meetings of this nature would have been inconceivable prior to the Locarno period of relative normalization and by their very occurrence demonstrated that German–Polish relations were not frozen into immobile incompatibility. If anything, these conciliatory conferences indicated that without the present conflict over territorial claims, the negative historical legacy and differences

[16] AA, GA/3727/K176/K030 138–52.
[17] Letter, Moltke to Hey, February 10, 1932, *ibid.*, 201–10.

of national temperament, taken by themselves, did not in the long run present an insurmountable obstacle to good-neighborly relations. On the other hand, these meetings which proceeded on the fringe of public perception were equally indicative of the extremely thin veneer supporting reconciliatory efforts; the meetings were conducted privately, and only by withholding from the press those issues which had given rise to heated disputes could a general public reaction against these experimental stages of conciliation be avoided. By the same token, a certain flavor of the purely theoretical rather than the real hovered over these private assemblies, for in all of their discussions the central issue of the disputed territories had to be avoided, or if it was brought up, as in 1931, it produced an immediate obstacle that threatened to destroy the existing spirit of good will. In so far as the territorial question constituted the central issue between the two countries, the real test for the importance of these private conferences centered on their ability to subject the revisionist question to the same dispassionate discussion in the search for a common solution which until then had been reserved for more technical and less significant problems.

Actually, these discussions only confirmed what political experience had spelled out for so long: namely, that Poland would not peacefully submit to any territorial sacrifices, and the question arises whether there existed in Germany any sentiment in favor of a voluntary sacrifice of her revisionist claims in favor of securing an understanding with Poland. Although a few instances of such opinion can be traced in Germany of that period, these were far too sparse even to deserve the name of a distinct movement under an identifiable label. The ideal of sacrificing her revisionist policy on the altar of a German–Polish understanding found its most consistent champions in pacifists such as Helmut von Gerlach and Friedrich Wilhelm Foerster. The *Sozialistische Monatshefte* also adhered to this view, and Walter Maas pointed out in the same journal that the way to a reconciliation was not served by the present talk of revisionism.[18] Kaspar Mayr's booklet *Ist die Verständigung zwischen Polen und Deutschland Unmöglich?*, which was rooted in the author's belief in a Catholic Christian Europe, made a plea for a European order that functioned under the norms of Christian conciliation and common sense. In Mayr's view both Germany and Poland appeared as victims of an idealized, romantic vision of national power and greatness that lacked

---

[18] Walter Maas, "Polen nimmt Front Zum Meer," *Soz. Monatshefte* (1932): 1006 ff.

objectivity and rationality.[19] "We must have the courage to recognize that the mouth of the Vistula as the only access to the sea constitutes a question of life for Poland, not merely from the view of former [Mayr hoped, outdated] military power politics but also in the spirit of the new Europe. . . ." Mayr consequently advocated that Germany sacrifice her revisionist claims in favor of a policy of co-operation with Poland in the construction of a new European order.[20] Fritz Sellin's booklet, entitled *Die polnische Frage*, dismayed the Foreign Office because of its support of Poland's historical claims to the "Corridor." Sellin accused German revisionist policy of generating tensions and demanded its cessation in favor of a policy of co-operation with Poland; in a solution of this nature Germany would receive more than adequate economic compensation for her territorial losses.[21]

RECONCILIATORY ATTITUDES AMONG GERMAN POLITICAL PARTIES

While a few isolated voices in Germany spoke of a sacrifice of her territorial claims as a justifiable down-payment for a reconciliation with Poland, none of her political parties endorsed this stand. This rejection included even those parties, ranging from the Socialists to the *Volkspartei*, which otherwise favored a normalization of relations with Warsaw. The Nationalists, in a highly emotional political concept, viewed any policy of understanding with Poland as degrading and incompatible with German dignity and her domestic and foreign political interests. It was generally believed that more friendly relations with Poland would work to the detriment of the agrarian interests in Germany's eastern provinces and threatened to pave the way for a tacit and then a formal recognition of the existing frontiers. Dr. Weiss, the business manager of the DNVP, decried the efforts of private conciliatory groups which tacitly accepted the existing frontiers.[22] In the same manner, the Prussian Minority School decree of December 1928, which ironically had been instigated by the Foreign Ministry as an indirect instrument for revisionism, came under heavy attack from the Nationalists for providing "nests of espionage and Polish propaganda" which

[19] Kaspar Mayr, *Ist die Verständigung zwischen Polen und Deutschland Unmöglich?* (Vienna, 1931), p. 4.
[20] *Ibid.*, pp. 46–47.
[21] Fritz Sellin, *Die Polnische Frage* (Berlin, 1932), pp. 6–7.
[22] M. Weiss, *Politisches Handwörterbuch (Führer ABC)* (Berlin, 1928), pp. 378–79.

were not only tolerated but even financed by the Prussian authorities.[23] On April 3, 1930, Count zu Reventlow of the National Socialists acted as crown prosecutor of the entire Right wing when he delivered a scathing attack on Stresemann's former policy of understanding with Poland which he thought was now continued by the Brüning government. The policy of friendship at any price, thundered Reventlow, would indeed be at any price, namely at that of Germany's eastern policy and in particular at the expense of the eastern agrarian interests.[24]

In this particular context it is necessary to observe that the division into a pro- and an anti-Polish orientation in German political life did not run along party lines. The division was more amorphous and all moderate parties had champions of either approach within their ranks. To some extent this was a continuation of the situation which had existed prior to World War I, when there had been a keen rivalry between two opposing foreign policy concepts, both of which had their root in their adherents' respective attitudes toward Russia. On the one hand, there continued the old Bismarckian tradition of German–Russian co-operation, which stemmed from a basically anti-Western orientation and which helped suppress the national aspirations of Poland and the other nationality groups on the western periphery of the Russian Empire. Although this was generally the orientation of the German Right, it also had its followers among the "bourgeois" parties, especially in the Wirth wing of the *Zentrum*. The other main track of German foreign policy was dominated by strong fear of Russia. Its adherents responded to this fear by seeking an alliance with the West and by fostering the national aspirations of the Poles and other peripheral nationality groups in order to provide a protective shield of friendly states between Germany and the Russian colossus. This was predominantly the policy of the Socialists and the moderate parties, as, for example, the Erzberger wing of the *Zentrum*. From this group Bethmann–Hollweg's wartime efforts to restore an independent Poland had received their principal support. This anti-Russian foreign policy orientation even included some members from the conservative camp, for example, the well-known historian and publicist Hans Delbrück.[25]

On the whole, the "bourgeois" parties in the years between 1926 and 1930 supported the idea of improved relations with Poland, especially in

[23] *Unsere Partei (Sondernummer)*, VIII, August 6, 1930, p. 187.
[24] Reichstag, *Sten. Berichte*, 427, p. 4763.
[25] Immanuel Birnbaum, "German Eastern Policy, Yesterday and Tomorrow," *International Affairs* 31 (1955): 427–34.

the economic field, without retracting from the theme of the just nature of Germany's revisionist demands and their inevitable fulfillment, but no extreme urgency was assigned to the execution of this demand. In March 1927 Dr. Haas of the Democratic party drew the attention of the *Reichstag* to the fact that Poland was, after France, Germany's largest neighbor, and as the Polish economy was expanding—Haas rejected the belief in an economic collapse of Poland—it would provide an increasingly important market for German goods. "Just because we seek a peaceful alteration of the boundaries, it is necessary that satisfactory economic relations first be instituted. Nobody has been able to tell me yet that the Polish problem can be solved other than by first establishing economic relations with Poland."[26] The *Frankfurter Zeitung*, which represented the opinion of German liberals and was closely linked with the DDP, over this period displayed a consistently positive attitude toward Poland and the question of normalizing relations with her. Another great newspaper of the liberal camp, the *Vossische Zeitung*, exerted itself in the same direction, although until 1927 it had been more inclined to support a pro-Russian and anti-Polish foreign policy course for Germany.

In the Catholic Center party the attitudes toward Poland were probably more polarized than among the other "bourgeois" parties. On the one hand, there existed a strong commitment to the policy of Rapallo, which had been inaugurated during Wirth's chancellorship and whose *pique* was directed against Poland. On the other hand, the memories of the fate which this party had shared with the Polish representatives during the days of the *Kulturkampf* and its aftermath were still vivid and a variety of Catholic Church organizations helped to establish personal contacts. The concept of closer ties with Poland gradually won more adherents, especially as it became increasingly evident that co-operation with Russia fell far short of the initial expectations, and members of the *Zentrum* took a very active role in the German–Polish Friendship Committee and other cultural exchange activities. On March 21, 1927, Dirksen noted with concern that the *Zentrum* might abandon its former pro-Russian leanings and pursue a pronounced course of conciliation with Poland. At a recent party caucus the Rapallo policy had been subjected to strong criticism and even members of the pro-Russian Wirth wing had admitted that by aligning herself too closely with Soviet Russia, Germany's eastern policy had entered a dead-end road. Kuenzer,

---

[26] Reichstag, *Sten. Berichte*, 392, March 23, 1927, p. 9867.

one of the founders of the German–Polish Friendship Committee, obviously entertained strong sympathies for Poland and his position, Dirksen noted, was not an isolated one in his party. A few *Reichstag* members
of the *Zentrum* were even contemplating a trip to Warsaw, and, in
Vienna, Chancellor Seipel, apparently acting under clerical influence,
had interceded with Zaleski for the resumption of trade negotiations with
Germany. Dirksen urged that Stresemann and Schubert talk with *Zentrum* leaders in an attempt to restore what had previously been a united
front of German political parties toward Poland.[27] Early in 1928 Cardinal
Hlond, the newly appointed Primate of Poland, on his return journey
from Rome where he had received his cardinal's hat, spent some time
visiting the cardinals of Munich, Cologne, and Breslau. Ambassador
Schurman considered the visit significant as part of "the general relaxation of German–Polish relations." The American embassy in Berlin had
learned that Cardinal Hlond's visit had been encouraged by the Polish
government with a view to promoting a "good understanding with the
Center and other Roman Catholic forces in Germany."[28]

Because of the conservative bent in the *Volkspartei* there existed,
akin to the attitudes which plagued the Nationalists, some strong emotional reservations to the policy of normalization. But under Stresemann's powerful influence and the urging of the industrialists who supported the DVP and who desired improved trade relations with Poland,
the party generally responded to the call of improved relations during
the Locarno phase.

As has been seen in connection with Locarno, the liquidation agreement, and the trade treaty, the Socialists had been the most consistent
and most articulate spokesmen in favor of a reconciliation with Poland
and gave evidence of having penetrated the underlying psychological and
historical factors of German–Polish relations more thoroughly than any
other group. In making a plea before the *Reichstag* for a German–Polish
understanding, Breitscheid, the foreign affairs expert of the SPD, turned
to the deputies on the Right and reminded them that they had formerly
ridiculed the efforts of his party in bringing about a détente with France
which they had styled impossible, but such a détente had in fact
been achieved. "In the same manner the understanding with Poland will
also come about some time, simply because it has to come and because
these two states are economically dependent on one another. Therefore,

27 AA, StS/2339/4569H/E168 975–77.
28 Report, Schurman, January 27, 1928, SD, 760c. 62/77.

it would be a misjudgment . . . to declare that we could never sit together on the [League] Council. I would even imagine that Germany and
Poland if they sat together on the Council would be in a better position
than today in solving certain disputes. . . ."[29] As a means of counteracting the hopes of those Rightist circles, who saw in the Berlin Treaty of
1926 a golden opportunity for a German–Soviet encirclement and an
eventual forceful reduction of Poland, the party paper *Vorwärts* urged
the immediate entry of Germany into the League, thereby preventing
the Berlin Treaty from acquiring a meaning which it was not intended to
have. A Polish–French encirclement of Germany and a new German–
Soviet encirclement of Poland, it warned, would renew the fateful character of the pre-war power blocs and would impair the prospects for
peace; it would be better if Germany, France, Poland, and Russia (if she
so desired) were all represented in the League of Nations.[30]

Despite their distinct preference for a reconciliation with Poland,
the Socialists never formally renounced Germany's revisionist claims.
The difference between them and other political parties on this particular issue was not one of basic doctrine but one of priorities. Theirs
was a distinctly passive approach toward the territorial question which
accepted the infeasibility of a frontier rectification in the foreseeable
future and therefore focused on the issues which were more pressing and
more close at hand, namely, the normalization of relations with Warsaw.
On January 17, 1927, *Reichstagspräsident* Loebe delivered a speech in
Łódź in which he acknowledged that the Polish element constituted a
majority in the "Corridor" area. He also called for German–Polish co-
operation in improving the transportation and communication facilities
between East Prussia and the rest of the *Reich*. There was nothing very
original or extraordinary in Loebe's common-sense observations, but the
mere fact that a leading German politician had gone on record as recog-
nizing the realities of the existing situation and was willing to base German foreign policy on this realization, created wide attention in the Polish and international press and greatly alarmed the German Foreign
Ministry.[31]

In the same year *Vorwärts* published a significant article on Ger-

---

[29] Reichstag, *Sten. Berichte*, 389, March 23, 1926, p. 6507.
[30] *Vorwärts*, April 28, 1926.
[31] AA, GA/3727/K170/K026 996. In a telegram of January 22, 1927, Wallroth
instructed Germany's legations abroad to interpret Loebe's speech as having been
made in full realization that the present Polish majority in the "Corridor" was the
result of forced evictions and that Loebe had not renounced the doctrine of peaceful
revisionism (*ibid.*, 997).

man–Polish relations which revealed considerable insight into the fundamental nature of the problem. The article underlined the Socialists' desire to come to grips with the realities of the present situation without formally renouncing Germany's territorial claims. It noted that Poland's behavior had given no indication of a voluntary surrender on her part of those territories Germany now claimed, nor could one realistically expect Warsaw to yield under pressure from a peaceful collective diplomatic action, even if this included France. Those who saw in a general European war the solution to the problem should be warned that after another catastrophe of such magnitude there would be greater concerns than over the ownership of the "Corridor." At Locarno, Germany had provided France with guarantees for her present possession of Alsace-Lorraine; strong emotional barriers had prevented Germany from extending this guarantee to the "Corridor" and Upper Silesia. Germany's emotional resistance was as easily comprehensible as Poland's objections to the differential treatment which she had been accorded at Locarno. But leaving emotional reservations aside, it was necessary to base neighborly relations with Poland on the concrete reality that at Locarno Germany had agreed to refrain from the use of force. Consequently, as Poland presently refused to submit to a peaceful revision and as Germany had pledged to limit herself to peaceful means, a kind of de facto East–Locarno had already been reached that should provide an adequate basis for good-neighborly relations.[32]

After 1930 both the capacity and the incentive of the Social Democrats to influence German foreign policy in the direction of a reconciliation with Poland diminished substantially. Following the break-up of the Müller Cabinet, the Socialists were no longer represented in the government and thus exerted far less leverage over the formulation of foreign policy. Also their attitudes toward Poland became considerably less sympathetic as the Piłsudski régime gradually shed its democratic trimmings and thus forced the PPS into an opposition role. Driven by sympathy for their ideological colleagues in Poland and by concern for the fate of democratic institutions in Europe, German Socialists adopted an increasingly hostile stand toward official Polish policy and thereby seemed to echo the anti-Polish sentiments of the other political parties in Germany, even though their criticism was motivated by quite different considerations.

[32] *Vorwärts*, September 7, 1927.

RAUSCHER AND THE POLICY OF RECONCILIATION

The conciliatory spirit and pragmatic approach to the revisionist question, which characterized the position of the SPD vis-à-vis Poland, also formed the essential element of Rauscher's diplomacy. During the period under discussion here, Rauscher had devoted himself more fully to the cause of a German–Polish understanding than any other individual in Germany, and a chapter that traces the reconciliatory elements in the relations of the two countries would, indeed, be incomplete without some reference to the work of this remarkable diplomat.

If Rauscher had taken up his delicate position in Warsaw as a devoted pacifist and a champion of Poland, this would have made a pleasant symbolic exception to the negative attitudes which prevailed among German politicians and diplomats. For its implications on policy, it was infinitely more important that he did not act on the basis of some friendly personal sentiments, which might easily have withered after the disillusioning experience of conducting German–Polish negotiations and which could not have been communicated to his anti-Polish countrymen, but that he was motivated entirely by a rational conception of German national self-interest. It was the realization of the real priorities of German foreign policy, and not any sentimental commitment to the Polish cause, which provided the reconciliatory imperatives in Rauscher's strategy and gradually undermined his support for Germany's revisionist policy. What was even more significant was the indication that Rauscher's experience was not an isolated case but had some contagious effect on men like Stresemann and leading members of the SPD.

Rauscher viewed as his primary task the promotion of a normally functioning relationship with Poland on routine issues and the advantageous exploitation of their mutual economic interests. Second, he sought to explore and to exploit the opportunities for a peaceful territorial revision. After some years of empirical evidence, Rauscher became convinced that a peaceful territorial revision, at least for the foreseeable future, was not only impossible but its pursuit was also incompatible with his primary objective of normalizing relations. It would be difficult to assign a particular date to Rauscher's rejection of active revisionism as a suitable tool for German foreign policy. The approximate period for this seems to have fallen into the immediate timespan after Piłsudski's return to power in 1926, and it is not inconceivable that the subsequent economic stabilization of Poland functioned as a catalyst in forming this opinion. In December 1925 he had still expressed himself favorably on the plan of bargaining for a territorial revision in return for an international stabilization loan to Poland.[33] But six months later, soon after Piłsudski's take-over, he left no doubt that he had definitely discarded the feasibility of a peaceful revision as a result of the multiple schemes that were then being advanced by the Foreign Ministry. In his view it was unreasonable to expect that one could "solve territorial questions in conjunction with financial ones," and that there could ever "exist in Poland such a measure of impoverishment . . . that any Polish government would be in a position or willing to pay for her financial salvation by a territorial sequestration."[34]

Although he had come to discount the prospects of a successful revisionist outcome in the foreseeable future and regarded the pursuit of an active revisionist policy as an obstacle to his conciliatory efforts, Rauscher preferred a suspension of Germany's revisionism to a formal renunciation of her territorial claims. The latter would burn the bridges to an eventual territorial recovery that might occur under a drastically revised, and yet indeterminable, power constellation in Europe. Moreover, a formal renunciation would produce an acutely hostile reaction in Germany and would thus obstruct rather than support his conciliatory endeavors. In the opinion of his colleague Laroche, Rauscher, like the rest of his countrymen, did not view the eastern boundary provisions of the Versailles treaty as final. But given Germany's disarmed state, he rejected the concept of a military recovery. "Il y avait intérêt à améliorer les rapports des deux voisins et, qui sait? amorcer plus tard une revision pacifique."[35]

Rauscher's commitment to seek an understanding with Warsaw transcended the immediate and direct gains of such a détente; instead, he saw in a German–Polish conciliation the necessary prerequisite for the fulfillment of Germany's more essential and broader foreign policy goals. The German envoy subordinated his Warsaw tasks to what he considered to be the precepts of German foreign policy at large. To Rauscher the road to Germany's full restoration to membership in the international system in the capacity of a Great Power would have to proceed by way of an international conciliation with the Western Powers and in particular with France. In his conception, Paris figured as the central tar-

[33] AA, StS/2339/4569H/E168 435–40; December 4, 1925.
[34] Letter, Rauscher to Dirksen, June 11, 1926, ibid., 775–78.
[35] Jules Laroche, La Pologne de Pilsudski. Souvenirs d'une ambassade 1926–1935 (Paris, 1953), p. 67.

get of German foreign policy and a German–French reconciliation as its primary goal. During his student days at Strasbourg, Rauscher had acquired fluent command of French and to become ambassador in Paris was apparently his greatest personal ambition. Rauscher had realized that until German–Polish relations had at least assumed the character of normalcy, they would constitute an inevitable obstacle to the full consummation of the French–German Locarno union. Thus serving as the prerequisite to Germany's principal foreign policy goal, the normalization of German–Polish relations became to Rauscher a matter of utmost importance. He did not suffer from the common ambassadorial disease of regarding his present post as the navel of the world, Rauscher once assured State Secretary von Bülow, but the vital importance of German–Polish relations could hardly be over-estimated, both for its direct consequences and the indirect significance of Germany's standing in Paris and Geneva.[36]

In the face of this realization, the experience of unending political obstacles on either side, the feeling of not receiving sufficient support from his own government, and the constant flow of criticism from Rightist circles would have proved sufficiently harassing and frustrating to have discouraged a less optimistic and less energetic individual than Rauscher.[37] Once, half in jest and half indignantly, he compared himself to the enchained Prometheus, "who is convinced that he possesses the necessary light and fire but is hardly in a position to make use of it."[38] Viewing a German–Polish conciliation in the broader perspective of Germany's over-all foreign policy goals, Rauscher consistently referred to it as the critical component of Germany's *grosse Politik*. In a political report of November 11, 1926, he warned "that in the interest of our *Gesamtpolitik* [over-all policy], especially now, one ought to avoid at all

[36] Private letter, Rauscher to Bülow, August 13, 1930, AA, RAM/1430/2945H/D575 227–28.

[37] Rauscher's Socialist connections and his conciliatory approach toward Poland made him a favorite and constant target of the Nationalists. The *Kreuz-Zeitung* of April 1, 1922, styled Rauscher's appointment to Warsaw an April fool's surprise of the government. When Schubert proposed Rauscher as a candidate for succeeding Brockdorff-Rantzau in Moscow, Hindenburg vetoed the choice; he not only considered it unwise to dispatch as ambassador to Moscow a man who had previously been accredited to a power which was notorious in its anti-Soviet position, but he also had personal objections to the person of Rauscher, especially on account of his Socialist background. (See Schubert's note to Stresemann regarding his conversation with Hindenburg, October 12, 1928, AA, Brockdorff-Rantzau Papers, 3432/9101H/H226 595–600.)

[38] AA, StS/2224/4483H/E094 981–82; October 25, 1928.

costs drawing the attention of the world repeatedly to the German–Polish controversy and by the mass of disputes represent it as being virtually incurable." Such policy would only provoke international pressure for formal recognition of the territorial status quo, precisely what German diplomacy had dexterously managed to avoid at Locarno. No German government could yield to such demands, but a refusal would mean the collapse of the French–German détente. The exaggerated anti-Polish campaign in the German press negatively affected German foreign policy interests, and it was therefore essential that Berlin decide to put an end to these perpetual quarrels, or at least to refrain from giving them so much publicity. This would not only strengthen Rauscher's own position in Warsaw, but he was also convinced that Poland herself, because of all the internal confusion, could provide much more effective material in support of German demands than Germany's own propaganda machine.[39]

On August 13, 1930, Rauscher took time out on a rainy day during his holidays on Lake Constance to write a lengthy personal letter to State Secretary von Bülow, and although he jokingly referred to it as a monstrosity of a letter, for which he expected a severe reprimand from his superior, it so eloquently summarized his entire political outlook that, in view of his death soon after, it deserves to serve as his political testament. In this letter, Rauscher repeated his previous objections to the petty "Corridor" propaganda in which Germany continued to engage. Such a policy could only lead to a postponement of the territorial question *ad calendas graecas* or to a minimal frontier rectification such as the solution proposed by Count d'Ormesson. Revisionist statements, such as the unfortunate one recently made by Treviranus, which publicly paraphrased Stresemann's most fatal and never publicly used expression: "Settlement in the West for a free hand in the East," were regarded in Warsaw as proof of the perpetual German threat, especially after the evacuation of the Rhineland. They could only lead to unsatisfactory solutions, such as envisaged by d'Ormesson, or a "general reaction against Germany, the disturber of peace, dressed in moral and pacifist terms, and thereby a stiffening of the front of *status quo* powers, even on this point where there certainly exists already today a platonic understanding for our claims." One could not exaggerate the significance of normal relations between Berlin and Warsaw because of their influence on Germany's general relations with Paris and the West.

[39] Political report, November 11, 1926, AA, GA/3727/K170/K026 743–50.

It is a second axiom of mine that the deterioration of German–Polish relations, which in fact or in appearance has been instigated by us, has always injured us internationally. This is not founded on any—hardly existing—esteem for Poland on the part of the others or on any affection by France, which is certainly no longer present to any significant degree in the *Quai d'Orsay*. But it is simply based on the fact, excepting a certain sentimentality for the resurrected Poland, that a poor German–Polish relationship because of its unpredictable consequences frightens the other governments; the time has not yet come when one dares to eliminate the obvious reasons for such a poor and menacing relationship; consequently one remains content with pressing for the respect of the *status quo* which is the most comfortable approach and, moreover, accords with the heart's desire of all victors of the War.

The moral of all this, Rauscher concluded, was that in her relations with Poland, Germany should not let herself be guided by emotions and resentments—Bismarck had once observed that in the preference for or antipathy against a particular country, there already lay the first root of infidelity against one's fatherland—but by the dictates of the most calculating policy of national interest [*kühlste Interessenpolitik*]. But policy decisions of such weighty concern could not be made by the diplomatic envoy but only by the central authorities, namely, the director of the Eastern Division of the Foreign Ministry and, for the most important decisions, by the state secretary and the foreign minister. "But here," he concluded, "such a wide field opens up that it eludes the writer of letters on a rainy day."[40]

In his efforts to bring German–Polish relations to a workable denominator, Rauscher received Stresemann's growing support. The Foreign Minister and his envoy in Warsaw not only shared identical views on Germany's larger foreign policy goals but also revealed a close kinship of personal traits. In their personal life the Berlin politician and the Swabian diplomat both enjoyed a robust optimism, an earthy joviality, and an enormous energy for work; both displayed a zest for witty company, good food, and drink. Both by virtue of their middle class backgrounds and previous careers were strictly speaking "outsiders" to the *Auswärtiges Amt*, but had shown a great capacity for letting themselves become integrated into the Foreign Office, without, however, assimilating the rigidities of thought and prejudices of the *Wilhelmstrasse*, which enabled them to develop a cool and calculating policy of national interest

[40] Private letter, Rauscher to Bülow, August 13, 1930, AA, RAM/1430/2945H/ D575 226–29.

in dealing with Poland rather than letting any personal antipathy toward that country force them into a policy of passive hostility.

Before 1927 Stresemann had not actively exerted himself in favor of improved relations with Poland and on such issues as the development of the trade war in 1925 he had played a distinctly negative role. His personal anti-Polish sentiments, the speculation of the economic collapse of Poland, the lack of German domestic support for a conciliatory effort, and other policy preoccupations can all be mentioned in explanation of the Foreign Minister's position. But from 1927 to his death, Stresemann functioned as an active champion of a policy of normalization. In March 1927, Olszowski reported that after two significant conversations with Lord D'Abernon at San Remo, Stresemann had made the decision to improve relations with Poland, to make concessions, and to refrain from raising the frontier issue at that time.[41] Like Rauscher before him, Stresemann came to adopt this new position via a Western policy orientation; a position confirmed by a series of disappointing experiences in connection with the anticipated economic collapse of Poland, with the Lithuanian exchange solution and with Soviet co-operation on the Polish question. The counsel of the venerable Lord D'Abernon, that diplomatic Nestor, no doubt confirmed this general experience and may have hastened Stresemann's decision, but it would be difficult to accept Olszowski's version which casts the British ambassador in the role of an apostle who converted the German Foreign Minister. The apostles in this case were Time, Experience, and Stresemann's own good judgment.

Both Stresemann and Rauscher were in agreement that German foreign policy had to accord primacy to the reconciliation with the West, and in particular with France, and that a workable relationship with Poland constituted a prerequisite for a successful engagement in the West. German policy toward the Polish question had traditionally been a subordinate function of German–Russian relations. During the Stresemann–Rauscher partnership, which enjoyed its most fruitful period of collaboration between 1927 and 1929, relations with Warsaw increasingly began to figure as a function of Germany's Western rather than Eastern policy. Rauscher himself throughout his tenure in Warsaw remained curiously silent on the subject of German–Soviet relations.

The most concrete achievements in the improvement of German–Polish relations—the liquidation and trade treaties—can be said to have emerged as the result of the Stresemann–Rauscher partnership, and if

41 Report, Olszowski, March 7, 1927, AMSZ, P 11, fol. 4493.

the trade agreement failed to be ratified, it was to no small degree on account of death's premature dissolution of this partnership. Stresemann had given his Minister in Warsaw the privilege of writing to him directly and privately, a privilege of which Rauscher frequently availed himself during critical periods. Rauscher's colorful imagination exerted a stimulating influence on Stresemann, who himself demonstrated a greater capacity for incorporating and implementing the original ideas of others than for conceiving them. Stresemann's tragically early death terminated the partnership before it had been permitted to reach its most fruitful potential, namely, the appointment of Rauscher to the post of state secretary, for which Stresemann had him earmarked.

The work of Stresemann and Rauscher on behalf of an understanding with Poland was duly recognized in Warsaw. At the opening of the League Council meeting in January 1930, Zaleski, in his dual capacity as president of the Council and as Polish foreign minister, paid warm tribute to the memory of Stresemann, pointing out that if he and the German Foreign Minister had on occasion differed in this or that matter, they had both been "unis par le même sentiment de la nécessité d'une bonne entente polono-allemande pour assurer la paix en Europe."[42] The obituaries in the Polish press on the occasion of Rauscher's sudden death in December 1930 displayed both genuine sympathy and appreciation for his reconciliatory role that far exceeded normal diplomatic courtesy. *Kurjer Polski* of December 19 referred to him as an "unusually engaging personality" and a "skillful negotiator," while *Gazeta Polska* of the same day praised his objectivity, tact, and noble intentions which had facilitated the difficult relations between the two nations. "He was convinced," the article stated, "that the two countries which complemented one another in many aspects, especially economically, would sooner or later have to find the basis for a *modus vivendi.*"

POLISH RECONCILIATORY INITIATIVES AND RESPONSES

In Poland the idea of improving relations with Berlin generally met with a more positive response and produced less political controversy than in German circles. In the first place, the *beati possidentes* usually have a more conciliatory disposition than the losers of a dispute. In Germany there lingered the morbid suspicion that any form of concession and agreement with Poland might pave the way for a renunciation of

---

[42] AA, StS/2366/4587H/E185 471–74.

her territorial claims, whereas the Poles approached the matter with the full confidence that a territorial concession was unthinkable and that therefore no political party or group would ever exchange Polish territorial rights for a rapprochement with Germany. Third, after Locarno, France supported the cause of improved relations between Berlin and Warsaw, and, consequently, a policy of normalization with Germany did not force on Polish decision-makers a Kierkegaardian "Either . . . Or" choice which many Germans imagined they had to make between Moscow and Warsaw. Finally, the Poles accorded to Germany more attention than Germany accorded to the Poles in foreign policy calculations, with the result that German policy was somewhat slower in responding to the Locarno challenge of creating a more friendly climate of neighborly relations.

Traditionally, the parties of the Left, in particular the PPS, and the minority bloc favored more friendly relations with Germany. Among the German minority, conflicting short-term interests and long-range ambitions produced a mixed response. On the one hand, they favored an improvement because of the prospects it offered for getting better treatment from the Polish authorities. On the other hand, the German minority in Pomorze and Upper Silesia was concerned lest this improvement act as a prelude to a revisionist sacrifice. The National Democrats, Christian Nationalists, and conservative peasant groups had traditionally been opposed to closer collaboration with Germany. But after Locarno, French support for a policy of understanding mellowed the objections of the Francophile National Democrats; Piłsudski's growing dependence on the Right brought conservative circles into alignment with the government's efforts at normalizing relations with Berlin; agrarian groups showed an increased interest in harmonious trade relations with Germany; and in 1927 Stroński, the leader of that wing of Christian Nationalists which had refused to join the government bloc and had kept their alliance with the National Democrats, called for more intimate cultural contacts between Germany and Poland.

The leading figures in the Polish Foreign Ministry who were concerned with the conduct of Polish–German relations strove for an improvement of the situation. Between 1926 and 1930, in his formal addresses to the *Sejm* Foreign Affairs Committee, Foreign Minister Zaleski did not once miss the opportunity to express his wish for improved relations with Berlin. This was not merely public posturing on his part, for as has been seen in connection with the liquidation agreement, the trade

treaty, and the settlement issue in 1928, Zaleski supported an accommodation on these questions, even though his efforts frequently failed to
sway his more truculent Cabinet colleagues. In his guidelines of December 1926, Olszowski had pleaded for an earnest attempt to settle the
current disputes with Germany in the hope that this might at least temporarily deflect the inherent dangers of war. From the Polish Foreign
Ministry records, as well as from Rauscher's reports, it becomes clear that
the leading figures in the Western Division of the Foreign Ministry,
persons like Jackowski, Lipski, and Wysocki, strove for the same end and
that their efforts had the full backing of Prince Janusz Radziwiłł, the
chairman of the parliamentary Foreign Affairs Committee. In May 1928
the Western Division held a conference for the purpose of evaluating the
effects of the recent German elections on German–Polish relations. The
meeting concluded that the gains of the Left in Germany were favorable
to Polish interests, and while it advised caution until the foreign policy
course of the new government could be ascertained, it recommended several measures which would help pave the way for a Polish–German understanding. The Press Department of the Foreign Ministry was to instruct
the Polish press to keep to strictly factual reporting and to refrain from
vitriolic attacks against Germany. An effort was to be made to get an
early agreement on some technical questions, such as those relating to
social insurance and valorization; to apply more lenient standards in
granting visas to German citizens—even von Kries, the father of the
disreputable "Kries notes" was to be issued a short-term visa—; to establish closer personal contacts with members of the *Auswärtiges Amt*, the
SPD, and Catholic circles in Germany; and to reach agreement on the
liquidation and trade issues.[43]

The basis for Marshal Piłsudski's wish for an understanding with
Germany followed logically from his concept of an independent foreign
policy for Poland. This concept was nourished by his keen awareness of
Poland's great historical past and the recent experience of dependence
on France and other Entente Powers, which to Piłsudski was both
humiliating and unreliable. But a policy of greater self-reliance for Poland necessitated a direct understanding with her two more powerful
neighbors. Beck summarized the position of his master as follows: "Le
Maréchal a toujours déclaré qu'il était particulièrement utile pour un

[43] Memorandum signed by Lipski, May 23, 1928, AMSZ, P 11, fol. 4617, pp.
62–77. Zaleski accepted the terms of reference of the recommendation but urged
that one move cautiously in resuming trade negotiations.

pays d'être capable de s'entendre directement avec ses voisins; il en retire une liberté réelle pour règler toutes les autres relations internationales, et son politique gagne en indépendance."[44]

Piłsudski's desire for an understanding was intensified by the fact that he, like many of his countrymen from the eastern part of Poland, was inclined to view Germany as a lesser evil than Russia; moreover, as a factor which might be enlisted against the greater evil. These precepts were reflected in Piłsudski's own wartime behavior. This particular foreign policy orientation was reinforced by the fact that the Marshal harbored no personal resentments toward Germany. His open admiration for the military achievements of the German soldier, which as an old soldier he could both respect and fear, was mixed with appreciation for the high standards of discipline and order in German work and administration which he found somewhat lacking among his own countrymen.

Contrary to some expectations, Piłsudski refrained from any dramatic overtures toward Germany after his return to power in 1926. By appointing someone like Prince Janusz Radziwiłł foreign minister or envoy in Berlin, the new government in Warsaw would have made a clearly recognizable gesture of its earnest wish to start a new chapter in German–Polish relations. By appointing Zaleski instead, German uncertainties about Warsaw's intentions continued, for Zaleski was relatively unknown in German political circles, and, from what could be surmised, he seemed more inclined to continue Skrzyński's policy which favored international conciliation through the League of Nations and intimate ties with London rather than a direct reconciliatory offensive toward Germany. Given Piłsudski's attitude favoring an understanding with Germany, his cautious strategy in putting this into actual diplomatic practice may seem surprising. But the Marshal was temperamentally disinclined to take any prolonged and active interest in the procedural and technical minutiae of routine matters, such as the negotiations on liquidation and trade matters, and these questions were thus left in the hands of diplomats and other officials and continued to proceed at the customary limping pace. A real breakthrough in German–Polish relations, as Piłsudski recognized, would have to await a fundamental revision of German attitudes and an acceptance of the territorial status quo. One could hope that in the long-run political realism would

[44] Józef Beck, *Dernier rapport. Politique polonaise 1926–1939* (Neuchâtel, 1951), p. 5.

assert itself in Germany, but this was a function of German psychology and German domestic politics and would have to be internally resolved. The Marshal was disinclined to interfere in German domestic politics to try to accelerate this process.

Despite this rather cautious and passive strategy, one can detect certain specific Polish initiatives in favor of a reconciliation which were made outside formal diplomatic channels. One such attempt was undertaken by the Marshal himself, and was thus *sui generis* official. Other initiatives, such as Diamand's visit in 1926 and Prince Michał Radziwiłł's conversation with Stresemann in 1928, can at best be styled semi-official. These were private initiatives which had been inspired by Piłsudski's wish to bury the German–Polish conflict. But these private conversations did not proceed on the basis of specific instructions from the Marshal; at the most, he had advance notice of their occurrence, and he had found no reason to impose a veto.

The first conciliatory intervention of this type occurred little over a month after Piłsudski's *coup d'état*. In June 1926, the Socialist *Sejm* deputy, Dr. Diamand, visited Berlin in order to explore the attitudes of German officials and politicians on the question of a comprehensive settlement in German–Polish relations. Given the close ties which at that time still existed between the PPS and the Marshal, it is quite possible that the latter had known of Diamand's journey and had approved of the idea of privately sounding out German opinions. Under these circumstances it is indeed tempting to take the position of Gąsiorowski, who concludes that Diamand came to Germany as Piłsudski's emissary.[45] But evidence, and in some cases lack of evidence, would dictate a more cautious conclusion. In the first place, there is no mention of Diamand's mission in the Polish Foreign Ministry records. Rauscher, who constantly scanned the diplomatic horizon for meaningful signals of improved relations, did not believe there was anything official or important in the visit and ridiculed "the private diplomacy" of Dr. Diamand.[46] Also, Diamand's position was so vague that it seems safer to conclude that he was functioning as a self-appointed ambassador of good will and not as Piłsudski's official emissary. After some preliminary conversations with Schubert, Diamand himself seemed to perceive that his conciliatory propositions, e.g., agreement regarding the settle-

[45] Zygmunt J. Gąsiorowski, "Stresemann and Poland after Locarno," *Journal of Central European Affairs* 18, no. 3 (1958): 301.
[46] Letter, Rauscher to Schubert, July 9, 1926, AA, D/2339/4569H/E168 809–12.

ment of German nationals and improved transit facilities through the "Corridor," might be out of touch with official government policy, and he consequently returned to Warsaw to convince himself of his government's definite wish to come to an understanding with Germany.[47] Whatever Diamand's credentials, Stresemann considered this dialogue worth exploring and received him on his next German visit a month later. On this occasion Diamand showed more specific interests than just to advertise Poland's conciliatory sentiments. He asked Stresemann to support the plan which would admit Poland to a nonpermanent seat on the League Council under a formula that would determine her eligibility for re-election on the basis of a simple, rather than a two-thirds, majority vote. Poland would reciprocate with considerable concessions. Without specifying the nature of these concessions, Diamand emphasized Piłsudski's extraordinary interest in friendly relations with Germany and his anti-Russian attitude. Stresemann expressed the hope that in the future Germans and Poles would no longer regard each other as enemies and pretended to be disinterested in Polish ambitions for a Council seat.[48]

At their meeting in Geneva in December 1927, Piłsudski tried and, as has been seen, succeeded in making a favorable impression on Stresemann and in convincing him of his desire to reach an understanding with Germany. His loud praise for the heroic achievements of the German army, while expressing his sincere admiration, appears to have been calculated to befriend the German Foreign Minister, who was not unsusceptible to such patriotic flattery. Having paid public tribute to the German army during the famous luncheon, Piłsudski continued in the same vein when he privately told Stresemann how his own father had always singled out East Prussia as a model of efficient administration and good agricultural practices.[49] The Marshal had used the Geneva encounter to establish his credentials of good will and sincerity with regard to Germany and to win the confidence of the German Foreign Minister. As it involved the foremost statesmen of both Poland and Germany, the meeting had official character. But with the exception of Stresemann's suggestion to settle those disputed liquidation claims that were pending before the Paris Mixed Tribunal and to come to terms

---

[47] Note by Schubert, June 30, 1926, *ibid.*, 789–91.
[48] Memorandum, Stresemann, July 28, 1926, AA, D/2771/5462H/E368 941–45.
[49] Note by Stresemann, December 9, 1927, AA, RAM/1428/2945H/D573 409.

on the W*iederkaufsrecht* question—Piłsudski showed himself agreeable on both points—no specific proposals for a reconciliation were made. Discounting the Marshal's reassuring remarks that nobody in Poland entertained any annexationist ambitions toward East Prussia, the key obstacle to a reconciliation, i.e., the territorial dispute, was not touched upon in their conversation. The silence on the territorial issue might have contributed to a mutual tragedy of errors. Piłsudski appears to have interpreted Stresemann's silence as an indication that a sense of rationality was gaining ground in Germany and that the latter would be inclined to base relations with Warsaw on the tacit acceptance of the existing frontiers. Stresemann, in turn, regarded the Marshal's conciliatory manner and Briand's mediatory role as confirmation of the wisdom and ultimate success of Germany's revisionist policy.

The territorial question which had remained unmentioned at the Geneva meeting was explicitly raised at a later conciliatory initiative in March 1928 when Prince Michał Radziwiłł visited Stresemann at Cap Martin on the French Riviera where the Foreign Minister was convalescing.[50] The Cap Martin meeting loses much of its inherent interest once it has been established that Prince Radziwiłł was not speaking as Piłsudski's official emissary but in a purely private capacity.[51] At their first meeting Radziwiłł had remained rather passive and Stresemann had done most of the talking. When they held a second talk, the roles were shifted. The Prince assured the Foreign Minister that Polish opinion would gladly endorse a settlement with Germany if such an agreement could be arranged. He revealed certain anxiety about the prospects of intimate relations between Paris and Moscow but felt that this danger would cease once both Poland and France had become fully reconciled with Germany.

Having dispensed with these preliminaries, Radziwiłł came to the point when he asked Stresemann what he viewed as indispensable to making the resignation from all further territorial claims acceptable to

---

[50] *Stresemann Papers*, 3149/7348H/H165 203–5.

[51] On March 12, 1928, Prince Michał Radziwiłł as an act of courtesy had provided Stresemann with a translated copy of his report to Piłsudski in which he gave a resumé of their Cap Martin talks. From this report one can easily gain the impression that Radziwiłł had undertaken his mission in an official capacity. But a recent survey of the Adjutants' Office of the Belweder Palace has unearthed the same memorandum, dated March 7, 1928, together with a covering letter, not contained in the *Stresemann Papers*, in which it is made quite clear that Radziwiłł had acted strictly on his own initiative and without instructions from the Marshal (AAN, *Adiutantura Belwederu*, vol. V; cited in Jerzy Krasuski, *Stosunki polsko-niemieckie, 1926–1932* [Poznań, 1964], II, p. 76).

German public opinion. Stresemann, who viewed this as an invitation for a German revisionist sacrifice, replied that he could not face the German people empty handed. The Foreign Minister repeated the German thesis that a reconciliation would follow a revision and outlined Germany's territorial claims. In his memorandum Radziwiłł did not specify what these claims were. This omission would indicate that there had been no deviation from Germany's normal claims for Danzig, the "Corridor" and Upper Silesia. In his behavior, Radziwiłł did deviate from the normal Polish response, for rather than rejecting this proposal as non-negotiable, he inquired whether such sacrifices by Poland could be matched by proper compensation "through great advantages in the east . . . in particular with respect to new outlets to the sea which might be secured for us." Radziwiłł's implied eastern exchange scheme seemed to lend credence to German speculations that Piłsudski still nourished his own version of a *Drang nach Osten* and would have been inclined to accept certain territorial sacrifices in the west for a free hand in the east. However, these calculations ignored the negative response of Polish public opinion to such a scheme and the growing conservatism of the Marshal; under the metamorphosis of age an adventurer's youthful dreams of imperial destiny in the east had turned into an elderly statesman's concern for preserving what his own efforts had created. Despite his contrary assurances to Chicherin, Stresemann registered no objections to Radziwiłł's proposal, which would have amounted to the annexation of Lithuania by Poland, if not even a greater expansion at Soviet expense. Stresemann also spoke of German financial compensation to Poland in the event of a territorial revision and, in concluding, asked Radziwiłł to try to arrange for a confidential meeting between himself and Piłsudski where these weighty matters might be discussed. Such a meeting might be staged at Marienbad or Carlsbad, where both statesmen could go for a cure and where they could meet "accidentally" and thus cure the ailments in the mutual relations of their countries.

Stresemann's answer to Radziwiłł had left no doubt that a real reconciliation was unalterably linked to a prior satisfaction of Germany's territorial claims, in return for which she would provide Poland with financial compensation and leave her a free hand in the east. We do not know Piłsudski's reaction to Radziwiłł's memorandum, but there was no response to Stresemann's bid for another meeting with the Marshal. The unofficial Cap Martin conversation merely served to underline the indelible differences between the reconciliatory strategies of the two countries. For Germany it was a reconciliation on the basis of a territorial alteration; for Poland under Piłsudski it was a reconciliation that would be based on a mutual respect of the existing frontiers, a transformation of attitudes, economic co-operation, an amicable settlement of disputes, improved transit facilities through the "Corridor," and, at the very most, some local frontier rectification. Piłsudski was willing to renounce all Polish aspirations with respect to East Prussia and no doubt expected similar guarantees from Germany for the rest of their existing common boundaries.

After Piłsudski's friendly encounter with Stresemann and the private initiatives of persons like Diamand and Prince Michal Radziwiłł had failed to create a fundamental breakthrough in the stalemate of German–Polish relations, little more survived these efforts than the tacit consensus on both sides to minimize frictions in their routine contacts. Even in this very truncated version of the reconciliatory theme, Piłsudski's presence had a useful impact on German–Polish relations, and the German government anxiously listened to the proliferating rumors and reports about the Marshal's declining health and intentions to retire from politics. In German estimates, either alternative to his withdrawal, the full restoration of parliamentary institutions or a military *camarilla*, threatened to lead to a further deterioration of relations and a repetition of the undesirable pre-Locarno state of affairs.[52]

In retrospect, the inherent incompatibility of the reconciliatory strategies pursued by the two sides becomes evident. There was no common ground between Germany's romantic Faustian strivings for the unattainable revisionist goal and Poland's search for the acceptance of the status quo. In the absence of consensus on this basic issue, private and official attempts concentrated on creating a more tolerable working climate in their routine relations. If the Great Depression had not prematurely reversed the trends which had begun to emerge after Locarno, even this delicately improvised German–Polish détente between 1926 and 1930 might have taken more permanent form and might eventually have mellowed German attitudes toward the revisionist question. The personal examples of Rauscher, and to some extent Stresemann, provide some supporting evidence for such speculation. But given the brevity of its existence, the tentative normalcy which was only beginning to emerge was unable to survive the stress of a major crisis. Viewing it from the perspective of the tragic events which followed, Beck tends to discount

[52] Letter, Rauscher to Stresemann, July 13, 1928, AA, StS/2339/4569H/E169 155–57.

altogether the importance of the conciliatory moves which were undertaken after Locarno. "La tentative faite en vue d'amener une détente entre Varsovie et Berlin," he wrote, "n'eut aucun résultat qui vaille la peine d'être mentionné, si l'on excepte les efforts continus de l'éminent ministre d'Allemagne à Varsovie, M. Rauscher, esprit large et homme de bonne volonté."[53]

[53] Beck, *Dernier rapport*, p. 5.

XI

The Disintegration of Relations, 1930–1933

WITH THE ECONOMIC COLLAPSE of 1930 and the accompanying political symptoms, the state of normalcy—an uneasy equilibrium of a working relationship at its best—which had begun to prevail in German–Polish relations during the last three years of the Stresemann era disintegrated to the level of tension and uncertainty which had prevailed in the immediate postwar years. The deterioration proceeded so far that a few days after Hitler's take-over the Polish Minister in Berlin told the German Foreign Office that he saw little use in appointing a Polish consul general to fill the vacant position in Königsberg since the two countries were on the verge of war.[1]

The disastrous effects of the collapse of the German economy, which resulted in three million unemployed in 1930, brought about the growth of extremist political groups. In the autumn elections of 1930, the Nazi party had received a vote of 6.5 million, as compared to the 800 thousand in 1928, and by July 1932 both the number of unemployed and the Nazi vote had more than doubled the 1930 figures. These gains by extremists had been made at the expense of those moderate parties that had identified themselves with the cause of normalization with Poland. The extreme groups in Germany were particularly apt to compensate for their economic frustrations by intensifying their revisionist clamor and by sharpening their chauvinistic slogans. Not only had the strength of the moderate parties in Germany been sapped numerically,

[1] Note by Meyer of his talk with Wysocki, February 17, 1933, AA, GA/3024/6601H/E495 037–40.

327

but their commitment to improving relations with Poland suffered heavily as the result of the Polish elections of 1930 and the decline of democratic institutions in that country. Being themselves engaged in an acute domestic struggle against anti-democratic forces, the moderate parties in Germany were bound to respond negatively and emotionally to the dictatorial measures of the incumbent régime in Warsaw. The economic crisis also made itself directly felt by the nonratification of the trade treaty, the imposition of prohibitive trade restrictions, and the sharp decline of trade between Germany and Poland after 1930.

At the same time the changing of the guard in the German Foreign Ministry worked to the detriment of German–Polish relations, as the Curtius–Moltke team replaced the Stresemann–Rauscher partnership. Comparing the stature of Curtius with that of his predecessor strictly in terms of foreign policy achievements would be distinctly unfair to Curtius who, by events out of his control, was deprived of the relative internal stability and economic prosperity upon which Stresemann could base his diplomacy. Curtius was a distinguished lawyer who directed the Foreign Office in the fashion of a talented advocate but lacked the dynamism, persuasiveness, and flexibility which had distinguished Stresemann's foreign policy. As minister of economics, Curtius had been an active promoter of an economic settlement with Poland. As foreign minister, he applied himself on behalf of the ratification of the liquidation and trade agreements in an attempt to retain a tolerable working relationship with Poland. It was mainly through Curtius's efforts that the trade treaty was accepted by the Cabinet, despite heavy opposition from Schiele, and was presented to the *Reichstag* for ratification. This policy followed a Cabinet decision of October 4, 1929, which had opted for the conclusion of a liquidation and trade agreement as part of the general continuation of the policy of normalization with Poland, instead of a policy of intensive revisionism which, it was realized, promised no hope for success in the foreseeable future and threatened to involve Germany in a war with Poland which she was totally incapable of waging.[2] Notwithstanding the Foreign Minister's genuine intentions, he was unable to stem the tide of the swelling revisionist campaign in which even his own Cabinet colleagues participated, and being less of a craftsman than

---

[2] Julius Curtius, *Sechs Jahre Minister der Deutschen Republik* (Heidelberg, 1948), pp. 98–99.

Stresemann in influencing the press and winning the people, he himself felt forced to make more frequent and more direct revisionist utterances in public than was compatible with his conciliatory aims.

Hans Adolf von Moltke, the new German minister to Warsaw, was in almost every respect the opposite of his predecessor Rauscher. Moltke, a Silesian by birth, was the son of a Prussian minister of state and nephew of the younger field-marshal. Moltke's aristocratic background was reflected in his impeccable courtesy and dignified, if somewhat aloof bearing, which differed visibly from Rauscher's informality. Where Rauscher had started as an "outsider" in the Foreign Ministry, Moltke was very much a product of that organization and his primary loyalty was to that body. Where Rauscher had been adventurously experimental and flexible in his approach, Moltke tended to be conservative and cautious to the degree of indecisiveness. Moltke had actually been slated for the position of undersecretary under Curtius, but his expertise in Polish affairs—he had served on the Upper Silesian Mixed Commission from 1922 to 1924 and had followed Dirksen as *Dirigent* and later as *Direktor* of the Eastern Division—had made him indispensable to that section and had prepared him admirably for his new Warsaw post.[3] As one might expect, in view of his background, Moltke was an adherent, though with caution, of the Bismarckian strategy of German–Russian co-operation. He had little personal sympathy for the Poles, but, in the words of Laroche, "il n'en laissait rien paraître,"[4] and generally enjoyed the respect of the Polish officials and received a favorable press. During the period under examination, Moltke never entertained the intimate relations with Curtius which Rauscher had enjoyed with Stresemann, and he played a far more passive role than his predecessor in trying to help shape the foreign policy vis-à-vis Poland. Moltke's primary importance in the history of German–Polish relations unquestionably does not fall into the Weimar period but into the Hitler era, where he was instrumental in conducting negotiations for the temporary German–Polish détente, even though it seems that he never fully believed in the prospects of a lasting German–Polish reconciliation and regarded Hitler's policy of friendship as a temporary but shrewdly Machiavellian tactical device for counterbalancing the French–Polish and, even more so, the French–Soviet alliance.

[3] Hans Roos, *Polen und Europa* (Tübingen, 1957), p. 67.
[4] Jules Laroche, *La Pologne de Pilsudski. Souvenirs d'une ambassade 1926–1935* (Paris, 1953), p. 125.

THE UNENDING FUGUE OF INCIDENTS

Relations between the two countries after 1930 witnessed an ever increasing cadence of incidents: German public agitation for a revision that elicited the sharpest Polish replies, hostile demonstrations on both sides, border incidents, and more intensified minority complaints, all of which revived the prospect of a German–Polish armed conflict. Varied as these incidents were, they all shared the quality of being grossly exaggerated by a hostile press and a clamorous public and thereby interfered with the normal process of adjustment by rational diplomacy.

Typical of such minor but exaggerated incidents was the speech which the German minister of transport, Treviranus, delivered on August 10, 1930. The speech, which referred to the day when all the lost territories in the east would be reincorporated into the *Reich*, followed the standard ritual which was almost daily repeated at political gatherings and in press statements throughout Germany. What heightened its negative impact was the fact that these words had been spoken by a minister of the *Reich* on the steps of the *Reichstag* building. The German government tried to mute the sting by publishing a communiqué in which it underlined that the government had had no previous knowledge of the speech. But this was only a partial apology which did not formally disavow the Minister. What particularly embittered Poland was that the German press generally praised Treviranus for the frankness of his statement. The Minister himself, speaking at Kassel a few days later, insisted that he felt no need to withdraw any part of his speech, for it constituted an open declaration on behalf of an active policy of revisionism without, however, involving any military threat.[5]

Treviranus's speech, following so shortly upon the Allied evacuation of the Rhineland, seemed to confirm Poland's worst fears that Germany would intensify her revisionist activities in the east once her hands had been freed in the west. Its reception by the Polish press was particularly violent and it prompted anti-German demonstrations across Poland. Zaleski summoned the German chargé d'affaires, von Rintelen, and delivered a formal protest. The Foreign Minister noted that he would resist the temptation to reply in the same vein, for in that case a point would soon be reached "which no longer permitted diplomatic relations between Germany and Poland." Zaleski expressed himself extremely

---

[5] Christian Höltje, *Die Weimarer Republik und das Ost–Locarno Problem, 1919–1934* (Würzburg, 1958), pp. 192–93.

pessimistically on the future of German–Polish relations. He found Treviranus's subsequent explanatory comments even more disturbing than the original speech, for they clearly demonstrated that Germany relied on peaceful methods of revision solely because of lack of military might; "from this the whole world had to conclude that Germany would make war on Poland if she had an adequate army."[6]

The Polish attempt to get more international mileage out of the incident failed. In London the Polish chargé d'affaires, Count Potocki, requested that the Foreign Office issue a formal statement of disapproval. A similar request had also gone to France. But the Foreign Office regarded the incident as closed and refused to comply with the Polish proposal, which it viewed as an unnecessary attempt to raise a storm in a teacup. "We cannot make a *démarche*," was noted in a marginal comment that characterized the supercilious attitude of that Ministry toward matters which affected Poland, "every time a blundering German transgresses the rule that 'toutes les vérités ne sont pas bonnes à dire'. . . . This is a relatively level country and we have no taste for going mountaineering on molehills."[7]

During the summer of 1930 there occurred a number of border violations by Polish military aircraft. In Germany the frequency of these violations left the impression that it was a case of systematic espionage rather than mere accident. German diplomatic and military authorities had tried to keep these incidents confidential to avoid a public clamor, but when the news leaked to the German press a great issue was made of it.[8] Rauscher found the Polish Foreign Ministry officials concerned and embarrassed and eager to remove this source of friction.[9] On August 2, the Polish government presented Rauscher with an *aide-mémoire* which promised to investigate all complaints and to punish individual culprits. In October the German Foreign Ministry noted with satisfaction that there had been only one further violation.[10]

[6] Telegram, Rintelen, August 14, 1930, AA, RAM/1430/2945H/D575 234–36.
[7] FO, 371/14370, pp. 83–84; August 15, 1930.
[8] The party organ of the DNVP called these violations an indication of Polish impudence and demanded stiffer action than mere diplomatic protest, suggesting that all intruding aircraft be shot down (*Unsere Partei*, 10, no. 1 [1932], p. 388).
[9] On May 15, 1930, Wysocki thanked Rauscher for having provided him with a precise account of the various air violation incidents which gave him ammunition against the General Staff and the Ministry of War (AA, RAM/1430/2945H/D575 060).
[10] Note for Undersecretary von Bülow, October 17, 1930, *ibid.*, 339–42.

At the time of these air space violations, three border incidents followed in short succession. Each incident, viewed in isolation, was of no more than minute importance; however, their repetition at brief intervals and the hysterically exaggerated and grossly misrepresented treatment which they were given in their respective national presses indicated the precarious state of relations and the difficulty in resolving even small differences.

The incidents involved clashes between border police and their rough treatment of the local population. The most serious clash occurred at Neuhöfen in the evening of May 24, 1930, when two armed Polish border patrol guards entered German territory in order to pick up secret information which they had been promised by German border officials who were eager to lay a trap for them. When they had been threatened with arrest on the German side, several other Polish border guards had rushed in to assist their colleagues in distress. In the course of the ensuing *mêlée*, one Polish guard was killed. The incident evoked much passion on both sides. Germany protested against the violation of German soil by armed Polish border guards, while Poland accused Germany of having lured her border guards into German territory and having killed one of them. The two governments, realizing that the mounting frequency of these frontier incidents and the public reaction which they produced might provoke an uncontrollable situation, agreed to institute measures for the prevention and settlement of further frontier incidents. In response to a suggestion by the Polish government, a mixed commission was established for this purpose, and even though the commission was unable to reach consensus on the factual evidence of the three border incidents, it was agreed that in the future frontier guards were not to cross the boundary without an official service order and without permission of the border officials of the other country; furthermore, border guards were urged to avoid any unnecessary harshness when dealing with the local population in regulating border traffic. The local authorities were instructed to co-operate with their counterparts across the border in the event of another incident.[11] The above agreement, which was, in all probability, accompanied by strict orders to respective frontier authorities, resulted in the successful elimination of further frontier incidents of this nature.

In his annual address to the *Sejm* Foreign Affairs Committee

[11] Undated note from approximately July 1930, *ibid.*, 196–97.

on January 10, 1931, Zaleski took a distinctly more outspoken position against Germany than was customary for him.[12] During a rally of the *Stahlhelmbund* which took place in Breslau at the end of May 1931, several revisionist and strongly anti-Polish slogans had been circulated. The public expression of these slogans in the vicinity of the Polish boundary naturally appeared highly provocative in Polish eyes and prompted critical, though generally restrained, comments by the Polish press. The Polish envoy called on the *Auswärtiges Amt* to draw attention to the unfortunate impression produced by these anti-Polish demonstrations in the vicinity of the Polish border. The German government rejected his request that similar demonstrations be avoided in future by insisting that the *Stahlhelmbund* was a private organization and official circles could therefore not be held responsible for its activities.[13]

The degree to which small incidents could incite a national storm was best illustrated by a trivial flag incident, which in its exaggeration was not without comical overtones. On July 31, 1932, the Warsaw population celebrated the festival of the Polish sea in the customary Polish manner by decorating the streets in a colorful array of flags and banners. Since this was not an official holiday and was moreover a celebration with a distinct *pique* against Germany, at whose cost Poland had become a sea power, Baron von Rintelen, the German chargé d'affaires, had lost his temper when he repeatedly found a Polish flag tied to the inside of his garden fence and twice removed the object of his irritation.[14] The Polish press represented the incident as a national insult and pressed for Rintelen's recall, while the conservative press in Germany made him an instant hero. In the diplomatic exchange that ensued, the Germans argued that the extraterritoriality of Rintelen's residence had been violated, while the Poles claimed that a German diplomat had insulted the Polish flag. Unlike previous minor incidents of this type, where both foreign ministries had tried to soothe frayed national tempers and an irate press, in this case only the German Foreign Ministry expressed its regrets, while Deputy Foreign Minister Beck—Zaleski was absent at the time—supported rather than restrained the hostile comments of the Polish press and insisted on Rintelen's recall.

Since 1930 the governments of the two countries had become victims rather than initiators of the rapid process of deterioration in their

[12] *Messager Polonais*, January 12, 1931.
[13] SD, 760c. 62/153; June 17, 1931.
[14] Telegram, Rintelen, August 2, 1932, AA, RAM/1430/2945H/D575 728–29.

mutual relations. Just as the impact of the international economic crisis and the lack of central economic planning and proper fiscal and monetary co-ordination left the governments unable to cope with the worsening economic situation, internal political reaction, especially in Germany, deprived decision-makers of the public support that would have been necessary to continue the process of normalization. In several instances official circles in Berlin and Warsaw tried to impose a brake on the accelerating deterioration of relations but they were unable to stem the tide. Diplomats on either side frequently sought a compromise solution to disputed issues like the 1930 air-space violations and border incidents, and they tried to avoid excess publicity over these issues of conflict. When the dissemination of hostile radio propaganda had reached a crescendo in March 1931, the Polish legation in Berlin approached the German Foreign Ministry with the proposal for a private agreement between the radio stations of the two countries which would eliminate hostile news broadcasts. Zechlin's immediate response had been noncommittal, for "we cannot possibly let our mouths be shut over the radio regarding Upper Silesia and the 'Corridor.' "[15] But Curtius promised to do his best to reduce the anti-Polish tenor of German radio broadcasts and noted privately that it would, indeed, be necessary to negotiate with German broadcasting officials on this matter.[16]

On March 31, 1931, the Director of the *Reichsrundfunkgesellschaft* and the Director of the Polish Broadcasting Company signed an agreement in which both sides promised to assume responsibility for creating all possible safeguards so that in the political, cultural, religious, economic, and intellectual spheres no breach would be committed against the spirit of international co-operation, although each country retained the right of conducting some active propaganda in those areas where national aspirations exerted themselves, as long as these did not injure the national sentiments of the listeners of the other country.[17]

The broadcasting agreement helped to infuse a more moderate tone to radio broadcasting than was to be found in the newspapers. The officials on both sides were satisfied with this arrangement, and it was not until the end of 1932, in connection with an undisguised revisionist program of the *Ostmarkenrundfunk* in Königsberg on December 28, 1932, that one of the signatories was forced to protest against the infraction of the

15 Note by Zechlin, March 24, 1931, *ibid.*, 590–92.
16 Note by Curtius, March 28, 1931, *ibid.*, 599–602.
17 *Deutsch–Polnisches Rundfunkabkommen*, March 31, 1931, *ibid.*, 793.

agreement. Foreign Minister Baron von Neurath received Wysocki's complaint in a sympathetic spirit. Neurath expressed his regrets over the incident and readily admitted that the German official censor of radio broadcasts had been negligent in his duties, probably because he had been away on a Christmas holiday. In turn, he asked for the assistance of the Polish Foreign Ministry in quieting the Polish press. Responding to Neurath's conciliatory statement, the Polish government agreed to calm its press and to refrain from publishing an official communiqué of the Neurath–Wysocki talk in order to spare the badly faltering German government any additional domestic embarrassment.[18]

Despite the increasingly hostile climate of German public opinion, Warsaw placed some hopes in the person of Chancellor Brüning and his government's conciliatory foreign policy. Brüning's religious convictions and scholarly and urbane manner gave him the appearance of a Catholic monsignor which, in Polish eyes, contrasted favorably from the otherwise violent and demagogic tenor of German politics. Lipski noted with satisfaction that on his tour to the eastern provinces, Brüning had avoided all inflammatory references to the revisionist question.[19] Brüning's foreign policy aims were principally dictated by the need to stabilize the domestic situation in Germany and to protect the democratic basis of German politics against the onslaught of extremist elements. The Chancellor expected relief for Germany's economic depression from a revision of the Young Plan and reparations obligations. He also sought to outmaneuver his nationalist opponents by procuring for Germany full equality in the military field as part of an international disarmament settlement. The success of his foreign policy, and with it the chances of his own political survival, depended on the responsiveness of the Western Powers. As Lipski correctly analyzed, Chancellor Brüning would not wish to risk losing international confidence in his policies by engaging in any drastic anti-Polish measures. The Polish diplomat therefore recommended that Poland avail herself of this opportunity "to make a further outward display of our good will," as had already been done by the decision to ratify the liquidation and trade treaties, in an attempt to establish a common basis of collaboration with those reasonable elements in Germany which strove for peaceful co-existence.[20]

The substance of his recommendation was soon put to the test when

---

[18] Telegram, Wysocki, January 3, 1933; note by Polish Foreign Ministry, January 4, 1933, AMSZ, P II, fol. 4937.
[19] Letter, Lipski to Wysocki, February 23, 1931, *Lipski Papers*, p. 27.
[20] *Ibid.*, pp. 30–31.

the news about the Austro-German agreement to enter into a customs union exploded like a bombshell on March 21, 1931.[21] Contrary to the strong opposition from countries like France and Czechoslovakia, Poland adopted a neutral stand toward the customs dispute.[22] On May 20, Lipski informed the Polish Minister in Berlin that in recent consultations with Zaleski and Beck, Marshal Piłsudski had approved "our intended policy toward Germany," i.e., the policy of détente and collaboration with reasonable elements in Germany. Because of the uncertainties which had been raised by the customs union dispute, Piłsudski had wished to retain freedom of action for Poland and thus preferred that the German–Polish trade treaty not be enforced for the time being. Apart from this general line of policy, Beck had backed Lipski's recommendation to seek agreement on such secondary matters as the liquidation of the Paris Mixed Arbitration Tribunal, the problem of insurance claims, and the Graebe–Naumann interpellation, whenever a favorable moment offered itself.[23]

Observing the situation directly from Berlin, Minister Wysocki was in a better position than his superiors in Warsaw to evaluate the problems and prospects of improved relations with Germany. In a letter to Lipski of July 8, Wysocki noted pessimistically that he had "come to the conclusion that Germany's attitude toward Poland has not improved in the least." Luther, the German *Reichsbankpräsident*, had vetoed Poland's election to the council of the Basel Bank; public officials contin-

---

[21] The League Council decided to ask for a ruling from the Hague Court as to whether the customs union, which Germany and Austria had agreed to conclude as a remedy to their economic crisis, was compatible with the treaty obligations of these two countries to refrain from *Anschluss*. The Court's decision on September 5, 1931, which seemed to be influenced more by political than by legal considerations, ruled against the establishment of a customs union.

[22] Poland's lack of concern on this question, as well as on the broader question of *Anschluss*, must strike us as surprising in view of the far-reaching political implications of such a move. In a letter to the German Minister in Prague on April 19, 1931, State Secretary von Bülow remarked that the customs union might eventually also include Czechoslovakia. This German-dominated economic bloc, together with German economic penetration of the Baltic States, would have the effect of isolating Poland economically. This would make Poland more susceptible to German revisionist demands in return for economic concessions (AA, StS/2385/4602H/E199 512–15; cited in F. G. Stambrook, "The German-Austrian Customs Union Project of 1931," *Journal of Central European Affairs* 21 [April 1961]: 43). In his argument, Bülow quite clearly echoed the sentiments which had prevailed in the *Auswärtiges Amt* before 1927 and which, one would have assumed, had been laid to rest.

[23] Lipski to Wysocki, May 20, 1931, *Lipski Papers*, pp. 31–33. The minority leaders, Graebe and Naumann, had protested with the League Council against land reform practices which discriminated against the German minority.

ued their negative pronouncements; Germany had failed to ratify the trade treaty and to extend the wheat agreement; and she now tried to isolate Poland economically by offering seductive trade deals to Hungary, Rumania, and Yugoslavia. All this led him to the conclusion that there existed no difference between the views of people like General von Seeckt and the policies of the *Reich* government. Wysocki was less convinced than Lipski of the yields which a conciliatory policy of small steps might bring. He therefore came up with a more ambitious and bolder scheme when he suggested that a direct meeting be arranged on neutral ground between the Polish Prime Minister and Foreign Minister and their German counterparts.[24] A few days later in a letter to Beck, Wysocki returned to his proposal for a Polish–German summit meeting at which he believed even such controversial matters as the frontier revision might be discussed. Once Germany had restored order to the financial situation and had settled the reparations and disarmament issue, she herself was bound to raise the "Polish question." It would therefore be advantageous for Poland to pre-empt the issue as long as Germany was still beset by internal weakness. In Wysocki's view, a "frank, even slightly brutal, but basic exchange of opinions between the prime ministers of both countries and their foreign ministers would lead not only to the conclusion of the trade agreement but also to a considerable relaxation in the field of propaganda and in the policy of economically isolating Poland."[25]

In Warsaw more cautious considerations prevailed, and there exists no evidence that Wysocki ever broached the question of a summit meeting in his discussions with German officials. Lipski adhered to Talleyrand's warning when he noted that too much zeal on the Polish side might be counterproductive as it might jeopardize Chancellor Brüning's delicate domestic position. He therefore instructed his Berlin envoy to conduct careful soundings to determine whether Germany's wish for some rapprochement with Poland, as recent reports from Berlin would indicate, was merely "a matter of strategy designed to evoke a desirable effect in the West," or whether it constituted a "genuine effort to normalize relations with Poland." Lipski recalled how Poland's earlier attempt to normalize relations with Germany by relying on mass media and the open parliamentary forum in order to publicize the benefits of the liquidation and trade agreements had failed because of the unrecep-

---

[24] Wysocki to Zaleski, July 9, 1931, *ibid.*, pp. 36–38.
[25] Wysocki to Beck, July 19, 1931, *ibid.*, pp. 38–39.

tive public opinion in Germany. He had thus become convinced that it would be preferable for Wysocki to approach certain leading political figures in Germany in a more confidential manner in order to determine the attitudes of the various political parties toward Poland and toward the question of normalization.[26]

Throughout the deteriorating situation, Wysocki followed this line of instruction and conducted confidential talks with German politicians from different parties but excluded the Nazis, Communists, and extreme Nationalists like Hugenberg. A quiet dialogue was thus kept open despite mounting tensions between Berlin and Warsaw. The Polish envoy later recalled the 1931–32 period as the worst of his official career. In Berlin he was constantly confronted by an irate press, a hostile public, and haughty officials, and he and his colleagues found themselves socially ostracized.[27]

Colonel Beck's strong personal involvement and reaction to the flag incident of 1932, where he had identified himself with the extreme position of the Polish national press, was a departure from the previous practice of not allowing the negative press clamor to set the tone for their foreign policy behavior and to seek a quiet diplomatic solution to the periodic incidents which troubled relations between Berlin and Warsaw. Both governments had generally adhered to this practice during Brüning's chancellorship when the situation had been tense but, at least as judged from Warsaw, not without hope for a distinct improvement. The fall of the Brüning Cabinet on May 30, 1932, and its replacement by that elegant anachronism, Franz von Papen, enhanced Polish concerns over domestic developments in Germany and may, to some extent, explain Colonel Beck's over-reaction to a clumsy performance by a junior German diplomat.[28]

It required Zaleski's return to Warsaw to lay the flag incident to rest. In what Moltke styled "an astonishing disavowal of Colonel Beck," Zaleski represented the incident as an exaggerated trifle [*"car elle est très petite"*] and allowed the matter to be forgotten. Beck's contrasting hard-line position not only reflected his own ascendancy in the Foreign Ministry and the rivalry with his superior Zaleski, but also a newly emerging style of Polish foreign policy which took a more independent, self-

[26] Lipski to Wysocki, October 20, 1931, *ibid.*, pp. 41–43.

[27] Alfred Wysocki, "Początek dramatu," *Tygodnik Powszechny*, No. 7 (525), February 15, 1959; cited in *Lipski Papers*, pp. 43–45.

[28] Rintelen, who had been due for a new post in any case, was quietly and somewhat prematurely recalled from Warsaw early in September 1932.

assertive, and impetuous course and had first been put to test in June of that year in the famous "Wicher" incident.

The ambitious, energetic, and elegant Colonel Beck presented a marked contrast to the conciliatory and somewhat colorless Zaleski. As deputy minister of foreign affairs, a post he had occupied since December 1930, Beck stood out from his senior colleagues in the Foreign Ministry because of his youth and middle class background. Also his career pattern, which rapidly projected him to the very top when he became foreign minister two years later, differed distinctly from that of his predecessors in that post. Previous foreign ministers had either emerged from the arena of parliamentary politics, like Dmowski and Seyda, or had climbed the rungs of the well-ordered ladder of professional diplomacy, like Zaleski himself, or they had shifted with ease between these two métiers, as had Skrzyński, Skirmunt, Sapieha, and Zamoyski. Beck was neither a professional diplomat nor a politician with a parliamentary background. He had briefly served with the Polish missions in Bucharest, Budapest, and Brussels and had been a military attaché in Paris from 1922 to 1923. After the French authorities had expelled him from his Paris post, Beck had gone to the Military Academy in Warsaw. After the 1926 coup, Piłsudski had appointed Beck as his *chef de cabinet* in the War Ministry. In 1929 Rauscher reported that Beck was regularly in the Marshal's company and exercised great influence over him.[29] When Piłsudski briefly replaced Sławek as prime minister in August 1930, he promoted his protégé to the post of minister without portfolio, in which capacity Beck conducted the routine functions which were normally performed by the prime minister but for which the Marshal showed little inclination. Following the 1930 election and Sławek's return to the prime ministership in December of that year, Beck was dropped from the Cabinet and sent to the Foreign Ministry to replace Wysocki as deputy minister. The British Minister in Warsaw expressed his regret over the departure of the conciliatory and competent Wysocki, a regret that became "still deeper in view of the personality of his successor, who has no official experience and enjoys an unenviable reputation as an unscrupulous and ambitious adventurer."[30]

Colonel Beck, with his dynamic personality and intimate contacts with the Marshal, soon began to over-shadow his nominal superior. Under these conditions it was almost inevitable that a strong rivalry

[29] AA, GA/3759/K190/K036 336–37; June 18, 1929.
[30] Erskine to Henderson, December 10, 1930, FO, 371/14820, p. 197.

should have developed between the two men. Beck's control over the personnel division of the Foreign Ministry allowed him to penetrate the organization with his supporters and to remove those officials who did not enjoy the full confidence of the Piłsudski group.[31] Beck thus occupied a strategic position from which he could gradually supplant his chief. Zaleski's stand was further weakened by his frequent attendance at international conferences and at the regular sessions of the League of Nations. During his absence from Warsaw, Beck had been able to take a harder line than was favored by Zaleski with respect to the flag incident and, more important, in dealing with Danzig.[32] When Zaleski returned from the 1932 autumn session at Geneva with the victory of Poland's re-election to the League Council in his pocket, he apparently felt sufficiently strong to risk a showdown with his unruly subordinate. When Piłsudski refused to remove Beck from the Foreign Ministry, Zaleski resigned on November 2, ostensibly for reasons of health, and Beck advanced to the vacated position.[33] In an article of November 4, *Gazeta Warszawska* aptly commented on the recent transfer by noting that before Zaleski's resignation there had been two foreign policies in Poland, an official one conducted by Foreign Minister Zaleski, and an unofficial one pursued by Beck. Henceforth, predicted *Gazeta Warszawska* there would only be one foreign policy.

MILITARY ASPECTS IN GERMAN–POLISH RELATIONS

Under the general climate of uncertainty which had descended upon Europe in the wake of the economic depression and which placed in doubt the very survival of the Weimar Republic, the perceived dangers of a military confrontation between Germany and Poland reached a level of seriousness which recalled the days of the Upper Silesian insurrections. In retrospect, these fears of a German–Polish military conflict in 1930–32 appear as the exaggerated product of a tension-ridden political situation which were not justified on the basis of the existing military preparations and plans.

Apart from the general atmosphere of distrust, the inherent strategic situation seemed unsatisfactory to both sides and thus added to a mutual feeling of insecurity. The flat terrain and the absence of natural obstacles on either side of the German–Polish boundary left each country exposed

[31] Report, Wiley, March 6, 1931, *SD*, 860c. 021/16.
[32] *SD*, 960c. 00/558; November 4, 1932.
[33] Laroche, *Souvenirs*, pp. 115–16.

and highly vulnerable to an aggressive surprise attack from the other side. For Germany, numerical inferiority in military manpower and arms and the proximity of Berlin to the border created particular anxieties. The Poles, on their part, were unnerved by the constant awareness of Germany's potential military superiority and their inherently inferior strategic position. The geographic shape of Poland was such that a rearmed Germany could easily block the narrow "Corridor" passage from the sea and penetrate it by land, in a pincer movement conducted from Silesia and Pomerania and supported by a back-door attack from East Prussia. In the 1939 campaign this was precisely the operational plan which Germany adopted and which allowed her to exploit her strategic advantage to the fullest.

Even though the terrain would seem to invite a strategy that was focused on an offensive thrust, the actual military arrangements on both sides were defensive rather than offensive in nature. Germany in her disarmed state simply did not dispose of the necessary means to contemplate an offensive strategy. At best, the German army could fall back to the Oder in an attempt to halt the enemy at that river. Pitted against the German army, whose total strength was frozen at 100,000—this figure was actually exceeded by different manipulative techniques—was the Polish army which was more than twice that size.[34] One-half of the Polish army was deployed along the German border where Poland maintained clear numerical superiority over Germany: five Polish army corps with fifteen divisions against three German infantry divisions (stationed at Königsberg, Stettin, and Berlin) and two cavalry divisions (situated at Frankfurt/Oder and Breslau).[35] When Briand complimented Stresemann on the enormous achievements of the *Reichswehr*, the latter replied that "he had been shocked when General von Seeckt in 1923, as later also General Groener, had been forced to admit that the *Reichswehr* did not even suffice against a small country like Czechoslovakia or Poland; moreover, that in the case of an attack by Poland, it would have to be withdrawn behind the Oder line, as it lacked all means of entering into an offensive."[36] In the same vein, when Colonel von Fritsch presented a plan which sought to counter a Polish surprise attack by a quick

[34] In 1930 the Polish army had a strength of 265,800, consisting of 17,900 officers; 37,000 NCO's; and 210,900 men. The Polish navy at that time had a strength of 3,387 and was composed of 307 officers, 800 petty officers and 2,280 sailors (*Groener Papers*, reel 25).

[35] Roos, *Polen und Europa*, p. 6.

[36] Note by Dr. Schmidt of the Lugano talks between Stresemann and Briand, December 3, 1928, AA, StS/2365/4587H/E184 580–81.

German offensive in the east, while relying on dilatory tactics in the west, the plan had been rejected on the grounds that Germany lacked the necessary numerical strength for its execution. The plan which was adopted instead, envisaged a purely defensive strategy in the east in anticipation of an intervention by the League.[37]

Despite her numerical superiority, Polish strategic plans also followed basically defensive lines. The Polish General Staff was aware of the liabilities of Poland's geographical location and realized that on the qualitative side her margin of superiority over Germany looked considerably less impressive than her numerical lead.[38] Even the offensive strategy for a Polish–French war against Germany seemed predominantly defensive. During Marshal Foch's visit to Warsaw in May 1923, Polish military planners had rejected his plan for a straight offensive drive to Berlin without regard for Poland's own exposed flank. They had therefore insisted on a plan which would first widen her access to the sea and eliminate East Prussia as a military threat before embarking on a general offensive.[39]

Military reports from Rauscher and his Warsaw staff generally tended to downgrade both Poland's ability to wage offensive warfare against Germany and the probability of such an attack. Following the Polish autumn maneuvers of 1928, Pannwitz praised the excellence of

[37] Walter Görlitz, *Der Deutsche Generalstab–Geschichte und Gestalt 1657–1945* (Frankfurt, 1950), p. 376.

[38] In 1930 the Polish General Staff produced a lengthy analysis of the German military budget for that year, which showed a total of 713,423,000 marks (516 million marks for the army and 197 million marks for her 15,000-man navy). The analysis noted that additional military appropriations were made from the budget of other government departments, particularly the Ministries of Transport and Interior, and from other secret sources. The total sum of these extra contributions was estimated at 272 million marks. The General Staff report noted that Germany maintained the most expensive professional army in the world. She paid twice as much per soldier as the British army, which was also a professional force.

The report listed the following comparative annual cost figures per man in the armed forces:

Germany	13,280 zł.
Britain	7,355 zł.
France	5,765 zł.
Poland	2,458 zł.

(AMSZ, P II, fol. 4756).

[39] Historical Commission of the Polish General Staff (ed.), *Polskie Siły Zbrojne w drugiej Wojnie Światowej*, Tom I, *Kampania wrześniowa 1939. Cz. I, Polityczne i wojskowe położenie Polski przed wojną* [The Polish armed forces in the Second World War, vol. I, The September Campaign of 1939, Part I. The political and military position of Poland before the War] (London, 1951), pp. 112–14. Cited in Roos, *Polen und Europa*, p. 6.

the Polish cavalry and—compliments of the French Military Mission— noted a distinct improvement in the infantry, but he found much left to be desired in the artillery, both from its technical and tactical aspects and because of the complete lack of communication with the infantry.[40] Rauscher observed that Piłsudski was carrying through a definite policy of replacing career officers of the former German, Austrian, and Russian armies with his legionairies, whose loyalty rather than military skill was responsible for their promotion. The Polish army had thus lost some of its most capable officers, and Rauscher concluded from this that the Piłsudski régime valued the army more for its role in internal politics than for its maximum military efficiency.[41]

In 1929 another report, this time by Count du Moulin, the military expert on the staff of the German legation in Warsaw, confirmed the defensive orientation in Poland's strategic planning. One characteristic in Poland's strategic concept, wrote du Moulin, was the fact that the Polish army, out of respect for the *Reichswehr* and Germany's industrial strength, considered itself inferior to the German army. In the event of a German war, Warsaw's primary target would therefore be the maintenance of the "Corridor" and a possible attack against East Prussia which, by promising success, might be used as a psychological booster at the opening of the war. "All these considerations will in the end lead to the conclusion that in addition to adhering to the principal idea of a defense, small tactical advances of the Polish army against East Prussia and perhaps against Pomerania are entirely conceivable." Du Moulin added that in the east the situation was radically different, for the Polish forces considered themselves far superior to the Red Army, and war plans against Russia were probably bolder than those against Germany.[42]

Despite the defensive nature of these military preparations, anxiety about a surprise attack existed on both sides. Poland was less concerned with the immediate present than with the future, when Germany would again be in a position to exercise her full military potential. Her diplomatic energy was therefore directed toward getting the disarmament provisions of the Versailles treaty enforced. But Poland was not represented on the international bodies which decided on these matters and her efforts to prevent the dissolution of the Inter-Allied Military Control Commission and to link the evacuation of the Rhineland with adequate security guarantees were frustrated by French compliance with Ger-

[40] Report, Pannwitz, November 2, 1928, AA, GA/3759/K190/K036 205–10.
[41] Report, Rauscher, May 10, 1929, *ibid.*, 300–7.
[42] AA, GA/3760/K190/K036 418–23, December 27, 1929.

many's growing demands. Germany's temporary military impairment gave Warsaw a period of grace in which to strengthen her own military posture and to approach those reasonable elements in Germany that might be won over to the idea of arranging a *modus vivendi* between the two countries. In Piłsudski's estimation Germany figured as a potentially greater military threat than the Soviet Union, while the ideological impact of international Communism as directed from Moscow posed a greater political danger to Poland than any of the forces which emanated from Berlin. Because of the mutually perceived threat of Communism and the common Western cultural tradition of Poland and Germany, the Marshal was inclined to place greater stress on a German–Polish understanding than on a similar arrangement with the Soviet Union. What made the idea of a settlement with Berlin particularly attractive to Piłsudski was the enhanced independence vis-à-vis the other Western Powers which such an arrangement promised.

Germany's anxiety about military entanglements was probably more acute and widespread at that period owing to her partially disarmed state and the vivid memories of the Upper Silesian insurrections. Although some of this insecurity was genuine, even if misplaced, much of it was artificially created by her policy-makers and military leaders for its domestic payoff and its international implications. Indeed, it must strike us as ironic that Germany complained most vociferously about the prevailing atmosphere of insecurity and tension in German–Polish relations when her own revisionist drive was the principal cause for this state of affairs.

In German domestic politics the parties of the Right tried to make political capital by accusing Poland of aggressive designs against Danzig, East Prussia, and Upper Silesia. The moderate parties did little to dispel these unsubstantiated charges. During the 1932 presidential election the Nazis had circulated wild rumors of a planned Polish strike against East Prussia. For fear of alienating nationalist sentiments, the government neither rejected these charges as pure political propaganda nor officially endorsed them. Hindenburg, Groener, and even Brüning, took the middle course in a number of public speeches in which they represented the Polish military threat as not being imminent but portrayed it as a potential danger against which they pledged to defend all German soil.[43]

Under normal circumstances governments are more inclined to camouflage their military weaknesses rather than to advertise such defi-

---

[43] Report by the Polish Legation in Berlin, June 1, 1932, AMSZ, P II, fol. 4503.

ciencies. But in this case the German authorities were of the opinion that by making constant reference to the exposed nature of their eastern flank and by stressing the threat of a Polish invasion they could persuasively communicate the need to lift the military restrictions of the Versailles treaty and to revise the eastern boundaries. On the eve of the League of Nations disarmament talks in 1932, when Germany hoped to regain a status of military equality, particular emphasis was given to this stratagem. To lend force to these arguments the *Reichswehr* conducted the largest military maneuvers up to that time in the area of Frankfurt/Oder during September 1932. Present on this occasion were Marshal Tukhachevsky—Schleicher had invited Tukhachevsky to give practical demonstration that even under Papen German–Soviet military co-operation would continue—and all foreign military attachés with the conspicuous exception of the Polish attaché. The military objective of the maneuver had been to test the defense of Berlin against a rapid cavalry attack by an enemy (obviously Poland). The exercise was largely a propaganda maneuver in Germany's quest for armament equality which sought to underline the fatal weakness of her present defense posture and especially the exposed position of Berlin to a Polish cavalry strike. The enemy was allowed to advance so rapidly and to cross the Oder without meeting serious resistance from the "Blue" (German) Division that even some German papers were prompted to note that in case of a real war the commander of the "Blue" Division would face a court martial within forty-eight hours as the result of this dismal performance.

German preoccupations with a Polish armed attack, and military preparations for this eventuality, were by no means confined to the period of intensified tension after 1930. Defense preparations had been underway ever since the days of the Poznań uprising and they had been increased immediately after the dissolution of the Inter-Allied Military Control Commission, following a decision of the Conference of Ambassadors on December 12, 1926. The absence of a system of international military inspection after 1927 enabled Germany to increase her force concentration and defense installations in the vicinity of the Polish frontier and to build up her secret *Grenzschutz* forces in that area. After the dissolution of the Military Control Commission there remained the provisions under Article 213 of the Versailles treaty which assigned to the League Council the responsibility for supervising disarmament measures in Germany. However, the functions were not to be exercised on a continuous basis but were reserved for an occasional verification of alleged German breaches of the disarmament clauses. In fact, the League

Council never resorted to an actual inspection; consequently, Poland gained little from her seat on the Council with respect to keeping Germany disarmed.[44]

Polish diplomacy had taken a strong stand against the dissolution of the Military Control Commission, but as she was not a member of the Conference of Ambassadors, Poland could do little more than warn her French ally of the dangerous consequences of the Commission's withdrawal. In this endeavor, Polish diplomats tried to make capital of the fact that Germany had violated Article 180 of the Versailles treaty by enlarging existing eastern fortifications and by constructing several new ones.[45] Even though Polish experts attached little military significance to these fortifications which, moreover, served a purely defensive role, their existence was used as an argument in favor of maintaining the IMCC.

The question of the eastern fortifications was discussed at great length at the 1926 December session of the League Council. Stresemann defended their existence on the ground that "in the Treaty of Versailles all signatory powers have granted us the right of defense against the east. This right is all the more important as Berlin today is a frontier city, and if Herr Piłsudski suddenly wishes to attack us, then he would be in the German capital within two days." Unless Germany could also modernize these fortifications, Stresemann argued, they would be no more than museum pieces in a few years.[46]

Despite Stresemann's apparent confidence, the German authorities were under no illusions about the illegality of these eastern fortification measures.[47] The Foreign Minister sensed the hostile mood at Geneva,

---

[44] When Poland had lobbied for a seat on the Council in 1924, the Council's disarmament functions vis-à-vis Germany under Article 213 had been advanced in support of Polish claims. (Instruction by Foreign Minister Zamoyski, July 5, 1924, AMSZ, Berlin Legation, W. 110; cited in Krasuski, "Reakcja Polski na zniesienie Sojuszniczej Komisji Kontroli Niemiec w 1926 r.," *Przegląd Zachodni* 17 [1961]: 287.)

[45] Report, Sokal of his conversation with Massigly, secretary-general of the Conference of Ambassadors, December 8, 1926, AMSZ, P I, W. 170, t. 2; cited in Jerzy Krasuski, "Reakcja Polski," *Przegląd Zachodni* 17 (1961): 289.

[46] AA, StS/2363/4587H/E183 108–20; December 10, 1926.

[47] Acting Undersecretary Koepke noted on March 23, 1929, that there existed no objection against the army's plans of constructing additional dugouts on the left bank of the Oder, for the agreement reached between General von Pawelsz and General Baratier of the IMCC had defined the zone of fortification restrictions as confined to the area to the east of the Oder, stretching from Küstrin to Brieg and reaching westward only in places at Glogau and Küstrin. Koepke further noted that the 1926 dispute had centered on the fortifications which the *Reichswehr* had con-

and he was too shrewd a tactician to jeopardize his major goal, i.e., the dissolution of the IMCC, by holding out on a relatively minor issue where Germany was very clearly in the wrong. He quickly abandoned his assumed attitude of self-righteous indignation and consented to have the question settled by international arbitration. Thus the last major obstacle to the termination of the system of international military inspection was removed. In the agreement reached between the Allies and Germany on January 31, 1927, Germany was permitted to retain fifty-four of the concrete dugouts which she had built since 1920 and to destroy the remaining thirty-four (seven at Glogau on the right side of the Oder, five at Küstrin, and twenty-two at Königsberg). On June 12 the Allied Powers were informed of the completed destruction of the said fortresses,[48] and after some initial reluctance Germany agreed to submit to an on-the-spot inspection by Allied representatives, which was carried out by French and Belgian officers in early July and met with their approval.

From the moment he moved into the *Bendlerstrasse* as minister of national defense in January 1928, General Groener devoted himself with great energy to the improvement of Germany's defense capability against Poland. Groener had been responsible for getting a professional military man appointed to the staff of the German legation in Warsaw as a de facto military attaché even though, as he explained to Zechlin, he otherwise placed no value on military attachés, but "Poland was the only country that interested him militarily."[49] Groener was primarily con-

---

structed at their own responsibility and in violation of Art. 180 of the Versailles treaty (AA, RAM/1611/3170H/D681 189–93).

[48] AA, RAM/1611/3170H/D680 951.

[49] Note by Zechlin, April 18, 1928, AA, GA/3527/9182H/E645 778–79. No official German military attaché was appointed to Warsaw until February 1933. The Polish General Staff had been advocating for the appointment of a military attaché to Berlin as early as 1924 (AMSZ, P II, fol. 4616, pp. 2–4; November 27, 1924). The appointment had bogged down partly because of difficulties in choosing a suitable candidate and partly over the broader question of whether Germany had the right to reciprocate by sending a military attaché to Warsaw.

In 1926 the Polish General Staff renewed its pressure for a military representative in Berlin. In their arguments they pointed out that Germany's entry into the League of Nations would hasten the dissolution of the Military Control Commission, which would make it imperative that Poland establish her own sources of military information through a military attaché (*ibid.*, p. 18; April 17, 1926). It was not until May 1928, however, that Major Morawski, a former officer of the Imperial German army, took up his post as first Polish military attaché in Berlin. Morawski's initial reports made special reference to the unexpectedly polite, and sometimes even friendly, reception which he was accorded by officials in the German Foreign and Defense ministries.

cerned with strengthening Germany's naval resources for an eventual war with Poland, and his name became closely linked with the construction program of armored cruisers, the so-called *Panzerkreuzer*. The history of the *Panzerkreuzer* belongs more properly to the annals of German parliamentary history, where it became a *cause célèbre* of conflicting party politics, and only certain aspects of the question need concern us here.

The Versailles treaty had given Germany the option to replace the six obsolete battleships which she had been allowed to retain by armored cruisers whose displacement was under 10,000 tons. Initially it had made little sense to construct armored cruisers of such small size, but technological advances made this an increasingly attractive option. On February 13, 1924, Stockhausen noted in his diary that Chancellor Marx agreed with Admiral Behnke, the de facto chief of naval staff, on the necessity of constructing armored cruisers. Stockhausen's comments that "in the Baltic Sea even a small fleet was of value in the face of certain Polish aspirations," left no doubt as to the country against which the *Panzerkreuzer* were directed.[50]

In his speech to the *Reichstag* on March 14, 1928, Defense Minister Groener defended the government's budgetary request of some nine million marks to commence construction on the first armored cruiser, the so-called *Panzerkreuzer* A. Groener justified this unpopular expenditure on the basis that it would help defend Germany against a military *fait accompli* until she could mobilize international assistance. While no specific power was named, it was obvious that the Minister had Poland in mind when he spoke of the danger of a military *fait accompli*. Heavy opposition by the Socialists in the *Reichsrat* forced the government to accept a moratorium on the construction program until after the elections, even though the *Reichstag* had already approved this particular appropriation. On August 10, 1928, the new Cabinet, under Chancellor Müller, agreed to proceed with the construction of the first armored cruiser. In defense of the government's decision, which came into immediate crossfire from Communists and Chancellor Müller's own Socialist party colleagues, Groener prepared a lengthy memorandum in which he outlined the strategic rationale for building the controversial armored cruisers. In his memorandum the Defense Minister drew attention to East Prussia's exposed position—Poland had stationed four divisions around the East Prussian periphery against the single division which

50 Max von Stockhausen, *Sechs Jahre Reichskanzlei* (Bonn, 1954), p. 106.

Germany maintained in that province—and he pointed out that Poland coveted both East Prussia and Upper Silesia. According to Groener's analysis, the German land forces would probably be incapable of penetrating the "Corridor" and were thus not in a position to relieve East Prussia in the event of an attack. In the absence of adequate ground forces and land communication, an effective naval force was thus indispensable for the defense of East Prussia. Such a force would help keep the sea lanes open, provide direct shore support to military operations on East Prussian soil, and protect the East Prussian coast against attack by Polish naval units. The armored cruisers would confront Poland with distinct risks and would thereby reduce the temptation to attack East Prussia. Moreover, the proposed cruisers, which could cope with any vessel in the Polish navy and might even deter a French naval intervention on behalf of Poland, would be of great value in protecting German neutrality in conflicts involving third powers, as for example a renewed Polish–Soviet war.[51]

In November some thirty copies of Groener's top secret memorandum had been circulated to members of the Cabinet and other senior party officials. As a result of some indiscretion, which might well have been calculated by domestic critics to embarrass the government cruiser program, the content of the secret memorandum reached Britain and its substance was divulged by the British journalist Wickham Steed in a sensational article in *The Review of Reviews*. The authenticity of this information, which was received with great indignation in Poland and in some German circles as well, was not contested by the German government. While rejecting the armored cruiser program on financial grounds, the Communists pointed out that they were the last ones to trust in the peaceful intentions of Poland, which they regarded as one of the most imperialistic bourgeois elements in all of Europe.[52] The Socialists, on the other hand, criticized the memorandum for having invoked the bogey of a planned Polish aggression which they considered groundless. "We have a lively interest," Stampfer told the *Reichstag*, "in seeing that this fearful image be brought to rest."[53] Sir Horace Rumbold speculated that Groener's scenario might have been influenced subconsciously by the

[51] For a complete text of Groener's memorandum, see *Groener Papers*, reel 25. An abridged version was published by Nauticus (pseud. for Wickham Steed), "New Germany's New Navy," *Review of Reviews*, January 1929.

[52] Reichstag, *Sten. Berichte*, 424, February 26, 1929, p. 1280.

[53] *Ibid.*, p. 1284.

thought of an aggressive war against Poland. Still, he thought it "far more probable that he, in common with most Germans, apprehends a Polish seizure of East Prussia."[54] Despite Polish newspaper protests against the insinuation of Polish aggressive intentions, the Warsaw government maintained an attitude of dignified resignation and kept strict silence. When Erskine urged Wysocki that Poland refrain from an official protest over the Groener memorandum, now that the two countries were so close to agreement on the liquidation and trade issues, he was assured that the Foreign Ministry planned no remonstrance. According to Wysocki the archives of the Ministry were stocked with similarly provocative statements by German officials regarding East Prussia and other areas; there was thus nothing new or surprising in Groener's memorandum.[55]

At the same time that the armored cruiser program was first adopted, the German navy drew up war plans for naval operations against Poland. These particular plans are of special interest for they were the only German war plans at that time which could be said to have had an offensive orientation against Poland. On January 16, 1930, the Defense Ministry informed the Foreign Ministry that recent naval studies on the subject of a German–Polish conflict had revealed the urgency of paralyzing the port of Gdynia immediately upon the outbreak of hostilities. Once Gdynia had been rendered useless by a military strike and if diplomatic intervention made Danzig unavailable for Polish use, foreign assistance would have great difficulty in reaching Poland. This situation might deter France and other powers from getting involved in such a conflict altogether.[56] In June, officials of the Foreign Ministry and the *Marineleitung* met to discuss the issue. In spite of the urgent appeals from the naval authorities, the diplomatic representatives adopted a cautious attitude and refused to commit themselves to an immediate naval and air attack on Gdynia in the event of an armed conflict with Poland. They insisted that in such a case all diplomatic means for a speedy termination of the conflict should first be brought to bear. Any military action against Gdynia or Danzig, if the neutrality of the latter could not be guaranteed, would come into question only if the diplomatic parleys to end the conflict had been futile and then only with the expressed permission of the political leadership. Once the decision in favor of a military action against

54 *FO*, 371/13632, p. 9; January 25, 1929.
55 Letter, Erskine to Chamberlain, January 24, 1929, *ibid.*, pp. 16–18.
56 *AA*, GA/3613/K7/K000 669–74.

Gdynia had been taken, the Foreign Office saw no need for further restrictions on the use of forbidden arms such as mines and aircraft which
the navy had already earmarked for use against Gdynia.[57]

On May 21, 1931, the Foreign Ministry clarified its position in a
written reply to the naval authorities in which it communicated its
agreement with the principle of an early military strike against Gdynia
in the event of a German–Polish conflict. But at the same time the
Foreign Ministry insisted that such an action would first have to await a
political decision. On the question of approaching Danzig to seek assurance that its harbor facilities and the Westerplatte ammunition depot
would not be available to Poland in the event of war, steps were to be
taken with utmost caution since it was impossible to predict when a
suitable opportunity for this diplomatic offensive might offer itself.[58]

Judging by the content of the 1931 war games of the German navy,
the latter seemed to take for granted that political permission to proceed
with a blitz attack on Gdynia would not be long in forthcoming. The
1931 war game produced a scenario of a German–Polish conflict which
opened on September 1, 1938—a remarkably prophetic date which pre-
empted real events by exactly one year—and erupted into open hostilities
by September 3. According to the plan Gdynia was to be put out of
action between September 4 and 5, within which period most of Poland's
submarines would also be destroyed. The scenario further assumed that
Britain and Italy would guard benevolent neutrality and that France
would mobilize but would not yet be at war during this early stage.[59]

Secret Grenzschutz Preparations in the East

The preparations for a war with Poland by Germany's regular
ground and naval forces were accompanied by secret parallel efforts at
organizing, training, and arming the illicit *Grenzschutz* or border militia
units. These particular units, it will be recalled, dated from the imme-

---

[57] Protocol of the discussion between the German Foreign Ministry and the
Navy, June 26, 1930, *ibid.*, 687–711.

[58] *Ibid.*, 732. In the case of a conflict, Danzig was to undertake immediate steps
with the League of Nations to guarantee its neutrality and prevent its facilities from
being used by Poland. The Foreign Ministry even considered the possibility of asking
a foreign power like Britain or Italy to occupy Danzig for the duration of the conflict
to guarantee that city's neutrality.

[59] *Geheime Kommandosache* (signed by Admiral Raeder), November 25, 1931,
ibid., 648–50.

diate domestic political turmoil and foreign complications following the
November 1918 armistice and had found their most important application during the Upper Silesian insurrection in 1921. The underground
activities of these paramilitary formations had been curtailed once the
German–Polish border had become firmly established. But the
Grenzschutz had never been entirely disbanded, and the withdrawal
of the Inter-Allied Military Control Commission in January 1927 provided German military and other circles with a renewed incentive to
press for an extension of the size and role of these forces.

On February 26, 1927, only one month after the departure of the
IMCC, the Cabinet of the *Reich* accepted an emergency defense program which had been prepared by the General Staff. To implement this
program successfully it was found necessary to establish a system of fruitful co-operation between the military and civilian authorities in supervising the storage of secret arms depots and in providing the *Grenzschutz*
with some measure of military training. In September the Cabinet discussed the *Reichswehr* proposals for an expanded role and improved
preparedness of the *Grenzschutz* in the defense of Germany's eastern
provinces. During this particular session, Stresemann had accepted the
necessity for these proposed preparations.[60] But discussions were broken
off without agreement having been reached because of the adamant opposition from Prime Minister Braun of Prussia whose co-operation was
indispensable. Braun quite correctly regarded these paramilitary units as
a threat to the democratic order in Germany and a liability to Germany's
credibility abroad, and he therefore hampered their activities wherever
possible.[61]

Following this delay, Schleicher reported to Stresemann and argued
forcefully for a Cabinet decision that would upgrade the military
effectiveness of the *Grenzschutz* in the east. In the view of Schleicher,
"a certain degree of military preparedness and, in the last resort, even
military instruction—for the time being at least for the *Grenzschutz*—
became simply a pressing necessity."[62] Schleicher's arguments were supported by a memorandum by Colonel von Fritsch of the *Truppenamt*.
In it, Fritsch reasoned that unlike the situation in the west, Locarno
offered Germany no protection against a Polish *fait accompli* in the east.

---

[60] Letter, Stresemann to Defense Minister Gessler, November 21, 1927, AA,
GA/3613/K6/K000 316.
[61] Memorandum, Koepke, November 21, 1927, *ibid.*, 312–15.
[62] AA, GA/3613/K6/K000 301–4.

Fritsch did not deny that the proposed defense measures constituted a blatant violation of the disarmament provisions of the Versailles treaty and the agreement which Germany had concluded with the Military Control Commission. To allay any government qualms, he pointed out that the militia defense program in East Prussia was already fairly complete and had produced no incidents. What was required now was to extend it to the other parts of the German–Polish frontier.[63] Koepke seconded Fritsch's observations regarding East Prussia when he noted that in that particular region the *Grenzschutz* had for some time functioned smoothly and with the full co-operation of all authorities. Koepke noted that the Foreign Ministry recognized the necessity for these measures, but he warned the Defense Ministry against keeping any official lists of *Grenzschutz* members. He also viewed the practice of offering training in the use of firearms to hand-picked militia members as unacceptable, for such exercises in the vicinity of the Polish border might easily be detected and could cause grave international complications. The Acting Undersecretary closed his memorandum with a stern warning that the Defense Ministry would be entirely misguided if it believed that Germany could achieve rearmament by the circuitous route of expanding the secret *Grenzschutz*.[64]

In order to provide the Cabinet with tangible proof of the necessity for maintaining a *Grenzschutz* in the east, the *Reichswehr* staged a war game of a Polish attack in January 1928. The game itself offers some interesting insight into German diplomatic and military thinking with reference to a German–Polish war. The game envisaged a growing period of tensions that was followed by the intrusion of Polish insurgents into East Prussia and finally a full-scale attack by Polish regular forces. In this game the *Reichswehr* was totally incapable of stemming the Polish aggression and within a period of a month the Polish forces had occupied all of Pomerania, Silesia, and East Prussia, except Königsberg, and had advanced to the Oder. Along this line a cease-fire had been arranged with the aid of the League of Nations. The Defense Ministry inquired whether there existed a possibility of keeping Britain and France out of a war if at this stage the Soviet army attacked Poland and Germany participated in the attack. (At this spot a marginal Foreign Ministry note reads: "The Defense Ministry has been notified orally that an intervention in

[63] *Ibid.*, 305–8.
[64] Memorandum, Koepke to the Ministry of Defense, November 21, 1927, *ibid.*, 309–15.

which Germany and Russia conduct a war against Poland, without having France and England come into play, is unthinkable.")[65]

In commenting on the recent war game, the Foreign Ministry noted that a German–Polish war that would not also involve France and other powers was inconceivable, even though France might stay out of the initial phase of such a conflict. Even if Poland were the aggressor and France came to her aid, it was still extremely unlikely that Britain would honor her Locarno commitment and aid Germany. Moreover, it would be futile to expect a Soviet attack under the outlined conditions; at best, Russia might be induced to create anti-Polish demonstrations and thus force Poland to withdraw some of her forces to the east. Germany's most secure defense still lay in the League of Nations, which might impose economic sanctions on Poland and thus at least provide a cushion against the attack.[66]

Following the war game, Groener and Blomberg met with Stresemann and Schubert for the purpose of finding a common platform of agreement on the *Grenzschutz* preparation measures. Blomberg pointed out that the maintenance of personnel lists was to be restricted to certain districts and to be handled by civilian authorities under the supervision of the Prussian Interior Ministry; in East Prussia this was already running smoothly but areas like Pomerania lagged behind. As for giving *Grenzschutz* members instruction in firing machine guns, this was to be conducted in utmost secrecy—Blomberg was obviously trying to cater to the reservations of the Foreign Ministry—and on a modest scale. Both Stresemann and Schubert repeated their previously voiced concerns, and the Foreign Minister insisted that under no circumstances were *Reichswehr* officers and noncommissioned officers to be permitted to assist in firearms practice sessions which, it had been decided, were to be held under the camouflage of ordinary civilian shooting matches [*Schützenfeste*]. Blomberg and Groener accepted these terms of the Foreign Ministry and the Defense Minister added that he would still have to iron matters out with Prime Minister Braun and, in so doing, he

[65] Letter of the *Truppenamt* to the Foreign Office, January 14, 1928, *ibid.*, 337–50. It is interesting to notice that both sides tended to attribute an exaggerated strength to the enemy. While the German war game wrote off East Prussia as a quick loss, Rintelen reported from Warsaw that in the Polish war game of 1929, which had concentrated on the conquest of East Prussia, it had been concluded that the planned forces were insufficient for their task and could not penetrate the interior of East Prussia until considerably reinforced (AA, GA/3759/K190/K036 387; November 7, 1929).

[66] Note by Martius, January 28, 1928, AA, GA/3613/K6/K000 342–44.

considered himself empowered to state that the Foreign Ministry backed the plan. To this Stresemann registered no objections.[67]

From these secret negotiations it becomes evident that in 1928 the systematic creation of a *Grenzschutz*, which seems to have been operational in East Prussia as early as 1927, was well on its way for the other portions of the German–Polish border. A secret memorandum of May 12, 1928, listed the conditions under which the Foreign Ministry had given its assent to the guidelines which had been worked out with respect to civilian-military co-operation in the management of the clandestine militia. The memorandum concluded that since the *Reichswehr* itself was unable to cope with a sudden military invasion, Germany had to undertake measures to defend her frontiers and to prevent a *fait accompli*. The Foreign Ministry supported the plan, in full realization that it constituted a violation of the Versailles treaty. The execution of these measures was to be the responsibility of the Defense Ministry, but the *Auswärtiges Amt* demanded that nothing be undertaken that might endanger Germany's general foreign policy and noted that a *Grenzschutz* for the west was entirely out of the question.[68] In 1929 the Cabinet unanimously accepted these expanded *Grenzschutz* functions on the basis of the above guidelines.[69]

In the years that followed the eastern *Grenzschutz* developed a numerical strength that has been estimated at 30,000.[70] The majority of its members was recruited from the *Stahlhelmbund* or other paramilitary organizations of veterans. In East Prussia, where these secret militia preparations had developed further than anywhere else and found the most enthusiastic response from the local population, the SA and SS also played a prominent part in the *Grenzschutz* activities and developed intimate ties with the commander of the East Prussian military district, General von Blomberg, and his chief of staff, Colonel Reichenau, and other *Reichswehr* officers. In this manner East Prussia became a training ground for a new breed of senior *Reichswehr* officers with a much more sympathetic disposition toward the Nazi movement than was held by their more conservative colleagues in the *Bendlerstrasse*. The picture of Nazi involvement in the *Grenzschutz* activities was not, however, uniform. To the great indignation of Hindenburg, Hitler had prohibited

---

[67] Top secret note by Schubert, February 6, 1928, *ibid.*, 367–68.
[68] *Ibid.*, 388–89.
[69] Hans Gatzke, *Stresemann and the Rearmament of Germany* (Baltimore, 1954), p. 101.
[70] Görlitz, *Der Deutsche Generalstab*, p. 361.

a similar co-operation between SA and militia units in Pomerania because the latter collaborated with the civilian authorities of the existing democratic régime which the Nazi movement sought to destroy.

The principal functions of the eastern *Grenzschutz*, which were exercised in close collaboration with the local army commands and the district civilian government authorities, consisted of the supervision of the widely dispersed depots for arms and ammunition; the maintenance of personnel lists of men who were eligible for military service; scouting and patrol exercises in the border districts; theoretical training in defensive frontier fighting; and practical instruction in the use of small arms for a selected group of militia members.[71] The Defense Ministry and the *Reichswehr* were responsible for taking the initiative in drawing up the plans and providing the supervision for these militia tasks. The Prussian Ministry of Interior came next in importance, and unlike the enthusiastic support and endorsement which came from the Defense Ministry, it generally exercised a restraining role. It grudgingly admitted to the need of some secret militia preparation measures in the immediate frontier districts in the east. But persons like Prime Minister Braun insisted that these activities be confined to the immediate border districts and limited to local residents of these regions; that the *Reichswehr* not get directly involved in the militia; and most of all, that these paramilitary organizations assumed no active role in German domestic politics. But unlike the reservations of the central agencies of the Prussian government, its local civil authorities, especially in East Prussia, were only too willing to assist in the expansion of the size and role of the *Grenzschutz* and to turn a blind eye to the army's involvement in it.

The eastern *Grenzschutz* was the most developed and active component of a wider self-defense or *Landesschutz* organization which began to play a more important role after 1930, when under the direction of General von Schleicher it was systematically expanded into a national reserve army which could be rapidly mobilized and transferred to active duty in the case of an emergency. By 1932 these *Umbau* [transformation] plans had been completed, and it was envisaged that by 1938 at the latest, Germany would in case of mobilization be able to call to immediate service 7 active divisions (143,000 men), 14 reserve divisions (340,000), and 34 *Grenzschutz* divisions (320,000). This was to be supplemented by

[71] Memorandum on the functions of the militia, November 12, 1928, AA, GA/3613/K6/K000 384–87.

an *Ergänzungsheer* of approximately 2 million men which would include all other veterans and reservists.[72]

Whatever military effectiveness these secret reserve units might have acquired in the long run, there can be no doubt that the *Grenzschutz* as it existed in 1930–32, with its small, dispersed, poorly armed, and insufficiently trained units, which Groener described in the unflattering term of *Mist* [rubbish], was of little military significance and would have been no match against Poland's professional army.[73] It might have been of some use in dealing with Polish armed insurgents. On the whole, it was kept as a sop to Rightist demands and as a tranquilizer for nervous officials in the eastern provinces. It was also viewed as the hard core of Germany's military revival, a source for keeping alive the spirit of resistance and revisionism, and a prospective pool for military recruits. In view of the limited military significance of the *Grenzschutz*, it is not without certain historical irony that it should have exerted such a pernicious influence both on internal developments in Germany and German–Polish relations. These paramilitary cadres became easy converts of the Nazi movement and perhaps the frustration of impotence and anonymity as members of the *Grenzschutz* made them all the more receptive to exchange their previous role for the glory of the SA brownshirt. Furthermore, when the Brüning government dissolved the SA and SS in April 1932, because of the threat which these organizations posed to the survival of the democratic order of the Weimar Republic, it exposed itself to charges from military and Rightist circles that it had thereby undermined the role of the *Grenzschutz* in the defense of East Prussia at a time when Germany was faced with the threat of an imminent attack by Poland. These arguments, especially as they were

[72] Georges Castellan, *Le Réarmement du Reich 1930–1935. Vu par le 2° Bureau de l'État-Major Géneral Français* (Paris, 1954), p. 391.

[73] In 1928 Braun asked Groener whether he saw any military significance in the *Grenzschutz*. Groener denied that it had any real military utility but found it necessary for calming the local population in their fear of a Polish invasion. (Otto Braun, *Von Weimar zu Hitler* [New York, 1940], pp. 265–67). It is interesting to note that another soldier, Marshal Piłsudski, also thought little of the military potential of these paramilitary organizations. In 1932, after Papen became Chancellor, the Marshal told Wysocki that one should not exaggerate the importance of these units: "There are a lot of appearances which are misleading, but they have not the real values of a true soldier. . . . Observers of the exercises and organization of these units repeatedly stated that beyond *paraden marches*, roll-calls, and speeches, not much is happening there. And there is no question of comparing the value of such organizations with regular soldiers." (*Lipski Papers*, pp. 51–52.)

echoed by persons like Generals Hammerstein, Blomberg, and Schleicher, may have been an important factor in persuading President Hindenburg to drop Brüning as chancellor.[74]

The weight of this historical irony becomes even more pressing when one takes into consideration not only the absence of any convincing evidence that Poland was in fact planning aggressive military measures at that time but also the highly unreliable nature of the SA contribution to the defense of the eastern frontier. There is good reason to assume that in the event of military complications with Poland, the East Prussian *Grenzschutz* would have been deserted by the SA, as the latter would have exploited the situation to stage a Nazi takeover. In a campaign address in the small Pomeranian town of Lauenburg, Hitler himself had stated that he would not sacrifice his storm-troopers for the defense of Germany's borders until the supporters of the democratic order in Germany had been annihilated.[75] That this was more than a momentary emotional outburst during an election campaign was verified by further evidence on this point. Baron von Aretin, a prominent Bavarian monarchist, notes in his memoirs that on April 10, 1932, he heard from the Berlin correspondent of the *Münchener Neueste Nachrichten* that a secret order had been given to the SA that in the event of an attack against East Prussia, they were to get control of the ammunition depots, march on Königsberg, and refuse to engage in any fighting against the invading Polish forces as long as the campaign was not directed by Hitler himself in the capacity of commander-in-chief.[76] The authenticity of this report was confirmed by documentary evidence which the Prussian police discovered when it searched the Berlin headquarters of the SA following its ban. If this secret order was in fact given, it shows that Hitler intended to utilize the turmoil of an invasion to seize power himself, regardless of its consequences to German national security at a time of

---

[74] Several historians have viewed this as one of the primary reasons for the fall of Brüning (Richard Breyer, *Das Deutsche Reich und Polen 1932–37* (Würzburg, 1955), p. 34; Roos, "Zum Sturze Brünings," *Vierteljahrshefte für Zeitgeschichte* 1 (1953): 261–88). Schleicher might have availed himself of the same argument with Hindenburg in order to prepare the way for Brüning's fall, but he himself does not seem to have attached much weight to it. In his discussions with Groener, Schleicher did not advance the eastern security argument at all but warned that the dissolution decree would have a negative effect on conservative voters in the impending Prussian election (*Groener Papers*, reel 25).

[75] Erich Eyck, *A History of the Weimar Republic* (Cambridge, Mass., 1963), II, p. 364.

[76] Freiherr Erwein von Aretin, *Krone und Ketten. Erinnerungen eines bayerischen Edelmannes* (Munich, 1955), pp. 78–79.

extreme danger. It becomes difficult to understand how a person like Aretin, writing in 1955, would try to explain Hitler's motives in terms of his desire to join forces with the Poles; Hitler, according to Aretin, as an Austrian was a "true friend" of Poland and wanted an understanding with her and only in 1939 became an enemy of Poland over the "Corridor" question.[77] If Brüning had possessed an ounce of the propaganda wizardry of a Goebbels, the exploitation of the issue, which clearly showed that the Nazis were willing to further their own career at the expense of German security, could have served as a trump card in unmasking the Nazis before the whole nation. As it was, Hitler's blackmailing tactics triumphed over Brüning's cautious and conservative nature which shrank from taking foreign political risks in order to combat greater domestic dangers. Hitler threatened to expose the whole scheme of Germany's secret defense efforts in the east if the government publicized his order to the SA, and Brüning consequently urgently requested that it be kept secret lest the revelation of Germany's secret defense efforts darken the propitious outlook for the approaching Lausanne conference.[78] Brüning's decision was all the more unfortunate as it seems unlikely that the publication of these documents would have produced much of a negative international reaction. In the first place, Germany's neighbors would have applauded a more active policy by Brüning in combatting the growing Nazi danger. Furthermore, the existence of the *Grenzschutz* in the east was known in great detail to both Poland and France. Both had learned of the existence of these particular SA documents and the nature of their content. Three days after the SA ban, Wysocki reported a conversation with the French ambassador to Berlin, François-Poncet, in which the latter had told him that these documents were concerned with Germany's eastern defense efforts and disclosed the intimate relations which existed between the *Reichswehr* and the SA. The SA was to be placed under the command of the army in the event of war with Poland, but at the same time the documents had provided evidence that the storm-troopers had secretly been instructed to disobey the army and to obey the party alone. A week later, Wysocki confirmed that the documents in question were believed to contain evidence that the Nazis sought to exploit the event of a war with Poland in order to create a social revolution in Germany. The Polish Minister advised that this information be treated with cau-

[77] *Ibid.*, pp. 136–37.
[78] *Ibid.*, pp. 135–36.

tion as it might have been spread merely for the purpose of obscuring the real situation.[79]

In Poland the German *Grenzschutz* was not viewed as a purely defensive mechanism but as testimony of her neighbor's bad faith in keeping the provisions of the peace treaty and as the first effort to a complete rearmament which would culminate in a German aggression against Poland. The existence of the *Grenzschutz* thus kept alive the image of Germany as the incorrigible enemy of Poland. These fears were reinforced when Polish army intelligence in 1930 gained surprisingly accurate information on the nature of the German–Soviet military collaboration, which it passed on to the French General Staff.[80]

After 1930 Poland viewed with growing alarm the international efforts of the Brüning government for Germany's equality of armaments and the mounting strength of the Nazi party with its militant nationalism, uncompromising revisionism, and hatred of Poland. *Polonia* of July 28, 1931, called Germany's policy catastrophic and accused the *Stahlhelmbund*, the SA and SS, and similiar organizations of keeping German policy on an anti-Polish track. Three days later *Kurjer Poranny* singled out the activities of the *Stahlhelmbund* and accused Germany of actively preparing for war against Poland; even the economic assistance program to the eastern provinces, the *Osthilfe*, was viewed as playing an aggressive military role. On April 28, 1932, *Gazeta Warszawska* viewed the rise of Hitler not merely as a passing aberration but as a fundamental movement for the creation of a new Germany. Hitler would soon come to power, the article predicted prophetically, and would be celebrated for having saved Germany from Communism, economic depression, and military defeat. Hitler's anti-Polish feeling already represented the true feelings of the entire German people. Once Hitler came to power, Germany would terminate reparations payments, end her armament restrictions, and then cash in on her revisionist demands. The article enjoined all threatened states to combine in opposing Germany and not to believe that she would be satisfied with any half measures.

MILITARY SCARES AND PREVENTIVE WAR CONSIDERATIONS

Piłsudski expressed himself in an equally pessimistic vein on the long-term prospects of German–Polish relations when he confided to Ambassador Noël that "nous aurons fatalement une guerre avec

---

[79] Reports, Wysocki, April 15 and April 21, 1932, AMSZ, P II, fol. 4503.
[80] Castellan, *Réarmement Clandestin*, pp. 186–89.

l'Allemagne. Il faudra s'y préparer. . . . Les Russes, on les bat toujours, dès qu'ils sortent de chez eux et nous les battrons en toutes occasions. Les Allemands, c'est une autre affaire. . . ."[81] The Marshal's policy of preparation in the face of Germany's mounting military activities acquired three distinct aspects. In the first place, it involved assembling a superior Polish force along the German frontier even in peace-time; second, it sought to protect Poland from the danger of a two-front war by improving relations with the Soviet Union; and third, it involved a conscious policy of intimidation [*Einschüchterungspolitik*] against Germany by way of organized public anti-German demonstrations, military maneuvers in the proximity of the German border, and calculated incidents which involved Danzig.

In line with Piłsudski's first approach, the Polish army kept a numerical superiority in the ratio of 3:1 over the *Reichswehr*. Although there was some acceleration in the activities and movements of Polish forces during the critical 1930–33 period, neither a major change in the disposition of forces nor any significant reinforcement of Poland's western garrisons took place

In conjunction with the maintenance of military superiority on her western boundary, Poland undertook steps to improve the situation on her eastern flank. The events of Japan's invasion of Manchuria in 1931 and Russia's subsequent preoccupation in the Far East played into Warsaw's hands, for it made Moscow equally interested in freezing conditions along their common frontier so that both could ease their complicated Janus role and concentrate on their outside problems. The outcome was the Polish–Soviet nonaggression pact of July 1932. Even though Krestinski may have spoken in all sincerity when he assured Dirksen that the pact with Warsaw entailed no change of political course [*politische Richtungsänderung*],[82] it made it possible for Poland to step up her policy of military and political intimidation against Germany and it also lent more credibility to these demonstrations.

Coming at a time of general tensions, these measures added to Germany's feeling of insecurity and contributed to the proliferating number of nervous reports by German military authorities and by local officials. Although subsequent investigations usually exposed these rumors and speculations as having been exaggerated or without foundation, and even though the German legation in Warsaw denied that there existed any

---

[81] Léon Noël, *L'Aggression allemande contre la Pologne* (Paris, 1946), p. 68.
[82] Telegram, Dirksen, July 25, 1932, AA, RAM/1417/2860H/D562 335.

immediate danger of a Polish attack, these strong measures produced a general war scare among German political and military leaders. This sentiment was shared by much of German public opinion, as the following minor incident demonstrates. Wysocki was a very eager gardener, a hobby which offered the harassed diplomat some relief from his frustrating diplomatic tasks. In the summer of 1932, his neighbor, an elderly lady, expressed surprise that the Wysockis would spend so much time and effort cultivating their garden when it was obvious that their labor of love would soon come to naught as war with Poland was bound to start any moment. The old lady in question "added that her son said so, and he was in the Stahlhelm, where this was common talk."[83]

The fear of a simultaneous domestic uprising by Communists and Nazis and a Polish military intervention in East Prussia and Upper Silesia greatly burdened the Brüning government and its successors. Brüning commented on these anxieties after World War II in a letter to Rudolf Pechel, the editor of the *Deutsche Rundschau*, in which he wrote:

> The failure of the League of Nations to take action against the Japanese occupation of Manchuria in the fall of 1931, together with a new Polish mobilization plan, of which we received news in that same year by way of a foreign power [Soviet Union] heightened Schleicher's nervousness. The Polish mobilization plan was designed in such a manner that it left no doubt of the clear intention to take all of Silesia in a coup at an opportune moment. Since the German government would have to use the entire German army and police force against a possible simultaneous uprising of Nazis and Communists, we convinced the reluctant Hindenburg to consent to the withdrawal of several garrisons from Silesia to Brandenburg and Saxony in case the Polish attack was launched simultaneously with the Nazi and Communist uprising.[84]

Although Brüning's letter is of great interest in describing the tense atmosphere which existed in Germany at that time, it contains several major inaccuracies which are all the more remarkable in view of the fact that it was written after the war and not in the heat of the 1930–33 confrontation. In his letter Brüning treats as an established fact Poland's decision to pounce on Silesia at the first opportune moment. No reliable information which existed then or which has subsequently come to light

[83] *Lipski Papers*, p. 44.
[84] Heinrich Brüning, "Ein Brief," *Deutsche Rundschau*, vol. 70, no. 7 (1947): 1–22.

confirms this assertion. Brüning's own supporting evidence is extremely weak. He speaks of a new Polish mobilization plan which was geared to exploit the threat of a Nazi and Communist uprising in Germany. But there existed no new Polish mobilization plan. The Foch plan of 1923 was still in force and it could not have foreseen and prepared for a joint Communist–Nazi uprising in Germany. There are other inaccuracies in Brüning's explanations. He speaks of the SA ban having been decided on too hastily by the army and the Interior Ministry during his absence from Berlin, but it is a matter of undisputable record that he not only participated but also took a driving role in the final stages of the decision to ban the SA. Finally, in view of the fact that his fall in 1932 intensified the crisis in German–Polish relations, it is difficult to accept Brüning's version that he had been able to improve relations with Poland to such a degree that at the time when he left office there existed some assurance that an internal uprising would not provoke a Polish attack.

Although Brüning is altogether too undiscriminating in treating over-anxious speculation as clear evidence for aggressive Polish plans, his testimony does accurately portray the nervousness which existed in German military and political circles. General Adam, the chief of the de facto general staff, later testified in the Krupp trial that in 1931 he had been haunted by the vision of a Polish invasion of East Prussia and Upper Silesia.[85] In order to counteract this military threat, Germany undertook some emergency defense measures and tried to tighten the military collaboration with Russia. In June 1931 Germany renewed the 1926 Berlin Treaty and in the autumn of that year General Adam traveled to the Soviet Union, as did Colonel Fischer in April of 1932, apparently with the purpose of persuading the Red Army not to reduce its forces on the Russian–Polish frontier.[86] There even exists some indication that during Schleicher's chancellorship a German–Soviet military agreement was reached regarding Poland and that a common operational plan had been drawn up by their general staffs.[87]

In March 1932 Groener traveled through East Prussia to warn the Polish government in speeches and writings not to attempt an invasion of German territory. At the same time, in a haste that represented panic, the military authorities began with the construction of a provisional de-

---

[85] Testimony of General Adam, *Krupp Prozess, Verteidigungs Dok. Buch,* 2b, No. 103. Cited in Roos, *Polen und Europa.* p. 38.

[86] *Ibid.,* p. 43.

[87] *Ibid.,* p. 57.

fense line in the Heilsberg triangle of East Prussia—permitted by the provisions of the Versailles treaty—in order to detain a Polish advance on Königsberg. The danger was perceived as being so acute that General Adam was forced to cancel his planned May visit to the Soviet Union.[88]

Germany's internal political weakness and military inferiority permitted little more than purely defensive preparations. Even though her army had information of the Polish operation plan, the German "General Staff" refused to draw up its own operation plan for a war with Poland. Its tactics were confined to resisting Polish forces as long as possible in East Prussia and on the Oder–Neisse line, while surrendering Upper Silesia.[89]

At the time of the Westerplatte crisis in 1933 General Adam repeated that a war against Poland and France was entirely hopeless; even a war against Poland alone offered little more than the chance of holding the Oder line. "At this time we cannot conduct a war. We have to do everything to avoid one, even at the price of diplomatic defeats. We cannot prevent a war, if the others desire to conduct it preventively. It would be senseless to prepare operation and marching plans for this eventuality."[90]

Brüning's fall and Papen's amazing projection from well-deserved obscurity into the spotlight of the *Reichskanzlei* prompted an immediate storm reading on the barometric scale of German–Polish relations. Polish assessments of Brüning had been mixed, but the balance had been favorable. In Warsaw it was feared that Brüning might exploit his considerable international reputation to gain military equality for Germany. At the Geneva Disarmament Conference in April 1932, Prime Minister MacDonald of Britain and the United States secretary of state, Stimson, had indicated their approval of Brüning's proposal to raise Germany's military forces to 200,000, to reduce the period of military service from twelve to six years, and to permit her to acquire those weapons which had been prohibited under the Versailles treaty.[91] On the day of his resignation, Brüning also received news of Premier Herriot's responsiveness toward German wishes on this question. Ambassador Chłapowski therefore was somewhat relieved by the news of Brüning's fall, which he felt

    88 *Ibid.*, pp. 41–42.
    89 Testimony of Dr. Wirth, *Krupp Prozess*, V.D.B. 2a, No. 141. Cited in Roos, *Polen und Europa*, p. 7.
    90 *Krupp Prozess*, V.D.B. 2b, No. 104. Cited in Roos, *Polen und Europa*, p. 68.
    91 Eyck, *Weimar Republic*, II, pp. 377–78.

would destroy French illusions about the possibility of French–German friendship.[92]

On the whole, however, Poland's reaction to his fall was negative. Brüning had been seen as a reasonable man of good intentions and credit had been given to his moderate statements on the Eastern question. Moreover, Brüning's chancellorship had been regarded as a guarantee against a take-over by Hitler. In July 1931 Lipski had indicated to Moltke that a consolidation of domestic politics in Germany would be in the Polish interest, for a take-over by the radical Left or by Hitler would have dangerous implications for Polish–German relations.[93] Wysocki noted in the same vein that even though Brüning stood closer to the Nationalists than to the Socialist camp, it was still to Poland's advantage that he remained chancellor so that Hitler's access to power might be blocked."[94]

In the estimates of Warsaw, the emergence of Papen represented a significant shift to the Right, a movement which was viewed with great concern. This over-all negative impression could not be erased by Papen's personal background as a Roman Catholic, his apparently moderate sentiments toward Poland, and his previous reservations about Germany's Rapallo policy,[95] all of which would otherwise have made him *persona grata* in the eyes of Warsaw. Papen's "Cabinet of Barons," which gave an overwhelming representation to those groups which traditionally had been the most implacable foes of Poland, was enough evidence for suspicion. This was enhanced by the fact that the Cabinet's other feature member and principal political impressario, General von Schleicher, offered sufficient assurance that German policy would continue to navigate on a pro-Soviet course regardless of the Chancellor's private predilections and sensibilities on that score. Another serious Polish objection to Papen arose from the latter's grandiose scheme for a military alliance with France, which he revealed to Premier Herriot during the Lausanne Reparations Conference in June 1932. The price for such an alliance would,

[92] Report, Chłapowski, June 3, 1932, AMSZ, Berlin Legation, W. 391; cited in Jerzy Krasuski, *Stosunki polsko-niemieckie, 1926–1932* (Poznań, 1964), II, pp. 268–69.

[93] Deutsches Zentralarchiv Potsdam, *Wirtschaftsministerium*, 2814/2; cited in Krasuski, *Stosunki polsko-niemieckie*, II, p. 303.

[94] Report, Wysocki, May 2, 1932, AMSZ, P II, fol. 4503.

[95] Dirksen notified Bülow on June 2, 1931, that the formation of the Papen Cabinet had caused serious concern in the Kremlin regarding the future of German–Soviet co-operation, especially since Papen was credited with an anti-Soviet position (AA, RAM/1417/2860H/D562 323).

by implication, have consisted of French acquiescence in German re-armament and a revision of the eastern frontier.[96] Furthermore, by re-voking the SA ban, the new government tended to give aid to the Nazi movement and to augment the secret military preparations in the eastern provinces.

To Papen the hostile reaction from Warsaw came as an unpleasant surprise. The Chancellor did not subscribe to the pronounced anti-Polish sentiments of his Cabinet colleagues—perhaps the *Herrenreiter* harbored some appreciation for a nation that took such pride in its cavalry—and had the naive impression that an understanding could be negotiated on the basis of a peaceful revision. Such a program, of course, entirely ig-nored the realities of German–Polish relations of the last decade, which had made clear that a peaceful revision, at least in the foreseeable future, was totally unacceptable to Poland and its mere proposal an additional strain on their relations. Papen's plan apparently even exceeded the aim of normalizing relations and envisaged a military alliance with Warsaw. On June 25, 1932, Dr. Reuter, the editor of the *Führerbriefe*, mentioned in the Foreign Office that he had recently attended a talk which Papen had given before an audience of prominent political figures at the exclu-sive *Herrenklub*, the Chancellor's favorite stage for political operations. In his address Papen had expressed himself in favor of the formation of a German–French alliance which would be joined by Poland and whose *pique* would be directed against the Soviet Union. In the framework of this alliance certain territorial revisions would be undertaken on the east-ern frontier of Germany, and the strength of the German and French armies was to be fixed by mutual agreement of their general staffs at a ratio of 3:5.[97]

Although the suggestion had been made quite informally and at a time when Papen still played a minor political role, his elevation to the chancellorship soon after gave the proposal a more official and significant stamp. The Polish legation in Berlin knew of this particular conversation and the Communist *Berliner Volkszeitung* published a fairly accurate version of this intimate session at the *Herrenklub*.[98] However, there is no evidence that during Papen's chancellorship this proposal was ever formally raised in Warsaw. The immediate hostile reaction which his government encountered from Poland would have precluded it. And after Papen had failed to warm French hearts and those of his own Cabi-

[96] Roos, *Polen und Europa*, p. 46; Laroche, *Souvenirs*, p. 109.
[97] AA, RAM/1417/2860H/D562 329; June 23, 1932.
[98] Josef Korbel, *Poland between East and West* (Princeton, 1963), p. 276.

net to his spontaneous and clumsy alliance offer at Lausanne, it is unlikely that another attempt was made to peddle his plan on the Warsaw
market.

Piłsudski's policy of a strong hand with Germany found its most
obvious application in a threatening military gesture which took place on
June 15, 1932, when Poland dispatched the destroyer *Wicher* [the term
ironically means "gale"] into the Danzig harbor on the occasion of a
British fleet visit. This high-handed initiative, which had immediate
international repercussions, was not only meant to act as a forceful persuasion for Danzig to settle its disputes with Poland in a manner that
would respect the latter's rights and interests but also sought to fire a
shot of warning over the bow of the German ship of state.[99]

Danzig had long been a most sensitive seismographic instrument in
measuring the tremors of German–Polish relations. During the years
when Berlin and Warsaw had enjoyed a relative relaxation in their relations, dealings between the Danzig Senate, where a coalition government of Socialists and moderates exercised control, and Warsaw for
once proceeded harmoniously. In 1928 Poland and Danzig concluded a
number of agreements on various long-standing disputes, and when
Prime Minister Bartel subsequently visited the Free City, he received
a warm welcome. But the economic catastrophe, the political upheaval
and the rise of the Nazi party, and the increasingly hostile attitudes which
swept across Germany were all mirrored by similar developments in
Danzig. All this led to a rapid deterioration of relations between Warsaw
and the Free City.

Several simultaneous disputes in 1931 aggravated Polish–Danzig
relations to the utmost: Danzig had submitted a complaint to the League
on the grounds that Poland was boycotting its harbor in favor of Gdynia;
Poland, on the other hand, had complained to the League because of
the poor treatment which Danzig accorded to the resident Polish minority and, furthermore, charged the Free City with abusing the agreement
under which it was permitted to import certain quantities of goods from
Germany to be "finished" in Danzig by introducing large quantities of
these duty-free goods on the Polish market.

Along with the customs dispute and the problem of equal use of

[99] The *Wicher* incident is examined in greater detail in Stefan Benedykt,
"Zajazd O.R.P. 'Wicher' na Gdańsk," *Wiadomości*, no. 108, April 25, 1948; Bohdan
Dopierała, "Beck and the Gdańsk Question, 1930–1935," *Acta Poloniae Historica* 17
(1968): 82–83; T. Morgenstern, "Wejście O.R.P. 'Wicher' do Gdańska w 1932 r.,"
Bellona, no. 1 (1953): 44–48.

the Danzig harbor was the sensitive issue of Polish rights to use the harbor facilities for her warships. By the original *port d'attache* agreement of October 8, 1921, Danzig had accorded to Polish warships the right of free entry and use of the harbor facilities without special permission. Upon its expiration, a provisional agreement was drawn up with the help of the League high commissioner, Count Gravina, and this remained in force until May 1, 1932. When this provisional accord, too, expired, the Danzig authorities unilaterally set up a new system of regulations for the use of the port by foreign ships-of-war. Under these Poland was accorded preferential treatment but was required to seek permission of the Danzig authorities before sending a warship into the Danzig harbor. The regulation warned that any violation of this provision would constitute an *action directe*.[100]

By its uncompromising behavior, Danzig not only tried to retaliate against Poland for the number of unsettled disputes, but the Free City also responded to Germany's wish to have Poland's naval role in that harbor reduced and eventually eliminated altogether. Warsaw refused to accept the legality of these recent provisions and regarded the former accord as still being in force.[101] Both parties had thus embarked on a clear collision course.

The visit of three British destroyers in June 1932 brought the disputed issue to an immediate showdown. Senate President Ziehm had urged Count Gravina to persuade Britain to dispatch some Royal Navy vessels on a good will visit to Danzig in order to indicate British support for Danzig and thereby make Poland more accommodating to the wishes of the Free City.[102] Despite Warsaw's request to postpone the visit until some bilateral settlement had been reached which would regulate the presence of Polish warships in the Danzig harbor, Britain proceeded with these plans and dispatched three destroyers to the Free City.[103] The fleet visit provided Piłsudski with an opportunity to force a showdown with the Danzig authorities and to make them more receptive to the necessity of coming to terms with Poland by invoking the specter of a military coup. The Marshal therefore gave orders, which he personally

---

[100] According to the definition of the League Council of March 13, 1925, an *action directe* was "an action . . . which might endanger or prove a serious obstacle to the maintenance of public security in Danzig or which might jeopardize good relations between Danzig and Poland."

[101] AA, GA/3803/K217/K057 074–76.

[102] E. Ziehm, *Aus Meiner Politischen Arbeit in Danzig, 1914–1939* (Marburg, 1960), pp. 104–7.

[103] Dopierała, "Beck and the Gdańsk Question," p. 82.

supervised, for the Polish destroyer *Wicher* to come alongside the *Westerplatte* on the morning of June 15 in order to exchange the customary courtesy calls with visiting foreign ships in accordance with the expired Polish–Danzig accord of January 30, 1923. In addition, the *Wicher* had been directed "to take the nearest public building of Danzig under fire if during the entry of the British destroyers and the welcome ceremonies the Polish flag suffered any insults."[104] No such drastic measures were applied, however, for the Danzig population remained calm and the *Wicher* left that same afternoon once her courtesy call had been returned by the Royal Navy.

The Danzig Senate immediately protested against the unannounced visit of the Polish warship, which it viewed as a violation of its rights and as an *action directe*. The whole episode produced a strong and immediate reaction from the League Council which was then in session in Geneva. Poland's precipitate and provocative action was generally condemned, even by her French ally, for the latter feared a further deterioration of the international atmosphere and was in no mood to jeopardize the current French–German negotiations.[105] Both Herriot and Simon pressed Zaleski for an assurance that Poland would refrain from similar actions in the future.[106] Poland gave no such assurance at Geneva, but when the German warship *Schlesien* and two torpedo boats visited Danzig later that summer no Polish vessel appeared to do the honors. This was generally construed as an implicit guarantee of Poland's future good behavior.[107]

The guns of the *Wicher* had been fixed on a much wider target than

---

[104] Józef Beck, *Dernier rapport. Politique polonaise 1926–1939* (Neuchâtel, 1951), p. 17; Wojewódskie Archiwum Państwowe Gdańsk, *Komisariat Generalny Rzeczypospolitej Polski*, no. 592, pp. 2–4; cited in Bohdan Dopierała, "Beck and the Gdańsk Question 1930–1935," *Acta Poloniae Historica* 17 (1968), p. 82. Both of these sources leave no doubt that Piłsudski not only authorized but also personally directed the sudden visit of the *Wicher*.

[105] Dufour (Geneva) to Bülow (Lausanne), June 17, 1932, AA, GA/3803/K217/K057 205.

[106] Telegram, Meyer to Moltke, June 18, 1932, *ibid.*, 149.

[107] The visit of the German ships had been scheduled long before the *Wicher* incident. As the visit had already been publicly announced, the German government was unwilling to cancel it even though it was alarmed that the visit might produce a more serious crisis than the *Wicher* incident; moreover, one where Germany was directly involved. Admiral Förster had been instructed to be meticulous in keeping the protocol of salutes and courtesy calls with the Polish ship if one came to greet them. (AA, GA/3803/K217/K057 150). One day before the German visit, Poland informed the Danzig Senate that she would not dispatch a ship for the occasion, and the visit proceeded without incident.

"the nearest public building" in Danzig; they were aimed at several governments and organizations simultaneously. Their most immediate target, both in the narrow military as in the broader political sense, was the Free City itself. By demonstrating its determination and willingness to take certain risks, the Warsaw government tried to impress the Danzig Senate of its unshakable resolve to protect Polish rights and interests in the Free City. From his conversation with Beck, Ambassador Laroche, who considered the Polish action extremely unfortunate, also gained the impression that Poland had first and foremost resorted to this provocative measure in order to bring an end to the uncertainties in her relations with Danzig and to arrive at an acceptable agreement on the *port d'attache* question.[108] Piłsudski's policy of showing a strong hand was not without consequence and brought almost immediate dividends. On August 13, 1932, the somewhat chastised Danzig Senate concluded two reconciliation protocols with Warsaw. In line with Polish wishes, the first of these regulated the entry of Polish warships into the Danzig harbor on a preferential basis over foreign warships. The second protocol arranged for a mutual suspension of their current economic boycotting measures.[109]

But Polish calculations went beyond Danzig. The *Wicher* incident had also been staged in order to test the reaction of her French ally and thereby to gain a better impression of French determination to resist German revisionist policies. At the same time, it was probably meant to convey a warning to other powers as well, so that they would stop meddling in the Polish–Danzig dispute (as the British fleet visit was construed) and would relinquish their pro-Danzig bias, which in Polish opinion characterized the behavior of the League of Nations and its High Commissioner in Danzig. According to the Polish general commissioner in Danzig, Papée, Piłsudski had told him that the incident was "an attempt to use new methods toward the League of Nations and the Gdańsk Senate, and that it marked the end of the former Polish policy of submission."[110]

Aside from Danzig, Piłsudski's move was mainly directed toward Berlin, and there he sought to use the incident to test German reactions and to give a firm warning that Poland would unhesitatingly resist any

---

[108] Telegram, Moltke of his conversation with Laroche, June 19, 1932, *ibid.*, 161–62.
[109] Dopierała, "Beck and the Gdańsk Question," p. 83.
[110] Wojewódskie Archiwum Państwowe Gdańsk, *Komisariat Generalny*, no. 592, pp. 2–4; cited in Dopierała, "Beck and the Gdańsk Question," p. 83.

encroachments of her rights in Danzig and *a fortiori* any violation of her territorial integrity. The German press accorded it little notice and the Foreign Ministry's nervousness was little more than routine. At any rate, this particular warning did not deter Berlin from going ahead with the scheduled visit of German warships to Danzig a few weeks later. If there really existed an immediate threat of a German–Polish armed conflict as the result of the *Wicher* incident, it would not so much have originated as the consequence of an uncontrollable explosion of events— even if Danzig had suffered damage or invasion, Germany was hardly in a position to do more than acquiesce while appealing to the League— than from Piłsudski's deliberate plan to make this the starting point to spark a preventive war. Certain evidence may be presented to support this hypothesis. Toward the end of 1931 Tytus Filipowicz, the Polish Ambassador to Washington, reportedly informed President Hoover that Poland was threatened by German irregular troops and would consequently have to march into Germany "to settle the thing once and for all."[111] In a later speech before the New York Piłsudski Institute, General Emer Yeager, who had served as United States military attaché in Warsaw between 1929 and 1932, recalled that Piłsudski had shown him plans for an aggressive action against Germany in 1932.[112]

By lumping the *Wicher* incident with later events like the sudden reinforcement of the Polish garrison on the *Westerplatte* in March 1933, analysts have tended to pre-empt later developments when the accession of Hitler forced Piłsudski to give serious consideration to the idea of launching a pre-emptive military strike against Germany. The question of Poland's preventive war considerations has become a rich source for historical analysis and speculation.[113] But as this issue applies to a later period it is of less immediate interest to us here. While preventive war thoughts may well have been on the Marshal's mind throughout the period of deteriorating relations with Germany, all evidence that has be-

---

[111] Roos, *Polen und Europa*, p. 38.

[112] Höltje, *Das Ost–Locarno Problem*, p. 197. But according to a report of the U.S. *chargé* in 1932, Yeager himself had dismissed these alarmist speculations as rumors devoid of military foundation. (Report, Flack, April 6, 1932, SD, 760c.62/171).

[113] The literature on the subject of Poland's preventive war plans is voluminous and most diplomatic accounts of that period make some reference to this question. The comments of Beck, Laroche, and Noël are of particular importance here. An excellent summary of the preventive war question is given by Wacław Jędrzejewicz, "The Polish Plan for a 'Preventive War' against Germany in 1933," *Polish Review* 11 (1966): 62–91.

come available indicates that it was only after Hitler came to power that Piłsudski seriously contemplated this drastic course of action and began to take soundings in Paris to determine the French reaction. Because of his strong distrust and disdain for bureaucrats and professional diplomats, Piłsudski preferred to entrust these delicate sounding operations to individuals who stood close to him rather than pursue them through official diplomatic channels. In the beginning of 1933, he therefore dispatched his former aide-de-camp, Count Jerzy Potocki, on a secret mission to Paris to speak with Foreign Minister Paul-Boncour. Soon thereafter Piłsudski's aide-de-camp, Colonel Wieniawa-Długoszowski, held conversations with the French Intelligence Service, and in November 1933, before he finally committed himself to enter into serious negotiations with Germany on the conclusion of a nonaggression pact, another private individual was sent to Paris. This time it was the poet Morstin who was commissioned to determine the nature of the expected French military response in the event of a Polish–German war.[114]

There is no evidence that similar soundings had been conducted in Paris in 1932, and the surprised and indignant French reaction to the *Wicher* episode tends to confirm that Piłsudski had acted without prior knowledge and approval from Paris. It is unlikely that Piłsudski, with his high respect for the caliber of the German army, would have embarked on as serious a venture as a preventive war without seeking prior assurance of the co-operation, or at least benevolent neutrality, of his French ally, as was demonstrated by the soundings which he conducted in 1933 when he was seriously contemplating this course of action. The preventive war question was not mentioned when the newly appointed undersecretary of state, Count Jan Szembek, was sent on a good will mission to Paris and London in November 1932. This was largely a get-acquainted tour, but Szembek probably gave expression to Polish concerns over Germany's internal political developments and her demand for military equality. No reference to the preventive war option was made during this visit; in fact, throughout this period Szembek remained unaware that the Marshal and his immediate confidants were giving serious consideration to a military solution of this kind.[115]

---

114 *Ibid.*, pp. 81–82, 85–86.

115 In a letter to Count Edward Raczyński of August 31, 1942, Szembek recalled that "ever since I had the post of undersecretary of State (from 1932 on) not a whisper of such negotiations came to my knowledge. Did Marshal Piłsudski carry on such talks through his military channels with the highest French authorities?—I do not know. But I must deny that any official steps connected with this matter were

Even with respect to events after Hitler came to power, the notion that Poland drew up preventive war plans against Germany tends to over-dramatize the true state of affairs. If plans are defined as blueprints for a specific course of action which are matched by parallel military preparations, then no preventive war plans against Germany were involved. No new war plans were drawn up for this occasion and no major force movement or changes in force disposition took place at that time. It would, therefore, be more proper to speak of preventive war considerations rather than war plans. These considerations came closest to the more concrete planning stage when Piłsudski prepared a decree which provided for the creation of a Government of National Unity and Defense in the event of a war with Germany. He drew up this decree on April 18, 1933, and the fact that it was signed by President Mościcki on the same day would indicate its urgency.[116] Perhaps the nature of the whole situation is best described by Beck himself, who notes in his memoirs that before signing the nonaggression pact with Germany, Piłsudski had considered the pros and cons of a preventive war against Germany, but "la faiblesse de nos alliés éventuels à cette époque nous fit abandonner l'idée d'une guerre préventive. . . ."[117]

Even though one can observe a distinct hardening in Poland's confrontation tactics after Hitler's *Machtergreifung*, the *Wicher* incident had certain features that were similar to the reinforcement of the Westerplatte garrison in 1933. Both events were purposely designed to probe for German intentions and reactions, to test the firmness of the Western Powers, and, in particular, to clarify the position of France. Both cases remained mere incidents without escalating into open violence. If Germany had offered any resistance they might easily have escalated into an international conflict, a risk which Piłsudski was willing to take.

As a counterpart to these provocative measures, Warsaw continued to demonstrate its desire for an accommodation with Germany. The fluctuation between confrontation and détente tactics was not as diamet-

---

taken by the Polish Government in Paris." (*Lipski Papers*, Piłsudski Institute, New York, file 1; cited in Wacław Jędrzejewicz, "The Polish Plan for a 'Preventive War' against Germany in 1933," *Polish Review* [1966]: 79.)

[116] When Piłsudski's aide-de-camp, Major Lepecki, was handed this particular manuscript for typing and asked the Marshal whether Hitler intended to attack Poland, Piłsudski instructed him that "even if we attack him, it will also be a defense." (M. B. Lepecki, "Marshal Piłsudski i przewidywana w r. 1933 wojna z Niemcami," *Wiadomości*, no. 169 [1949]; cited in Jędrzejewicz, "The Polish Plan for a 'Preventive War'," p. 83.)

[117] Beck, *Dernier rapport*, p. 66.

rically opposed as might appear at first sight, for by his policy of intimidation, Piłsudski tried to pressure German policy-makers into accepting
the necessity for an accommodation with Poland. But it should be
realized that by this simultaneous application of the carrot and the stick,
Piłsudski handled the punitive preventive war aspect not merely as a
tactical device to get German compliance but treated it as a real strategic
alternative which he seriously considered.

RELATIONS DURING THE LAST PHASE OF THE WEIMAR REPUBLIC

The 1932 long "hot" summer in German–Polish relations gave way
to a somewhat more relaxed atmosphere in autumn. The Danzig reconciliation protocols helped ease the explosive situation which had
prompted the *Wicher* incident. Wysocki's analysis of the German domestic situation helped to convince Piłsudski that Germany's internal
conflicts and preoccupations were on the increase and would "obviously
weaken the aggressive impetus of that nation externally."[118] Wysocki's
reports about Hitler's future prospects also tended to be reassuring. The
Polish envoy held the convenient and conventional opinion, which then
enjoyed wide currency both in German political circles and among foreign observers, that Hitler's talents as a demagogue and publicist were
not matched by similar skills as an administrator and that as head of a
government he would quickly discredit himself by his inability to govern
and his failure to fulfill his campaign promises. Consequently, it was believed that Hitler would prefer to remain under the protective shelter
which his opposition role granted him. Nevertheless, if he remained in
opposition too long he was bound to alienate many voters. Thus, according to this reassuring argument, Hitler could not win either way. Wysocki
reasoned that the Nazis could not prolong their double-dealing with the
government much longer; either they would have to revert to the role of
a radical opposition or they would have to accommodate themselves with
the present government and join its ranks. In his opinion the latter was
the more likely course.[119]

The German November election confirmed the view that the swelling tide of the Nazi movement might yet be stemmed. In the foreign
field Papen's plans for an alignment with France had failed and internal

[118] *Lipski Papers*, p. 51.
[119] Report, Wysocki, August 10, 1932, and December 11, 1932, AMSZ, P II,
fol. 4502. This is also the argument which he used when he briefed Piłsudski in 1932
(*Lipski Papers*, p. 51).

political unrest and a series of inconclusive elections deprived the German Chancellor of a platform from which he could conduct the kind of energetic foreign policy that might have threatened Poland.[120]

As a gesture of its good intentions, the Warsaw government had instructed Szembek to make Berlin the last diplomatic whistle-stop on his tour, which had first taken him to Paris and London. Szembek had been instructed not to make any mention of the basic conflicts which existed between Warsaw and Berlin, but merely "to declare that relations between the two countries were in a state of tension which could produce God knows what consequences if some reasonable *modus vivendi* could not be found."[121] His discussions with Foreign Minister von Neurath proceeded in a frank and cordial atmosphere and touched on a number of current issues which might be settled in a satisfactory manner. German press commentaries speculated about a new orientation of Polish policy,[122] and *Gazeta Polska* even spoke in terms of a possible German–Polish nonaggression pact.[123]

Szembek's visit and the reference to a nonaggression pact seem to have been designed as an olive branch with which to induce the Papen government to revise its negative stand toward Poland and to come to terms with that country. But this trial balloon burst almost immediately when Schleicher took his brief stand at the helm of the drifting ship of state on December 2, 1932. Schleicher's role in building the secret *Grenz-schutz* and in designing the mobilization plan, his loyal adherence to the principles of making German–Soviet co-operation the bedrock of Germany's foreign and military policies, as much as his energetic application in favor of a German–French alignment, all made him appear as the very embodiment of all those aspects of German policy which seemed objectionable and menacing in Polish eyes. Polish reaction to Schleicher's appointment was given fresh impetus when he reaped by a windfall profit that which more properly belonged to the Brüning government in the form of the Five-Power Declaration of December 11, 1932, which in principle conceded to Germany equality of armaments in a system that gave security to all nations. The declaration was doubly objectionable to Warsaw, for not only did it promise to break the dam that had stemmed

---

[120] See Piłsudski's statement to the French military attaché in Warsaw, General d'Arbonneau, on October 24, 1932; cited in Laroche, *Souvenirs*, p. 111.

[121] Letter Szembek to Raczyński, August 31, 1942; cited in Jędrzejewicz, "The Polish Plan for a 'Preventive War'," p. 79.

[122] *Schulthess' Europäischer Geschichtskalender*, vol. 73 (1932), p. 349.

[123] Roos, *Polen und Europa*, p. 56.

the flood-tide of German official rearmament but it also opened the gates for a German–French alignment at the expense of Poland. The effects of the Five-Power Declaration in driving a wedge between Paris and Warsaw were considerable, and when in January of 1933 France presented her disarmament and security plan draft for Warsaw's endorsement, Poland came forward with her own plan, on the grounds that she had not been consulted on the French proposal. Paris regarded this as *"une faute grave de tactique,"*[124] and in the vote of February 23, 1933, the Polish delegate did not support the French project. Warsaw's growing alienation from Paris helped lay the groundwork which later enabled Hitler to score his decisive breakthrough in relations with Poland in 1934. Schleicher's irreconcilable hostility to Poland seems to have mellowed in no way by the sobering experience of political office in the *Reichskanzlei*. In handing over the reins of government he is reported to have advised Hitler to form an entente with France and Russia and to liquidate Poland. Hitler's apparent reply to Schleicher's counsel was a simple rebuttal: "Und ich werde das Gegenteil machen" [I shall do the reverse].[125]

Despite this accumulation of discouraging evidence, Wysocki executed his earlier instructions and continued to make the rounds among German political leaders from the moderate parties in order to explore the ground, and hopefully widen the support, for an understanding with Poland. The Polish envoy went to the Social Democrats first, as he was most likely to find a favorable reception there. As on previous occasions, he found in Loebe a sympathetic partner and a co-operative force. Loebe regretted the deterioration of relations over the preceding two years, a development for which both sides had to accept responsibility. At the same time, the resurgence of extreme nationalism across the European continent had played its part in contributing to the unfortunate situation. Loebe recognized the danger of an open Polish–German conflict, but he was convinced that even Schleicher would not risk a war with Poland. According to Loebe, the situation was not beyond repair, despite the multiple obstacles. He therefore urged Wysocki to expand the basis of his talks so that members from other parties like the *Zentrum* and the Democrats would also be included.[126] Wysocki's conversation with

124 Laroche, *Souvenirs*, p. 119.

125 Jan Szembek, *Journal 1933–1939*, (Paris, 1952), p. 33. The story was related by Goring during his good will visit to Warsaw in 1935. There is no proof of the authenticity of this comment by Hitler, and Goring may well have invented it in order to underscore the friendly attitude of Hitler toward Poland in contrast to that of the Weimar Republic.

126 Report, Wysocki, January 5, 1933, AMSZ, P II, fol. 4502.

Dietrich, a leading member of the DDP and former finance minister in Brüning's Cabinet, proceeded in an equally cordial and positive atmosphere. When the Polish Minister had insisted that the boundary question was non-negotiable for his country, Dietrich had replied that there were several other issues that could be profitably negotiated. In his personal opinion, a revision of the frontier was clearly of secondary interest to Germany when measured with the need for an economic agreement with Poland and the Balkans.[127]

Of even greater interest than the content of the preceding conversations was the discussion that Wysocki had with Papen during the latter's brief interregnum between his chancellorship and vice-chancellorship. Papen had readily consented when the Polish diplomat had asked him for an audience, but had insisted from the outset of their talk that a territorial revision was a *sine qua non* for placing German–Polish relations on a regulated and friendly basis. Wysocki appealed to Papen's notorious vanity when he expressed his regrets that the latter did not conduct negotiations for the normalization of German–Polish relations, a task for which he was eminently suited because of his outstanding personal qualities—qualities which have subsequently eluded historians—and his close ties to Hindenburg. Papen repaid the Polish diplomat in the same coin when he praised Marshal Piłsudski's great wisdom and statesmanship. In Papen's opinion the Marshal, in all his wisdom, could not but realize that a rectification of the Polish–German frontier was a small matter in comparison with the overwhelming common interest in combatting Communism. Three days after their initial conversation, Papen visited Wysocki in the Polish legation in order to resume its thread.

On this occasion the ex-Chancellor outlined a definite procedure which he felt ought to be followed if relations were to be normalized. At first an attempt ought to be made to clear the general atmosphere. This could be achieved by settling a long series of outstanding issues of secondary importance. Then the stage would have to be set for both sides to apply themselves to resolve the major disputes which divided them. Papen related how, during their meeting at Geneva, Herriot had insisted that France herself could not raise the territorial question in the League or in Warsaw because of Poland's solid opposition. In reply, Papen had warned him that time was quickly running out, for the present moment was uniquely suited for a settlement of the frontier dispute.

[127] *Ibid.*, January 13, 1933.

In Germany there was Hindenburg, and in Poland there was Piłsudski. These two alone were in a position to come to terms on the territorial dispute and to conclude an agreement *"von Mann zu Mann"* [from man to man] which would not involve parliament or the press. The last comment in itself betrays with brutal clarity Papen's disdain for parliamentary institutions and democratic politics as well as his belief, which was either grossly naive or blatantly totalitarian, that whole provinces could be made to change hands by the command of a single person.[128]

In Wysocki's discussions with German political leaders the question of Germany's territorial claims had dominated the talks. Nevertheless, the Polish envoy felt encouraged by what he had heard and his report to Warsaw was fairly optimistic. He was above all struck by the sharp contrast between the pleasant tone of these political conversations and the shrill notes of German public propaganda. In Wysocki's estimate these talks proved that Poland could enter into negotiations with Germany for the normalization of relations and that she could do so without the mediating services of third powers; furthermore, that one could talk in this vein with all German political parties except the Nazis and Communists. Even with such extreme nationalists as Papen one could negotiate all questions except the territorial one, and with many Germans—Dietrich was an example—the desire for an economic agreement with Poland far outweighed their wish for a territorial revision.[129]

With respect to German domestic politics, Wysocki also retained some optimism to the last day of the Weimar Republic. In his opinion, the Nazis had become more cautious after their recent electoral setback and might even decline the option of forming the government if the opportunity should present itself.[130] Only one day before the fateful January 30, when he commented on Schleicher's resignation, the Polish envoy noted that those "iron chancellors," of which Germany used to boast, faded from the scene like ghosts. In his estimate, German politics had come to the crossroads: either there would be a clear break from the Weimar Constitution as the system moved toward a presidentially directed government under Hindenburg, or the storm would be weathered as the government was reconstituted on the basis of a much broader

---

128 *Ibid.*
129 *Ibid.*
130 Report, Wysocki, January 14, 1933, *ibid.*

coalition. Wysocki himself attached greater probability to the latter course of events.[131]

When Hitler came to power, the Polish envoy, like so many others, did not at first view this as a basic change in German politics and in the international politics of the European Powers. On February 12, 1933, he noted that the National Socialists were in a minority in the Cabinet and that it was not Hitler but Hindenburg and Papen who controlled ministers like Blomberg, Neurath, and Schwerin-Krosigk, with the result that the army, police, foreign affairs, and finance lay beyond Hitler's grasp. Hindenburg's son Oskar and his state secretary, Otto Meissner, had reassured Wysocki in almost identical terms that if Hitler stayed in power for as long as a year, his inability to govern would have become evident and his government would collapse in a general debacle.[132] But the Polish Minister was soon forced to revise his earlier assessment. Only two weeks after the above report he informed his government that, like an octopus, Hitler was rapidly extending the tentacles of control over the entire government apparatus; that he was determined to stay in power, and that there was little hope that Hindenburg and Papen could any longer dismiss him at their pleasure.[133]

During the last phase of the Weimar Republic, relations with Poland had notably deteriorated and tensions had become so extreme that rumors of an imminent military conflict were widely circulated and met with credulity in the highest military and political circles in Berlin. On the German side, the primary interest at that time was to prevent a Polish military attack which she was unprepared to counter because of the military restrictions under which she was forced to operate and because of the domestic political crisis with which she was convulsed. Poland was better equipped to pursue a policy of intimidation, but at the same time she was more committed to the idea of coming to an understanding with Germany. One notes from the instructions which went to Wysocki and from his activities in Berlin that toward the very end of the Weimar Republic Warsaw never abandoned the goal of normalizing relations between the two countries and the thread to a dialogue was never entirely broken.

[131] *Ibid.*, January 29, 1933.
[132] *Ibid.*, February 12, 1933.
[133] *Ibid.*, February 26, 1933.

XII

Conclusion

FROM THE ASHES of World War I both Germany and Poland had emerged as essentially restructured political units—Poland as a reconstituted state and Germany under a new political régime and a significantly deflated international status. Both sides were thus presented with an ideal opportunity to start their relations on a clean slate. The total record of their thousand years as neighbors provided a sufficiently rich variety of examples of friendly associations and joint enterprises to outweigh the antagonistic elements which had prevailed in their recent history. Their historical legacy, if properly interpreted, therefore, did not have to be an insurmountable barrier to the renewal of friendly relations. The newly formed governments in Berlin and Warsaw were beset by internal turmoil and confronted by an unstable and unfriendly international environment. To try to master this uncertain future through mutual co-operation and assistance might have seemed like a natural choice for both sides under these circumstances. The concept of a *Schicksalsgemeinschaft* [community of fate] which the Germans were so fond of invoking with reference to their relations with the Soviet Union could have been applied with equal relevance to their relations with Poland.

But these opportunities remained unexplored, and the history of German–Polish relations during the Weimar period became a story of failure. The concept of a broader partnership between the two countries was never clearly articulated and was not reflected in their actual relations at that time.

380

But the situation was not one of unmitigated conflict. After Locarno, attempts were made on both sides to improve the climate of their relations. On the Polish side one can refer to Marshal Piłsudski's friendly overtures to Stresemann in Geneva in 1927, to Olszowski's plea in 1926 for the rapid conclusion of a trade and liquidation treaty, to Wysocki's suggestion of 1931 for a summit meeting, and to his subsequent efforts to win the support of various German political leaders for a policy of accommodation. In Germany, as well, one could observe a positive reaction. During the Locarno era, Germany's Social Democrats and other moderate political parties, economic interest groups (particularly from the industrial sector), and various peace organizations all actively promoted a policy of economic co-operation and political accommodation between the two major powers in the Central European area. Between 1927 and 1929 their aims coincided at least temporarily with the policies of the German government, when Stresemann also pursued a détente with Warsaw in order to provide the missing link in his over-all foreign policy strategy.

Compared with Germany's efforts, Poland's reconciliatory attempts were not only more continuous but they also had more official backing. In Warsaw there was never any doubt that Germany—defeated or victorious—was a Great Power which would have to be included in all major Polish foreign policy calculations. Also, Polish reconciliatory initiatives were in line with her status quo orientation and the desire to stabilize relations on the basis of existing realities, including the reality of the established frontier. Finally, Warsaw's interest in better relations with Germany proceeded from the wish to reassert Poland's status as a Western power and to protect herself from the threat of isolation from Western Europe. These were not considerations which affected Germany.

Yet, the actual course of relations between Berlin and Warsaw did not significantly respond to these emerging conciliatory considerations because the revisionist question proved to be an insurmountable obstacle at that particular period. The territorial dispute so infected the general atmosphere that it negatively affected every other facet of their relations, and it thus prevented a natural accommodation between the two countries within the new constellation of power in Europe. As long as Germany retained her territorial claims and exploited every available opportunity to conduct her revisionist campaign before the international forum, Poland, associating a revision with the prelude to a fourth partition, feared for her national existence. The barren political and emotional climate of this elementary conflict prohibited the growth of an effective reconciliatory settlement.

The introduction of historical guidelines could not resolve their overlapping territorial claims, as each side found ample precedent in support of its demands, and, furthermore, no historical proof, no matter how persuasively documented and argued, could have induced the Poles to part with their present possessions. Similarly, to determine the right of ownership in terms of need, that is to say according to whether Poland's need for a direct access to the sea outweighed Germany's need for an unbroken connection with East Prussia, was hardly a realistic proposal, for not only was there no accepted way of calculating such ratios of relative need but no argument of this nature could have persuaded Poland to make any territorial sacrifices. It may be added that under a system of mutual co-operation Germany could have entered East Prussia through a Polish "Corridor" just as Poland could have enjoyed access to the sea across German territory without suffering intolerable burdens.

From these observations the natural question arises as to whether the sacrifice of the disputed territories, or respectively of the claims thereto, as the necessary price for a reconciliation would not in the long run have served Poland's national interests better than the obstinate defense of the status quo. Even if the surrender of the "Corridor" and of Upper Silesia had represented the true national interest of Poland, especially since she was the more exposed and weaker power and thus in greater need of German friendship than vice versa, it was realistically inconceivable that Poland would ever surrender areas which were presently her possession and to which she felt historically and ethnically entitled. In so far as the sacrifice of a claim or of an illusion would seem to be more easily accomplished than the more tangible sacrifice of actual territory, it would have been more logical for Germany to have shouldered this sacrificial role herself. It is difficult to see how Germans could have remained totally imperceptive to the impact of the quadruple argument that the disputed area was presently in Polish hands; that the majority of the population in these areas was Polish; that Poland had not offered the slightest indication that she would ever submit to a voluntary revision; moreover, that the European powers in the last resort tended to seek refuge from this dilemma by upholding the status quo against Germany's revisionist demands. Yet it was precisely this conclusion which Germany refused to draw.

Germany's uncompromising demand for a revisionist solution constituted a refusal to bow to the dictates of reality and may be said to have demonstrated a natural German tendency, as the philosopher Keyserling sees it, of according imagination precedence over reality. Perhaps in her mystical crusading spirit against the Versailles treaty, under the spell of which Germany spun all sorts of revisionist solutions and tried to engage the services of everybody from the Pope to London bankers, the Faustian qualities of the German mentality [Faust: "I have merely desired and attained and still craved and so come through my life, never for an instant satisfied."] in its perpetual romantic strivings for an unattainable ideal came to the surface.

With respect to Poland, Germany's failure to adjust to the reality of the situation was accentuated by the fact that German public opinion was unable to disassociate itself from the habit of judging everything connected with Poland as inferior. The relative ease with which German opinion generally accepted the loss of Alsace-Lorraine can to no small extent be attributed to the fact that German opinion respected France as an equal or superior power and thus more readily acquiesced in that loss than in the loss of territory to a supposedly inferior power which might eventually be forced to relinquish its gains.

The habit of assigning an inferior status to Poles as persons and to Poland as a power not only complicated the adjustment of current disputes but also tended to obliterate the judgment of German statesmen in evaluating the importance of Poland as a partner for Germany. This tendency was cemented by the continued adherence—even under radically altered circumstances—to the traditional concept of seeing in Russia her natural partner in the east. But the history of the Weimar Republic repeatedly demonstrated the inherent limitations of a partnership between Germany and Communist Russia. The fiction of friendship could not forever be maintained under the extraordinary situation where the primary goal of one's supposed friend was directed toward the overthrow of one's own government. Even in the economic sphere, where Germany's free-market economy experienced considerable difficulties in dealing with the state-controlled Soviet economic system, results fell short of expectations. In this respect it is interesting to note that even at a time when Germany was engaged in a trade war with Poland while she enjoyed treaty-regulated trade relations with Russia, the value of her trade with Poland exceeded that with the Soviet Union.

Certainly by 1926 the initial German concept of Poland as a *Saisonstaat* had given way to a realistic acceptance of the existence of the

Polish State as an undeniable factor in Europe's political life. What Germany refused to accept, however, was Poland's postwar territorial composition where it interfered with German claims. Germany's revisionist crusade sought a solution by the use of propaganda and diplomacy rather than by the use of force. The responsible leaders of the Weimar Republic had realistically accepted Germany's limited military posture as totally inadequate for a military venture against Poland, and the illicit creation of the *Grenzschutz* and the construction of eastern fortifications were exclusively defensive. Furthermore, men like Stresemann gave evidence of gradually accommodating themselves to the realization that even if Germany should regain her natural military superiority over her eastern neighbor, the German–Polish problem could not be settled by a "clean" surgical military incision that would avoid a general European war. German revisionist efforts were consequently confined to propagandistic, economic, and diplomatic means.

When the initial explorations for solving the Polish question in conjunction with Russia had pointed toward a solution by force, German diplomacy shifted its emphasis almost exclusively in the direction of the Western capitals, thus furnishing the most tangible proof of her commitment to a peaceful solution. The apparently sympathetic reception which her policy of a peaceful revision encountered in the West during the Locarno era tended to sustain her belief in the practicability and efficacy of this policy. Yet despite the numerous tactical gains which her diplomacy initially seemed to score on this issue, it was, as events after 1930 demonstrated, fundamentally a chimerical goal she was pursuing, for when confronted by the clash between Germany's more active pressure for a revisionist solution and Poland's unwavering resistance, the Western Powers resorted to the defense of the status quo as the most reliable means of preserving the peace.

As long as Germany engaged in her relentless revisionist crusade, she denied herself the benefits concomitant with an understanding with Poland. An understanding between Berlin and Warsaw not only held out immediate economic rewards for both parties but also promised to alleviate the effects of the territorial loss by giving Germany greater leverage in influencing Polish minority policy and by allowing her to retain an economic foothold in the lost regions. Furthermore, the most direct route for a lasting German reconciliation with France, as Rauscher never tired of emphasizing, and for the disruption of the anti-German element in the French continental coalition structure, was the road of a German–Polish understanding. Finally, seen in its long-range perspective the principal objective of an understanding between the two major powers in the Central European area invariably was provided by the imperative of preserving a united European front against the mounting threat of Communist Russia.

Even if the German government had correctly evaluated the potential of Poland as a partner and had been willing to sacrifice its revisionist claims on the altar of a reconciliation, it remains open to serious question whether German popular opinion under the democratic process could have been induced to accept a solution of this nature. Perhaps a gradual extension of the policy of the Social Democrats and certain economic interests groups, who formally upheld Germany's revisionist claims but did not actively press them and assigned priority to the settlement of other outstanding issues, might have produced a general decline in German revisionist sentiments, if this process had been accompanied by an intensive public information campaign.

But the government's public information efforts proceeded in the opposite direction and forever tried to keep alive the relentless striving of the entire nation for a revisionist solution. Under these conditions German public opinion did not soften either on the revisionist issue or on the general question of relations with Poland. To change public opinion on a fundamental foreign policy issue is a long-term process under any circumstances. In our own generation we have witnessed that more than two decades elapsed before a major breakthrough in German public opinion on the recognition of the Oder–Neisse frontier could be registered. The life-span of the Weimar Republic was considerably shorter than that, and the German government at that time was unwilling, and in view of the internal instability of the system probably also unable, to provide the kind of foreign policy leadership which might have acted as a catalyst in altering public opinion on this sensitive and highly emotional matter.

In the light of the experience during the Weimar period, Hitler's boast that he alone could find a solution to the German–Polish problem was not without validity, for unlike the Weimar government he exercised sufficient power over public opinion to enforce an unpopular settlement with Poland, and he could also seemingly by-pass the territorial issue as he suffered from none of the compunctions which had prevented his predecessors from planning for an eventual solution by force.

It was the tragic fate of both Germany and Poland, as also that of Europe, that the two major powers which formed the *Raumgemein-schaft* in Eastern Central Europe and whose far-reaching national interests—if only properly conceived—were mutually complementary should have been unable to come to a lasting understanding. The history of Germany's foreign policy vis-à-vis Poland during the Weimar period is a story of failure, both in political perception and in practical application. Its only redeeming grace is to be found in the firm commitment on the part of the German government to seek a revisionist solution solely by peaceful means, and in the fact that despite most formidable obstacles and frustrations her diplomats succeeded in guarding a peace—however precarious.

Appendix I

LIQUIDATION CLAIMS OF THE GERMAN GOVERNMENT ON BEHALF OF PRIVATE
PERSONS AGAINST THE POLISH STATE, 1929
(in million RM)

Nature of claim	Amount demanded	Amount realizable	Amount to be paid or already paid under war compensation bill[a]
1. Application of the Annulment Decree			
a. 4,000 *Ansiedler*	80	65	55
b. *Domänenpächter*	90	53	18
c. *Personnes royales*	30	20	2
d. Corporations	11	7	—
2. Additional claims of liquidated persons			
a. 960 *Ansiedler*	45	23	11
b. Private property of land	38	32	5
c. Private urban property	18	12	4
d. Claims by Prince von Thurn und Taxis	36	25	3
e. Claims by Dessau Public Utilities Co.	91	47	4
f. Liquidations in Congress Poland	4	3	1
3. Bail for emigrants	8	—	—
4. Chorzów	25	25	—
5. Damages by insurrection	47.7	—	—
6. Other	15	—	—
TOTAL	538.7	312[b]	103

[a] No new financial burden originated from this for the *Reich*, as these sums
had already been authorized.

[b] The additional burden, if total compensation were granted, would amount
to 200 million marks.

Source: Condensed from AA, RAM/1429/2945H/D574 353–55.

Appendix II

LIQUIDATION CLAIMS OF THE POLISH GOVERNMENT ON BEHALF OF PRIVATE
PERSONS AGAINST THE GERMAN REICH, 1929
(*in million RM*)

Nature of claim	Amount demanded	Amount realizable
Requisition measures	192	15
Requisitions in Germany	2	1
Treaty claims	14	12
Claims by workers	315[a]	45
Claims collected by the Westmarkenverein	300[a]	17
Claims of prisoners of war	9.25	—
TOTAL CLAIMS	832.25	90

[a] No definite sums given as yet by Poland.
Source: Condensed from AA, RAM/1429/2945H/D574 355.

388

Appendix III

BALANCE OF GERMAN–POLISH TRADE, 1924–34[a]

Year	Movement from Germany to Poland		Movement from Poland to Germany	
	German exports to Poland according to German statistics	Polish imports from Germany according to Polish statistics	Polish exports to Germany according to Polish statistics	German imports from Poland according to German statistics
	(in million marks)			
1924	395.3	408.8	438.3	456.2
1925	422.2	377.7	412.9	455.7
1926	260.8	172.4	269.6	304.5
1927	430.9	346.3	378.2	366.2
1928	496.0	424.3	403.5	377.9
1929	425.4	400.4	412.9	376.0
1930	328.7	284.6	294.4	263.0
1931	187.7	169.5	148.8	132.2
1932	93.4	81.8	83.1	81.7
1933	82.4	68.8	79.2	77.1
1934	55.6	50.0	78.0	75.8
	(Percentage of total trade)			
1924	6.0	34.5	43.2	5.0
1925	4.5	30.7	40.4	3.7
1926	2.5	23.7	25.4	3.0
1927	4.0	25.5	32.0	2.6
1928	4.1	26.9	34.2	2.7
1929	3.2	27.3	31.2	2.8
1930	2.8	27.0	25.8	2.5
1931	2.0	24.5	16.8	2.0
1932	1.6	20.1	16.2	1.8
1933	1.7	17.6	17.5	1.8
1934	1.3	13.5	16.6	1.7

[a] Statistics compiled from Jerzy Krasuski, Stosunki polsko-niemieckie, 1926–1932 (Poznań: Instytut Zachodni, 1964), p. 294; Reichstag, Sten. Berichte, Anlagen, 442, No. 2138, pp. 85–88.

Appendix IV

THE POPULATION OF POLAND BY NATIONALITIES, 1921–31[a]

By nationality, according to census of 30.IX.1921			By mother tongue, according to census of 9.XII.1931		
	Number in thousands	*% of total population*		*Number in thousands*	*% of total population*
Poles	18,814	69.2	Polish	21,993	68.9
Ruthenians	3,898	14.3	Ukrainian	3,222	10.1
			Ruthenian	1,220	3.8
"Locals" [*tutejsi*]	49	0.2	"Locals"	707	2.2
White Russians	1,060	3.9	White Russian	990	3.1
Jews	2,110	7.8	Yiddish	2,489	7.8
			Hebrew	244	0.8
Germans	1,059	3.9	German	741	2.3
Lithuanians	69	0.3	Lithuanian	83	0.3
Russians	56	0.2	Russian	139	0.4
Czechs	31	0.1	Czech	38	0.1
Others	16	0	Others	11	0
No answer	13	0	No answer	39	0.1
TOTAL	21,177	100	TOTAL	31,916	100

[a] *Sources: Rocznik statystyki, 1925–1926,* Tab. 5; *Stat. Polski,* Ser. C, Zesz. 94a (1938), Tab. 10; cited in Werner Markert, ed., *Osteuropa Handbuch—Polen* (Cologne: Böhlau Verlag, 1959), p. 37.

Selected Bibliography

UNPUBLISHED DOCUMENTS

Germany

Akten des Auswärtigen Amtes [Records of the Foreign Ministry]. Archiv des Auswärtigen Amtes, Bonn. Microfilmed copy, National Archives, Washington, D.C. For a convenient guide to these microfilms, see George Kent, ed. *A Catalogue of Files and Microfilms of the German Foreign Ministry Archives, 1920–1945.* 3 vols. Stanford: The Hoover Institution, 1962–64.

Department	Microfilmed serial no.	Subject
Büro des Reichsministers	2860H	Russia
	2945H; 3170H	Poland
Büro des Staatssekretärs	4509H; 4562H	Locarno Security Pact
	4569H	Polish affairs 1925–30
	4570H–4571H	Danzig, Upper Silesia
	4483H	German–Polish trade treaty negotiations
	4587H	League of Nations sessions 1926–30
	4622H	"Corridor" questions
Deutsche Botschaft Moskau	1563H–1565H	German–Soviet relations
Geheimakten	K 162–K 167; K 202–K 205	German–Polish economic relations
	6173H–6177H; K 170; K 175–K 177	Political relations; boundary questions

Department	Microfilmed serial no.	Subject
	6188H–6191H; 6698H; 8960H; 9192H–9193H; K 186–K 189	Poland's internal affairs and relations with third countries
	6197H–6200H; 9092H; K 171–K 172; K 197; K 201; K 225; K 238	Minority questions
	6202H–6207H; 6601H–6602H; 9068H–9071H; K 216–K 223	Danzig
	K 7; K 190–K 191	German–Polish military matters
	6192H–6195H; K 182	League of Nations affairs; security pact
Handakten von Dirksen	5462H	Liquidation treaty; trade agreement; boundary question; conciliation attempts
Handakten von Moltke	5544H	Upper Silesian school dispute
Handakten Trautmann	5551H	"Corridor" question
Handakten Wallroth	5265H	Polish politics and economics 1924–28
Brockdorff-Rantzau Nachlass	9101H	Brockdorff-Rantzau's correspondence with Ernst Rantzau, Maltzan, and the Foreign Ministry

Professor Alfred Herrmann Nachlass [Herrmann Papers]. Bundesarchiv, Coblenz.

General Wilhelm Groener Nachlass [Groener Papers]. Bundesarchiv, Coblenz. Microfilmed copy, National Archives, Washington, D.C.

General Kurt von Schleicher Nachlass [Schleicher Papers]. Bundesarchiv, Coblenz.

General Hans von Seeckt Nachlass [Seeckt Papers]. Bundesarchiv, Coblenz. Microfilmed copy, National Archives, Washington, D.C.

Nachlass des Reichsministers Dr. Gustav Stresemann [Stresemann Papers]. Archiv des Auswärtigen Amtes, Bonn. Microfilmed copy, National Archives, Washington, D.C. For a guide to the microfilmed copy, see Hans Gatzke. "The Stresemann Papers," *Journal of Modern History* 26 (1954).

Sahm, Heinrich. Diary and unpublished manuscript, "Erinnerungen aus meinen Danziger Jahren." Private collection.

Poland

Akta Juliusza Twardowskiego [Twardowski Papers]. Archiwum Akt Nowych, Warsaw.
Archiwum Ignacego Paderewskiego [Paderewski Papers]. Archiwum Akt Nowych, Warsaw.
Archiwum Ministerstwa Spraw Wewnętrznych [Records of the Ministry of Interior]. Archiwum Akt Nowych, Warsaw. Files dealing with the German minority, internal security matters, and border police.
Archiwum Ministerstwa Spraw Zagranicznych [Records of the Ministry of Foreign Affairs]. Archiwum Akt Nowych, Warsaw. Files of Political Division II (Western Europe), including reports and memoranda of that Division, as well as correspondence with the Polish legation in Berlin and consulates in Germany. Of particular relevance to German–Polish relations from 1919 to 1933 are folders 4477 to 4950.
Protokoły Posiedzeń Rady Ministrów Rzeczypospolitej Polskiej [Protocols of the Council of Ministers of the Polish Republic]. Archiwum Akt Nowych, Warsaw.

Other

Records of the British Foreign Office. Public Record Office, London.
Records of the U.S. State Department. National Archives, Washington, D.C.

PUBLISHED DOCUMENTS, YEARBOOKS, GOVERNMENT AND PARTY
PUBLICATIONS

Actes et Documents de la Conférence polono-allemande tenue à Vienne du 30 avril au 30 août 1924. Vienna: Manz, 1925.
Archivkommission des Auswärtigen Amtes. *Ein Französischer Diplomat über die Bolschewistische Gefahr. Berichte des Botschafters der Französischen Republik in Moskau, Jean Herbette, aus den Jahren 1927–1931.* Berlin: Deutscher Verlag, 1943.
Beck, Józef. *Beiträge zur Europäischen Politik. Reden, Erklärungen, Interviews, 1932–1939.* Essen: Essener Verlagsanstalt, 1939.
Diplomat in Berlin, 1933–1939: Papers and Memoirs of Józef Lipski, Ambassador of Poland [Lipski Papers]. Ed. by Wacław Jędrzejewicz. New York: Columbia University Press, 1968.
Documents on British Foreign Policy, 1919–1939. Ed. by E. L. Woodward and R. Butler, later series by W. N. Meddlicott, D. Dakin, and M. E. Lambert. London: H. M. Stationery Office, 1946–.
France, Ministère des Affaires Etrangères, *Pacte de sécurité: neuf pièces rela-*

tives à la proposition faite le 9 février 1925 par le gouvernement allemand et à la réponse du gouvernement français. Paris: Government of France, 1925.

League of Nations, *Official Journal.*

──────. *Treaty Series,* 54–55 (1926–27).

Piłsudski, Józef. *Erinnerungen und Dokumente.* 4 vols. Essen: Essener Verlagsanstalt, 1935–36.

"Polens Aussenpolitik zwischen Versailles und Locarno: Runderlass des polnischen Aussenministers Skirmunt an alle Missionen, August 2, 1921." *Berliner Monatshefte* 18 (1940).

Reichstag. *Verhandlungen der Verfassungsgebenden Deutschen Nationalversammlung.* Vols. 326–43. This contains the *Stenographische Berichte; Anlagen;* and *Sach-und Sprechregister.*

──────. *Verhandlungen des Reichstags.* Vols. 344–457. It contains the *Stenographische Berichte; Anlagen;* and *Sach-und Sprechregister.*

Schulthess' .Europäischer Geschichtskalender. Ed. by Ulrich Thürauf. Munich: Becksche Verlagsbuchhandlung, 1919 ff.

Stresemann, Gustav. *Vermächtnis.* Ed. by Henry Bernhard. 3 vols. Berlin: Ullstein Verlag, 1932.

Temperley, H. Ed. *A History of the Peace Conference of Paris.* 6 vols. London: Hodder & Stoughton, 1920–24.

Toynbee, Arnold. Ed. *Survey of International Affairs.* London: Humphrey Milford, 1920 ff.

Unsere Partei. Party organ of the DNVP. Berlin, 1919 ff.

Zaleski, August. *Przemowy i deklaracje.* 2 vols. Warsaw: [n.p.], 1929, 1931.

MEMOIRS AND DIARIES

Aretin, Erwein Freiherr von. *Krone und Ketten. Erinnerungen eines bayerischen Edelmannes.* Munich: Süddeutscher Verlag, 1955.

Braun, Otto. *Von Weimar zu Hitler.* New York: Europa Verlag, 1940.

Curtius, Julius. *Sechs Jahre Minister der Deutschen Republik.* Heidelberg: Universitätsverlag, 1948.

D'Abernon, Viscount Edgar. *An Ambassador of Peace.* 3 vols. London: Hodder & Stoughton, 1929–30.

Dirksen, Herbert von. *Moskau, Tokio, London.* Stuttgart: W. Kohlhammer, 1949.

François-Poncet, André. *Souvenirs d'une Ambassade à Berlin.* Paris: Flammarion, 1946.

Kessler, Graf Harry. *Aus den Tagebüchern, 1918–1937.* Munich: Deutscher Taschenbuchverlag, 1965.

Laroche, Jules. *La Pologne de Pilsudski. Souvenirs d'une ambassade 1926–1935.* Paris: Flammarion, 1953.

Noël, Léon. *L'Aggression allemande contre la Pologne.* Paris: Flammarion, 1946.

Piłsudski, Józef. *The Memoirs of a Revolutionary and Soldier.* Transl. by D. R. Gillie. London: Faber & Faber, 1930.

———. *L'Année 1920.* Paris: La Renaissance du Livre, 1929.

Sforza, Count Carlo. *Makers of Modern Europe.* Indianapolis: Bobb-Merrill Co., 1928.

Stockhausen, Max von. *Sechs Jahre Reichskanzlei. Von Rapallo bis Locarno. Erinnerungen und Tagebuchnotizen, 1922–1927.* Ed. by Walter Görlitz. Bonn: Athenäum–Verlag, 1954.

Szembek, Count Jan. *Journal 1933–1939.* Paris: Libraire Plon, 1952.

———. *Diariusz i teki Jana Szembeka, 1935–1945.* 3 vols. Ed. by Tytus Komarnicki. London: Polish Research Centre, 1964–65.

SELECTED GENERAL WORKS

Bagiński, Henryk. *Poland and the Baltic—The Problem of Poland's Access to the Sea.* London: Oliver & Boyd, 1942.

Bahr, Richard. *Volk Jenseits der Grenzen; Geschichte und Problematik der deutschen Minderheiten.* Hamburg: Hanseatische Verlagsanstalt, 1933.

Balcerak, Wiesław. *Polityka zagraniczna Polski w dobie Locarna.* Warsaw: Instytut Historii Polskiej Akademii Nauk, 1967.

Beck, Józef. *Dernier rapport. Politique polonaise 1926–1939.* Neuchâtel: Editions de la Bacounière, 1951.

Bertelsmann, Heinz Otto. "The Role of the German Parliament in Foreign Affairs 1919–1926. Four Tests of the Weimar Republic." Columbia University Dissertation, 1956.

Bierschenk, Theodor. *Die Deutsche Volksgruppe in Polen, 1934–1939.* Kitzingen: Holzner Verlag, 1951.

Blücher, Wipert von. *Deutschlands Weg nach Rapallo.* Wiesbaden: Limes Verlag, 1951.

Böhmert, Victor. *Die Rechtsgrundlagen der Beziehungen zwischen Danzig und Polen.* Berlin: Verlag Emil Evering, 1933.

Brackmann, Albert, et al. *Deutschland und Polen. Beiträge zu ihren geschichtlichen Beziehungen.* Berlin: Verlag Oldenburg, 1933.

Bradley, Pearle E. "The National Socialist Attack on the Foreign Policies of the German Republic, 1919–1933." Stanford University Dissertation, 1954.

Bretton, Henry L. *Stresemann and the Revision of Versailles. A Fight for Reason.* Stanford: Stanford University Press, 1953.

Breyer, Richard. *Das Deutsche Reich und Polen 1932–1937. Aussenpolitik und Volksgruppenfragen.* Würzburg: Holzner Verlag, 1955

Bromke, Adam. *Poland's Politics: Idealism vs. Realism.* Cambridge, Mass.: Harvard University Press, 1967.

Broszat, Martin. *Zweihundert Jahre deutsche Polenpolitik.* Munich: Franz Ehrenwirth Verlag, 1963.

Carr, Edward H. *German–Soviet Relations Between the Two World Wars, 1919–1939.* Baltimore: The Johns Hopkins Press, 1951.

Castellan, Georges. *Le Réarmement Clandestin Du Reich 1930–1935. Vu par le 2° Bureau de l'Etat-Major Géneral Français.* Paris: Libraire Plon, 1954.

Conze, Werner. *Polnische Nation und Deutsche Politik im Ersten Weltkrieg.* Cologne: Böhlau Verlag, 1958.

Craig, Gordon and Gilbert, Felix. Eds. *The Diplomats.* Princeton, N.J.: Princeton University Press, 1953.

D'Abernon, Viscount Edgar. *The Eighteenth Decisive Battle of the World. Warsaw, 1920.* London: Hodder & Stoughton, 1931.

Debicki, Roman. *Foreign Policy of Poland, 1919–1939.* New York: Frederick Praeger, 1962.

Dmowski, Roman. *Polityka polska i odbudowanie państwa.* 2nd ed. Warsaw: 1926.

Donald, Sir Robert. *The Polish Corridor and Its Consequences.* London: Thornton Butterworth, 1929.

Douglass, Paul F. *The Economic Independence of Poland—A Study in Trade Adjustments to Political Objectives.* Cincinnati: Ruter Press, 1934.

Duroselle, Jean Baptiste, ed. *Les Relations Germano–Soviétiques de 1933 à 1939.* Paris: Libraire Armand Colin, 1954.

Dyck, Harvey Leonard. *Weimar Germany and Soviet Russia, 1926–1933.* New York: Columbia University Press, 1966.

Dziewanowski, M. K. *Joseph Pilsudski: European Federalist.* Stanford: Stanford University Press, 1969.

Eyck, Erich. *A History of the Weimar Republic.* 2 vols. Transl. by Harlan Hanson and Robert Waite. Cambridge, Mass.: Harvard University Press, 1963.

Fischer, Louis. *The Soviets in World Affairs.* New York: Vintage Russian Library, 1960.

Franzius, Enno. "German Foreign Policy, 1923–1926. Stresemann and Press Opinion." Columbia University Dissertation, 1954.

Freund, Gerald. *Unholy Alliance. Russian–German Relations from the Treaty of Brest–Litovsk to the Treaty of Berlin.* New York: Harcourt, Brace, 1957.

Gatzke, Hans W. *Stresemann and the Rearmament of Germany.* Baltimore: The Johns Hopkins Press, 1954.

Geiss, Imanuel. *Der Polnische Grenzstreifen 1914–1918.* Hamburg: Matthiesen Verlag, 1960.

Gentzen, Felix-Heinrich. *Deutschland und Polen. Ein Überblick über die deutsch-polnischen Beziehungen.* Leipzig: Urania Verlag, 1956.

Gessler, Otto. *Reichswehrpolitik in der Weimarer Zeit.* Stuttgart: Deutsche Verlagsanstalt, 1958.

Górecki, Roman. *Polens Wirtschaftliche Entwickelung.* Warsaw: Bank Gospodarstwa Krajowego, 1931.

Görlitz, Walter. *Der Deutsche Generalstab—Geschichte und Gestalt 1657–1945.* Frankfurt: Verlag der Frankfurter Hefte, 1950.

Halecki, Oscar. *A History of Poland.* New York: Roy Publishers, 1956.

Heike, Otto. *Das Deutschtum in Polen 1918–1939.* Bonn: Selbstverlag des Verfassers, 1955.

Helbig, H. *Die Träger der Rapallo-Politik.* Göttingen: Vandenhoeck & Ruprecht, 1958.

Heyl, Friedrich W. *Die Tätigkeit des internationalen Gerichtshofs, 1922–1928, unter besonderer Würdigung der deutschen Minderheitenfrage in Polen.* Ochsenfurt: Buchdruckerei Fritz Rappert, 1930.

Hilger, G., and Meyer, A. G. *Incompatible Allies.* New York: The Macmillan Co., 1953.

Höltje, Christian. *Die Weimarer Republik und das Ost–Locarno Problem, 1919–1934.* Würzburg: Holzner Verlag, 1958.

Horak, Stephen. *Poland and Her National Minorities, 1919–1939.* New York: Vantage Press, 1961.

Junckerstorff, Kurt. *Der Schulstreit der deutschen Minderheit in Polnisch-Oberschlesien nach dem Genfer Abkommen.* Berlin: Verlag Reimar Hobbing, 1930.

Kaeckenbeeck, G. *The International Experiment of Upper Silesia. A Study of the Working of the Upper Silesian Settlement, 1922–1937.* London: Oxford University Press, 1942.

Komarnicki, Tytus. *The Rebirth of the Polish Republic.* London: W. Heinemann, 1957.

Korbel, Josef. *Poland Between East and West. Soviet and German Diplomacy Toward Poland, 1919–1933.* Princeton, N.J.: Princeton University Press, 1963.

Krasuski, Jerzy. *Stosunki polsko-niemieckie, 1919–1925.* Poznań: Instytut Zachodni, 1962.

———. *Stosunki polsko-niemieckie, 1926–1932.* Poznań: Instytut Zachodni, 1964.

Kraus, Herbert. *Das Recht der Minderheiten.* Berlin: Verlag Georg Stilke, 1927.

Kuźmiński, Tadeusz. *Polska, Francja, Niemcy 1933–1935.* Warsaw: Państowe Wydawnictwo Naukowe, 1963.

Kwiatkowski, E. *The Economic Progress of Poland.* Warsaw: The Polish Economist, 1928.

Laeuen, Harald. *Polnische Tragödie.* Stuttgart: Steingrüben Verlag, 1955.

Machray, Robert. *Poland 1914–1931*. London: George Allen & Unwin, 1932.

Manteuffel-Szoege, Georg Baron von. *Geschichte des polnischen Volkes während seiner Unfreiheit, 1772–1914*. Berlin: Duncker & Humblot, 1950.

Markert, Werner, ed. *Osteuropa Handbuch—Polen*. Cologne: Böhlau Verlag, 1959.

Martel, René. *La Pologne et Nous*. Paris: André Delpeuch, 1928.

Mayr, Kaspar. *Ist die Verständigung zwischen Polen und Deutschland Unmöglich?* Vienna: Internationaler Versöhnungsbund, 1931.

Mornik, Stanislaus. *Polens Kampf gegen seine nichtpolnischen Volksgruppen*. Berlin: Walter de Gryter, 1931.

Morrow, Ian F., and Sieveking, L. M. *The Peace Settlement in the German–Polish Borderlands. A Study of Conditions Today in the Pre-War Prussian Provinces of East and West Prussia*. London: Oxford University Press, 1936.

Pajewski, Janusz, ed. *Problem polsko-niemiecki w Traktacie Wersalskim: praca zbiorowa*. Poznań: Instytut Zachodni, 1963.

Paprocki, S. J. *Polen und das Minderheiten Problem*. Warsaw: Institut zur Erforschung der Minderheitsfragen, 1935.

Petrie, Sir Charles A. *The Life and Letters of the Right Hon. Sir Austen Chamberlain*. 2 vols. London: Cassell & Co., 1940.

Puchert, Berthold. *Der Wirtschaftskrieg des Deutschen Imperialismus gegen Polen, 1925–1934*. (East) Berlin: Akademie-Verlag, 1963.

Rabenau, Friedrich von. *Seeckt. Aus seinem Leben, 1918–1936*. Leipzig: von Hase & Koehler Verlag, 1940.

Raphaël, Gaston. *Allemagne et Pologne*. Paris: Librarie Delagrave, 1932.

Rauschning, Hermann. *Die Entdeutschung Westpreussens und Posens*. Berlin: Verlag Reimar Hobbing, 1930.

Recke, Walter. *Die polnische Frage als Problem der europäischen Politik*. Berlin: Verlag Georg Stilke, 1927.

Roos, Hans. *Polen und Europa. Studien zur polnischen Aussenpolitik 1931–1939*. Tübingen: Mohr, 1957.

———. *Geschichte der polnischen Nation 1919–1960*. Stuttgart: Kohlhammer Verlag, 1961.

Rosé, Adam C. *La politique polonaise entre les deux guerres*. Neuchâtel: Editions de la Bacounière, 1945.

Rosenbaum, Kurt. *Community of Fate: German–Soviet Diplomatic Relations 1922–1928*. Syracuse, N.Y.: University of Syracuse Press, 1965.

Roth, Paul. *Die Entstehung des polnischen Staates*. Berlin: Verlag Otto Liebermann, 1926.

———. *Deutschland und Polen*. Munich: Isar Verlag, 1958.

Rothschild, Joseph. *Piłsudski's Coup d'Etat*. New York: Columbia University Press, 1966.

Rudershausen, Jutta. *Die polnische Seehandelspolitik.* Königsberg: Ost–Europa Verlag, 1936.

Schneider, Oswald. *Die Frage der wirtschaftlichen Unabhängigkeit Polens.* Königsberg: Graefe & Unzer Verlag, 1933.

Seeckt, Hans von. *Deutschland zwischen West und Ost.* Hamburg: Hanseatische Verlagsanstalt, 1933.

Sellin, Fritz. *Die polnische Frage.* Berlin: Selbstverlag des Herausgebers, 1932.

Seraphim, Peter-Heinz. *Die Handelspolitik Polens.* Berlin: Volk & Reich Verlag, 1935.

Sikorski, W. *Le problème de la paix: Le jeu des forces politiques en Europe orientale et l'alliance franco-polonaise.* Paris: 1931.

Skrzyński, Count Alexander. *Poland and Peace.* London: Allen & Unwin, 1923.

Smogorzewski, Casimir. *Abrégé d'une Bibliographie relative aux Relations Germano–Polonaises.* Paris: Gebethner & Wolff, 1933.

Starzyński, Stefan. *Polish Economic Conditions in 1926.* Warsaw: Ministry of Finance, 1927.

Stone, Julius. *Regional Guarantees of Minority Rights: A Study of Minorities Procedure in Upper Silesia.* New York: The Macmillan Co., 1933.

Strassburger, H. *German Designs on Pomerania.* Toruń: Baltic Institute, 1934.

——— et al. *Danzig et quelques aspects du problème germano-polonais.* Paris: Publications de la conciliation internationale, 1932.

Studnicki, Władysław. *Polen im politischen System Europas,* Berlin: Verlag E. S. Mittler, 1936.

Swart, Friedrich. *Diesseits und Jenseits der Grenze. Das deutsche Genossenschaftswesen im Posener Land.* Leer: Verlag Rautenberg & Möckel, 1954.

Szklarska-Lohmannowa, Alina. *Polsko–czechosłowackie stosunki dyplomatyczne w latach 1919–1925.* Warsaw: Polska Akademia Nauk, 1967.

Thimme, Annelise. *Gustav Stresemann.* Hannover: Norddeutsche Verlagsanstalt O. Goedel, 1957.

Turner, Henry Ashby. *Stresemann and the Politics of the Weimar Republic.* Princeton, N.J.: Princeton University Press, 1963.

Umiastowski, Roman. *Russia and the Polish Republic 1918–1945.* London: Aquafondata, 1945.

Van Husen, Paul. *Das Minderheitenrecht in Oberschlesien.* Berlin: Brückenverlag, 1930.

Waite, Robert. *Vanguard of Nazism. The Free Corps Movement in Postwar Germany 1918–1923.* Cambridge, Mass.: Harvard University Press, 1952.

Walters, F. P. *A History of the League of Nations.* 2nd edition. London: Oxford University Press, 1960.

Wambaugh, Sarah. *Plebiscites Since the World War*. Washington, D.C.: Carnegie Endowment for International Peace, 1933.
Wandycz, Piotr S. *France and Her Eastern Allies 1919-1925*. Minneapolis: The University of Minnesota Press, 1962.
Wellisz, Leopold. *Foreign Capital in Poland*. London: Allen & Unwin, 1938.
Wertheimer, Fritz. *Deutschland, die Minderheiten und der Völkerbund*. Berlin: C. Heymann, 1926.
Worgitski, Max. *Geschichte der Abstimmung in Ostpreussen*. Leipzig: K. F. Kochler, 1921.
Zelle, Arnold. *100 Korridorthesen*. Berlin: Volk & Reich Verlag, 1933.
Zimmerman, Ludwig. *Deutsche Aussenpolitik in der Ära der Weimarer Republik*. Göttingen: Musterschmidt Verlag, 1958.

ARTICLES

Benedykt, Stefan. "Zajazd O.R.P. 'Wicher' na Gdańsk." *Wiadomości* 108 (1948).
Birnbaum, Immanuel. "Germany's Eastern Policy, Yesterday and Tomorrow." *International Affairs* 31 (1955).
Beneš, Eduard. "After Locarno: the Security Problem Today." *Foreign Affairs* 4 (1926).
"Benesch und die tschechische Aussenpolitik 1918-1935." *Berliner Monatshefte* 16 (1938).
Breitscheid, R. "Das aussenpolitische Programm der Sozialdemokratie." *Europäische Gespräche* 4 (1926).
Brüning, H. "Ein Brief an R. Pechel." *Deutsche Rundschau* 70 (1947).
Cleinow, Georg. "Wege eines deutsch-polnischen Ausgleichs." *Europäische Gespräche* 8 (1930).
Curtius, J. "Der Polnische Korridor." *Europäische Gespräche* 11 (1933).
Dąbrowski, Stanisław. "The Peace Treaty of Riga." *Polish Review* 5 (1960).
Dopierała, Bohdan. "Beck and the Gdańsk Question, 1930-1935." *Acta Poloniae Historica* 17 (1968).
Epstein, Julius. "Der Seeckt Plan." *Der Monat* 1 (1948).
Erdmann, Karl D. "Das Problem der Ost—oder Westorientierung in der Locarno—Politik Stresemanns." *Geschichte in Wissenschaft und Unterricht* 6 (1955).
Forst de Battaglia, Otto. "Polen und Deutschland, Tatsachen, Gedanken und Möglichkeiten." *Europäische Gespräche* 5 (1927).
Gąsiorowski, Zygmunt J. "Did Piłsudski Attempt to Initiate a Preventive War in 1933?" *Journal of Modern History* 27 (1955).
———. "Stresemann and Poland before Locarno." *Journal of Central European Affairs* 18, no. 1 (1958).
———. "Stresemann and Poland after Locarno." *Journal of Central European Affairs* 18 no. 3 (1958).

————. "The Russian Overture to Germany of December 1924." *Journal of Modern History* 30 (1958).

Gatzke, Hans W. "Von Rapallo nach Berlin: Stresemann und die deutsche Russland Politik." *Vierteljahrshefte für Zeitgeschichte* 4 (1956).

Hoetzsch, Otto. "Polens aussenpolitische Stellung." *Osteuropa* 6 (1930-31).

Jędrzejewicz, Wacław. "The Polish Plan for a 'Preventive War' against Germany in 1933." *Polish Review* 11 (1966).

Korodi, Lutz. "Das Problem der nationalen Minderheiten." *Preussische Jahrbücher* 203 (1926).

————. "Die nationalen Minderheiten und Deutschland." *Preussische Jahrbücher* 210 (1927).

Krasuski, Jerzy. "Wpływ Traktatu w Rapallo na stosunki polsko-niemieckie." *Przegląd Zachodni* 17 (1961).

————. "Reakcja Polski na zniesienie Sojuszniczej Komisji Kontroli Niemiec w 1926 r." *Przegląd Zachodni* 17 (1961).

————. "Political Significance of the Polish–German Financial Accounting in 1919–1929." *Acta Poloniae Historica* 15 (1967).

Kruszewski, Charles. "The Polish–German Tariff War (1925–1934) and its Aftermath." *Journal of Central European Affairs* 3 (1943).

Landau, Zbigniew. "Bank Dillon Read and Co. a Polska." *Sprawy Międzynarodowe* 13 (1960).

————. "Polish Economy of the Years 1918–1939 in Polish Postwar Publications." *Acta Poloniae Historica* 5 (1962).

Lapter, K. "Międzynarodowe tło przewrotu majowego." *Sprawy Międzynarodowe* 9 (1956).

Leber, Annedore, ed. "Ausgewählte Briefe von Generalmajor Helmuth Stieff." *Vierteljahrshefte für Zeitgeschichte* 2 (1954).

Mendelssohn-Bartholdy, A. "Deutschland und Polen." *Europäische Gespräche* 8 (1930).

————. "Kondominium?" *Europäische Gespräche* 9 (1931).

Morgenstern, T. "Wejście O.R.P. 'Wicher' do Gdańska w 1932 r." *Bellona* 1 (1953).

D'Ormesson, Comte Wladimir. "Frankreich–Deutschland–Polen." *Europäische Revue* 2 (1927).

Pliska, Stanley. "The 'Polish–American Army' 1917–1921." *Polish Review* 10 (1965).

"Polens Mysterium des nationalen Instinkts." *Preussische Jahrbücher* 228 (1932).

Radziwiłł, Prince Janusz. "Gliederung der polnisch-deutschen Probleme." *Europäische Revue* 6 (1930).

Rheinbaben, Werner Freiherr von. "Deutschland und Polen." *Europäische Gespräche* 6 (1926).

————. "Deutschland und Polen: Zwölf Thesen zur Revisionspolitik." *Europäische Gespräche* 9 (1931).

Riekhoff, Harald von. "Piłsudski's Conciliatory Overtures to Stresemann." *Canadian Slavonic Papers* 9 (1967).

Roos, Hans. "Die 'Präventivkriegspläne' Piłsudskis von 1933." *Vierteljahrshefte für Zeitgeschichte* 3 (1955).

Rose, Karol. "Deutschland und Polen." *Europäische Gespräche* 4 (1926).

Rosenfeld, Günther. "Stosunki polityczne polsko-niemieckie po Rapallo i Locarno." *Kwartalnik Historyczny* 70 (1963).

Senn, A. E. "The Polish–Lithuanian War Scare, 1927." *Journal of Central European Affairs* 21 (1961).

Seraphim, P. H. "Die Kapitalverflechtung zwischen Deutschland und Polen." *Osteuropa* 7 (1931/32).

Silesius, M. "Die polnische Mentalität." *Deutsche Rundschau* 209 (1926).

Sokulski, H. "Wojna celna Rzeszy przeciw Polsce w latach 1925–1934." *Sprawy Międzynarodowe* 8 (1955).

Steinert, Hermann. "Polens Seehandelspolitik." *Osteuropa* 8 (1932/33).

Symmons-Symonolewicz, Konstantin. "Polish Political Thought of the Eastern Borderlands of Poland, 1918–1939." *Polish Review* 4 (1959).

Targ, Alojzy. "Zarys działalności Związku Polaków w Niemczech." *Przegląd Zachodni* 18, nos. 3–4 (1962).

Thimme, Annelise. "Die Locarnopolitik im Lichte des Stresemann-Nachlasses." *Zeitschrift für Politik* 3 (1956).

Volz, Wilhelm. "Und Oberschlesien?" *Deutsche Rundschau* 191 (1922).

Wandycz, Piotr. "General Weygand and the Battle of Warsaw of 1920." *Journal of Central European Affairs* 19 (1960).

Wojciechowski, Marian. "Polska i Niemcy na przełomie lat 1932–1933." *Roczniki Historyczne* 29 (1963).

Wroniak, Zdzisław. "Nawiązanie stosunków dyplomatycznych przez Polskę z Niemcami w 1918 roku." *Historia* 6 (1964).

————. "Geneza Rządów Paderewskiego." *Historia* 4 (1959).

Wrzesiński, Wojciech. "Geneza Związku Polaków w Niemczech." *Przegląd Zachodni* 18, nos. 3–4 (1962).

Zieliński, Henryk. "La Question de 'L'Etat Indépendant de Haute-Silésie' après la Première Guerre Mondiale, 1919–1921."*Acta Poloniae Historica* 4 (1961).

————. "Znaczenie traktatu wersalskiego dla rozwoju stosunków polsko-niemieckich po 1 Wojnie Światowej." *Kwartalnik Historyczny* 70 (1963).

NEWSPAPERS

Berliner Tageblatt.
Frankfurter Zeitung.
Germania.

Kölnische Zeitung.
Neue Preussische Zeitung (Kreuz-Zeitung).
Völkischer Beobachter.
Vorwärts.
Vossische Zeitung.

Index